Ruling Women

Stacy S. Klein

Ruling Women

Queenship and Gender in Anglo-Saxon Literature

University of Notre Dame Press
Notre Dame, Indiana

Library of Congress Cataloging-in-Publication Data

Klein, Stacy S., 1967–
Ruling women : queenship and gender in Anglo-Saxon literature /
by Stacy S. Klein.
    p.   cm.
Includes bibliographical references and index.
ISBN-13: 978-0-268-03310-1 (pbk. : alk. paper)
ISBN-10: 0-268-03310-2 (pbk. : alk. paper)
1. English literature—Old English, ca. 450–1100—History and criticism.
2. Queens in literature. 3. Women in literature. 4. Sex role in literature.
5. Christianity and literature—England—History—To 1500. 6. Civilization,
Anglo-Saxon. I. Title.
PR179.W65K55   2006
829'.09358—dc22

                                                      2006003879

For my parents

Contents

Acknowledgments

It is a great pleasure to thank the many people who provided help with this book. *Ruling Women* began as a dissertation at Ohio State University, and I am grateful to my committee members Lisa Kiser and Karen Winstead for their unfailing support and excellent teaching. Most of the book was written during a period as a visiting scholar at Harvard University (2001–3), made possible by the generous support of the American Council of Learned Societies and by Rutgers University, both of whom have my deepest gratitude. I am also grateful to fellow visiting scholar Nicola Nixon, whose keen intellectual curiosity has helped to invigorate my own work, and whose comments and conversation have much improved both my project and my prose. Mary-Jo Arn, Dan Donoghue, Joe Harris, and Nicholas Watson responded to my work and, just as importantly, welcomed me to the community of Harvard medievalists, making my time in Cambridge a pleasure. I am also grateful to Fiona Griffiths, who read all of the chapters as they evolved, and on whose intelligence, candor, and graciousness I have had the good fortune to be able to rely.

My colleagues in the English Department at Rutgers have been equally supportive. Chris Chism, Susan Crane, and Larry Scanlon provided insightful reflections on the book as a whole. I will always be grateful to Chris for her willingness to discuss ideas and to work through critical problems, and for her good humor while doing so. I am also grateful to my former chair, Cheryl Wall, who reminded me that one has little control over the reception of one's work but much control over its completion. My current chair, Richard Miller, has been most helpful, as has the FAS dean of Humanities, Barry Qualls, whose ability to blend administrative savvy with human decency I admire greatly. My research assistant at Rutgers, Jennifer Garrison, has been astute and resourceful throughout.

Many people commented on various portions of the book or in other ways played an important role in its genesis. The names that I now list in alphabetical order are a constant reminder to me of the rewards of intellectual companionship and the pleasures of being an Anglo-Saxonist: Tom Bredehoft, Stewart Brookes, Dan Donoghue, Roberta Frank, Timothy Graham, Tom Hall, Toni Healey, Dave Johnson, Clare Lees, Hal Momma, Robin Norris, Robert Stanton, Mary Swan, Paul Szarmach, Elaine Treharne, Jon Wilcox, Cynthia Wittman-Zollinger, and Charlie Wright. The list is indeed long, and I believe it testifies to the intellectual generosity that characterizes my field. To read a book once is generous; to read and offer comments on it several times is little short of heroic. For this, I thank Nick Howe, Roy Liuzza, and Katherine O'Brien O'Keeffe, who read the book in various stages and then again at its completion. My work has benefited greatly from their deep knowledge of Anglo-Saxon literature and from their willingness to share it with others. *Ruling Women* is much indebted to their intellectual rigor, as well as to the standards set by their own scholarship.

It is my great good fortune that *Ruling Women* found a home at the University of Notre Dame Press. I doubt that anyone could have had a better editor than Barbara Hanrahan. She supported this book from the start and found two brilliant readers, whose thorough and insightful responses to the manuscript helped me to realize the book's larger aims. I will always be grateful to Barbara and to those anonymous readers for their intelligence and forthrightness and also for their kindness. My manuscript editor, Margo Shearman, has been a pleasure to work with, and I am deeply grateful for her meticulous editing. Rebecca DeBoer and Margaret Gloster have also been extremely helpful.

An earlier version of chapter 2 appeared as "Reading Queenship in Cynewulf's *Elene,*" *Journal of Medieval and Early Modern Studies* 33 (2003): 47–89. An earlier version of chapter 5 appeared as "Beauty and the Banquet: Queenship and Social Reform in Ælfric's *Esther,*" *Journal of English and Germanic Philology* 103 (2004): 77–105. Permission to reprint these materials is acknowledged. I would also like to thank Michael Cornett for his help with chapter 2 and Charlie Wright for assistance with chapter 5.

This book owes more than I can ever acknowledge fully to my former dissertation director, Nicholas Howe. Nick taught me Old English and provided, through rigorous instruction and the inspiration of his own stellar work, a model for combining research, teaching, and service to one's field and university. I was privileged to be able to work with such a wise scholar and teacher, and it is an honor for me to make clear how much he has meant to me—as my teacher, mentor, and dear friend.

My greatest debts are indicated in the dedication. My parents, Marc and Dorothy Klein, have provided unfailing support during the many years I worked on this book. As fellow educators, they seemed to understand the rigors of writing and completing a large-scale project, and offered steady support throughout. I am grateful for their support and for their love.

Many Old English personal names have not survived into modern English. There is also little consistency in their recorded spellings; such names regularly appear in different forms and dialects throughout the Anglo-Saxon period. Those names that have survived into modern English (e.g., Alfred, Edgar, Edith) are cited in their modern forms. The many names that have not survived appear in either the simplest or the best known of their Old English variants, except in cases where I cite directly from a particular manuscript (e.g., *Ælfgifu* generally, but *Ælfgyfu* when quoting from the frontispiece to London, British Library, Stowe 944). Scandinavian and Frankish names appear in the forms most readily recognizable to modern readers. With respect to abbreviations, I have retained notae and abbreviations for *æ*, treating *æ* and *ę* as interchangeable, but have expanded abbreviations for *þæt*. I have rendered the Old English letter *wynn* and the insular form of the letter *g* as modern *w* and *g*, and I have not reproduced stress marks. All translations are my own unless otherwise noted.

King Canute and Queen Ælfgyfu place a cross on the altar of the New Minster. London, British Library, Stowe 944, fol. 6. Courtesy of the British Library.

Introduction

She stands, hand outstretched toward the altar cross, a gift to the New Minster from her and her husband, Cnut, who is positioned directly opposite. The diadem encircling her brow marks her status as a married woman, while the rubric arcing over her upper body designates her as *Ælfgyfu regina,* queen of the English. Together, she and Cnut fill much of the composition's center, reversing the customary iconographic hierarchy of early medieval donor portraits, in which saints and the celestial court are usually figured as larger than, and thus symbolically superior to, earthly donors.[1] Yet here it is the queen who looms large—almost equal in stature to her husband and larger than the Virgin, Saint Peter, or even Christ.

This image forms the frontispiece to the *Liber Vitae* of the New Minster, Winchester (A.D. 1031), the book containing the names of the abbey's brethren, monks, associates, and benefactors, living and dead, who were commemorated in the monks' prayers.[2] One of the two surviving pre-Conquest drawings of an Anglo-Saxon queen, the frontispiece testifies to the social importance and symbolic complexity of queenship in Anglo-Saxon culture.[3] A flying angel hovers over the queen's head, holding her veil and gesturing toward the mandorla-enclosed Christ above to suggest that Ælfgifu's queenship is both derived from and sanctioned by the celestial ruler. The queen stands directly below the Virgin, her dress and pose likening her to the Queen of all Queens, and conveying the promise that Ælfgifu and Cnut will look after the minster on earth, much as its two patron saints, Mary and Peter, watch over the house in heaven. In exchange for such generous patronage, the cluster of tiny monks housed in their stalls below the feet of the royal couple offer up prayers, joining Saints Mary and Peter in their intercessory efforts to ensure a place in heaven for the king and queen. Indeed the judgment looks promising for the royal couple, as the frontispiece is followed in the manuscript by a glorious depiction of Saint Peter with key in hand, welcoming the righteous through the open gates of the celestial city and into heaven.

I begin my study of queenship in Anglo-Saxon literature with the *Liber Vitae* miniature because it poses a question that is central to this book, namely, how did queens function as imaginative figures within the writings of pre-Conquest England? The miniature points to the malleability of the queen, her clothing and accessories suggesting cogent differences between her imaginative potential and that of her husband's in the minds of early medieval writers. While the king's side-fastened cope, crown, and sword clearly distinguish him from Peter and Christ, with their bare feet and saintly clothes, the queen is a more homogeneous figure, whose royal status is far less conspicuous than that of her husband: her headgear is little different from that worn by any other married woman or cloistered nun, her very shoes almost identical to those of the Virgin.[4] The generic clothing that enables the queen to shade so easily into an image of wife, nun, or Queen of Heaven emblematizes how very ill defined queens' roles were in Anglo-Saxon England—so ill defined that J. M. Wallace-Hadrill, in his classic study of early Germanic kingship, was led to claim that the Church "lacked any definition of the role of queens beyond what was required of all Christian wives."[5] Although Wallace-Hadrill offers little further discussion of either queens or Christian wives, his suggestive linking of the two nevertheless offers a central insight into the analysis of queenship that this book takes up. Anglo-Saxon literature and culture offer us far more resources for studying queens than they do for Christian wives. Might representations of royal women in Anglo-Saxon literature be used to investigate broader cultural ideals of femininity in early medieval England? And what might representations of queens, the richest and most powerful women in Anglo-Saxon society, have meant to audiences—male and female, lay and monastic—who enjoyed far less access to wealth or privilege?

But the drawing also raises questions about what is not or cannot be represented. Textual representations of living royal figures were a delicate affair, requiring Anglo-Saxon writers to weigh carefully the pleasures of candid self-expression against the potential hazards of offending men and women capable of wielding extreme power and privilege. Even setting forth more generic models of exemplary royal conduct could have been perceived as risky, for such models could be easily interpreted as suggesting gaps between the model and the contemporary king or queen. The *Liber Vitae* miniature adumbrates these kinds of artistic anxieties, reflecting a distinct effort to conform to Cnut's own wishes regarding his public self-presentation. A Dane by birth, Cnut worked tirelessly throughout his reign to ease the English people's acceptance of a foreign ruler by presenting himself as the darling of both their own clergy and their queen.[6] Not surprisingly, the drawing conveys a sense of harmony between court and cloister, depicting necessarily a symbiotic relationship in which the royal family's material wealth is effortlessly exchanged for the monks' spiritual capital and its attendant promise of eternal riches. So too the miniature offers an image of marital harmony, the serene expression on the queen's face veiling the fact that she stands opposite the man who had alienated her from her two eldest sons and married her in an attempt to shore up his claim to the throne: if the English queen loved him, perhaps her people might follow suit.[7] But how would an Anglo-Saxon writer have represented queens if he were a bit less constrained? What might a medieval monk have to say about queens if he were not—as the *Liber Vitae* monks quite literally are—under the feet of the royal family?

There are few discussions of either contemporary queens or models of queenship in Anglo-Saxon writings. The most substantive accounts of living queens and their roles within both the court and society at large are found in the *Encomium Emmae Reginae* (1041–42) and the *Life of King Edward Who Rests at Westminster* (1065–67), the former detailing Ælfgifu-Emma's life during the early years of Cnut's reign, the latter recounting Edith's participation in Edward's court before the Norman Conquest.[8] Both are Latin texts, generally presumed to have been written on the Continent and commissioned by the particular queen who figures centrally within the narrative. Not surprisingly, both texts offer highly flattering portrayals of their royal female protagonists, so scripted that historians have often remarked on the strong resemblance between the two women featured in these texts.[9] Yet the scarcity of contemporary representations of queens in Old English writings is probably not indicative of a lack of clerical interest in royal women or even due simply to fears about offending the royal family. Rather, this textual gap is more accurately explained as a product of the common medieval practice of negotiating contemporary cultural concerns through retrospection, specifically, through textual accounts of the past.[10] While the extant Anglo-Saxon corpus contains few depictions of living queens, it is nevertheless replete with rich and imaginative accounts of queens from distant, bygone worlds, queens from the Old Testament, from Germanic paganism, and from Christian late antiquity, whom Anglo-Saxon writers resurrected from the past to inhabit the mead halls and mythic courts of their verse and prose. *Ruling Women* traces Anglo-Saxon writers' preoccupation with legendary queens to consider the cultural work that they performed for their Anglo-Saxon authors and audiences. Focusing on five major pre-Conquest works—Bede's *Historia Ecclesiastica,* Cynewulf's *Elene, Beowulf,* and Ælfric's alliterative prose versions of the Old Testament Kings and Esther—I argue that Anglo-Saxon writers used legendary royal wives to model cultural ideals of queenship during a historical period in which queenship was itself undergoing profound changes; and to participate in the creation of ideologies of gender, family, spirituality, and politics which were both instantiated in and extended far beyond the rarified realm of the royal palace.

Unlike their later medieval successors, pre-Conquest writers seldom used female figures to register overt misogyny; to ventriloquize feelings of disempowerment, marginality, or compassion; or to gain access to the spiritual privileges that were thought to be available by identifying with the "weaker sex."[11] Rather, Anglo-Saxon writers drew on legendary royal wives to explore and to express their views on the most difficult and debated issues of Anglo-Saxon society: conversion, social hierarchy, heroism, counsel, idolatry, and lay spirituality. While their topical focuses, thematic interests, and formal strategies vary a great deal, Anglo-Saxon writers nevertheless exhibit a shared sense of the queen as a mediatory figure, a hybrid character who usually hails from a foreign kingdom and who offers the potential to bridge differences between groups of people, social structures, and systems of belief. Anglo-Saxon queens' ever-fluctuating social status and their strong associations with intercession, combined with legendary queens' ability to traverse temporal, territorial, institutional, and symbolic boundaries, further established a powerful link between queens and the idea of transition. Anglo-Saxon writers thus consistently mobilized queens to negotiate sustained tensions, and sometimes overt antagonisms, between neighboring tribes, between Church and state, between ecclesiastical and lay culture, between paganism and Christianity, and between competing conceptions of heroism. Yet the queen's intermediary capacity for different peoples, institutions, and ideologies is accompanied by a dangerous ability to destroy the very bonds she fosters. Thus, unlike evil, tyrannical kings, who are often permitted to exist within their communities, queens who refuse to work toward the bridging of differences are usually forcibly reformed, exiled, or killed. As focal points for encounters between past and present, between traditional and revisionist models of belief and social practice, legendary queens in Anglo-Saxon texts are poised at moments of cultural instability or change, and they exert a powerfully ambiguous potential: to accomplish exemplary negotiations that alleviate cultural strain, or, more fearfully, to break apart existing unities and to show how tenuous and constructed they really are. Early medieval writers' relationships to legendary queens were thus underwritten by a constant dialectic of hope and fear: the hope that exemplarity was the lens through which these female figures would be perceived, thus making them a potentially powerful means of influencing contemporary politics, patterns of thought, and social practice; and the fear that legendary queens might function as dangerous exemplars and lead readers to social and spiritual transgression.

In spite of the pervasive presence of queens in both Anglo-Saxon literature and historical documents, Anglo-Saxon queenship remains an elusive concept. Unlike fourteenth-century France or Elizabethan England, in which heated debates on gynecocracy thrust queenship into the arena of both oral and written discourse, Anglo-Saxon England has left us no general tracts or treatises on queenship, no historical documents designating queenship as a public office or position with attendant rights and responsibilities. While the roles of other key political players, such as kings and bishops, were laid out in coronation ceremonies, ecclesiastical treatises, and monastic rules, queens' roles were far less clearly defined—so much so, that historians have questioned whether queenship as an institution actually existed during the early Middle Ages, or whether early medieval queenship is a presentist assumption imposed on the early Middle Ages by modern historians.[12] Throughout this study, my interest is in reconceptualizing queenship—in viewing it not as a construct manufactured by rigid institutional definitions that have evaded modern historical sensibilities, but as an idea that took shape within the particular contexts in which it was enacted. The richly imagined courts within Anglo-Saxon literary and historical writings offer a unique set of such contexts—in part because these texts were driven less by their authors' recapitulation of objective truths than by their authors' desire to create exemplary fictions. As Barbara Raw points out, images of the past in medieval art were usually intended not to provide objective pictorial recollections for teaching individuals about Christ's life or biblical history, but rather to focus the mind on the present and the heavenly future, and to elicit specific emotional and behavioral responses from medieval audiences.[13] The idea that textual representations of the past had similar formative power and could provide models of living for contemporary audiences is famously captured in the opening lines of Bede's *Historia Ecclesiastica,* in which Bede maintains:

> Siue enim historia de bonis bona referat, ad imitandum bonum auditor sollicitus instigatur; sue mala commemoret de prauis, nihilominus religiosus ac pius auditor siue lector deuitando quod noxium est ac peruersum.[14]

———

> Should history tell of good men and their good estate, the thoughtful listener is spurred on to imitate the good; should it record the evil ends of wicked men, no less effectually the devout and earnest listener or reader is kindled to eschew what is harmful and perverse.[15]

Although the drive toward queenly exemplarity in Anglo-Saxon texts necessarily shades away from any direct representation of the lives of contemporary royal women, that impulse nevertheless displays a textual and cultural negotiation of queenship that illuminates social attitudes that affected the lives of Anglo-Saxon queens.

Any consideration of the cultural work of queens in Anglo-Saxon literature speaks, of course, to a larger vexed problem with cultural studies generally in Anglo-Saxon criticism. Difficulties of securely locating Old English poetry, either temporally or geographically, have deterred all but a very few scholars from reading the poetic corpus through the lens of cultural criticism, or from exploring Old English verse in the context of the more firmly dateable pre-Conquest Latin and vernacular prose.[16] The slipperiness of Anglo-Saxon queenship as a historical institution, exacerbated by queens' powerful typological and symbolic resonances, has encouraged scholars to focus on legendary queens more as residual products of Latin and Germanic textual traditions than as compelling cultural artifacts, whose very alterations from their precursors reveal their authors' profound engagement with distinctly Anglo-Saxon social, spiritual, and political formations.[17] This book works to redirect the critical treatment of queens in Anglo-Saxon literature away from examining them mainly as products of different textual traditions and toward understanding them as complex sites of intersection between literary and cultural formations. In so doing, *Ruling Women* provides a revisionist perspective on earlier typological studies of queens that have sought to identify royal women's symbolic associations with particular virtues, biblical figures, or institutions, as forged through biblical exegesis and patristic commentaries.[18] Rather than taking the identification of each queen's symbolic significance as a goal in itself, I seek to understand how medieval writers exploited legendary queens' symbolic associations for contemporary Anglo-Saxon audiences. It was precisely because legendary queens carried such strong quotidian significance that they were so appealing to Anglo-Saxon writers—because writers could count on their audiences' knowing, for example, that Elene represented the successful union of Church and state, that Jezebel stood for the dangerous seductions of earthly glory, or that Esther symbolized the potential benefits of pious intercession. These meanings were backed by the weight of biblical and patristic authority, as well as the sense that the female figures to which these meanings adhered were timeless and transcultural. However, legendary female figures proved remarkably protean in the hands of early medieval writers, who seized hold of these powerful cultural symbols, cloaking them in Anglo-Saxon dress and habits of thought, divorcing them from particular (and foreign) contexts, and placing them within hazy, generic geographical environs so as to render them more accessible exemplars for contemporary audiences. As the mountains and rivers of Jerusalem and Rome recede, biblical and late antique women are transformed into strikingly Anglo-Saxon exemplars with the power to convey partisan, culturally specific ideas vested with the authority of tradition. By examining how Anglo-Saxon writers mobilized and refigured both legendary queens and their symbolic associations, *Ruling Women* seeks to revive typology as the historically and culturally engaged hermeneutic approach that it once was for medieval writers, as opposed to the reductive, closed system of analysis that it has tended to become in the hands of some medievalists.

Queens are the most ubiquitous female figures in the surviving corpus of Anglo-Saxon writings and have thus generated significant interest but also great ambivalence among feminist scholars.[19] Viewed generously, the numerous richly detailed accounts of legendary queens in pre-Conquest writings offer feminist medievalists an opportunity to undertake important recovery work and to balance a literary history that has for quite some time taken long-haired kings and mail-coated warriors as its main objects of investigation. Viewed less so, the prevalence of queens in Anglo-Saxon writings threatens to focus feminist energies on a very small subset of extremely privileged women, and thus to further the production of an elitist literary history already weighted with "great kings and conquerors." While feminist scholars have duly cautioned against using women of privilege to generalize about Woman as a unitary group, Anglo-Saxonists have, understandably, been attracted to a small but significant body of lexical, thematic, figural, and historical evidence suggesting that the line between queens and women of lesser social status can be productively conceptualized as a very fluid boundary. Numerous metaphors of queenship—the queen as the spiritual mother of all Christians or as the chaste body of the Church—emphasized roles and virtues that were equally available to a broad range of women in Anglo-Saxon society.

Lexical evidence reinforces the fluidity between Anglo-Saxon queens and women of lesser social status. The strong feminine noun *cwen* was used as a title for queens, as in the *Anglo-Saxon Chronicle*'s 722 entry, which recounts, "Her towearp Æþelburh cwen Tantun" (In this year, Queen Æthelburg destroyed Taunton);[20] yet the term was also used in a more general capacity to refer to any noblewoman or wife, as in Riddle 80's claim that "cwen mec hwilum / hwitloccedu hond on legeð, / eorles dohtor, þeah hio æþelu sy" (sometimes a fair-haired woman lays her hand on me, an earl's daughter, although she is noble).[21] The weak feminine *cwene*, which ultimately led to the archaic *quean*, had an even broader valence and was used to refer to a wide range of women, including ordinary laywomen, concubines of priests, prostitutes, and the Virgin Mary.[22] Indeed, the word "queen" is derived from the proto-Indo-European **gwen*, a word originally meaning "woman" and from which is derived the Greek *gyn*, a prefix that denotes a generic non-class-specific womanhood.[23] Exemplary queenship in Anglo-Saxon texts thus comprehends, as I argue, not simply legendary royal wives but also ideals of normative femininity generally, pointing at once to recognizable queenly figures and to women who enjoy significantly less social stature, and about whom Anglo-Saxon sources are largely silent.

The mutability of the linguistic and cultural signifiers surrounding Anglo-Saxon queenship and, by extension, womanhood generally suggests that queens, perhaps even more so than the familiar and putative heroes of many Anglo-Saxon texts, are the actual register of the cultural climate. Legendary queens' historical and metaphorical richness made them particularly open to multiple interpretations and thus able to speak to different readerships, made them, as Claude Lévi-Strauss puts it, "bonnes à penser"—an ideological convergence of "good" to consider, "goods" to trade, and "maids" to employ as sexualized servants.[24] By examining representations of royal wives along with the cultural concerns they embody, *Ruling Women* offers a fresh perspective on the well-worn "Golden Age debates" among feminist medievalists of the 1980s and early 1990s over the relative power of women in pre-Conquest England.[25] I shift critical concern away from investigating how much power Anglo-Saxon women had, either individually or collectively, and toward illuminating what kinds of roles and power women are shown textually as taking up. Anglo-Saxon writers had, I argue, a strong sense of royal women's rightful place as not constrained to either the bedroom or the birthing chamber, but as expanding outward toward sociopolitical acts and endeavors that trouble traditionally conceived gender boundaries. This is not to say that gender is irrelevant or secondary within these texts, but simply that Anglo-Saxon writers mobilize contemporary understandings of gender to explore and to express their views on a far broader range of issues.

In arguing that Anglo-Saxon writers use queens to address issues that reach beyond the boundaries of either queenship or gender, I also strive to stake a somewhat bolder claim, namely, that it is to a large extent their gender that made queens so attractive to Anglo-Saxon writers as vehicles for social commentary and cultural critique. Placing a woman in the middle of a text, particularly in a traditionally male role or story, as in *Elene,* or asking readers to view an event through the eyes of a woman, as in the Finnsburg episode in *Beowulf,* is an effective strategy for upsetting an audience's expectations, forestalling their primary reactions and creating a space of cultural critique. It is a strategy that works particularly well in heroic poetry, where queens are typically relegated to a position outside, or rather, just alongside, the cycle of violent action that organizes heroic life. Forced

to act as involved observers rather than direct participants in heroic violence, queens are thus able to offer powerful commentary upon it. This
special perspective is not limited to queens; rather it is ascribed to any "disenfranchised" or, one might say, "feminized" voice, including the voices of
most women, old men, children, monks, poets, and all those deemed "un-
manly" by virtue of their inability to occupy the heroic position prescribed
by the narrative. Writing—and reading—from a "woman's" point of view
was a powerful tool, perhaps one of the few available in nondidactic texts,
for social critique.

Throughout this study, I consider Anglo-Saxon queenship not as a rigidly defined historical institution but as an idea that took its relative meanings from the particular contexts in which it was enacted. Because these
contexts include not only the fictional courts in Anglo-Saxon literature but
also the material courts in early medieval England, I offer here a brief overview of the history of queenship in pre-Conquest England and the social
roles that were available to queens during this period. My remarks are not
intended to be comprehensive but simply to highlight common issues that
emerge in the fictions and practices of Anglo-Saxon queenship, and also to
provide a few key examples that underscore the ill-defined, ever-changing,
and extremely volatile nature of queenship in Anglo-Saxon England.[26]

Anglo-Saxon queens were almost always queens consort; that is, they
became queens through marriage rather than inheritance. Although few
queens from the period actually held the throne, women were not techni-
cally excluded from royal succession; nor was their fitness for rule ever disputed. Unlike fourteenth-century France and Elizabethan England, where
heated debates raged over women's fitness for national rule, in Anglo-Saxon
England female rulership was never openly debated, nor do the Anglo-
Saxons seem to have been opposed to the idea. The 672 annal of the *Anglo-
Saxon Chronicle* matter-of-factly records that Seaxburh ruled Wessex for
one year after the death of her husband, King Cenwealh; the *Mercian Register* offers ample evidence that Æthelflæd ruled Mercia for at least eight
years after her husband's death (911–18); and the *Mercian Register* also suggests that when Æthelflæd died in 918, leaving only a daughter, Ælfwynn,
the Mercian nobility supported Ælfwynn as their next ruler.[27] It is also possible that Anglo-Saxon queens exercised direct rule by acting as regents
during a king's absence from court or when the heir-apparent was under-
age. However, most of the contemporary evidence points to the regency of

ealdormen or bishops during royal absence, and also to the fact that the Anglo-Saxons tended to prefer fraternal succession to minority rule.[28] It is thus unlikely that many Anglo-Saxon queens functioned as regents.

Although Anglo-Saxon queens occasionally exercised power through direct rule, they far more often claimed authority through informal channels, most notably, intercession and counsel. The idea that Anglo-Saxon queens might offer their husbands valuable counsel on both domestic and political affairs was backed by a long tradition of reverence for female counsel within Germanic culture.[29] As early as the first century A.D., Tacitus remarked on the extent to which Germanic men valued female counsel.[30] The Anglo-Saxons' esteem for female counsel is borne out in the frequent appearance of the wise and verbally adept aristocratic *ides,* "woman," in Old English poetry, as well as in such gnomic poems as *Maxims I,* which prescribes that a wife ought to "rune healdan . . . ond him ræd witan / boldagendum bæm ætsomne" (keep counsel . . . and know advice for them both, for both home-owners together).[31] It was perhaps in part the assumption that Anglo-Saxon kings would look to their wives for counsel that led such Continental churchmen as Pope Gregory the Great and Pope Boniface V to write to English queens in the seventh and eighth centuries, urging them to soften the hearts of their husbands, and to draw them away from their former pagan practices and toward Christianity.[32] During this early stage of England's Christianization, queens played prominent roles in promoting the Church. They functioned as patrons of monasteries and founders of churches; their coronation ceremonies were initially modeled on the rituals used for the making of an abbess; and seventh- and eighth-century queens who were either widowed or abandoned frequently founded and entered monasteries, usually appointing either themselves or one of their daughters as abbess.[33]

While seventh- and eighth-century queens do seem to have exercised significant influence in matters related to national spirituality, the authority of the queen during these centuries was very much dependent on her position as the king's wife. The amount and kind of power early Anglo-Saxon queens exercised thus varied a great deal, and was dependent on both the personality strength of the individual woman as well as the extent to which her husband wished her to participate in political life. So too the relative laxity of seventh- and eighth-century English marital practices left the queen vulnerable to losing her position. During this period, Anglo-Saxon kings regularly took concubines, any of whom might be called on to replace the queen.[34] Moreover, before the tenth-century Benedictine reforms, it was fairly easy to leave one's spouse and not uncommon for an Anglo-Saxon king to have several queens over the course of his life.

Perhaps no text better illustrates the extremely tenuous nature of the Anglo-Saxon queen's position than Asser's *Life of Alfred*. Writing in 893, Asser recounts a slanderous tale about a West Saxon queen living in the early ninth century, detailing how this queen's antipathy toward both her husband and her people led to her own expulsion from the throne as well as to strong public opposition to granting either titles or thrones to all subsequent West Saxon queens:[35]

> Gens namque Occidentalium Saxonum reginam iuxta regem sedere non patitur, nec etiam reginam apellari, sed regis coniugem, permittit. Quam controversiam, immo infamiam, de quadem pertinaci et malevola eiusdem gentis regina ortam fuisse, maiores illius terrae perhibent; quae omnia contraria seniori suo et omni populo ita peregit, ut non solum suum proprium odium mereretur, ut a reginali solio proiceretur, sed etiam omnibus suis subsequutricibus eandem pestiferam tabem post se submitteret. Pro nimia namque illius reginae malitia omnes accolae illius terrae coniuraverunt, ut nullum unquam regem super se in vita sua regnare permitterent, qui reginam in regali solio iuxta se sedere imperare vellet.[36]

> ──────

> For the West Saxons did not allow the queen to sit beside the king, nor indeed did they allow her to be called "queen," but rather "king's wife." The elders of the land maintain that this disputed and indeed infamous custom originated on account of a certain grasping and wicked queen of the same people, who did everything she could against her lord and the whole people, so that not only did she earn hatred for herself, leading to her expulsion from the queen's throne, but she also brought the same foul stigma on all the queens who came after her. For as a result of her very great wickedness, all the inhabitants of the land swore that they would never permit any king to reign over them who during his lifetime invited the queen to sit beside him on the royal throne.[37]

As Asser calls attention to the vulnerability of queens in ninth-century Wessex, he also reveals a sense of increasing debate and contention over queens' roles during this century. Although Asser characterizes the early ninth century as a period of popular consensus, with "omnes accolae illius terrae" (all of the inhabitants of the land) opposed to queens inhabiting the throne or possessing the title *regina*, he suggests that by the time that he was writing in the 890s, popular opinion on the social status of queens had become far more fragmented and diverse. Asser refers to public opposition to West Saxon queens inhabiting the throne as an "infamia" (disgrace, scandal, infamous practice) and also as a "controversia" (controversy), suggesting that late ninth-century attitudes in Wessex toward queens were divided and that some of the higher echelons of West Saxon society favored granting queens more status than had formerly been customary. So too Asser himself harshly condemns popular opposition to the queen's possession of public authority, characterizing such opposition as a "perversa illius gentis consuetudo" (perverse custom of that people) and also as a "detestabilis consuetudo in Saxonia" (detestable custom in the Saxon land)—a stance that probably derives from Asser's own cultural background, as he had come to Wessex from Wales, where queens were typically granted significant authority.[38]

The debates over queenship in ninth-century Wessex that Asser so vividly describes were enacted during a period when queens seem to have had relatively minimal political power. Unlike earlier and later annals of the *Anglo-Saxon Chronicle*, ninth-century annals do not refer to queens by either name or title, and they mention queens only for the purposes of explaining dynastic connections created through marriage. Similarly, studies of queens' signatures on pre-Conquest land-grant charters have shown that, while queens frequently served as charter witnesses in the eighth, tenth, and eleventh centuries, they did so far less often during the ninth century.[39] However, the ill-defined and unstable nature of Anglo-Saxon queenship that permitted a sharp decline in the status of ninth-century West Saxon queens allowed for exactly the opposite situation to obtain in the following centuries.

The tenth and eleventh centuries witnessed dramatic changes in the social and symbolic status of Anglo-Saxon queens. As reformers argued for increasingly strict marital laws, repudiating one's wife became increasingly difficult, affording queens additional security that they would be able to keep their positions. This period also saw the establishing of new titles for queens and queen mothers, the increased use of public anointing ceremonies for queens, the formal appointment of a queen as the official patron of female monasteries, the regular attendance of queens at meetings of the royal council, the enthronement of the first female ruler of central England, an increased esteem for royal maternal lineage, and the designation of queens as officially responsible for the conversion of heathens.[40] It remains unclear whether the increased social and symbolic status of tenth- and eleventh-century West Saxon queens was accompanied by increased power, or even any changes at all, in the practice of queenship. Because Anglo-Saxon queens' power and influence had, historically, been exercised mainly through informal channels, the increasing formalization of queenly roles might have limited queens' power by erecting institutional barriers that prevented queens from taking up roles that had not been designated as rightfully theirs. So too such changes as new titles for queens, formal coronation ceremonies, and increased esteem for royal maternal lineage may simply point to an increased emphasis on the symbolics and rituals of queenship, an emphasis that, as Paul Strohm points out, corresponded with a decline in queens' actual power during the thirteenth and fourteenth centuries.[41] It is also worth noting that many of the roles taken up by tenth-century queens, in practice, differed little from those of seventh- and eighth-century queens. Changes in late Anglo-Saxon queenship point less to the emergence of new roles for queens than to an increased interest in codifying and formalizing queens' roles by recording them in such official documents as the *Regularis Concordia* and coronation *ordines*. While the burgeoning references to queens in these writings may be explained in part by the greater documentary evidence surviving from the later period, they also point to an emerging sense of queenship as a social role accompanied by specific rights and responsibilities. New understandings of queenship in the tenth century may well have been facilitated by literary representations—for it was during this very period that all of the major Old English poetic codices, as well as a significant portion of the prose texts, were copied and circulating.

In light of the highly unstable nature of Anglo-Saxon queenship, reading legendary queens historically is less a process of situating them within a fixed (or even debated) institutional discourse than a practice of reading them in light of the very few pre-Conquest references to general roles for queens and the more numerous references to roles assumed by individual royal women. Yet the lack of a clearly defined historical discourse of Anglo-Saxon queenship which renders it so difficult to historicize representations of queens in Anglo-Saxon literature may, paradoxically, be partly respon-sible for our having so many rich and complex depictions of queens to work with in the extant Old English corpus. In short, queens may have held a topical appeal for early medieval writers precisely because queenship was less a construction manufactured by rigid institutional definitions than a nascent interpretive possibility that writers took power and pleasure in shaping within the fictional courts of their texts.

Chapter 1, "The Costs of Queenship," investigates queens as agents of Christian conversion in Bede's *Historia Ecclesiastica* (A.D. 731). I argue that Bede exploits the historic synonymy between queens and the earthly wealth and power they offered kings through dynastic alliance in order to lessen the gap between the values of pagan warlords and the desires of Christian missionaries. Royal women become, for Bede, a means of synthesizing in-congruities between a history of pagan kings who viewed conversion as a one-time price for acquiring a well-connected royal wife, and Bede's own vision of conversion as an ongoing process of spiritual transformation ef-fected by recognition of the intrinsic beauty not of the worldly lovely wife but of the divine heavenly kingdom. Chapter 2, "Crossing Queens, Pleasing Hierarchies," interrogates how a queen serves to define and challenge social and gender hierarchies in Cynewulf's *Elene*. I argue that, in translating the Roman empress into an Anglo-Saxon queen, Cynewulf creates a provoca-tive and almost paradoxical female figure whose experience of subservience as productive of personal happiness works to naturalize and perpetuate highly conservative institutional and ideological formations, even as her own representation through Cynewulf's revisionist history encourages readers to imagine those formations as open to negotiation. Chapter 3, "*Beo-wulf* and the Gendering of Heroism," shows how royal women become vehicles for addressing the sustained tension in Anglo-Saxon culture be-tween competing models of heroic masculinity. The *Beowulf* poet uses royal feminine voices and tears to redefine the criteria for cultural memo-rialization, a challenging enterprise in a society that clung fiercely to the belief that heroism ensued from the strength of one's handgrip and the ca-pacity to terrorize neighboring kingdoms.

My final two chapters, "Queenship and Royal Counsel in the Age of the *Unræd*" and "Queenship and Social Reform in Ælfric's *Esther*," turn to Ælfric's discussions of the Old Testament queens Jezebel and Esther in his alliterative prose renditions of Kings (A.D. 992–1002) and Esther (A.D. 1002–5). Focusing on differences between Ælfric's queens and their biblical counterparts, I situate these differences in the context of contemporary changes in the social and symbolic power of Anglo-Saxon queens. "Queenship and Royal Counsel" demonstrates that Ælfric uses the Old Testament queen Jezebel to offer a veiled critique of late tenth-century royal counsel, a tense issue at this time given queens' increased participation in court politics and the young king Æthelred's notorious inability to distinguish between good and bad advice. Although it would be many years before the king's problems with royal counsel would be publicly codified in his unfortunate epithet "Æthelred the *Unræd*," Ælfric's efforts to articulate the social dangers generated by an ill-advised king reveals that Æthelred's early troubles were by no means overlooked by his contemporaries. "Queenship and Social Reform" focuses on Ælfric's threading of such issues as female beauty, spousal abandonment, and royal concubinage through the figure of Esther—his registering of the rather frenzied reassessment of gender emerging from tenth-century Benedictine reformers' efforts to bring the social and spiritual practices of the laity under heightened surveillance. Here, I explore how the biblical story of a queen who saves her people from a royal mandate of genocide becomes, for Ælfric, an occasion to propagate reformist ideologies of gender, marriage, and lay spirituality, and thus becomes a way to enhance our understanding of the role that literature played in the Benedictine reforms.

Considering queens as illustrative of reformist ideals returns us then to the question of what queens had to offer early medieval writers. It brings us back to the *Liber Vitae* drawing, in which Ælfgifu's outstretched hand recalls queens' potential to endow monasteries, and indeed long after her husband lay dead and entombed in an elaborate casket in Westminster, Ælfgifu continued to patronize the New Minster, enriching the foundation in 1040 with the much-coveted relic of Saint Valentine's head. Yet, unlike Cnut's hand, which firmly grasps the Cross, Ælfgifu's hand merely reaches toward this material object, ultimately effecting nothing except the division of the word *regina* on the manuscript into two distinct parts. The queen's suspended hand slicing through this word is a fitting reminder of the kind of queenship this book seeks to describe: one that is full of possibility, imbricated in the material and social practices of Anglo-Saxon culture, and both created and disrupted by representation.

Chapter 1

The Costs of Queenship

One of the roles most often attributed to early medieval queens by contemporary writers was in the service of Christian conversion.[1] The Germanic prototype of the proselytizing queen was Clotild, the sixth-century queen of the Franks, who, on her wedding night, was reputed to have taken the customary moment of marital consummation as an opportunity to urge her husband Clovis to burn his meaningless idols and to worship the Christian God.[2] Numerous other missionary queens, including Clotild's daughter (also named Clotild), Helena, Clotsinda, and Theudelinda, appear in the writings of such churchmen as Gregory of Tours, Pope Gregory the Great, Bishop Nicetius of Trier, and Paul the Deacon, who alternately praise and chastise queens for their valiant or inadequate efforts at spousal conversion.[3] Perhaps no text more powerfully grapples with the model of "conversion by marriage" than Bede's *Historia Ecclesiastica,* a work that is deeply concerned with conversion—in all of the term's complex senses. Understanding precisely what conversion meant in medieval culture has proved notoriously difficult for modern scholars, in part because "conversion" was less a term used to denote a particular spiritual event than a broad rubric to capture a variety of religious experiences, and in part because the defining characteristic of those experiences is their ineffability.[4] Conversion was understood to encompass such experiences as the formal adoption of a new faith, marked by a public ceremony such as baptism; the dramatic flashes of divine revelation that shatter the self so that it might be remade in the image of that which has been revealed; and the ongoing attempts to transform one's spiritual self, a process that Karl Morrison captures in his description of the High Middle Ages as a period when "all of life, rightly lived, was conversion."[5] These various aspects of conversion constitute both the *topos* and the *telos* of Bede's *Historia Ecclesiastica,* which details England's spiritual transformation from paganism to Christianity in order to inspire spiritual transformation in contemporary readers. While queens and royal women appear throughout the *HE,* Bede never illustrates a queen's conversion, focusing exclusively on the conversion of kings and their people.[6] One of the reasons that queens in the *HE* are never shown to convert may be that, generally speaking, they tended to come from Christian families—either Continental or recently converted English—and were thus already Christian. These queens were typically married to pagan husbands, leading numerous modern historians to believe that queens played a vital role in England's conversion and thus merited inclusion within the Anglo-Saxon historical record as well as modern histories of the period.[7] More recently, however, scholars have questioned the extent to which royal women participated in England's conversion, as well as the extent to which Bede's depictions of them can be taken as at all representative of women's roles in early medieval society.[8] Scholars have long recognized the profound biases in Bede's work—his Deiran and pro-Roman loyalties, or his reluctance to write extensively about the content of pagan practice—and Bede's lack of attention to women's contributions to the establishment of Christianity in England has been seen as arguably another symptom of his biases.[9] Viewed on the one hand as a mark of female presence within a largely male historical record, and on the other, as a mark of women's erasure, the figure of the queen in Bede's *HE* has occupied a rather vexed position within modern criticism.

My concern in this chapter is not to use the *HE* for historical insight into queens' participation in England's spiritual transformation; nor is my intent to use Bede's treatment of queens as evidence for the partiality of the *HE*'s account of a past that Bede hoped to have been rather than one that really was. To draw a rigid line between history and hope would be at odds with the historiographical principles of the *HE,* from which the twin pillars of eyewitness and exemplarity—the reports of the human and textual witnesses that Bede claims as his sources, and the intratextual examples that he hopes will spur the faith of his readers—emerge as equally crucial structural supports guiding the text's design. Rather, my intent is to trace the rhetoric of queenship, royal marriage, and "domestic proselytization" in the *HE*, and to elucidate the cultural work attempted through Bede's treatment of these gendered constructs.[10] My conviction is that Bede uses queenship and royal marriage in the *HE* to lessen the gap between the values of pagan warlords and the ideals of Christian missionaries. By foregrounding the historic synonymy between queens and the earthly wealth and power they offered kings through dynastic alliance, and then distancing queens narratively, geographically, and figuratively from conversion, Bede constructs a spiritual past that looks less like an unbroken trajectory of royal conversions motivated by kings' unadulterated desire for earthly gain, than one interspersed with spiritual transformations effected by recognition of the intrinsic beauty of Christianity and the heavenly kingdom. As Bede rewrites the traditional—and to him, overly secular—tale of the queen's role in her husband's conversion, he refigures such entrenched Anglo-Saxon queenly roles as secular peaceweaver and catalyst for dynastic alliances, suggesting that royal women might be used, instead, to weave peace with God and to forge alliances between kings and clergy. The result is an exemplary narrative that promises that bonds between men, and the military victory, peace, and secular gain that were thought to ensue from those bonds, were more readily and permanently accessed if forged through union in Christ rather than marital alliances with women. Yet even as the *HE* works to revise readers' views on the most effective routes to earthly gain, it also teaches that such gain is rightfully understood as one of the delightful fruits of, and never the ultimate rationale for, adherence to the faith. As Bede distances queens from royal conversion, he "remembers" an English past that naturalizes the separation of the sexes and minimizes the important social roles that royal women played in England's spiritual transformation, while inadvertently revealing queens' powerful social and symbolic functions in that process.

Irishmen Bearing Gifts

Bede's first reference to royal women is to an unnamed collective of Irish women, each of whom is seen as having the potential to become a queen when handed over to an all-male band of Pictish settlers on the condition that in cases of doubted succession, the Picts would choose their new king from the female royal line.

> Cumque uxores Picti non habentes peterent a Scottis, ea solum condicione dare consenserunt, ut ubi res ueniret in dubium, magis de feminea regum prosapia quam de masculina regem sibi eligerent; quod usque hodie apud Pictos constat esse seruatum. (*HE*, i.i, p. 18)[11]

———

> As the Picts had no wives, they asked the Irish for some; the latter consented to give them women, only on condition that, in all cases of doubt, they should elect their kings from the female royal line rather than the male; and it is well known that the custom has been observed among the Picts to this day. (*HE*, i.i, p. 19)

Precisely what Bede meant by this statement, as well as its historical veracity, are matters for debate. Cases of doubted succession may refer specifically to instances in which there was no brother to inherit the throne, or simply to any time that the question of succession arose (i.e., whenever the throne became vacant), while election of a king from the female royal line may refer either to matrilinear succession or to the actual occupancy of the throne by a woman.[12] Both Henry and Nora Chadwick argue that Bede's statement is devoid of historical truth and is simply a conflation of one of the various Irish *Cruithnig* myths with Bede's own misunderstanding of the principle of matrilinear succession as practiced in contemporary Pictish society.[13]

The difficulty of ascertaining either the meaning or the historical veracity of Bede's remarks ought not to obscure the fact that they nevertheless capture a number of undeniable truths about the symbolic function of the exchange of royal women in Anglo-Saxon culture and within the *HE*. Both the Picts and the Irish view women as commodities, a term that I am here using in its broadest sense, as any thing whose exchangeability has become its most socially relevant feature.[14] Yet for the Picts, women are interchangeable—Pictish women left at home are easily replaced by Irish women acquired along the way—whereas for the Irish, women are not interchangeable but simply exchangeable, and indeed valuable, goods whose value resides in the fact that they are, as Annette Weiner puts it, "inalienable possessions"—that is, when given away in marriage, they continue to maintain powerful and intimate connections to their families of birth.[15] Adherence to these two very different logics of female commodification creates a severe power differential between the Picts and the Irish: belief in women's interchangeability leaves the Picts little choice but to acquiesce readily to the demands of the Irish, whereas recognition of the supreme value that resides in women on account of their exchangeable bodies and inalienable blood creates a permanent avenue for Irish claims to Pictish land through female lineage. It is most likely these claims that Bede is invoking when he asserts, immediately after the exchange of the Irish women, that the Irish "sibimet inter eos sedes quas hactenus habent uindicarunt" (won lands among the Picts. . . . These they still possess; *HE,* i.1, pp. 18, 19).

From the outset of the *HE,* Bede thus reminds us that women are never given freely; rather, as with any gift, their reception is marked by contingencies that establish new relationships and power differentials between groups of men. The exchange of women for the purposes of forming dynastic alliances, and thus gaining access to military backing and material gain, was a common Anglo-Saxon practice, so common that it accounts for the majority of references to royal women within the Anglo-Saxon corpus. It is nevertheless striking that this association between women, marriage, and material gain appears as the first reference to royal women in the *HE.* From this position of narrative precedence, the association presides over the history of England's spiritual development, at once asserting a connection between women and worldly prosperity that profoundly informed Anglo-Saxon royal politics, while adumbrating the very crass idea that England's Christianization was driven solely by royal marriages contracted for worldly gain—an idea that Bede fiercely works to deny.

Bertha: A "Foreign" Queen Ever More Distanced

Throughout the *HE,* the reception of royal women is figured as contingent on a heathen king's agreement either to convert to Christianity or to tolerate Christian worship within his kingdom. Queens are thus acquired through bargains waged, at least in part, over the revision of spiritual practices, and as the *HE* progresses, the price of queens grows ever steeper. The Frankish princess Bertha is given to Æthelberht of Kent "condicione . . . ut ritum fidei ac religionis suae . . . inuiolatum seruare licentiam haberet" (on condition that she should be allowed to practise her faith and religion unhindered; *HE*, i.25, pp. 74, 75). Edwin of Northumbria is denied Æthelberht's daughter until he promises not only to tolerate Christianity, but also to consider accepting it himself: "promisit se nil omnimodis contrarium Christianae fidei, quam uirgo colebat, esse facturum. . . . Neque abnegauit se etiam eandem subiturum esse religionem" (he promised that he would put no obstacles of any kind in the way of the Christian worship which the maiden practised. . . . Nor did he deny the possibility that he might accept the same religion himself; *HE*, ii.9, pp. 162, 163). Peada of the Middle Angles is granted Oswiu's daughter Alhflæd on the strictest conditions of all: "nisi fidem Christi ac baptisma cum gente cui praeerat acciperet" (only on condition that he and his nation accepted the Christian faith and baptism; *HE*, iii.21, pp. 278, 279). Bede thus narrates England's history as a trajectory of spiritual progress, with each subsequent king more willing than his predecessor to accept Christianity, thus creating the general sense that the kings of England's past were open to the new faith, and that their lack of belief was less a function of active resistance than a lack of exposure to Christianity, much as was the case among the Old Testament patriarchs.

The increasing tolerance that kings evince toward the faith also effectively distances each subsequent queen in the *HE* further from the stock trajectory of the female saint's life—either that of the legendary virgin martyr, who is typically born within a royal or noble family, or that of the more contemporary royal female saint, an identity commonly conferred on Anglo-Saxon princesses and royal widows, who frequently entered monasteries, often as abbesses, and were eventually venerated as saints.[16] As beautiful and well-born Christian women in a largely pagan land, early queens in the *HE* bear an initial resemblance to female saints, but one that is quickly revealed as superficial. The primary trope marking the female saint's life is her staunch adherence to Christianity and willingness to suffer in its defense. In the case of the virgin martyr, this suffering takes the form of sexual and physical defilement that is threatened by pagan men of royal or noble birth; in the case of the royal female saint, suffering is a more interiorized response to the wealth, elegant clothing, and food that the saint is forced to endure and that she despises as interference with her spiritual discipline. Unlike the royal women of hagiography, queens in the *HE* almost never suffer in defense of their spiritual lives, for they are married not to kings who enact the stock hagiographic role of the evil pagan suitor who threatens his bride's devotional practices, but to kings who create sanctuary-like conditions for their new wives to continue their devotions unhindered.[17] The conditions of ease and lack of strife that characterize the spiritual lives of queens in the *HE* markedly contrast with the lives of the various bishops and missionaries in the text, who are continually shown to toil and labor on behalf of the faith.[18] Queens in the *HE* thus do not appear to be active proponents of even their own faiths, let alone those of others. Their Christianity is figured as merely another facet of their lineage, a way of life bequeathed to them from birth and remarkably removed from spiritual struggle or any other acts of piety or devotion that might suggest these women as fitting exemplars for influencing the spiritual lives of those around them.

The passive nature of queens' spirituality is evident in Bede's first account of royal conversion, which opens by directly invoking Æthelberht's Christian queen, Bertha:

> Qui haec audiens manere illos in ea quam audierant insula, et eis necessaria ministrari, donec uideret quid eis faceret, iussit. Nam et antea fama ad eum Christianae religionis peruenerat, utpote qui et uxorem habebat Christianam de gente Francorum regia, uocabulo Bercta, quam ea condicione a parentibus acceperat, ut ritum fidei ac religionis suae cum episcopo, quem ei adiutorem fidei dederant nomine Liudhardo, inuiolatum seruare licentiam haberet. (*HE,* i.25, pp. 72, 74)

> ――――――

> On hearing this [the preaching of Augustine] the king ordered them [the Augustinian missionaries] to remain on the island where they had landed and be provided with all things necessary until he had decided what to do about them. Some knowledge about the Christian religion had already reached him because he had a Christian wife of the Frankish royal family whose name was Bertha. He had received her from her parents on condition that she should be allowed to practise her faith and religion unhindered, with a bishop named Liudhard whom they had provided for her to support her faith. (*HE,* i.25, pp. 73, 75)

The lack of overt hostility and guarded tolerance that characterize Æthelberht's reception of the missionaries are figured as having a precedent in the king's reception of his wife, from whom he has received "some knowledge about the Christian religion." Yet whatever knowledge of the Christian religion had reached Æthelberht through Bertha appears to have had a rather minimal effect upon him. After over a decade of living with a Christian wife, Æthelberht still characterizes the missionaries' talk of eternal salvation as "words and promises that are beautiful enough," but which are nevertheless unacceptable due to their being "new and uncertain" ("Pulchra sunt quidem uerba et promissa quae adfertis; sed quia noua sunt et incerta, non his possum adsensum tribuere"; *HE,* i.25, p. 74; translation my own). The skepticism evident in Æthelberht's verbal response to the missionaries is echoed in his behavior. Refusing to meet the missionaries in any building, he demands that they meet in open air, which he believes will effectually diminish the potency of any magical arts that the missionaries might use to trick or deceive him.[19] Bertha is depicted as capable of transmitting "some knowledge," but not enough to convert her husband, or even to familiarize him with such basic Christian teachings as the promise of salvation. Nor does Bede suggest that Bertha was ever capable of influencing Æthelberht's religious beliefs, thus departing from the views of Pope Gregory the Great whose letter to Bertha in 601, urging the queen to further cultivate her husband's nascent piety,[20] in addition to other letters addressed to such Continental queens as Theudelinda and Brunhild, conveys a very real sense of Gregory's belief in the potential efficacy of the queen to effect spiritual transformation.[21] Bede drives a sharp wedge between Bertha and the conversion of Kent, omitting Gregory's letter from the *HE,*[22] and attributing the conversions of Æthelberht and the Kentish people not to the queen but to the simple and innocent living of the Roman missionaries and their heavenly doctrine:

> Crediderunt nonnulli et baptizabantur, mirantes simplicitatem innocentis uitae ac dulcedinem doctrinae eorum caelestis. . . . At ubi ipse etiam inter alios delectatus uita mundissima sanctorum et promissis eorum suauissimis, quae uera esse miraculorum quoque multorum ostensione firmauerunt, credens baptizatus est. (*HE,* i.26, p. 76)

To put it briefly, some, marvelling at their simple and innocent way of life and the sweetness of their heavenly doctrine, believed and were baptized. . . . At last the king, as well as others, believed and was baptized, being attracted by the pure life of the saints and by their most precious promises, whose truth they confirmed by performing many miracles. (*HE*, i.26, p. 77)

Immediately after Æthelberht's conversion, Bede recounts that Gregory "cui gloriae caelestis suo labore et industria notitiam prouenisse gaudebat" (rejoiced to think that Æthelberht had attained to the knowledge of heavenly glory by Gregory's own labour and industry; *HE*, i.32, pp. 110, 111). Gregory's remarks underscore the idea that Æthelberht's conversion was motivated solely by the mission that he had organized, while repeated references to Gregory's humility throughout the *HE* circumvent any possibility of viewing his interpretation of the king's conversion as motivated by undue pride or as anything other than an accurate reflection of events. Far from suggesting Bertha's involvement in Æthelberht's conversion, Bede's brief invocation of her as a Christian presence in the royal household and subsequent attribution of the conversion of the king and his people to the Augustinian mission only foreground the queen's absence in the process of royal conversion.

Excellent studies on Bede and the age of conversion offer us two broad explanations for Bertha's apparent lack of involvement in Æthelberht's conversion: her gender and her national identity. Feminist scholars tend to explain Bertha's very minor role in the *HE* as a product of Bede's misogynistic biases and as symptomatic of the larger biases attendant upon women in the Anglo-Saxon historical record. As Stephanie Hollis points out, throughout the *HE* and the *Life of Cuthbert*, Bede tends to de-emphasize women's contributions to the establishment of Christianity and to the promotion of its institutional structures within England.[23] Moreover, as Clare Lees and Gillian Overing have shown, because Bede's work constitutes such a significant part of the surviving historical record for the age of conversion, his views have led to a very partial understanding of the literal and symbolic roles that Anglo-Saxon women played in the cultural production of early medieval Christianity.[24]

Such historians as Henry Mayr-Harting and J. M. Wallace-Hadrill tend to emphasize Bertha's Frankish origins, arguing that Æthelberht's reluctance to accept Christianity from his wife can be attributed to the implications of political dependence that reception of conversion from another kingdom entailed, and to Æthelberht's reluctance to position Kent publicly as subordinate to the Franks.[25] Ian Wood, who has most recently revived the question of Frankish involvement in the conversion, argues that the Angles were eager for Frankish assistance, and that it was not fear of Merovingian domination but the Franks' unwillingness to offer the Angles religious assistance that ensured it was a Roman and not a Frankish mission that Christianized Kent.[26] The most widely accepted explanation for Bertha's apparently minimal role in Æthelberht's conversion, however, focuses not on actual Frankish influence (or lack thereof), but on Bede's fierce desire to portray England's conversion as a product of Roman influence alone. Indeed it is not only Bertha whom Bede downplays, but also Bertha's Frankish bishop Liudhard and the Frankish priest-interpreters that Augustine brought with him—all of whom might well have played a role in Æthelberht's conversion.[27] In order to enhance the historical importance of the Roman/Gregorian mission, Bede minimizes the role of any other possible evangelizing forces in sixth- and seventh-century England. These included not only Frankish but also native British Christians. Although by A.D. 600 the bulk of British Christianity was concentrated in the west, surviving historical and archaeological evidence suggests that pockets of British Christianity—albeit at a popular rather than ecclesiastical level—still existed in Kent at this time.[28] Not surprisingly, Bede takes pains to suggest that the Britons, much like the Franks, were wholly uninvolved in England's conversion, vilifying the former as inveterate sinners who had not only forsaken God but also abandoned the tenets of brotherly peace in their refusal to preach to the English and in their efforts to undermine Augustine's teachings.[29]

Both gender and national identity offer plausible reasons for Bede's minimizing of Bertha's role in the conversion. Yet arguments for Bede's misogynistic sapping of conversionary energy from the queens he represents, or for his potential rewriting of history to emphasize the influence of Rome, are not, of course, mutually exclusive, for questions of national identity were already bound up with gendered political alliances before Bede ever came to write the *HE*. Both Bertha's gender and her national identity were factors that highlighted the idea of conversion as an act of subjection and an act motivated by the desire to augment secular power via dynastic affiliation—neither of which being aspects of conversion that Bede wanted to emphasize.

In his classic study of England's conversion, Henry Mayr-Harting makes the compelling case that to adopt the religious views of another culture was to acknowledge political subservience to that culture.[30] Mayr-Harting's argument offers a powerful explanation for Bede's efforts to dissociate Bertha from Æthelberht's conversion: to portray Æthelberht's conversion as motivated by his Frankish wife would have been to suggest his subservience to the Franks and his willingness to subordinate himself and his people to another kingdom in exchange for their support.[31] In the case of Æthelberht, the issue may already have been a sensitive one, given his rather lackluster military reputation and, specifically, his inability to claim even a single outstanding victory that would have marked him as a fitting imperial leader chosen by God.[32] To portray Æthelberht's conversion as an act of acquiescence to his wife's spiritual leanings would have been to emphasize further the king's weakness by depicting his conversion as a kind of feminization. Precisely what "feminization" may have meant to Bede's readers during a period when Christianity was less than a century old is still an open question. However, for Bede, steeped in biblical and patristic writings that emphasized the husband as the rightful possessor of superior wisdom, to acknowledge the superior wisdom of one's wife may well have been accompanied by a sense of masculine failure or an unnatural gender hierarchy within the household. Christianity already brought with it certain well-known problems with respect to the subjection of the masculine self: a positive valuation of humility and a problematic stance toward retaliatory violence. To invoke Bertha as the underlying cause of Æthelberht's conversion would be to frame that conversion as coextensive with two additional forms of subjection: political subjection to Bertha's native land, and domestic subjection to her wishes as a woman and wife. Portraying the first conversion of an English king as synonymous with his spiritual, political, and marital subjection was most likely not how Bede wanted to remember the initial steps of the glorious march that would bring England ever closer to its rightful position as God's chosen nation and leader of the new *imperium*.

For all of Bede's efforts to minimize the association between conversion and subordination, wholly escaping the idea that Christian subjectivity entailed subordination proved nearly impossible. In her study *The Psychic Life of Power*, Judith Butler makes the compelling case that both the subject and the individual psyche are formed through subordination and subjection to power that is external to the self.[33] Rather than thinking of power as solely "what presses on the subject from the outside," Butler urges an extension of the Foucaultian understanding of the subject as formed through the regulatory forces of discourse, to the effect that "power is not simply what we oppose but also, in a strong sense, what we depend on for our existence and what we harbor and preserve in the beings that we are."[34] While Butler's concern is the formation of psychic life in the modern secular state, her ideas may help to delineate various aspects of thought in an emergent Christian state. Butler's theory that subordination of the self to greater power results in the formation of the subject is, of course, the basic premise of Christianity. It is also a crucial premise of such Anglo-Saxon forms of sociopolitical organization as the lord-retainer relationship and the dynastic alliance, both of which entailed subordination of the self—that is, the subordination of a retainer to his lord or of one dynastic leader to another—in the interests of self-actualization through the acquisition of power, prestige, and protection. This paradoxical process by which subjecting oneself to a greater power simultaneously subordinates and actualizes the self is usefully encapsulated in Butler's contention that "an irresolvable ambiguity arises when one attempts to distinguish between the power that . . . forms the subject and the subject's 'own' power . . . [for] [a]t some point, a reversal and concealment occurs, and power emerges as what belongs exclusively to the subject."[35] It was most likely the belief that power was fluid and ultimately detachable from its originary sources that, in part, made lord-retainer relationships and dynastic alliances so attractive to the Anglo-Saxons.

Such texts as the *Dream of the Rood,* which frames service to Christ in the context of a secular dynamic between lord and retainer, remind us that some Anglo-Saxon writers attempted to harness the Anglo-Saxons' familiarity with subjection as an aspect of their sociopolitical organization in order to acculturate the inherently subordinating aspects of Christianity. Yet whether one conceived of subjection to Christ as being just like subjection to a secular lord, or viewed Christianization as a transfer of allegiances from a pagan lord to a new and more powerful Christian one, for Bede Christianity still required that one internalize the idea of Christ as one's new lord, which may well, in the case of Æthelberht, never have taken place. Historians have long argued that the military and political ascendancy of Æthelberht was very much dependent upon his dynastic affiliations with

Frankia, and it is possible, as Higham suggests, that "his acceptance of baptism was arguably [another] diplomatic move, occasioned by his need in 595–6 to seek an accommodation with what looked like the winning side in Frankia."[36] If Æthelberht's conversion was in fact motivated by a desire to ensure positive relations with a new Frankish king, it was indeed motivated by the desire to serve a new lord, but that lord was not Christ but rather Childebert II, with Christ simply an ancillary to Æthelberht's main goal of preserving Frankish-Kentish relations, symbolized in the figure of Bertha. By distancing Bertha from the conversion, Bede concomitantly distances the idea that the conversion of the first English king was motivated largely by the desire to procure earthly power and prestige through secular alliance.

Precisely what motivated Æthelberht to convert, however, remains open to debate. While we cannot be certain that Æthelberht converted in order to solidify relations with the Franks, what we can be sure of is that Æthelberht's conversion made his kingdom look a lot more like that of the Franks—even more so than it already did. Archeaological evidence points to a strong Frankish presence in East Kenting by the seventh century, and Æthelberht's court was one in which Frankish customs, clothing, habits of thought, and language were arguably considered more fashionable than foreign.[37] The Frankophilic nature of the East Kentings sharply distinguished them from most of the rest of England, and because the Franks were Christian, the conversion of Kent was another act that would have accentuated this difference.[38] For Bede, Christianization was the single most important factor that would ultimately unite England into a nation of believers. To identify the beginnings of that process as reinforcing an existing ideological division between East Kenting and the rest of the English was contrary to such a goal. A sense of English unity under Christian belief was more effectively fostered by presenting all of the various English kingdoms as common heirs to a system of belief that was bequeathed solely from Rome, a national genealogical fantasy that would also ultimately justify English claims to the island via rightful spiritual inheritance from its former Roman Christian inhabitants over British claims based on physical incumbency.[39] To invoke the Frankish Bertha was to question the sense of Christian *imperium* as an unbroken line between Rome and England.

Bede's fierce attempts to keep that line intact are evident in his portrayal of the expansion of Christianity in England as an actual physical displacement of the Frankish queen by the Roman missionaries. When

Augustine and his men are given leave to practice their faith, they are said to take up residence in an "ecclesia . . . antiquitus facta . . . in qua regina, quam Christianam fuisse praediximus, orare consuerat" (church built in ancient times . . . in which the queen who, as has been said, was a Christian, used to pray; *HE,* i.26, pp. 76, 77). Yet while Bede succeeds in ousting a Frankish queen from the church, Frankish presence proves far more intransigent, seemingly as entrenched in Kent as the stone church itself, which was dedicated to Saint Martin, patron saint of the Franks.[40] That the Roman missionaries should take up residence, and that the first king of England should most likely be baptized, in a church guarded by such a strong Frankish presence is perhaps less an incident of historical irony than it is testimony to the actual course of history that Bede so desperately works to conceal through profound manipulations of the royal female presence.[41]

Æthelburh in Perspective

Bede's account of the conversion of Edwin, king of Northumbria, begins, much like that of Æthelberht, by invoking the king's marriage to a Christian princess: "Huic autem genti occasio fuit percipiendae fidei, quod praefatus rex eius cognatione iunctus est regibus Cantuariorum, accepta in coniugem Aedilbergae filia Aedilbercti regis, quae alio nomine Tatae uocabatur" (The occasion of the conversion of this race was that Edwin became related to the kings of Kent, having married King Æthelberht's daughter Æthelburh, who was also called Tate; *HE,* ii.9, pp. 162, 163). While Bede's remarks offer the initial impression that Northumbria's conversion was implicated in its new relationship to the recently converted kingdom of Kent, forged by Edwin's marriage to a Kentish princess, the actual course of events that are shown to convert Edwin effectively undermine any sense that either Kent or Æthelburh was at all involved. Henry Mayr-Harting characterizes Edwin's conversion as a "Herculean labour" that may well have taken approximately nine years.[42] In the *HE,* the conversion stretches over the course of six chapters, as Bede elaborates numerous events that bring the king ever closer to an acceptance of Christian truth and progressively further from his marriage to Æthelburh. As Dorsey Armstrong argues: "As Bede recounts the progression of events which lead to Edwin's final acceptance of the faith, the originary moment, represented by Æthelburh, recedes further and further from the focus of the narrative, until it disappears altogether."[43] Armstrong's identification of a significant temporal lapse between the king's marriage to Æthelburh and his conversion as one means by which Bede disrupts the sense of a causal link between the two events invites consideration of additional strategies mobilized to this same purpose. Bede effects the disappearance of the royal marriage as a possible force behind Edwin's conversion not simply through narrative distancing, but also through articulating Edwin's marriage and the Northumbrians' conversion from the perspective of three different churchmen, Pope Boniface V, the bishop Paulinus, and himself, each of whom envisions the queen as playing an ever lesser role in royal conversion: for Boniface, the queen will ideally teach her husband Christian doctrine and open his heart to conversion; for Paulinus, she will symbolize national conversion; and for Bede, she will play no role at all.

In a letter to Æthelburh (ca. 619–25) that appears in the *HE*, Pope Boniface V compares the queen's firm commitment to serving Christ with her husband's equally tenacious commitment to the worship of idols, arguing that religious difference interferes with true spousal unity, both in this life and the hereafter, and that the queen ought to repair her broken marriage by illuminating the spiritual chasm of darkness and detestable error that separated her from her husband Edwin (*HE*, ii.11, pp. 172–75).[44] That Boniface believes Æthelburh capable of playing a significant role in her husband's conversion is underscored by his letter to Edwin, which urges the king to convert by reminding him that his wife had already done so (*HE*, ii.10, pp. 168, 169), and also by his exhortations to Æthelburh that she should send him the good news of conversion in Northumbria, just as soon as a messenger became available. The tone of the letter is one of great respect: Boniface asserts a special relationship between the queen and God and recognizes her as a partner in the rule of Northumbria, explaining that God converted her for the express purpose of kindling the spark of religious orthodoxy in Edwin and "all the nation that is subject to you" (totius gentis subpositae uobis; *HE*, ii.11, pp. 172, 173). That Boniface views the role of queen as wholly compatible with that of domestic spiritual adviser is suggested by his accompanying gifts to Æthelburh of a silver mirror and a gold-adorned ivory comb, objects whose significant material worth at once emphasize her royal position even while they gently exhort her to move beyond mere physical beautification and to see herself as the pope does: as an agent of spiritual work who might effectively devote herself to cleansing the defiled nature of her marriage.

Boniface's view of royal marriage as a potentially powerful tool for converting a king and people subtly contrasts with that of Paulinus, the bishop who has been entrusted to escort Æthelburh to Edwin's court, and to whose innermost desires Bede claims access:

et sic cum praefata uirgine ad regem Eduinum quasi comes copulae carnalis aduenit, sed ipse potius toto animo intendens ut gentem, quam adibat, ad agnitionem ueritatis aduocans iuxta uocem apostoli uni uero sponso uirginem castam exhiberet Christo. (*HE*, ii.9, p. 164)

––––––

[A]nd so in the virgin's[45] train he came to Edwin's court, outwardly bringing her to her marriage according to the flesh. But more truly his whole heart was set on calling the people to whom he was coming to the knowledge of the truth; his desire was to present it [the people], in the words of the apostle, as a pure virgin to be espoused to one husband, even Christ. (*HE*, ii.9, p. 165)

For Paulinus, royal marriage is less a potential strategy than a symbol for—or, to borrow his imagery, a surface that conceals—the real work of conversion, which, for him, will take place on a far larger scale. Although charged with the duty of escorting the body of the virgin Æthelburh to a pagan king, Paulinus imagines his real calling as the escorting of the collective virginal body of the Northumbrians to marriage with the true King. Thus Paulinus labors with his whole heart in the hope that a single, localized union of the flesh will be superseded by a massive, national betrothal of the spirit. For him, the royal marriage is a symbol and his tending of that marriage an act that will ideally be revealed as merely a surface for his real spiritual work.

Numerous modern critics have nevertheless cautioned us against dismissing the importance of surfaces, arguing that such surfaces as clothing, physiognomy, and gender and rhetorical performance play crucial roles in the formation of the self.[46] Yet Bede's sketch of the dichotomy between Paulinus's external behavior and the true intention of his whole heart urges us to read this scene less through an understanding of behavior as formative of self than as a potential signifier of self—what we would today identify as a Freudian model of behavior, in which acts or emotions function as crucial indices of interior aspects of the self, typically ones that are prohibited expression. This is not to deny a constitutive function for behavior, rhetoric, or ritual within Anglo-Saxon literature or culture,[47] but merely to suggest that the relationship between behavior and interiority that Bede is here invoking is more akin to one in which the external surface of the self is less constitutive than it is revelatory, as is the stock model of surface found in hagiography in which the golden aura of the saint, for example, serves as a *tacen,* "sign," of a soul lit by truth. In the case of Paulinus, however, the bishop's behavior does not so much reveal as it does conceal his true intentions, a disjunction between exteriority and interiority that is often suggestive of falseness or disingenuousness, as in the case of the richly dressed pagan statesmen of hagiography whose bright exteriors serve as false markers of what are truly dark and sin-stained inner selves. Yet the disjunction between Paulinus's external behavior and inner desires does not, I think, point to a falseness in the bishop but rather to the disjunction between what he recognized the Northumbrian court was and what he believed it could be: a court whose paganism required him to act as the spiritual protector of an individual Christian woman, but whose potential for Christianization would, ideally, ultimately render that role obsolete.

Although both Pope Boniface V and Paulinus figure royal marriage through biblical (and mainly Pauline) rhetoric, they use Scripture to slightly different ends. For both churchmen, spiritual union between the king and queen offers the promise of literalizing Scripture through its enactment within the court. Citing Matthew 19:5, "they two shall be in one flesh," and 1 Corinthians 7:14, "the unbelieving husband is sanctified by the believing wife," Boniface urges Æthelburh to convert her husband so that "profecto sacrae scripturae testimonium per te expletum indubitanter perclareat" (the testimony of holy scripture will be clearly and abundantly fulfilled in you; *HE,* ii.11, pp. 174, 175). Paulinus also views royal marriage as, ideally, a living embodiment of the Holy Word: in his vision of national conversion, the royal marriage of Æthelburh and Edwin symbolizes the longed-for betrothal of the Northumbrians to God, and both are figured as re-enactments of the Corinthians' espousal to Christ (2 Cor. 11:2). Where the two churchmen differ is in the extent to which they interpret Scripture as delineating a practical role for queens in royal conversion. While Boniface draws on Scripture to convince Æthelburh that converting Edwin is her moral obligation as a Christian wife, Paulinus uses Scripture to elucidate the symbolic meaning of the royal marriage. Yet these differences in emphasis ought not to obscure the fact that both Boniface and Paulinus view the royal marriage as crucially important for the conversion of Edwin and his people. Indeed the two churchmen's respective distinctions between the royal marriage as either catalyst or symbol for national conversion recede greatly when read in the light of Bede's own depiction of Edwin's conversion, which accords the royal marriage no role in that process at all.

Immediately following Boniface's eloquent, emotionally charged case for the idea of the queen as an agent of Christian conversion, Bede states that Edwin's conversion, much like Æthelberht's, was effected not by his wife but by other factors, namely, a divine vision: "Sed et / oraculum caeleste, quod illi quondam exulanti apud Redualdum regem Anglorum pietas diuina reuelare dignata est, non minimum ad suscipienda uel intellegenda doctrinae monita salutaris sensum iuuit illius" (But a heavenly vision which God in his mercy had deigned to reveal to Edwin when he was once in exile at the court of Rædwald, king of the Angles, helped him in no small measure to understand and accept in his heart the counsels of salvation; *HE*, ii.12, pp. 174–75, 176–77). Bede thus acknowledges conversion by marriage as a model of conversion endorsed by some churchmen, but then uses the cases of both Æthelberht and Edwin to suggest its inefficacy. The point is underscored by Bede's description of Edwin's vision as an experience that helped him to recognize Christian truths "non minimum" (in no small measure); the rhetorical trope of litotes enhances the sense of Edwin's vision as the real force behind his conversion.

The vision to which Bede attributes Edwin's conversion is one that takes place while the king is in flight from Æthelfrith, his predecessor as king of Northumbria. Significantly, the king is far from his wife, wandering as a fugitive for many years through many places, until he finally arrives at the court of Rædwald, from whom he secures a temporary sanctuary. Yet the precarious status of protection elicited by allying oneself to an earthly king is soon revealed when Rædwald, motivated by either bribes or threats, decides to turn Edwin over to his enemy, Æthelfrith. Floundering in the depths of a despair brought on by learning of his imminent betrayal at the hands of his supposed protector, Edwin experiences the vision that catalyzes his conversion. In the vision, a mysterious stranger appears, claiming to know Edwin's troubles and someone with the power to free Edwin from all of them. The "someone" to whom the mysterious stranger is referring is, of course, God. Yet Edwin is in fact saved by Rædwald's pagan wife, who, after learning of her husband's plan to betray Edwin, advises him that "nulla ratione conueniat tanto regi amicum suum optimum in necessitate positum auro uendere" (it would not be fitting for so great a king to sell his best friend for gold when he was in such trouble; *HE*, ii.12, p. 180, my trans.). Persuaded by the queen's exhortations that sacrificing Edwin would undermine his own royal honor, Rædwald determines not only to abandon his plan of betraying Edwin, but also to help him gain the throne by providing military support. That Rædwald both follows his wife's advice and confides his plan to her "in secreto" (in secret; *HE*, ii.12, pp. 180, 181) suggests that their relationship is a close one, and it is indeed arguably the closest relationship between a husband and wife that appears in the *HE*. Numerous texts and cultural artifacts suggest that the powerful association between wives and counsel in pre-Christian Germanic culture survived long after England's Christianization.[48] Yet Bede depicts wifely counsel as a practice that is operative within the pagan courts of England's past, and which has no place in Christian royal households. The queen's capacity to provide sound advice is also shown to be limited to secular matters, a point that is driven home when she is depicted as one of the forces behind her husband's decision to relinquish his newfound Christianity. Moreover, Bede undermines the role of the pagan queen in Edwin's rescue by repeatedly urging that his good fortune be understood as a sign of God's beneficence. Following Edwin's rescue, Paulinus laboriously enumerates each aspect of Edwin's fortune as a gift bestowed upon him by God: "'Ecce' inquit 'hostium manus, quos timuisti, Domino donante euasisti. Ecce regnum, quod desiderasti, ipso largiente percepisti'" ("First," he said, "you have escaped with God's help from the hands of the enemies you feared; secondly, you have acquired by His gift the kingdom you desired"; *HE*, ii.12, p. 180, my trans.). It would be tempting to argue that Bede grants an important role to the pagan queen as the conduit of God's will had not Paulinus already claimed that role, in his self-characterization as the bearer of "uoluntati eius, quam per me tibi praedicat" (His will which is made known to you [Edwin] through me; *HE*, ii.12, pp. 182, 183).

Both Stephanie Hollis and Dorsey Armstrong argue that Bede's effacement of the role of queens in the *HE*'s depiction of Christianization heightens the relative importance of both kings and bishops. As Armstrong asserts, "In Bede, queens do not convert peoples—kings and bishops do."[49] To be sure, Bede emphasizes the role of kings and clergy over that of royal women in England's conversion. Yet the numerous references that Bede makes to the exemplary living of missionaries and bishops, their capacity to work miracles, and their ability to make known heavenly doctrine and Christ's will remind us that their role is less that of independent agent of conversion than that of intercessor between king and Christian truth. We are thus also reminded of Bede's intent to convey clearly the idea that conversion was ultimately never brought about by missionaries, bishops, kings, or indeed any individual, but by the truth of salvation and Christian doctrine—evident in the words and works of the Roman missionaries that so impress Æthelberht, or in the will of God as revealed to Edwin through Paulinus. Implicit in Bede's emphasis on the conversion of kings as effected by missionaries and bishops is a belief in their inherent superiority over queens to serve as rightful conduits of Christian truth.

Bede's conception of conversion as entailing the effacement of the queen and her replacement by the truth of Christian doctrine brought to the king through the intercessory efforts of churchmen is given additional weight by the *HE*'s narrative framework. Prefaced by a letter from Bede to Ceowulf, king of Northumbria, the *HE* is presented as part of an ongoing dialogue between a humble priest and a king who is eager for his teachings. Having already sent Ceowulf, at his request, a copy of the *HE* for his perusal and criticism, Bede once again sends the text, this time for copying and fuller study. Ceowulf is depicted as receptive to Bede's spiritual advice and desirous of seeing the *HE* more widely distributed, both for his instruction and for that of his people. The ongoing spiritual instruction of the king and the English people is portrayed as a process that hinges on close relations between churchmen and kings. Ceowulf's queen remains unknown, as distant from that process as the queens within the *HE*.

Hollis characterizes Bede's treatment of queens and bishops as suggestive of competition, arguing that "for the role of adviser to kings and peacemakers . . . bishops and queens were rivals," a framework that I think is both apt and open to fruitful extension.[50] Rivalry between bishops and queens was not only a struggle for control over such roles as adviser, peacemaker, or even intercessor, but was also a struggle between what each group represented—namely, two different understandings of how one might acquire worldly prosperity and, by extension, two fundamentally different attitudes toward it. Throughout the *HE*, Bede never tires of asserting an inextricable causal link between faith and worldly prosperity, offering numerous examples of such kings as Edwin and Oswiu, whose prosperity is figured as a reward for their belief. But marriage to a well-connected for-

eign princess, like Bertha or Æthelburh, in effect promised the same results, simply via a different route: military victory, territorial expansion, and
earthly glory accrued by trust in the power of dynastic affiliation rather
than that of God. Distancing queens from the process of Christian conversion creates the sense that the conversion of England was driven by a recognition of God's power to provide for his people on earth, a belief that is
perhaps nowhere more evident than in Bede's account of the pagan high
priest Coifi's decision to relinquish his allegiance to his pagan gods in the
hope that Christ would prove more able to ensure his reception of benefits
and honor within the Northumbrian kingdom (*HE*, ii.13).

If part of the message that the *HE* seeks to convey is that faith would
be rewarded by prosperity in this world, the other part of that message is
that such prosperity was incomparably inferior to that which would be
found in the afterlife. It is worth recalling that Coifi's decision to embrace
Christianity on account of its potential to ensure his worldly success is followed by a very different rationale for conversion: when another of the
king's advisers offers the famous image of earthly life as comparable in its
brevity to the flight of a sparrow through the mead hall (*HE*, ii.13). In its
rejection of the earthly kingdom as incomparably inferior to the kingdom
of heaven, the speech of the nameless adviser offers a gentle corrective to
that of Coifi, revealing the pagan high priest's attitude toward earthly glories, and his rationale for conversion, as slightly benighted. The fact that
the members of Edwin's court do not agree to convert until they have heard
the adviser's meditations on the promises of eternal life suggests their internalization of the respective merits of earthly and heavenly life. Thus even
as the *HE* fosters the sense of worldly prosperity as a reward for faith, and
acknowledges that kings converted to better their lives on earth, it also reinforces the idea that earthly wealth was merely a very minor fruit of conversion, and that the kings in England's past recognized eternal glory as the
more important reward.

That conversion necessarily entails a reprioritization of earthly and
heavenly rewards is stressed again later on in Bede's account of the conversion of Peada, king of the Middle Angles, which begins, much like the conversions of Æthelberht and Edwin, with bargaining over a royal princess:

> uenitque ad regem Nordanhymbrorum Osuiu, postulans filiam /
> eius Alchfledam sibi coniugem dari. Neque aliter quod petebat
> inpetrare potuit, nisi fidem Christi ac baptisma cum gente cui

praeerat acciperet. At ille, audita praedicatione ueritatis et promissione regni caelestis speque resurrectionis ac futurae inmortalitatis, libenter se Christianum fieri uelle confessus est, etiamsi uirginem non acciperet. (*HE,* iii.21, p. 278)

———

He thereupon went to Oswiu, and asked for the hand of his daughter Alhflæd. But his request was granted only on condition that he and his nation accepted the Christian faith and baptism. When Peada heard the truth proclaimed and the promises of the kingdom of heaven, the hope of resurrection and of future immortality, he gladly declared himself ready to become a Christian even though he were refused the hand of the maiden. (*HE,* iii.21, p. 279)

Although the use of force to effect conversion may well have been acceptable among some factions of Anglo-Saxon society, Bede articulates an adamant opposition to this practice. After Æthelberht converts, he is said to have "nullum tamen cogeret ad Christianismum . . .[d]idicerat enim a doctoribus auctoribusque suae salutis seruitium Christi uoluntarium, non coacticium esse debere" (compelled no one to accept Christianity . . . [for] he had learned from his teachers and guides in the way of salvation that the service of Christ was voluntary and ought not to be compulsory; *HE,* i.26, pp. 76–79).[51] Bede also depicts compulsory conversions as ineffective in the long term, when he describes the large-scale apostasy precipitated by Eadbald as enacted by people "who had accepted the laws of faith . . . either out of fear of the king or to win his favour" (*HE,* ii.5, p. 151). When Peada states that he is "gladly . . . ready to become a Christian even though he were refused the hand of the maiden," the first point that Bede is making is that Peada's conversion was not forced upon him by the Northumbrian king, Oswiu, in exchange for his daughter, but was instead a voluntary decision inspired by Peada's exposure to the proclamation of Christian truth. The second point is that Peada's conversion was motivated not by a desire to procure worldly prosperity, but by a desire to gain access to the eternal joys of heaven. Significantly, when Peada declares himself willing to convert even if he is refused the hand of Alhflæd, his declaration is accompanied by repeated assertions of Christianity's promises for benefit in the afterlife, with not the slightest interest in what it might offer him on earth. When Peada dissociates his own rationale for conversion from his reception of Alhflæd, he implicitly asserts an internalization of the idea that the real fruits of conversion are not the earthly gains made possible by marriage to a well-connected bride but rather the "hope of resurrection and of future immortality" guaranteed by union with God.

Indeed while a king might gain access to worldly prosperity through either conversion or marriage, it was eternal rewards, such as resurrection and everlasting life, that clearly distinguished God's offerings from those promised by a well-connected queen. Movement away from the idea of the queen as an agent of conversion was thus, at the same time, a movement away from the idea that the early kings' investment in and adherence to Christianity were solely a function of secular bargains designed to procure wealth, power, military victory, and temporal glory—everything that royal women represented as accessible through dynastic connections, and everything that, as such historians as Mayr-Harting, Wallace-Hadrill, and Higham have so elegantly argued, was precisely what motivated the early Germanic kings to convert. It was a logic of which Bede and indeed all of the early missionaries were well aware, but one whose emphasis on earthly wealth and secular power rendered it a less than exemplary model of conversion for contemporary readers. And for Bede, factual truth was less important than moral truth—the truth of Christian faith that transcended mere history.[52]

Gendering Apostasy

The letters of Pope Gregory the Great and Pope Boniface V reveal that at least some of Bede's near contemporaries imagined conversion as entailing an increased proximity between husband and wife. Gregory focuses on Bertha's potential to edify her husband "adhortatione assidua . . . sollicitudo" (through constant exhortation [and] solicitude) so that they might then both reign happily over the English ("ut et hic feliciter cum glorioso filio nostro, conjuge vestro regnetis"),[53] while Boniface, as we have seen, focuses on Æthelburh's potential to convert her husband, and thus to bridge the chasm of spiritual difference separating them. For Bede, however, increased proximity between husband and wife tends to be associated with apostasy.

Moreover, when kings draw closer to women, it is not only their own spiritual progress that is compromised but also that of their people. Describing the accession of Eadbald, for example, Bede relates that at this time

> magno tenellis ibi adhuc ecclesiae crementis detrimento fuit. Siquidem non solum fidem Christi recipere noluerat, sed et fornicatione pollutus est tali, qualem nec inter gentes auditam apostolus testatur, ita uxorem patris haberet. Quo utroque scelere occasionem dedit ad priorem uomitum reuertendi his qui sub imperio sui parentis, uel fauore uel timore regio, fidei et castimoniae iura susceperant. (*HE*, ii.5, p. 150)

———

> there followed a severe setback to the tender growth of the Church. Not only had he [Eadbald] refused to receive the faith of Christ but he was polluted with such fornication as the apostle declares to have been not so much as named among the Gentiles, in that he took his father's wife. By both of these crimes he gave the occasion to return to their own vomit to those who had accepted the laws of faith and continence during his father's reign either out of fear of the king or to win his favour. (*HE*, ii.5, p. 151)

The apostasy of Rædwald is similarly connected to his uxoriousness. Although Rædwald had accepted Christianity while away from his wife and kingdom on a visit to Kent, Bede claims that the king's initiation into the mysteries of the Christian faith was

> frustra; nam rediens domum ab uxore sua et quibusdam peruersis doctoribus seductus est, atque a sinceritate fidei deprauatus habuit posteriora peiora prioribus. (*HE*, ii.15, p. 190)

———

> in vain; for on his return home, he was seduced by his wife and by certain evil teachers and perverted from the sincerity of his faith, so that his last state was worse than his first. (*HE*, ii.15, p. 191)

Bede's treatment of the apostasy of Eadbald and that of Rædwald are no doubt motivated by very different concerns.[54] In the case of Eadbald, the characterization of a marriage between son and stepmother as a "severe setback to the . . . Church" stems from opposition to a common Germanic practice, whose rationale is outlined in detail in Augustine's fifth question to Gregory (*HE*, i.27, pp. 84–87).[55] In the case of Rædwald, Bede's account of the king's resumption of pagan worship upon returning to his kingdom most likely reflects actual pressures placed on Rædwald by his wife and advisers occasioned by their unwillingness to allow him to adopt the religious affiliations of Kent and thus subject them to Kentish overlordship.[56] Nevertheless, the two accounts of apostasy share the belief that spiritual decline is contiguous with illicit sexuality or seduction, a belief that is rooted in the pervasive formulation within biblical and patristic writings of apostasy as spiritual fornication.[57] As they reinforce the language of the fathers, Bede's accounts of apostasy imagine it as prompted by a greater proximity between the sexes. And this idea finds fuller expression in its logical corollary: conversion imagined as a movement away from women.

While Eadbald's marriage to his stepmother precipitates a "severe setback to the tender growth of the Church," the king's subsequent decision to leave his wife is figured as an act that is both coextensive with his conversion and which leads to a general promotion of the Church: "Atque anathematizato omni idolatriae cultu, abdicato conubio non legitimo, suscepit fidem Christi, et baptizatus ecclesiae rebus, quantam ualuit, in omnibus consulere ac fauere curauit" (So he banned all idolatrous worship, gave up his unlawful wife, accepted the Christian faith, and was baptized; and thereafter he promoted and furthered the interests of the Church to the best of his ability; *HE*, i.6, pp. 154, 155).

The idea that conversion entails a movement away from women is further evident in Bede's treatment of those kings who sought out the highest form of conversion, namely, the renunciation of secular life in order to enter a religious community or to travel to Rome on a lifelong pilgrimage.[58] To advocate or even to countenance royal resignation for the sake of religious life was highly controversial, and would have been especially so for Bede, given that it meant contradicting the views of his esteemed forefather, Pope Gregory the Great, who strongly believed that a Christian king's duty was to remain in this world and not to opt out.[59] Yet far from criticizing monk-kings for abandoning their worldly obligations, Bede depicts these men in a very positive light. He tells us of Cenred, who had ruled Mercia *nobilissime* (very nobly) but "nobilius multo regni sceptra reliquit" (with still greater nobility renounced the throne of his kingdom; *HE*, v.19, pp. 516, 517) in order to travel to Rome and live out his life as a monk. We also hear of Cenred's traveling companion, Offa, heir to the East Saxon throne, who, "pari ductus deuotione mentis reliquit uxorem" (inspired by a like devotion, left his wife; *HE*, v.19, pp. 516, 517), along with his property, kinsmen, and native land, to become a monk so that he might receive the hundredfold reward in this world as well as everlasting life in the next. Perhaps the most interesting of the monk-kings in the light of gender concerns is Sebbi of the East Saxons, a king whose predisposition for prayer and almsgiving would have led him to take up monastic life "si non obstinatus coniugis animus diuortium negaret" (had not his wife obstinately refused to be separated from him; *HE*, iv.11, pp. 364, 365). Bede's expansive account of Sebbi's thirty-year-long efforts to gain his wife's permission before entering a monastery most likely reflects Bede's efforts to perpetuate Church teachings on the indissolubility of marriage as well as on the need to obtain spousal consent before embarking on a life of continence.[60] Yet the extreme difficulties that Sebbi must overcome in order to convince his wife to allow him to take up monastic life also work to convey the idea that a royal wife is not an aid but rather an obstacle to her husband's spiritual progress.

Even those kings in the *HE* who do not permanently relinquish their wives in order to undergo spiritual transformations do temporarily move away from women as part of the process of conversion. It is worth recalling how many kings in the *HE* convert while physically distanced from their wives: Edwin, Rædwald, Æthelwealh, and Peada all convert while away from home. Those kings such as Æthelberht who do convert within their own kingdoms are depicted as spiritually immune to wifely influence, having opened their hearts instead to the counsels of missionaries and bishops. In Bede's eyes, the king's home space and domestic life appear as wholly inadequate sites for fostering spiritual change. Royal conversion is shown to be contingent instead on a disruption of those sites: home must be either temporarily abandoned through a king's physical departure or transformed through an influx of missionaries and bishops in order to allow exposure to the kinds of influences sufficiently powerful to effect spiritual change. In this respect, Bede's views on royal conversion sharply diverge from those of his near contemporaries, many of whom saw the royal household and marriage as highly opportune sites for initiating conversion.

In the eyes of such churchmen as Pope Gregory the Great and Pope Boniface V, religious difference within the royal household was indeed a lamentable situation but one that was nevertheless charged with spiritual potential. A Christian wife was, to borrow Boniface's imagery, the spark that could ignite a pagan king with religious fervor and thus set the whole nation afire with the warmth of divine love (*HE*, ii.11). For Bede, however, this sense of the royal household as a site of spiritual opportunity is wholly lacking. Apparently convinced, or at least intent on convincing his readers, that queens were powerless to effect kingly conversions, Bede consistently figures spiritual division within marriage not as a catalyst for individual or national change but as an inert and static condition to be remedied only by the intercessory efforts of kings, or more typically, churchmen.

A good example is the marriage between the pagan Æthelwealh and the Christian Eafe, king and queen of the South Saxons. Although Eafe was born to a Christian family and had been baptized in her own homeland, the South Saxons are seemingly unaffected by her belief, remaining "diuini nominis et fidei . . . ignara" (ignorant of the divine name and of the faith; *HE*, iv.13, pp. 372, 373) until the arrival of Wilfrid, bishop of York, whose evangelizing leads to their baptism. Wilfrid's efforts are greatly supported by the recently converted Æthelwealh, whose rationale for accepting Christianity is also dissociated from Eafe: it takes place while the king is away from home "in prouincia Merciorum, praesente ac suggerente rege Uulfhere" (in the province of the Mercians, at the suggestion and in the presence of [their] king Wulfhere; *HE*, iv.13, p. 372; my trans.).

A similarly static condition of spiritual division between husband and wife is found in Bede's depiction of the marriage of Oswiu and Eanflæd, who practice different forms of Christianity: while Eanflæd observes Easter according to the Roman calendar, her husband follows the Irish tradition. Spousal differences of faith appear to have little effect on them, leading neither to marital discussions nor to personal change, but simply to a divided kingdom, in which the king and queen occupy separate spheres, with the king in Easter Sunday and its attendant implications of feast and celebration, and his wife still taken up with the ascetic strictures of the Lenten fast (*HE*, iii.25).[61]

Yet another case in which one spouse is Christian and seemingly powerless to convert his or her pagan counterpart is found in the marriage of Rædwald, who, like Æthelwealh, had accepted Christianity while physically separated from his pagan wife during a visit to Kent. Rædwald's conversion appears to have little effect on either his wife or his advisers and merely results in a condition that is sometimes referred to as "syncretism," in which an individual or community holds two faiths at the same time. As Bede puts it:

> Ita ut in morem antiquorum Samaritanorum et Christo seruire uideretur et diis, quibus antea seruiebat, atque in eodem fano et altare haberet ad sacrificium Christi et arulam ad uictimas daemoniorum. (*HE*, ii.15, p. 190)

> After the manner of the ancient Samaritans, he [Rædwald] seemed to be serving both Christ and the gods whom he had previously served; in the same temple he had one altar for the Christian sacrifice and another small altar on which to offer victims to devils. (*HE*, ii.16, p. 191)

The dramatization of religious difference between husband and wife in the *HE* is less indicative of a force potentially leading to England's spiritual transformation than it is illustrative of the island's early state of spiritual division—evidenced in both the enormous gulf between paganism and Christianity and the less vast but equally pernicious divide between Irish and Roman Christianity. Yet if national spiritual division is figured through images of broken marriages and spousal alienation due to religious differences between husband and wife, the reparation of that national problematic is not figured as a mending of those marriages. Rather, national spiritual unity in the *HE* entails an even greater distancing between husband and wife: the narrative and geographic displacement of queens as agents of kingly conversion, the figural displacement of the body of the virgin queen Æthelburh by the body of the Northumbrian people, and the depiction of kingly conversion as coextensive with a movement away from women. Thus even as alienation between man and wife in the *HE* symbolizes the lamentable state of England's spiritual disunity, the fact that its reparation entails an even greater distancing of royal men and women naturalizes and endorses a separation of the sexes that is wholly consistent with everything we know about Bede's largely misogynist gender politics. [62] Yet if examining Bede's attitudes toward royal women and conversion has brought us to a familiar place, it has nevertheless done so via a slightly new route. Bede's efforts to erase royal women from the history of England's conversion are driven not by straightforward misogyny or fear of female power. Rather they are motivated by a complex set of issues, at the heart of which lies Bede's desire to rewrite a very secular history of politically motivated royal conversions, and which, paradoxically, attests to the importance of royal women and marriage in the eyes of the early Anglo-Saxon kings.

Refiguring Queenly Roles

As Bede works to shift the grounds for royal conversion away from opportunistic marriages and toward Christian truth mediated through churchmen, he constructs a powerful corrective to the familiar tale of the queen as an agent of Christian conversion. Yet rather than simply dismissing normative queenly roles, Bede mobilizes and refigures them to his own ends. Capitalizing on the idea of the queen as a catalyst of dynastic alliances through marriage, Bede refigures that idea, suggesting that a queen's truly valuable intermediary capacities lie in her ability to forge relations not between kings but between kings and bishops. Æthelberht's marriage to Bertha, for example, offers him access to the bishop Liudhard; similarly, Edwin's marriage to Æthelburh offers him access to the bishop Paulinus. And if Bede's desire to dissociate Æthelberht's conversion from Frankish influence leads to a rather truncated account of Æthelberht's newfound access to Liudhard, once Frankish influence is no longer a problem, as in the case of Edwin's conversion, readers are given an account of royal marriage in which Edwin's nascent relationship with his bride's spiritual adviser threatens to overshadow his new relationship with the bride's family, and even the bride herself. Glossing quickly over the Northumbrian-Kentish alliance that resulted from Edwin's marriage, Bede instead emphasizes the new relationship forged between Paulinus and Edwin, as well as the extensive benefits of that relationship for Edwin. Unlike Edwin's newfound Kentish family, who are notably absent during his military exploits, Paulinus and God are seemingly ever-present and powerful allies, willing and able to save Edwin in his many moments of political distress. For Bede, the real dowry that Æthelburh brings to Edwin is not the possibility of acquiring earthly wealth and military protection through an alliance with Kent, but the sure access to spiritual wealth and divine protection offered through an alliance with Paulinus.

As Bede refigures the familiar concept of queens as catalysts for dynastic alliances, he also revises the stock Anglo-Saxon idea of queens as peaceweavers. The *HE* offers a variety of conflicted images of royal women's capacities to effect longstanding peace between tribes. In recounting the relationship between Alhfrith, the son of Oswiu, king of Northumbria, and Peada, king of the Middle Angles, Bede claims a friendship between the two men formed by Alhfrith's marriage to Peada's sister Cyneburh (*HE*, iii.21, pp. 278, 279). In the case of Irish-Pictish relations, however, Bede's statement that the Irish took lands from the Picts "uel amicitia uel ferro" (by friendship or by the sword; *HE*, i.1, p. 18, my trans.) suggests that the marriage of Irish women to Pictish men resulted in a friendship but one that was not sufficiently strong to ensure a permanent laying down of weapons. In the case of Penda, Bede depicts an aborted peace-marriage that ultimately leads to war: Penda attacks Cenwealh for repudiating his sister. The relationship between Oswald and Cynegisl offers a telling scenario of Bede's sense of how true peace between men might be forged. When Cynegisl converts, Oswald attends his baptism, standing as godfather to the new Christian convert and enacting a relationship that is "lovely indeed and well-pleasing to God" (pulcherrimo prorsus et Deo digno consortio; *HE*, iii.7, pp. 232, 233). Oswald later receives Cynegisl's daughter as his wife, with the bride given as reward for, and evidence of, bonds between men forged through acceptance of Christ rather than through the exchange of women. The idea that true peace between men is catalyzed by Christ rather than women is more fully evident in Bede's discussion of the Northumbrian princess Osthryth, his most expansive account of peace-marriage in the *HE*. Although Osthryth is married to the Mercian king Æthelred, her peace-marriage is dismally ineffective in creating amity between the Northumbrians and the Mercians. The two kingdoms are depicted as engaged in terrible strife, in which Osthryth's brother is killed, leading to even greater hostility. Osthryth is powerless to help and is ultimately assassinated by Mercian nobles. Only when the archbishop Theodore intervenes can the blood-feud be set to rest. In a lucid reading of this scene, Hollis contrasts Osthryth's failure to allay violence with Theodore's success, arguing that "Bede glances at the royal woman as peaceweaver only in order to celebrate the superior peace-making of a man of God."[63] While peace-marriage is not always depicted in the *HE* as a wholesale failure, its unpredictability suggests that it is, at best, an unreliable method of facilitating sustained national peace. True peace, Bede insists, will be the fruits not of the exchange of women but of the exchange of paganism for Christianity. Yet unwilling to wholly abandon the familiar idea of peaceweaving, Bede rewrites this idea, suggesting, in the cases of both Edwin and Oswiu, that a king might use his daughter to weave peace—by offering her not to another tribal leader but to Christ.

In the already charged atmosphere of Easter evening, Edwin is attacked and wounded by a poisonous sword blow delivered by a would-be assassin sent by Cwichelm, king of the West Saxons, under the pretext of delivering a more innocuous message. As Edwin and his men labor with great difficulty to subdue the foreign messenger, Edwin's Christian queen, Æthelburh, labors in a remarkably easy childbirth that results in a daughter (*HE*, ii.9, pp. 164, 165). Upon learning from the bishop Paulinus that Christ was responsible for the queen's safe and relatively pain-free delivery, the still-pagan and severely wounded Edwin declares that his new daughter shall be consecrated to Christ as a pledge that he would renounce his idols if Christ would agree to grant him life and military victory over Cwichelm. And the pledge appears to work. As soon as the king has recovered from his bodily wounds, he and his men march upon the West Saxons and kill or force surrender from those who plotted against him, with the smashing success of the Northumbrians offering a clear testament to God's readiness to ensure victory for those willing to serve Him.

The idea that offering one's daughter to Christ is a more effective means of ensuring national safety than negotiating exchanges with one's enemies is even more clearly rendered in the case of Oswiu, king of Northumbria. Like Edwin, Oswiu is in dire military straits, having been exposed to the savage and intolerable attacks of Penda for some time, and subsequently reduced to offering the Mercian king an incalculable store of royal treasures as the price of peace. Such peace pledges prove worthless, as Penda is determined to annihilate all of Northumbria and is immune to bargaining. As a last resort, Oswiu declares his intent to turn to God, subsequently offering a remarkably lucid comparison of the futility of seeking peace from a secular lord over the very real possibilities of securing peace through Christ: "'Si paganus' inquit 'nescit accipere nostra donaria, offeramus ei, qui nouit, Domino Deo nostro'" ("If the heathen," he said, "will not accept our gifts, let us offer them to Him who will, the Lord our God"; *HE,* iii.24, p. 290;

my trans.). Like Edwin, Oswiu also offers Christ his infant daughter in exchange for military victory, yet while Edwin simply agrees to have his daughter baptized, Oswiu vows to have his daughter consecrated to God's service as a child oblate and to give twelve estates for the establishment of monasteries: "Vouit ergo quia, si uictor existeret, filiam suam Domino sacra uirginitate dicandam offerret, simul et XII possessiones praediorum ad construenda monasteria donaret" (He vowed that if he gained the victory he would dedicate his daughter to the Lord as a holy virgin and give twelve estates to build monasteries; *HE*, iii.24, pp. 290, 291). Once again, relinquishing one's daughter to Christ is figured as an unequivocally effective means of ensuring national peace. Although Oswiu's tiny army marches against heathen forces rumored to be over thirty times as great, he and his men meet their foes trusting in Christ, and destroy or put to flight the heathens, their success further assisted by the convenient occurrence of a massive rainstorm that causes the channels of the Winwæd to overflow and drown the bulk of the heathen troops. The episode is a classic illustration of the principle that military victory, and the national peace and security that were believed to be its fruits, depended not on brute force but on divine favor, attained in this instance through the peace-marriage of the royal daughter to God.

Early feminist scholars tended to view representations of royal female oblation, such as those found in the *HE*, as fairly straightforward evidence of early medieval culture's devaluation of the female sex.[64] More recent scholars, however, have begun to understand representations of female entrance to monastic life as far more complex, and indeed a number of factors urge a more careful scrutiny of these scenes of royal female oblation before interpreting them as indicators of misogyny.[65] For one, the oblation of male and female children was widely accepted throughout the early medieval West, and seems to have been a well-established practice in the early Anglo-Saxon Church.[66] Bede was himself a kind of child oblate, handed over by his relatives in 679 or 680, at age seven, to Benedict Biscop, and subsequently admitted to Biscop's foundation of Saint Peter's in Wearmouth—and soon after to its sister-house at Jarrow—for a lifetime of monastic service.[67] Oswiu's oblation of his infant daughter, Ælfflæd—who would eventually become abbess and joint ruler of Whitby with her mother, Eanflæd—was precisely the kind of oblation that mirrored Bede's own and which he would have celebrated: the dedication of a child at an early age, followed by a lifetime of service to Christ. Although some Anglo-Saxon parents no doubt viewed child oblation as a purely practical act, and the monastery as little more than a convenient place for child rearing, in Bede's eyes, the dedication of children carried strong symbolic weight, suggesting an internalization of the extreme worth of both God and child. To dedicate one's offspring to God was to acknowledge that He was the original source of all gifts, and thus merited counter-gifts of one's most precious "possessions." Having been duly acknowledged by an unreserved gift of that which was quite literally a part of the donor's self, God would then reward such parental sacrifices with appropriate compensation. For this reason many parents turned to child oblation during times of great duress, as in the cases of both Edwin and Oswiu.[68] Indeed the dire political conditions that motivate both kings to offer their daughters to Christ further militate against reading these scenes as indicative of early medieval misogyny. Far from devaluing their daughters, both Edwin and Oswiu clearly view their infant girls as precious gifts, evidenced by the fact that each king expects his gift to be recognized by Christ as worthy of almost astonishingly weighty recompense. Edwin believes that he ought to be spared from death and ensured a successful retaliation against those who tried to kill him, and Oswiu is hoping that all of the Northumbrians might be spared from genocide at the hands of a barbarous king from whom nothing else has been able to save them. Moreover, if we recall that royal daughters were commonly viewed as powerful tools for forging political alliances, these kings' rather lofty expectations make a great deal of sense, especially in the case of Oswiu. When Oswiu offers his daughter for oblation, he abandons a potential earthly peaceweaver—that is, one who would potentially weave dynastic alliances—and seeks, instead, to weave peace with God. Oswiu's oblation of his daughter in exchange for the benefits of divinely sanctioned warfare does not point to his disregard for the female sex but rather to his newfound regard for Christ's power and his understanding of the relative merits of earthly and spiritual alliances.

Susan Ridyard urges modern critics to employ a more careful terminology when discussing medieval monastic life, pointing out that the characterization of female monasteries as "dumping grounds" for unmarried daughters or unwanted wives, or as "refuges" for royal women in the face of political turmoil, may well perpetuate inaccurate understandings of Anglo-Saxon women religious and their contributions to the Church during the age of conversion.[69] While it is indeed likely that the oblation of female children was occasionally undertaken to rid families of "less marriageable" daughters, thereby preserving available patrimony for male children, to read Bede's depictions of early kings offering their daughters to Christ as indicative of a dumping or devaluation of female children is to miss the crucial cultural work these scenes perform, namely, to refigure the concept of female peaceweaving, in an attempt to convey the idea that kings could achieve military victory and national peace more effectively by using their daughters to form relationships with God rather than with other men.[70]

For all Bede works to refigure familiar queenly roles, however, he has no real interest in exploring their implications within monastic life. Even when royal women are housed in monasteries, Bede continues to insist upon a very minimal role for them in the establishment of Christianity and the early Church. Ridyard argues convincingly that female monastic leaders of royal birth used their wealth and familial ties to advance the conversion-age Church significantly, yet her evidence is necessarily drawn largely from non-Bedan sources, for on this topic Bede has very little to say.[71] While the *HE* does feature several royal abbesses and nuns, it rarely portrays these women actively using their familial connections or wealth to further Church interests. Far from suggesting that a royal woman's familial ties or wealth might make her particularly likely to benefit the Church, Bede repeatedly depicts a royal woman's entrance into monastic life as an act that necessarily entails renunciation of her secular status and all of its markers. A case in point is Æthelthryth, daughter of Anna, king of East Anglia, and wife of Ecgfrith, king of Northumbria. When Æthelthryth joyfully exchanges her linen clothing, gold and pearl necklaces, and marriage to King Ecgfrith for woolen garments, a divinely inflicted neck tumor, and marriage to the King of Heaven, she underscores the incompatibility of earthly and heavenly queenship, and the overwhelming superiority of the latter (*HE*, iv.20).[72]

The well-born abbess Hild, princess of Deira and great-niece of Edwin, is also distanced from the material manifestations of her former secular status through Bede's account of the dream of Hild's mother, Breguswith, which features a shining necklace whose bright splendor is then described as being truly fulfilled by Hild's life, which becomes "exempla operum lucis" (an example of works of light; *HE*, iv.23, p. 410; my trans.). The shining light of earthly riches is depicted as a part of Hild's infancy and as wholly unnecessary in her later life, when she herself will become a living embodiment of a light so bright that it can illuminate all of Britain (*HE*, iv.23). If Hild's entrance into monastic life demands that she sever her former ties to earthly wealth, her subsequent career as an abbess is dedicated to ensuring that other nuns follow suit: Bede claims that Hild established Whitby so that "nullus ibi diues, nullus esset egens, omnibus essent omnia communia, cum nihil cuiusquam esse uideretur proprium" (no one was rich, no one was in need, for they had all things in common and none had any private property; *HE*, iv.23, pp. 408, 409).[73] Bede's efforts to suggest that exemplary living for nuns of royal birth necessarily entails a sharp break with their former secular wealth and familial connections is matched by his condemnation of monasteries in which that break has not taken place. Bede's *Letter to Egbert*, for example, deplores the fact that there are monasteries in England run by abbesses who have been appointed to these positions by their wealthy husbands.[74]

Nor does Bede have all that much to say about queens as patrons or supporters of the Church. While later writers would routinely laud queens for their patronage of the Church and its monasteries, the *HE* contains only two very brief references to queens' channeling royal wealth toward Church interests: Eanflæd, who convinces her husband, Oswiu, to donate land for monastic use as expiation for his role in the murder of her kinsman, Oswine (*HE*, iii.24, iii.14); and Osthryth, who, in conjunction with her husband, Æthelred, venerated and enriched the Bardney monastery (*HE*, iii.11).[75]

Although the *HE* grants royal women only the most minor roles in the history of England's spiritual development, I would nevertheless argue against reading the text as a wholly successful elision of royal women's power or participation in the age of conversion. To be sure, Bede does not elaborate on queens' contributions to the promotion of the Christian Church. Nor does he ever suggest, as do other early medieval churchmen from this period, that royal women might serve as allies in the fight against spiritual darkness.[76] However, in using the *HE* to construct a powerful counterdiscourse to the model of conversion by marriage, Bede underscores how much force that model must have had within early medieval culture. There are many ways of construing how this model might have worked in practice: conversion as an act motivated by a king's desire to mollify his wife; conversion as an act forced upon a king by his wife's native family as a bride-price; conversion as an act voluntarily agreed upon by a king seeking powerful dynastic connections; or conversion as an act undertaken by a king as a result of his wife's persuasive counsel on the merits of Christianity. In Bede's eyes, not a single one of these scenarios offered an adequate ground for conversion, which was limited to the recognition of the truth of God's Word mediated through missionaries, popes, bishops, and priests—the very model of conversion that Bede foregrounds in the *HE,* and a model that, as we have seen, leaves little room for royal women. Nevertheless, as Bede painstakingly works to elide the power of Christian wives in England's spiritual development and to reconfigure that power so that he and people like himself have a share in it, his efforts are themselves a sign of royal women's power during the age of conversion.

In his study of Augustine's spiritual career, Robert Markus reminds us that conversion is typically accompanied by an element of disenchantment: conversion entails not only a movement toward new things to be embraced, but also a movement away from old things to be left behind.[77] Although Anglo-Saxon churchmen worked tirelessly to emphasize continuities between pre-Christian sociopolitical organization and Christianity, conversion nevertheless asked pagan kings to leave behind many things, most notably, their belief that earthly wealth and secular glory represented the highest of all possible achievements, and their conviction that both were most readily secured by politically savvy marriages that would result in enhanced wealth and military backing. In using women to symbolize earthly wealth and glory gained through the manipulation of sociopolitical relations with other kingdoms, and then fiercely asserting that women were *not* the forces motivating the early kings' conversions, Bede grants royal women a crucial symbolic importance as indices of a king's movement away from his former pagan values and toward new Christian ones. In so doing, Bede also inadvertently underscores the very real truth of women as points of access to, and symbols of, all that was most dear to the Anglo-Saxons and most consistently valued within their world. It is little wonder that there are so few references to the concept of dowry in the Anglo-Saxon corpus, but a veritable obsession in the law codes and other pre-Conquest writings with what a man might pay to acquire a wife.[78] As Bede and the convert kings knew well, wives, and particularly royal ones, offered access to everything that was valued in Anglo-Saxon culture, and they thus came at a high price. For Bede, it may have been all right for that price to be a king's willingness to relinquish Woden, but it could never be part of the bargain in his adoption of Christ.

Chapter 2

Crossing Queens, Pleasing Hierarchies

One of the best-known queen proselytizers in Anglo-Saxon England was Helena, the fourth-century Christian empress who was believed to have recovered the lost Cross as well as the obscure history of the Crucifixion. Helena appears as an exemplar of queenly proselytization in a letter that Gregory the Great sent to Bertha just a few years after he had dispatched Augustine to convert the English in 596. Gently scolding the Christian queen for failing to convert her husband, Æthelberht, Gregory urged Bertha to take the successes of her legendary royal counterpart as a model for how she might convert her husband, as well as the entire race of the English.[1]

> Nam sicut per recordandæ memoriæ Helenam matrem piissimi Constantini imperatoris ad Christianam fidem corda Romanorum accendit, ita et per gloriæ vestræ studium in Anglorum gentem ejus misericordiam confidimus operari. Et quidem jamdudum gloriosi filii nostri conjugis vestri animos prudentiæ vestræ bono, sicut revera Christianæ, debuistis inflectere, ut pro regni et animæ suæ salute fidem, quam colitis sequeretur.[2]

For as through Helena of illustrious memory, the mother of the most pious Emperor Constantine, He kindled the hearts of the Romans into Christian faith, so we trust that He works in the nation of the Angli through the zeal of your Glory. And indeed you ought before now, as being truly a Christian, to have inclined the heart of our glorious son, your husband, by the good influence of your prudence, to follow, for the weal of his kingdom and of his own soul, the faith which you profess.[3]

In viewing Helena as a model of how a queen might ideally direct her energies, Gregory was not alone. Throughout late antiquity and the early Middle Ages, writers frequently drew on Helena as an exemplar of queenship, invoking the well-known empress as a shorthand for praising and influencing their own empresses and queens. In his *Church History* (440s), Theodoret, for example, commemorates the fourth-century empress Aelia Flaccilla, wife of Theodosius the Great, in terms that bear a striking resemblance to the discussion of Helena in Rufinus's *Church History* (ca. 402).[4] Empress Aelia Pulcheria was honored at the 451 Council of Chalcedon as the "New Helena."[5] Gregory of Tours, in his *Glory of the Martyrs* (585–95), claims that the Frankish queen Radegund "is comparable to Helena in both merit and faith."[6] And Baudonivia's early seventh-century *Life of Radegund* likens Radegund's efforts to secure relics of the True Cross to Helena's, claiming that "what Helena did in oriental lands, Radegund the blessed did in Gaul."[7] The practice of using Helena as an exemplar of queenship continued long after Gregory's death, as illustrated by Pope Hadrian's 787 letter to the widowed empress Irene and her son, Constantine VI, urging them to restore the Eastern Church's former practice of image veneration and thus be called "another Constantine and another Helena."[8]

For Gregory the Great, as for so many late antique and early medieval writers, Helena's appeal lay in the fact that she was a powerful empress who used her political power to promote Christianity. Moreover, as the mother of Constantine—the first royal figure in Western Europe to bring Christianity under the official recognition of the state—Helena was strongly associated with the emergence of a unity between Church and state, the very unity that Gregory so desperately longed to establish in England. To invoke Helena was to invoke a powerful historical precedent for the idea that religion and politics should and in fact could be united, and, more specifically, that it was incumbent upon queens to foster this union. Repeatedly held out before royal women as an exemplar and occasionally lauded as an earthly, more political counterpart of the Queen of all Queens, the Virgin Mary, Helena held extraordinary cultural capital throughout late antiquity and the early Middle Ages, functioning, in short, as a kind of originary Christian queen.[9]

But like most originary figures, Helena was surrounded by a myriad of myths and legends, all of which could be shaped and refigured to create an image of Christian queenship that might speak to the needs of a particular culture. To celebrate the queen's *inventio* of the Holy Cross was, like all interpretive acts, to perform an act of "invention"—to engage in a critical praxis poised between the word's medieval connotation of finding that which already exists and its more modern sense of creating something wholly new.[10] Each retelling of the *Inventio* legend thus invested Helenè with different meanings, and it is the complex meanings of the queen in Cynewulf's *Elene*, the only extant pre-Conquest poetic account of the legend, that this chapter takes as its subject.

Because *Elene* is one of the longest Old English poems to survive and because it deals with a host of issues central to Anglo-Saxon literature and culture—namely, cross veneration, conversion, and conquest—both the poem and its female protagonist have generated a wealth of critical interest.[11] Critical responses to *Elene* have taken primarily one of two forms, neither of which is unique to the poem; rather each is broadly representative of a major strain of criticism within Anglo-Saxon literary studies. The first is Germanic formulaic analysis, which, in its more recent incarnations, takes as its object of investigation not only poetic diction but also stock scenes and characters found within Germanic literary culture. Through this critical optic, Cynewulf's female heroine is seen as akin to the Old Norse *valkyrie*, the Old Norse whetting woman, the aristocratic Germanic *ides*, the female *miles Christi*, and the Anglo-Saxon *freoðuwebbe*.[12] The second approach is typology, which transforms woman into a feminized virtue, a biblical figure, or an institution. It is through the latter interpretive lens that Elene has most often been viewed, as numerous critics, beginning in the 1970s, took up the idea of Elene as a militant *Mater Ecclesia* battling the Synagogue, a type of the New Law struggling against the Old.[13]

Despite their evident differences, both formulaic analysis and typological interpretation share a tendency to lose sight of a central force driving all Old English poetry: the contemporary culture in which these texts were produced and circulated. Taking as they do the textual as their main context—the former privileging vernacular, Germanic literary works; the latter, Latin biblical writings and patristic commentaries—both approaches tend to gloss over the historical specificity of Old English poetry and hence overlook the kind of cultural work these texts might have done for their contemporary audiences. More recently, however, such critics as E. Gordon Whatley, Clare Lees, and Joyce Tally Lionarons, have read *Elene* through a wider range of critical sensibilities, exploring Cynewulf's characters as complex sites of intersection between Germanic and Latin textual traditions, and as poetic amalgams that reveal their author's deep imbrication in distinctly Anglo-Saxon social, spiritual, and political formations.[14] Perhaps nowhere are the intersections of these different textual traditions and cultural formations more provocative than around the figure of Elene. As a queen, Elene bears obvious typological importance as, for example, a figure of *Ecclesia,* and obvious ideological importance as representative of the royal women who figured so centrally in Anglo-Saxon literature and culture. Elene thus offers a nexus between the sweeping historicity of typology and the more immediate historical embeddedness of cultural criticism, and a site around which accrue the many symbols, images, and ideas commonly associated with queens in Anglo-Saxon culture. And it is precisely because of her ability to evoke these associations that Cynewulf's queen has the capacity to do so much, and such complex, cultural work.

Any attempt to understand the cultural work of a queen who appears in an Old English poem, however, must confront a larger, vexed problem with cultural studies generally in Anglo-Saxon criticism. As is the case for all Old English poems, the language of *Elene* does not allow us to know either when or where the poem was originally composed. Traditionally seen as Anglian in origin, the poem could be dated, according to R. D. Fulk's linguistic analysis, as not earlier than around 750, if Mercian, and not earlier than around 850, if Northumbrian.[15] While many scholars concur with Fulk's dating and view the poem as either an eighth- or ninth-century composition, the issue is by no means settled; debates have forcefully re-emerged with Patrick Conner's recent reassessment of both *Elene* and the entire Cynewulfian canon as possible products of the late tenth-century Benedictine reforms.[16]

If we are unable to locate the text either temporally or geographically, how, then, are we to historicize and understand the cultural work performed by Elene, or indeed any character within the poem? How, in other words, can the queen be shown to have demonstrable historical meaning if the poem in which she appears cannot be firmly rooted in either time or place? Indeed, it is precisely our inability to date Old English poetry that is, in part, responsible for how very few attempts have been made to read the poetic corpus through the historical or cultural paradigms that can be more easily mobilized to address the vernacular prose, much of which we can date.[17] Difficulties of dating should not, however, deter Anglo-Saxonists from reading the poems as cultural artifacts: while we cannot know either the date or provenance in which *Elene* was originally composed, we do have access to a fairly close approximation of the Latin source with which Cynewulf was most likely working and can therefore use major discrepancies between the Latin and the Old English texts as a viable means of identifying aspects of *Elene* that are the product of a distinctly Anglo-Saxon cultural sensibility. Moreover, we know that the manuscript in which the poem is contained, the Vercelli Book, was copied at the end of the tenth century in England, where it remained for at least part of the next century.[18] Contextualizing the queen within the social and symbolic roles available to royal women during the period of the manuscript's reception thus offers a means of ascertaining how *Elene* might have been understood by one, and indeed the only, group of Anglo-Saxon readers whom we can be reasonably certain had access to the poem.

We begin, then, with questions of interpretation: What hermeneutic strategies does Cynewulf invite as most appropriate to an understanding of his queen, Elene, and how might he have intended his audiences to read her? From here we move to the actual representation of queenship in the poem. Focusing on key changes Cynewulf makes to his probable source text, the fifth-century *Inventio Sanctae Crucis,* I argue that he encases Elene in the linguistic, material, and social trappings that were particular to Anglo-Saxon discourses of queenship.[19] Such conspicuous displays of queenliness concomitantly familiarize and defamiliarize Elene, at once bringing the Roman empress more in line with the multivalent rhetorics of Anglo-Saxon queenship and imbuing her with an aura of royal legitimacy that dissociates her from the more unsavory aspects of her historical precursor's questionable sexual past. Such transformations enhance the queen's ability to function as an exemplar, but one impelled by ideological goals that reach far beyond the mere fashioning of model roles for royal women. Cynewulf uses the queen as an exemplar to naturalize and perpetuate a very traditional and highly conservative social hierarchy, figured as coextensive with righteous belief and as critical to the production of communal harmony and personal happiness. Yet he also produces this exemplarity as poetically and interpretively revisionist. In translating the fourth-century Roman empress into an Anglo-Saxon queen, Cynewulf creates a female figure whose renewed, culturally specific potentiality and own capacity to revise history implicitly destabilize his own poetic vision of social hierarchy because they invite historical revision. The reinvented queen thus suggests that highly conservative hierarchies of rank and gender might be reimagined and traditional forms of institutionalized subservience re-envisioned. Cynewulf's multifaceted treatment of queenship in *Elene* reveals his profound interest in using religious poetry to engage with the more secular aspects of the culture in which he lived, marking *Elene* as a text that offers rich insight into the complex social functions that poetry served in Anglo-Saxon culture.

Reading Elene

It is indeed not at all surprising that the typological reading of Elene as a figure of *Ecclesia* has proved so powerful. It is a critical stance that derives force from no less an authority than the poet himself—abstract, symbolic interpretation is precisely the kind of reading that Cynewulf encourages throughout the poem. *Elene* is filled with such richly allusive and overdetermined figures as the archetypally Judaic Judas, the anachronistically placed protomartyr Stephen, and the first Christian emperor, Constantine. As the mother of this emperor, Elene is a similarly overdetermined figure, her strong association with maternity easily evoking images of the Church, which was commonly identified in both patristic and early medieval writings through the metaphor of *Mater Ecclesia*—a metaphor rooted in the belief that one was reborn in the Church through baptism.[20] While Cynewulf never explicitly identifies the queen mother Elene as a figure of *Mater Ecclesia*, he nevertheless encourages readers to interpret Elene's maternity symbolically by characterizing it, as the poem progresses, through increasingly abstract forms of mothering. As several critics have noted, Elene enters the poem as Constantine's biological mother, then takes up the role of spiritual mother to Judas in his conversion, and ends up as the textual mother-muse of Cynewulf himself—the subject of a Latin source that inspires and motivates the poet, liberating him from both spiritual lethargy and writer's block.[21]

Cynewulf's transformation of Elene from literal to symbolic mother stands as an apt example of the kind of interpretive practice privileged in *Elene:* the acceptance of Christianity inscribes a necessary movement from literal to more symbolic orders of representation. One of the most pervasive themes in patristic and early medieval anti-Jewish polemics was that the Jews were unable to read figurally, that, unlike Christians, who understood the Old Testament as a prefiguration of the New Testament, Jews were bound to the literal letter of the Old Testament and unable to penetrate its deeper spiritual significance.[22] In keeping with this belief that a fundamental distinction between Jews and Christians lay in their very different kinds of hermeneutic practice, Cynewulf depicts Judas's conversion as an entrance into symbolic interpretation. After the newly converted Judas emerges from his pit, he eagerly recounts Old Testament history and correctly interprets it as a prefiguration of Christian events: Joseph's bones anticipate the Holy Cross, Creation foreshadows Revelation, and he himself becomes the new Moses. The unconverted Jews in the poem are depicted, by contrast, as strictly literal readers, obdurately impervious and willfully blind to symbolic meaning. Hence, they always read Elene as a literal queen, as a very real spokesperson from a powerful family whom they have somehow offended. When Elene accuses the Jews of multiple transgressions against God, for example, they innocently respond:

> ne we eare cunnon
> þurh hwæt ðu ðus hearde,   hlæfdige, us
> eorre wurde;   we ðæt æbylgð nyton
> þe we gefremedon   on þysse folcscere,
> þeodenbealwa   wið þec æfre.
>
> (399b–403)

We do not know clearly, lady, why you thus have become so severely angry with us. We do not know the transgression which we have committed against this people, of evils against you ever.[23]

Given that the Jews are depicted throughout the poem as blind, obstinate, and misguided, their strictly literal understanding of Elene as a real queen from a powerful family stands as an example of failed or misreading. To read Elene on a strictly literal level, then, would be misguided, for it would, in fact, be to read her precisely as do the Jews in the poem.

It is crucial, however, to recognize that the Jews' misreading of Elene is not that they read her as a queen but that they read her *only* as a queen; their hermeneutic failure lies not in recognizing the literal but in being unable and unwilling to move beyond it. As Erich Auerbach has so thoroughly shown, medieval figural interpretation—except among the fiercest of spiritualists—did not work through discarding literal, historical reality, but by preserving the historicity of both the early event or figure and its deeper meaning: "The two poles of the figure are separate in time, but both, being real events or figures, are within time, within the stream of historical life."[24] This sense of figural interpretation as preserving both literal and more abstract levels of meaning is very much borne out in *Elene*. For while Cynewulf privileges abstract over literal interpretation, he never discounts literal reading; instead, he prompts readers to see it as the necessary first step in Christian understanding, a point neatly illustrated through the poem's treatment of its main theme, conversion. If, as numerous critics have argued, *Elene* is a poem that is largely about conversion and the individual's discovery of Christianity, this quest for spiritual enlightenment is depicted as a very literal search mission.[25] Discovering the meaning of the Cross is shown to be profoundly dependent upon first actually finding it.

The poem's depiction of good hermeneutic work as crucially reliant on both literal and symbolic reading is, moreover, part of its broader characterization of the recovery of meaning as complex process rather than singular event, a point highlighted by the poem's expansive rendition of Elene's voyage to Jerusalem: finding the meaning of the Cross is depicted as a lengthy and arduous journey, rather than an instant revelation. So too the queen's recovery of the Cross is shown to be only one part of a much larger and far more complicated project of making known the Cross's many meanings. While Elene's recovery of the Cross does indeed effect a metonymic recovery of the Lord's presence—when the recovered Cross reanimates the corpse of a young boy—the full meaning of the Cross is shown to be revealed only by situating it within a wide variety of contexts: oral and written, past and present, psychic and social. Such contexts include the vision of the Cross and interpreting angel which appears to Constantine in a dream, the holy books from which Elene gleans knowledge of the Cross's history, and the advice of the king's wise advisers, who collectively explicate and reveal the

Cross's many mysteries. Moreover, the Cross's meanings are most power-fully revealed through their effects on the characters within the poem—effects that, the poem insists, are time-bound, culturally specific, and extremely personal. While the penitent, eschatologically minded narrator at the end of the poem may indeed model Cynewulf's own ideal imagined reader of *Elene,* the narrator's sorrow for his sins of the past and increased reverence for the hereafter reveal a newfound spiritual awareness that he has arrived at only through previous engagement with the meanings of the Cross in his own earthly life, meanings that the poem insists will vary from person to person. For Constantine, the meaning of the Cross inheres in its potential to ensure swift victory against the seemingly endless hosts of Huns and Goths who threaten his homeland; for the nameless Christian converts in the poem, the meaning of the Cross lies in its ability to resurrect the dead; for Cynewulf, the meaning of the Cross emerges from its power to unlock creative energy and allow him to produce poetry. While the Cross is no doubt a unique cultural artifact, Cynewulf's insistence on its multi-valence is, I would suggest, less unique than it is symptomatic of his treatment of characters and events throughout the poem—particularly his treatment of Elene. Moreover, to read Cynewulf's Elene as signifying on diverse levels is simply to acknowledge that the queen is not a replication of the queens found in any single Anglo-Saxon discourse but a conglomerate figure crafted from the dense web of roles that queens are shown enacting within multiple discursive arenas: Latin biblical writings and commentaries, vernacular literature, and the historical writings that offer modern critics a refracted view of the cultural and material worlds in which royal women lived. Such roles do not work in isolation but reinforce, complement, and occasionally conflict with one another. Attending to how they do so offers a powerful means of discerning the complex ways in which images of queenship signified in Anglo-Saxon England, and by extension the cultural work that *Elene* might have performed for both its author and audiences.

The Displays of Queenship

The *Inventio* most often refers to Helena by her proper name, rarely referring to her by the title *regina* or *domina.* Cynewulf, however, tends to replace the proper name *Helena* with more generic terms: most often *cwen,* and occasionally *hlæfdige*. He also frequently embellishes these terms, refer-ring to Elene as *sigecwen*, "victorious queen" (260a, 997a); *guðcwen*, "battle-queen" (254a, 331a); *þeodcwen*, "people-queen" (1155b); *æðele cwen*, "noble queen" (275b, 662a); *tireadig cwen*, "glorious queen" (605a); *Cristenra cwen*, "queen of the Christians" (1068a); *cwen selest[e]*, "best queen" (1169a); *ar-wyrðe cwen*, "honorable queen" (1128b–29a); and *rice cwen*, "powerful" or "high-ranking queen" (411b). This diverse array of epithets for the queen must be in part attributed to the formal demands of the alliterative half-line, as well as to the Anglo-Saxon poetic practice of variation. However, Cynewulf's preference for naming his female protagonist by the generic terms *cwen* or *hlæfdige* as opposed to the personal name "Elene" also sug-gests an interest in transforming Elene from a particular queen into a more generic exemplar of queenship, an image of female royalty whom Anglo-Saxon readers might view not simply as a phenomenon of a bygone Roman past but as a figure who might be found within their own Germanic world.

Repeated use of the terms *cwen* and *hlæfdige* also serves as a means of invoking Elene's typological status, for both terms were commonly em-ployed to symbolize Church, or the collective congregation of believing Christians; in Ælfric's formulation: "Seo cwen hæfde getacnunge þære hal-gan gelaðunge ealles cristenes folces" (The queen was a type of the holy congregation of all Christian people).[26] Moreover, it is not simply the Chris-tian narrator who invokes Elene through generic terms. So too do the Jews consistently refer to Elene as both *cwen* and *hlæfdige*, their ease with these typologically laden titles attesting to their collective spiritual state—a knowledge of the inherent superiority of the Church but a refusal to ac-knowledge this knowledge as truth. Repeatedly referring to Elene as *cwen* (533b), *hlæfdige* (400b), or *hlæfdige min* (656b), the Jews seem never to tire of voicing a collective awareness of the supreme power and authority right-fully due to the Church. Yet such iterations of humility are rapidly revealed as mere lip service, undermined as they are by subsequent interactions with the queen indicative of far less respect: the Jews challenge Elene's views on the preservation of textual history, stake claims for their own deep under-standing of Scripture, and demand that she enlighten them as to how they have offended her, her lord Constantine, and her people. The irony of these scenes is rich, for by refusing to reveal the whereabouts of the Cross and, more importantly, to recognize the divinity of Christ, the Jews have indeed gravely offended the triumvirate of Elene, her lord, and her people—not, as they believe, in the form of secular wrongs done to another social group, but in the form of spiritual offenses against the Church, her Lord (Jesus Christ), and her people, the collective body of Christian believers. Yet while the poem maintains a distinction between secular and spiritual offenses—by depicting the Jews as recognizing only the former—it concomitantly blurs this boundary. Drawing on the power of the terms *cwen* and *hlæfdige* to signal the Jews' offense against Elene as both secular leader and the Church, the poem sanctifies royal authority as it backs Christianity with the power of the state. Resistance to the state and resistance to God are conflated as reciprocal offenses, a point driven home in the poem through Cynewulf's use of the term *þeoden*, "prince," as a title for both Constantine and God (267b, 487a).[27]

For late tenth-century readers, the terms *cwen* and *hlæfdige* would have borne not only typological weight but also very particular cultural implications, in light of the new titling practices emerging for queens and queen mothers. As Asser notes in his *Life of King Alfred*, ninth-century West Saxon queens possessed little power, partially reflected by the fact that they were not permitted to be called *regina* but were referred to instead as *coniunx regis*, "consort of the king."[28] However, by the mid-tenth century, queens had gained more official status and power, one indication of which was increasing usage of titles for queens and queen mothers. As Stafford has argued, it was in the mid-tenth century that the first queen of Wessex was formally granted the title *regina*.[29] The closest Old English equivalent for *regina* was *cwen*, and frequent use of the term throughout the poem would probably have been understood by readers as a title serving to heighten and call attention to Elene's social status. Moreover, the term *cwen* appears to have carried a greater sense of official status and power than the more generic *hlæfdige*, which was commonly used to denote the female head of any landed household that contained servants.[30] Contemporary writings suggest that consecration may have been the distinguishing factor between the two titles. The 1051 entry in manuscript E of the *Anglo-Saxon Chronicle* states that Edith was a *hlæfdige* who had been consecrated as *cwen*, and witness lists to Anglo-Saxon charters reveal that Ælfthryth, the first English queen who was certainly consecrated (ca. 973), was the first to witness charters as *regina*.[31] Although this distinction between *cwen* and *hlæfdige* was often ignored—consecrated and nonconsecrated Anglo-Saxon queens were commonly referred to by both titles—the term *cwen* was, by the late tenth century, a title used to stress the queen's official status and the power deriving from her regal position.

Because we do not know precisely when and where Cynewulf was writing, it is difficult to ascertain whether the terms *cwen* and *hlæfdige* would have signified for him as titles or whether such recognition would have been confined to later readers. That Cynewulf may indeed be employing these terms in an attempt to heighten Elene's social status, however, is further suggested by the various adjectives that he uses to describe the queen. Unlike Ælfric's very brief homily for the Invention or, more notably, Cynewulf's own source text, both of which tend to modify references to Helena with adjectives denoting her piety and sanctity, Cynewulf's poem tends to describe Elene with adjectives that convey a sense of her secular nobility.[32] Over half of the references to Helena in the *Inventio* are accompanied by some form of the adjective *beata*. Cynewulf, however, only very occasionally refers to Helena through such Anglo-Saxon equivalents as *eadig* (619a) or *eadhreðig* (266a), and instead refers to her four times by the adjective or substantive *æðele*, "noble" (275b, 545a, 662a, 1130b), once as *geatolic*, "adorned" or "magnificent" (331a), once as *tireadig*, "glorious" (605a), and once as *rice*, "powerful" or "high-ranking" (411b).

Cynewulf also enhances the queen's social status by surrounding her with all of the trappings of Anglo-Saxon royalty. Unlike the *Inventio* author, who never refers to Helena's clothing, Cynewulf claims that when three thousand of the Jewish wise men approach Elene, they find the "geatolic guðcwen golde gehyrsted" (magnificent battle-queen adorned with gold; 331). And when the queen receives the nails with which Christ was crucified, she bursts into tears, which fall "ofer wira gespon" (over a web of wires; 1134a), a phrase suggesting that Elene wears some type of gold-embroidered garment or perhaps a pendant ornamented with gold.[33] Moreover, Cynewulf's Elene has both a *salor*, "hall" (382b), and a *cynestol*, "throne" (330a)—in the *Inventio* she has neither—and Cynewulf clearly depicts the queen receiving visitors from a seated position on the throne, as he states: "þær on þrymme bad / in cynestole caseres mæg, / geatolic guðcwen" (there the kinswoman of the emperor waited on the throne in glory, the magnificent battle-queen; 329b–31a).

Cloaking Elene in elaborate royal garb, Cynewulf departs significantly from his Latin source and produces an image of queenship that lands squarely within stock depictions of queens and upper-class women in Old English poetry. The *goldhroden*, "gold-adorned," or *beaghroden*, "jewel-adorned," queen makes frequent appearances in such poems as *Beowulf* and *Widsith*; draped in jewels and other finery, she circulates throughout the hall, dispensing gifts and serving guests. *Maxims I,* which proclaims that "gold geriseþ on guman sweorde, / sellic sigesceorp, sinc on cwene" (gold is fitting on a man's sword, an excellent ornament of victory, treasure on a queen), suggests that such conspicuous displays of royal wealth in the fictional courts of heroic poetry may not be too far from Anglo-Saxon social practice.[34] The richly adorned body of the queen may well have served as a means of publicly signaling the wealth and power of her kingdom, inviting traveling guests to broadcast afar that hers was a kingdom with great monetary reserves and hence one that would not prove an easy target of conquest.

Cynewulf's emphasis on the richness of Elene's clothing also brings the queen more in line with her typological status as Church, which homilists—invoking images found in the Psalms, the Song of Songs, and the Apocalypse—often described as an elaborately adorned royal woman decked out for her bridegroom.[35] These textual representations of the Church have a material analogue in the Anglo-Saxon custom of decorating churches with elaborate metal and artwork—a cultural practice that Barbara Raw argues was designed to ensure that the earthly church might be understood as a symbol of the heavenly city, and a material means of emphasizing that the riches of the Church were far superior to the wealth of any secular hall.[36] Elene's throne further enhances her typological significance, the royal seat bringing her more closely in line with images of Mary and the Church, which homilists frequently invoked as Christ's enthroned queen. As Ælfric puts it: "we sprecað be þære heofonlican cwene endebyrdlice æfter wifhade þeahhwæðere eall seo geleaffulle gelaþung getreowfullice be hire singð. þæt heo is geuferod 7 ahafen ofer engla werodum to þam wuldorfullum heahsetle" (We speak about the heavenly queen, as is usual, according to her womanhood, yet all of the believing congregation sing truly about her that she is honored and raised up to the glorious throne over hosts of angels).[37] While Elene's throne does not place her over hosts of angels, it does place her above all of the denizens of Jerusalem, for when the Jews are brought en masse into her hall, Cynewulf claims that the queen "wlat ofer ealle" (looked over everybody; 385b), a phrase that both reiterates that Elene is physically elevated over the entire assembly and signifies that she has a far-reaching understanding of Christianity in contrast to the Jews' limited vision.

For later readers of the poem, Elene's throne would have had particular cultural significance, in light of changing attitudes toward Anglo-Saxon queens' use of actual material thrones. Asser claims that during the ninth century "the people of the West Saxons did not allow the queen to sit beside the king" (Gens namque Occidentalium Saxonum reginam iuxta regem sedere non patitur), a custom that arose because of the wicked queen Eadburh whose alleged antagonism toward both her husband (whom she poisoned) and her people led to her "being expelled from the queen's throne" (a reginali solio proiceretur) and to the West Saxons' swearing "that they would never permit any king to reign over them who invited the queen to sit beside him on the royal throne" (ut nullum unquam regem super se in vita sua regnare permitterent, qui reginam in regali solio iuxta se sedere imperare vellet).[38] But a little over a century later, West Saxon queens appear to have recovered their right to sit on the throne, although there was no ritual for the enthronement of the queen during the coronation ceremony as there was for the king.[39] The frontispiece of the *Encomium Emmae* (1040–41) depicts Emma seated on the throne, with the Flemish monk who wrote the text presenting it to her, and two of her sons, Edward and Harthacnut, watching.[40] Similarly, the anonymous author of the mid-eleventh-century *Life of King Edward Who Rests at Westminster* states that both custom and law decreed that a throne at the king's side should always be ready for the queen, Edith. However, in extolling Edith's (his patron's) many virtues, the author also approvingly notes that Edith usually rejected the throne except on very public occasions, suggesting that even by this late date, the queen's sitting on the throne was still not completely customary.[41] It is difficult to ascertain precisely when cultural attitudes toward the queen's sitting on the throne began to change. The sources that attest to legal sanction of this formerly prohibited cultural practice date from the early to mid-eleventh century. However, public acceptance of the queen's throne was very likely another aspect of the increasing social status granted to late tenth-century queens. For late tenth- and eleventh-century readers of the poem, then, Elene's throne would have carried multiple meanings, functioning as an object that emphasized her regal status and also brought her more in line with the queens found in Anglo-Saxon texts and culture.

The depiction of queenship in *Elene* is one that places a great deal of interpretive pressure on its audiences, asking them to recognize the queen as hailing from a broad array of discursive arenas—poetry, homiletic writings, history—but more fundamentally, as inhabiting a vast expanse of time. As a figure of the Church, image of and exemplar for queens in pre-Conquest England, and a symbol of the heavenly city, the queen was a figure who inhabited all cultural moments—past, present, and future. She thus demanded that readers embrace an understanding of Christian history as timelessly eternal and view her as part of typological history, whose emphasis on recursiveness and claim to provide explanatory force for all historical moments have led many critics to characterize it as a spatial rather than temporal conception of history.[42] Yet *Elene* also offers readers a slightly less grand, more linear, and, perhaps most important, more culturally particular means of understanding the queen as a historical figure: the queen as an agent of Christian conversion.

Elene is the only major character in the poem who does not herself convert; rather, throughout the text, she functions as a mediator, a catalyst in the process of helping others to discover Christian truth.[43] Significantly, it is not Elene who actually finds the material remnants of the lost Cross, but Judas, for Elene has already discovered the Christian truth symbolized by those fragments, and her role is to convince others to do so as well. By the end of the poem, Elene has converted Judas and a multitude of unnamed Jews, and she has also effected a metaphorical conversion upon the poet himself—rescuing Cynewulf from both his former spiritual sloth and his inability to write.

Cynewulf's emphasis on Elene's role as an agent of Christian conversion appears to be a fairly accurate depiction of the historical circumstances that eventually drove the fourth-century empress to leave Rome and travel east. As Jan Drijvers has convincingly shown, Helena's "pilgrimage" from Rome to Palestine and her travels throughout other eastern provinces were motivated less by personal piety than by Constantine's programmatic efforts to convert the still largely pagan population of the eastern portion of his empire.[44] Having conquered the eastern provinces in 324, Constantine then sent his mother to travel throughout his newly claimed lands, overseeing his church-building initiatives to render Christianity visible, giving liberally to the poor, and freeing Christian prisoners—all of which, Drijvers argues, were part of the emperor's attempts to convert his new subjects.[45]

But the particular tactics that Elene uses to convert the Jews—the verbal denigration of their community and intellectual traditions, and the actual physical torture of their leader, Judas—are also implacably anchored in a sentiment that was widespread throughout Anglo-Saxon England: that violence was both a precondition for and an intrinsic part of strengthening and extending Christian *imperium*. Texts such as *The Battle of Maldon* and Asser's *Life of King Alfred* consistently frame Anglo-Saxon warfare as righteous campaigns of *Christiani* against *pagani*.[46] And as E. Gordon Whatley observes, even the most devout and cultured Anglo-Saxon churchmen, such as Bede and Alcuin, championed kings who waged brutal military campaigns that were deemed necessary to secure a sufficiently peaceful environment for missionaries to wage safely their battles of the spirit.[47] In Anglo-Saxon culture, violence and conversion were inseparable, and their imbrication finds voice in Elene's chilling treatment of the Jews—an aspect of the poem that renders it highly disturbing for modern readers and most likely further distances us from its contemporary reception, as there is some evidence to suggest that the anti-Judaic violence of the *Inventio* legend was in part responsible for its popularity.[48]

For tenth-century readers, the image of Elene as an agent of Christian conversion would not only have invoked early Christian Rome or conversionary aggression but would also have resonated with contemporary changes in English queenship, as the image of a proselytizing queen was wholly consistent with new attitudes toward the royal family ushered into England by tenth-century reformers and very much in accord with the emphasis placed on "spiritual queenship" during this period. By the tenth century, the English were indeed converted; however, invasions and settlements in England by pagan Scandinavians rendered conversion a pressing issue throughout the century. The prayer accompanying the giving of the ring in late Anglo-Saxon queens' coronation *ordines* explicitly conveys the sense that during the late tenth century, conversion of the barbarians was considered a duty for which queens were formally responsible:

> Accipe anulum fidei. signaculum sanctae trinitatis. quo possis omnes / hereticas prauitates deuitare et barbaras gentes uirtute dei praemere. [*sic*] et ad agnitionem ueritatis aduocare.[49]

––––––

> Receive this ring of faith, a sign of the Holy Trinity, by means of which you may be able to avoid all heretical depravities and urge barbarian peoples to the power of God and summon them to the knowledge of truth.

It is also helpful to recall that throughout late antiquity and the Middle Ages, "conversion" was understood less as a single event than as an ongoing process, namely, as a life marked by constant attempts to remake oneself, and be remade, more closely in accordance with the image of God.[50] To convert, then, might be thought of not merely as wholesale change from heathen to Christian but also as a metaphor for spiritual improvement, a social enterprise, which, during the tenth century, was increasingly falling under the control of the royal family.[51] Tenth-century reformist writings, most notably the *Regularis Concordia,* granted both the king and queen increased control over England's religious life, depicting the royal couple as spiritual guardians of the nation, with Edgar and his queen, Ælfthryth, responsible for the welfare and protection of England's monks and nuns.[52] Similar sentiments are apparent in the period's art, which placed heightened emphasis on the idea of the royal family as earthly representatives of the heavenly court and as intercessors for the people's spiritual welfare. As Robert Deshman points out, it was during this period that iconographic depictions of the crowned Christ, the crowned Magi, and the Coronation of the Virgin first appeared in England, as did unusual ruler portraits likening the king to both Christ and the ideal abbot Benedict and the queen to the Virgin Mary.[53]

While the emphasis that tenth-century reformers placed on spiritual queenship was new, the idea itself was not. It was an idea that was part of England's own history of conversion and was, I would suggest, resurrected by tenth-century reformers as part of an attempt to promote stricter religious life in England through nostalgic invocations of a glorious English past. As such historians as Antonia Gransden and Patrick Wormald argue, the tenth-century Benedictine reform was a movement driven by a profound sense of nostalgia that found voice in monks' and bishops' eloquent expressions of longing to return to a faraway Anglo-Saxon golden age, with its firmly entrenched monastic episcopacy and freedom from Danish invasions.[54] Within this climate of retrospection, the image of Elene as an agent of Christian conversion would have resonated in multiple ways: for tenth-century readers, Elene would have invoked both the spiritual queenship promoted by contemporary reformers and also memories of queens' participation in England's early conversion efforts. Papal letters to the seventh-century kings and queens of Kent and Northumbria testify to the fact that many English and Roman churchmen considered Christian queens a potential means of introducing the faith to pagan kings, which was thought to be the first step to converting the entire race of the English.[55] We might recall Pope Boniface V's letter to Æthelburh (ca. 624), which specifically charges the queen with the duty of converting her pagan husband, Edwin, and also Boniface's letter to Edwin, which urges the king to convert by reminding him that his wife had already done so.[56] Similarly, several versions of the Mildreth legend offer suggestive links between Mercia's conversion under the reign of Wulfhere and the king's marriage to Eormenhild.[57] And many of the abbesses who took part in the eighth-century missions to convert the Continent were either former queens or the offspring of royal families.

For tenth-century audiences, then, Cynewulf's textual celebration of the late antique Christian queen offered an experience of reading that was distinctly historical. For them, Elene might be read not only as a figure who lived during various moments within typological history, but also as a figure who inhabited three different moments of distinct relevance to their own cultural identity: early Christian Rome, from which the Anglo-Saxons derived so many of their social and psychological formations; tenth-century England, in which they were living; and a golden age of English conversion nostalgically produced by reformers. While interpreting Elene as a figure who inhabited an Anglo-Saxon cultural past as opposed to a typological past required a slightly different, namely more linear, conceptualization of history, both methods of reading relied on a deep engagement with the past and an ability to keep multiple levels of meaning in one's mind simultaneously. Reading Elene as a multivalent historical presence within the Anglo-Saxons' cultural past may thus have reinforced and helped encourage the hermeneutic skills necessary for understanding her typologically, a way of reading that the poem presents as integral to and synonymous with conversion and a comprehension of the Cross's true meaning.

As Cynewulf worked to transform Elene into an exemplar of queenship that might be readily recognizable in terms of the literary, typological, and historical roles available to queens within Anglo-Saxon culture, he would have known that his own portrayal of the queen was only one of many factors that might determine how contemporary audiences understood her. As historian William Sewell reminds us, "What things in the world *are* is never fully determined by the symbolic net we throw over them—this also depends on . . . the different symbolic meanings that may have been attributed to them by other actors."[58] And indeed, as Cynewulf no doubt knew, the symbolic meanings attributed to Elene by other actors in Anglo-Saxon culture were many; she was one of the best-known female figures in Anglo-Saxon England. Celebrated twice a year at the annual Invention and Exaltation of the Cross festivals, the queen was also invoked repeatedly in English calendars, homilies, coins, litanies of the saints, public church dedications, saints' lives, letters, Church histories, and other versions of the *Inventio* legend besides Cynewulf's.[59] While Cynewulf could expect his readers to know about the queen, precisely what they would know might very well be cause for concern. Cynewulf's insistent emphasis on Elene's nobility and his efforts to endow the Roman empress with all the accoutrements of Anglo-Saxon royalty is, I would argue, an attempt to familiarize the queen and hence create a more culturally accessible exemplar of queenship for Anglo-Saxon audiences. However, the poet's painstaking construction of Elene as a noble and regal queen may have been given additional impetus by information circulating in England at this time regarding Helena's actual social status and, by extension, Constantine's dubious descent.

According to late antique pagan and Christian historians, Helena was born into an extremely lower-class family. Because Roman law forbade men of high rank to marry beneath their social station, it is most likely that Helena was never legally married to Constantine's father, Constantius Chlorus (who belonged to the provincial aristocracy of Dalmatia), but served as his concubine for approximately nineteen years (ca. 270–89).[60] The fourth-century pagan writer Eutropius, in his *Breviarium historiae Romanae,* claims that Constantine was born "ex obscuriore matrimonio" (out of an obscure marriage).[61] Likewise, Ambrose twice calls attention to Helena's low social status in his funeral oration for Theodosius I, claiming that "Christ raised her [Helena] from dung to power" and referring to her as a *stabularia,* a term suggesting that Helena worked in a stable or, because in late antiquity stables were often associated with inns, that she was a female innkeeper or servant at an inn.[62] During this time, such positions possibly entailed enforced prostitution and certainly brought with them very low social prestige.[63] Overt references to Helena as a concubine include Ambrose's early fifth-century *Origo Constantini,* in which he refers to Helena as *vilissima,* "cheapest" or "most common" of women; the mid-fifth-century writer Philostorgius, who claims that Constantine "had emanated from Helena, a common woman not different from strumpets"; and the late fifth-century Zosimus, who refers to Constantine as "the son of the illegal intercourse of a low woman with the Emperor Constantius" and "the son of a harlot."[64]

Precisely how Anglo-Saxon writers learned of Helena's low birth and illicit marriage is difficult to ascertain.[65] Nonetheless, the fact that Helena was a concubine appears to have been fairly common knowledge among

Anglo-Saxon writers. Aldhelm's prose *De virginitate* refers to Constantine as "Constantii filius in Britannia ex pelice Helena genitus" (son of Constantius born in Britain of the concubine Helena).[66] Bede states in his *Historia Ecclesiastica* that "hic Constantinum filium ex concubina Helena creatum imperatorem Galliarum reliquit" (he [Constantius Chlorus] left a son Constantine, who was made emperor of Gaul, being the child of his concubine Helena).[67] Similarly, in his *De temporum ratione,* Bede again refers to Constantine as "Constantii ex concubina Helena filius" (son of Constantius from the concubine Helena).[68] And the Old English *Orosius* claims that "on þæm dagum Constantius, se mildesta monn, for on Brettannie 7 þær gefor, 7 gesealde his suna þæt rice Constanti[n]use, þone he hæfde be Elenan his ciefese"[69] (in those days, Constantius, the mildest man, traveled to Britain and died there and gave that kingdom to his son Constantine, whom he had by his concubine Helena).

Apparently, neither Bede nor the *Orosius* translator viewed Constantine's descent from a concubine and subsequent inheritance of his father's Western empire as in any way problematic. Both the *Historia Ecclesiastica* and *Orosius* describe Constantine in terms commonly used to designate legitimate male offspring, *filius* or *sunu,* as opposed to terms used to refer to illegitimate male offspring, such as *nothus,* "born out of wedlock but of a known father," *spurius,* "born of an unknown father," *hornungsunu,* "illegitimate son," and *hornungbrothor,* "illegitimate brother."[70] Moreover, both texts matter-of-factly relate Constantine's regnal inheritance in the same line as they describe his mother as a concubine. The fact that neither Bede nor the *Orosius* translator exhibit any concern over Constantine's descent from a concubine is perhaps explained as a recognition of the fact that concubinage was a common practice among Roman emperors.[71] So too this apparent lack of concern may be read as tacit acknowledgment of the frequency with which royal concubinage was practiced in early Anglo-Saxon culture and of the hereditary rights commonly granted to the children of such unions.[72]

By the tenth century, however, Constantine's descent from a concubine was likely to have become a less acceptable part of the Helena legends, for cultural attitudes toward concubines and their children had undergone significant shifts in the previous two centuries. Beginning in the eighth century, Anglo-Saxon churchmen launched increasingly strong attacks against concubinage, and particularly royal concubinage, attempting to redefine this traditional Anglo-Saxon practice as both illegal and immoral and to bar concubines' children from their previous rights of inheritance.[73] In 786, a legatine commission visited England from Rome, drawing up a series of injunctions to the Anglo-Saxons, the twelfth chapter of which prohibits the children of concubines from acceding to the throne, stating that "kings are . . . not to be those begotten in adultery or incest" and "neither can he who was not born of a legitimate marriage be the Lord's anointed and king of the whole kingdom and inheritor of the land."[74] By the tenth century, prohibitions against a concubine's child succeeding to the throne had tightened to the point where the social and somatic status of the queen at the time of her son's birth began to figure centrally in disputes over a particular prince's "throneworthiness." The period witnessed a host of succession debates, in which accusations that sons such as Æthelstan and Edward were the sons of concubines or women of low birth appear to have impeded temporarily their claims to the throne.[75] Leading churchmen such as Dunstan and Æthelwold played a major role in these debates, casting aspersions on the sexual proclivities of various queens and conducting investigations into their lineage to create arguments discrediting particular princes' claims to the throne.[76] Given the increasing tensions around the topic of royal concubinage during the tenth century, Helena's historical status as concubine had the potential to be particularly inflammatory for contemporary readers, or at least to interfere with her being taken up as a symbol of unity between leaders of Church and state.

Regardless of when Cynewulf was writing, however, Elene's historical status as concubine had the potential to pose problems, in that it directly conflicted with her typological status. Indeed, a woman associated with concubinage was a rather unfortunate choice as a symbol of the Church, for throughout the early Middle Ages, commentators typically used the concubine as a symbol for Synagogue, reserving the legally recognized wife as the usual figure for the Church.[77] Hence Jews were depicted as the illicit offspring of such concubines as Hagar, and Christians as the freeborn children of such legally recognized wives as Sarah and Ruth, and thus by extension, as the offspring of Christ's true spouse, the Church.[78] Such comparisons appear in numerous biblical commentaries, including those by Hrabanus Maurus and Isidore of Seville.[79] Thus, if Elene's historical status as mother and also mother of the first Christian emperor rendered her particularly suitable as an allegorical figure of the Church, her historical status as concubine made her a somewhat less than ideal figure for performing this kind of symbolic work.

There are no references to Helena's low social status in any of the Latin texts that most likely served as immediate sources for Cynewulf's *Elene*. However, this information would have been available to Cynewulf through both late antique and Anglo-Saxon writings, and it is probable that he was aware of Constantine's precarious parentage and—given the popularity of the Helena legends—could have reasonably expected some of his readers to be aware of it as well. Given the social and symbolic difficulties presented by Elene's historical status as concubine, Cynewulf may have had some anxiety about offering her to readers—either as an exemplar of queenship or as an image of the Church. One way to ameliorate these difficulties was to elevate Elene's social status, which is what other writers did when discussing both Constantine and Elene.[80] The late ninth-century translators of Bede's *Ecclesiastical History,* for example, translate Bede's reference to Elene as *concubina* with *wif*—a term that was commonly employed in Anglo-Saxon England to designate a man's lawful wife—thus transforming Constantine from the king's bastard into his legitimate son and rightful heir.[81] And I would suggest that this is precisely what Cynewulf did: he painstakingly constructed Elene as a noble queen, surrounded by all of the royal props that Anglo-Saxon readers would have associated not with a low-born concubine but with the legally recognized widow of a deceased ruler and the honored mother of a legitimate king.[82]

Queenship, Hierarchy, Christian Community

While Cynewulf's portrayal of a heroic battle-queen, encased in all the social and symbolic trappings of royalty and successfully spreading the Word, might seem a straightforward and delightfully refreshing example of a pre-Conquest writer endorsing the autonomy of royal women, such is not wholly the case. As many critics have pointed out, Elene's autonomy, and indeed her entire role in Cynewulf's poem, is in many ways seriously diminished in comparison with her Latin counterpart in the *Inventio*. Earl Anderson, for example, argues that Cynewulf presents Elene as a physical surrogate for her imperial son and her mission to Jerusalem as an extension of Constantine's will; and E. Gordon Whatley contends that Cynewulf invokes the emperor's name and imagines his physical presence more often than the *Inventio* does, all of which serves to "re-emphasize Elene's dependence on her imperial son for direction," to enhance Constantine's role in the integration of the Holy Land into the Christian empire, and to diminish Elene's.[83]

Yet if critics insist that Cynewulf takes pains to emphasize Elene's devotion and subservience to Constantine, what has gone largely unexamined is the larger matrix of human relationships in which the queen's interactions with her son are situated. While Cynewulf emphasizes Elene's close relationship with Constantine, this relationship is but one example of Cynewulf's efforts to portray the queen as firmly ensconced within a larger network of kin and community. Throughout the poem, the queen is never far from her own people but is almost always surrounded by a group of her own armed warriors: when the vessels land on the eastern shores, the ships are left until the queen should seek them again "gumena þreate" (with a band of men; 254b); the warriors are said to be "ymb sigecwen siðes gefysde" (around the queen ready for the journey; 260); Elene embarks toward Jerusalem "heape gecoste, / lindwigendra" (with an excellent band of shieldbearers; 269b–70a) and "secga þreate" (with a band of men; 271a); and when the group finally arrives in the city they are described as "corðra mæste, / eorlas æscrofe mid þa æðelan cwen" (a great company, illustrious warriors, with the noble queen; 274b–75). With her son frequently in her thoughts, her own men always around her, and her regular correspondence with the imperial court, Elene is hardly ever alone or lacking in company. And when her mission is completed, the queen happily prepares to return to her *eðel*, "homeland" (1219a). Cynewulf's effort to foreground kinship and community as central forces in Elene's life is notable as a sharp departure from the *Inventio*, which rarely mentions Helena's ties to her own people. In fact, the Helena of the *Inventio* is so infrequently represented within a community that she seems to have been abandoned in Jerusalem; although we are told that she enters Jerusalem with a mighty army, this army scarcely appears thereafter, and the end of the *Inventio* simply states that Helena left many gifts with the bishop and then died, making no mention of her intent to return to Rome.

The strong sense of community that Cynewulf's Elene experiences is by no means unique to the queen. All of the Christians in the poem are presented as firmly embedded within a community, which is figured as a felicitous by-product of Christianity, a reward for and feature of faith. Every time someone converts or any portion of Christian history is brought to light is an occasion for communal celebration, public rejoicing, and collective interaction. When Constantine learns that the Cross in his vision is a sign from God, Cynewulf adds that all of the Christians rejoice. As soon as the Old English Constantine receives baptism, he begins to proclaim publicly the Word of God day and night, unlike the Latin Constantine, who heads to his books for solitary study. The *Inventio's* description of Judas's release from the pit is figured as a private matter between Judas and Helena: after enduring seven days of starvation, Judas promises to show Helena the Cross, and when he is released he hurries off to Calvary. In *Elene,* by contrast, Judas's newfound freedom is the occasion for a public ceremony of communal reintegration: Elene orders a group of retainers to release Judas; he is led up "mid arum" (with honor; 714a); a troop of people then rush off with him to Calvary to search for the Cross (716); and when Judas finally unearths three crosses, he rejoices and lifts them up "mid weorode" (before the host; 843b). In the following episode, the *Inventio* simply states that Judas brought the crosses into the city. In Cynewulf's version, the finding of the crosses prompts a procession of guests and noblemen, who enter the city to witness a ceremonious presentation of the crosses at Elene's knees. After the crosses are brought into the city, the *Inventio,* once again, portrays a rather dull state of affairs: the people simply sit and wait for the glory of Christ. However, in Cynewulf's text, the wait is portrayed as a communal celebration: the people sit around, raise up song, and rejoice in their newfound glories, and Cynewulf explicitly states that "þa þær menigo cwom / folc unlytel" (many came there, not a few folk; 870b–71a). Similarly, when a young dead boy is then brought into the city so the people might distinguish which of the three crosses has life-giving power and is thus the True Cross, Cynewulf states that the bier is both carried and surrounded by a large group: "gefærenne man / brohton on bære beorna þreate / on neaweste" (They brought the dead man into the neighborhood on a bier, with a band of men; 871b–73a).

In *Elene,* then, to be Christian is to be surrounded by an ever-present community that is loving and harmonious, an idea that coheres most forcefully when Elene teaches the converted Jews that they must not only love God but also keep friendship and peace among themselves:

> þa seo cwen ongan
> læran leofra heap   þæt hie lufan dryhtnes
> 7 sybbe swa same   sylfra betweonum,

freondræddenne   fæste gelæston,
leahtorlease   in hira lifes tid.

(1204b–8)

Then the queen began to teach the beloved group, sinless in the time of their lives, that they should keep firmly the love of God and likewise peace, friendship among themselves.

Indeed, it is crucial for Elene to instruct the newly converted Jews in friendship and communal harmony, for, according to the poem's own logic, these are ideas as foreign to them as that of Christ as their savior. Cynewulf's depiction of Christianity as a kind of ongoing collective celebration enacted by members of a tightly knit community that functions harmoniously and abounds in peace and friendship presents a sharp contrast to his depiction of Judaism, which is characterized either as encouraging solitude or as producing a community rife with dissent, sadness, and acute anxiety. For example, when Judas is most insistently enacting his Judaism, that is, during his seven nights in the pit when he refuses to reveal the whereabouts of the Cross, he is most completely alone. Moreover, Cynewulf enhances Judas's solitude by claiming that Elene commanded her men to lead Judas "corðre" (away from the company; 691b), and by explaining Judas's sorrowful state of mind as in part due to his "duguða leas" (lacking a retinue; 693b). The Jewish elders do frequently come together for counsel, but such gatherings are filled with discord, confusion, and an anxious preoccupation with the expected fall of the Jews. While the appeal of Christian community is potentially overshadowed by the poem's more explicit and showy promise of Christianity's ability to guarantee military victory and hence protect against physical harm, I would argue that Cynewulf's depiction of loving community offers a powerful lure by promising protection against a less obvious but more insidious personal threat than that of invading armies, namely, that of loneliness. The poem holds out a delightful vision of Christianity as an effective bulwark against this painful state, assuring company—not the eternal company of the 144,000 virgins or the angels on high but an ever-present earthly fellowship—and acceptance within a family joined by bonds of belief as well as those of blood.

Yet the price for such fellowship is rather steep, requiring, as the poem makes clear, absolute conformity to a rigid social hierarchy that demands unquestioning obedience from every member. This obedience is felt quite palpably in Elene's utter subservience to Constantine; he is figured as unquestionably superior to her, and her own will as a mere extension of her sovereign son's desires. However, such subjection is not Elene's alone but a condition of harmonious Christian life. The queen's subservience to her son is mirrored in her people's to her; she is surrounded by servants and retainers who are ever-ready and eager to fulfill her every command. When Elene orders that Judas be pushed into a pit, Cynewulf claims that "scealcas ne gældon" (the servants did not delay; 692b), and when she commands that Judas be released from the pit, "hie ðæt ofstlice efnedon sona" (they performed that immediately, without delay; 713). Cynewulf emphasizes Elene's power to control her retainers, describing the queen as "sio þær hæleðum scead" (she who ruled over warriors there; 709b) and reinforces that power through repeated use of the verb *bebeodan*, "to command" (710b, 715b).

Moreover, Elene seems to have little trouble accepting her place within this hierarchy. She dutifully carries out her son's orders, offers requisite homage to both the newly appointed bishop and the nameless wise man skilled in God's mysteries, and appears, as Jackson Campbell has noted, to be a generally far happier character than that in the *Inventio*.[84] Far from challenging the notion of subservience to authority, Elene herself propagates it. The very last lesson that the queen teaches the people of Jerusalem is that they should be obedient to the instructions of the bishop:

> þa seo cwen ongan
> læran leofra heap   þæt hie . . .
> . . . .
> . . . þæs latteowes   larum hyrdon
> cristenum þeawum   þe him Cyriacus
> bude, boca gleaw;   wæs se bissceophad
> fægere befæsted.
>
> (1204b–5, 1209–12a)

Then the queen began to teach the beloved group that they . . . should obey the instructions of the leader, the Christian customs,

which Cyriacus, wise in books, proclaimed to them. The bishopric
was fairly established.

Nowhere in the *Inventio* is it stated that Helena taught the people to be
obedient to ecclesiastical authority, and Cynewulf's final, rather maximlike
comment that "the bishopric was fairly established," placed as it is after
Elene's teaching the people to obey authority, serves to highlight obedience
further as a defining characteristic of harmonious Christian community.
The queen's teachings are part of a rigid chain of command in *Elene*, in
which Constantine obeys God, Elene obeys Constantine, the retainers obey
Elene, the newly converted Christians obey the bishop, and the Jews are
utterly excluded. Even the animals seem to find Christianization a rather
ordering experience. Before Constantine's vision of the Cross, the beasts of
battle are divided between the Huns and the Romans and hence scattered
over approximately twenty-five lines (27b–30a, 52b–53a), yet after the emperor's vision, the rejoicing raven, dewy-feathered eagle, and forest-dwelling
wolf all line up neatly behind Constantine's troops, their descriptions tidily
completed in four short lines (110b–13a).

Within Cynewulf's formulation, hierarchy proves to be not only a rigid
but also an enduring construct, surviving as a hale and hearty presence well
beyond life on earth. The poem ends with a horrific vision of Judgment
Day, on which a terrifying God, flanked by a troop of angels, comes forth
to divide the human race into a hierarchy of his own making: a raging fire
composed of three tiers of flames which effect various levels of distress. No
one is exempt from the tripartite inferno, for it incorporates "folc anra
gehwylc / þara þe gewurdon on widan feore / ofer sidne grund" (all people
who have ever lived on the wide earth; 1287b–89a), and neither social rank
nor gender bolsters one's chances for securing a place within the uppermost,
or coolest, level of the fire. Rather, it is moral and spiritual righteousness
that emerge as the operative criteria for ranking within God's hierarchy,
as the "soðfæste" (truefast; 1289b), the "synfulle" (sinful; 1295b), and the
"awyrgede womsceaðan" (accursed evil-doers; 1299a) are all relegated to respectively lower tiers of flames, with descent accompanied by increasingly
uncomfortable temperatures and lack of physical mobility.

While it is not unusual to find depictions of social and spiritual hierarchy in Old English poetry, what is unusual about *Elene* is that it offers us
a glimpse of the complex strategies by which such poetry was mobilized,
and may have provided some of the impetus necessary, to sustain cultural

faith in these hierarchies. As Elene delves deeper and deeper into the Jewish heartland to create new Christian communities, she and the Roman community from which she hails model for these emergent communities an "ideal Christian social order," one in which the autonomy of every social actor is seriously compromised by Cynewulf's assertion of a Christianity circumscribed by a rigidly defined social hierarchy. Entrance into the faith entails acceptance of that hierarchy, but it also rewards such acceptance by a vision of community that is excitingly melioristic—it promises that the adoption of the hierarchy presages both personal happiness and ever-present human fellowship. To disregard the poem's larger portrait of human relationships is to risk viewing Elene's subservience to Constantine as merely another one of the numerous literary indices of medieval misogyny, and to overlook its crucial exemplary function with respect to the poem's broader and more ambitious ideological goals: to validate and naturalize contemporary ideologies of social hierarchy by projecting them back into a glorious Roman past, a move that brought with it the weight of tradition and the authority of founding figures.

Precisely how Cynewulf's depiction of a queen who was at once a powerful and effective agent of Christian conversion, and, at the same time, a humble and obedient servant to social hierarchy may have been received by contemporary audiences is a vexed issue. Historical evidence verifies that Mercian queens typically enjoyed a great deal of power and status, far more so than their West Saxon or Northumbrian counterparts.[85] If *Elene* was indeed composed in eighth- or ninth-century Mercia, as is often thought to be the case, contemporary Christian readers may have been all the more inspired by the tale of a queen-saint whose heroic exploits resonated with their own ideologies of queenship. Nonetheless, given their acculturation to queenly power, Mercian readers may also have been somewhat surprised by Elene's unquestioning obedience to both royal and ecclesiastical authority. For later readers, however, these images of queenly subservience may have been somewhat less startling, for while the tenth and early eleventh centuries indeed witnessed increased emphasis on the social and symbolic power of queens, these changes were nonetheless accompanied by ecclesiastical efforts to codify hierarchies of status and gender, and to create a social climate of unquestioning Christian obedience, much like the one envisioned in *Elene*.

The Benedictine reforms ushered into England a profound emphasis on hierarchy, specifically a demarcation of clear boundaries between various groups of people—clergy and laity, men and women—and the duties appropriate to people of different social stations.[86] As Clare Lees argues, while homilists constructed compelling visions of Christian community as an inclusive social space that incorporated all believers and based rank solely on good works, such images were overshadowed by more numerous depictions of Christian community as hierarchical, unequal, and reliant on conceptions of social rank as a series of fixed and natural states that it was the individual's godly duty to enact.[87] Late Anglo-Saxon homilies are rife with promises of an eternal kingdom free from social rank in exchange for happily enacting one's given rank on earth, definitions of the only true servitude as acquiescence to the rule of vices and hence subjection to not one but multiple masters, and injunctions that deviation from one's earthly rank would result in everlasting servitude in hell.[88]

Reformers' efforts to stress the importance of social hierarchy were accompanied, not surprisingly, by a hardening of gender boundaries. While modern historians have perhaps overstated the misogyny of reformers' policies and their deleterious effects on women, the reformist emphasis on priestly celibacy, monastic chastity, and the regulation of lay marriage tended to align women with notions of impurity, to insist on an increased separation of the sexes and a cloistering of women in monastic life, and to encourage general anxieties around the female body.[89] The royal status of queens did not exempt them from increasingly rigid attitudes toward gender. While the late tenth and early eleventh centuries indeed witnessed increased emphasis on the social and symbolic status of queens, royal women were still frequently abandoned by their spouses and their sexual behavior was subject to scrutiny.[90] Moreover, while the queen Ælfthryth was indeed formally named as the patron of nunneries, this position was less prominent than it would have been in earlier centuries, as the majority of the houses established during the tenth century were not nunneries but single male houses.[91] Read within such a cultural climate, the various hierarchies depicted in *Elene* seem to offer poetic affirmation of a traditional Pauline social vision of both rank and gender; even the queen is as carefully circumscribed as any other social actor and she, like her people, will eventually be free of earthly circumscriptions once admitted to the kingdom of heaven.

Critics have not failed to note the rather conservative gender dynamics at work in *Elene*. In a compelling reading of the poem, Joyce Tally Lionarons, for example, argues that Elene's power over Judas and her assumption of command over a host of armed men each constitutes a brief "citation

of 'masculine' categories of behavior [which] in the absence of any expec-
tation . . . of female reiteration, invariably forces her return to the performance of a normative 'feminine' role."[92] Within such logic, the poem's
gender dynamics enact a familiar drama of subversion and containment, in
which the queen's assumption of the role of Germanic warlord can only
"temporarily displace gendered norms," which are then powerfully reas-
serted when the queen subsequently "acts out a normative 'feminine' role as
spiritual daughter to Cyriacus and dutiful mother to Constantine."[93] Indeed, sustained gender transgression simply cannot be found in *Elene* at the
level of individual female behavior. For Elene is never truly free from her
subservience to Constantine; even her most potentially powerful moment—
her voyage to Jerusalem and assumption of command over a host of armed
men—is a performance of her son's will. Viewed solely in terms of her actions, the queen is always already contained—contained by a rigidly defined social hierarchy in which disobedience to the will of her earthly
þeoden, Constantine, would, because of the term's denotative indeterminacy, concomitantly entail transgression of the will of her heavenly *þeoden*,
behavior that would be unthinkable for a model Christian queen. Indeed,
far from a celebration of women's autonomy, the poem might easily be
read, if one focuses solely on Elene's actions, as a tale of female energy
channeled wholly into the fulfillment of male fantasy. In the first half of the
poem, Constantine worries about his martial prowess and dreams of a
jewel-encrusted Cross; in the second half of the poem Elene actualizes his
fantasies by recovering the Cross, decorating it with jewels, and sending
him the Crucifixion nails as adornment for his war-steed's bridle and guar-
antor of future military success.

While analysis of the queen's behavior reveals a severely compromised
portrait of female agency, I would nevertheless argue that *Elene* resists being
read as an unequivocal championing of a traditional and conservative social
order that requires female subservience. Revisionist possibilities may not
inhere in the autonomy of individual characters, but they are suggested else-
where. While Elene's unquestioning subservience to Constantine marks her
as an active participant in Cynewulf's attempts to promote a very traditional gender hierarchy, that hierarchy is rendered rather precarious by a
narrative emphasis and poetic investment that mark the queen as a clear
victor in the contest for Cynewulf's imaginative energy. To be sure, Cynewulf strains to focus his own and his audience's attention on the emperor,
creating an original opening for the poem that details Constantine's fierce

efforts to stave off invading barbarian tribes. Yet, attention to the emperor's military exploits quickly gives way to a wholesale absorption with the queen's spiritual warfare, and it is ultimately Elene who captivates the bulk of Cynewulf's creativity. Once past the poem's opening scenes, it is she who is the main beneficiary of the rich kennings, weighty verbs, appositions, and understatement—all the lexical choices and figurative devices that signal the supreme importance of a character or event in Old English poetry. As Elene embarks on her journey and the poem gains momentum, the emperor is relegated to a back seat and positioned in relation to the queen much as God the Father is to Christ in so many late medieval texts: as a familiar quantity and one whose expected appearance in incipit, coda, or short sequence functions primarily as a rote reminder of superior power positioned predictably outside the text's diachronic imperatives. And Cynewulf even seems to perceive the problem with his imaginative investment in Elene, intruding urgent, veiled injunctions throughout the text to the reader to recall that Rome is the real source of Christian conversion and Constantine the real leader of the mission.

As Rome and its masculine figurehead recede, both the queen and the symbolic value of femininity emerge in full force. Moreover, Cynewulf suggests that such an emergence is coextensive with the project of conversion and that a fluidity of gender hierarchy enables its accomplishment. Judas's conversion, for example, inscribes a reversal of the usual configuration of gender relations, in both hagiography-as-genre and Pauline logic. In torturing Judas, Elene reverses the typical hagiographical formulation of the female saint tortured by a male pagan, and Judas's subjection to a woman is figured as an enabling force in his conversion.[94] To be sure, the gender inversion inherent in Judas's subjection to Elene is rather brief. As Lionarons argues, such inversion is predicated in part on the patristic logic that Elene's Christianity renders her spiritually male while Judas's Judaism renders him spiritually female, a logic that explains why Elene's power over Judas is significantly lessened after he converts and is imbued with a newfound spiritual masculinity.[95] Nevertheless, I would argue that the brief span of time during which a Jewish man is placed under the power of a Christian woman unsettles traditional gender hierarchy by fiercely asserting that spiritual gender takes precedence over biological sex—that it is belief rather than the body that determines hierarchy.

That the coming of Christianity might usher in new and more fluid attitudes toward gender hierarchy which are more enduring than those witnessed in Judas's conversion is suggested in the poem's gendering of faith. Although widely known as a religion that places great importance on female genealogy and whose devotional texts are filled with powerful female figures, Judaism in *Elene* is imagined as an all-male faith that is sustained through a masculine intellectual tradition disseminated through patrilineage. There are no Jewish women in the poem, the end of Jewish supremacy is imagined as a period in which "sien . . . þa fæderlican / lare forleten" (the teachings of the fathers will be abandoned; 430b–32a), and the Jews' refusal to reveal the whereabouts of the Cross is the product of an oral tradition that has been passed from Judas's grandfather to Judas's father and finally to the young Judas (426b–53, 528–30). The queen's arrival in Jerusalem marks the intrusion of a woman into a formerly all-male space, a gender disruption that is figured as wholly positive by the Christian poet. The disruption of a biologically codified male space is further inscribed as a symbolically gendered transition from the wholly masculinized Judaism to the more feminized Christianity. The customs of the Jewish fathers give way before the teachings of the queen mother, Judas's conversion is followed by a heartfelt speech in which he twice acknowledges Mary (774–75, 782), and the prayer that ends the narrative component of the text depicts heaven as a female space, offering a rousing injunction that all people who remember the festival of the Cross might enjoy eternal bliss with Mary (1228b–35).

As it refigures traditional gender hierarchy, the poem concomitantly highlights the idea that tradition is itself a flexible, dynamic entity. The sheer act of rewriting the *Inventio* foregrounds the vitality of tradition, signaling that the social structures of the past—even a past as foundational to the Anglo-Saxons' cultural heritage as late antique Rome—were neither static nor fixed but perpetually open to revision. Similarly, the queen's most profound act, her conversion of Judas, powerfully asserts that the human relationships of the past need not, and indeed must not, be slavishly imitated but revised and rewritten. When Elene converts Judas Cyriacus, she radically revises a past that unfolded roughly three centuries earlier between Christ and Judas Iscariot. The breaking of bread and subsequent symbolic perversion of that act in the breaking of a trust are re-visioned when Elene convinces Judas to accept the spiritual loaf over which he has been dickering and to pledge eternal devotion to Christ—a rewriting of history that greatly irks the Devil, who appears midway through the poem to lament, "Ic þurh Iudas ær / hyhtful gewearð 7 nu gehyned eom / goda geasne þurh

Iudas eft, / fah 7 freondleas" (I was once made hopeful by a Judas and now again by a Judas, I am humiliated, bereft of goods, guilty, and friendless; 921b–24a).

But it is perhaps the interpretive strategies that the queen elicits which most profoundly destabilize any attempt to read the poem's depictions of social and spiritual hierarchy as straightforwardly prescriptive. "Remembering" the Roman empress through the various discourses of Anglo-Saxon queenship at his disposal, Cynewulf creates a queen whose typological, literary, cultural, and historical multivalence calls into question any unequivocal interpretation of a text. Just as it condemns slavish adherence to literal levels of textual analysis and insists at every turn that characters and events are polysemous, so too does *Elene* militate against reading any representation of social hierarchy as either temporally or historically fixed. To be sure, the poem lauds the benefits of inserting oneself into a Christian community and, in so doing, accepting highly traditional and conservative hierarchies of rank and gender. But it also demands that readers refuse to interpret these hierarchies as reductive prescriptions, through a complex and multivalent depiction of queenship that stakes a fierce claim for the utter banality and spiritual depravity of believing that a text means only and exactly what it says.

Chapter 3

Beowulf and the Gendering of Heroism

Although *Beowulf* contains more women than any other Old English poem, no reader can fail to note that its central focus is nevertheless on men and their actions. The poem's powerfully masculinist disposition is apparent in its largely male cast of characters and in the relatively minimal attention given to the women who do appear: of the eleven female figures in *Beowulf,* only five are named and only one speaks in direct address.[1] Hrothgar's characterization of Beowulf's mother as a woman basking in the reflected glory of her son's heroism (942b–46a) serves as a useful reminder that the women in *Beowulf* are identified primarily in relation to their male kin, most of whom are either prospective or former heroes.[2] The male-centered gaze of the poem finds fullest expression in its hero, whose obsession with fame and apparent lack of interest in women models a worldview that was adopted by the majority of early *Beowulf* critics. Until approximately the 1970s, much energy was lavished on Beowulf and his pursuit of heroism, but very little on the poem's female characters.[3] This dual tendency among early scholars to focus on heroism and to overlook women led some feminist critics to argue for a causal relationship between the two phenomena, and to view heroism and women as mutually exclusive or antagonistic critical concerns. In her survey of the past century of work on gender in *Beowulf,* Alexandra Hennessey Olsen, for example, writes: "Critics of *Beowulf* have tended to minimize the importance of women in the poem because of the obvious importance of male heroism."[4] Seth Lerer takes a similar view of the ill effects studies of heroism have had on gender criticism, but argues for the damage as more pervasive: "The traditional approach to *Beowulf* as a heroic poem . . . has excluded an analysis of women's roles and sensibilities in this as well as other documents of pre-Conquest narrative."[5]

Recent feminist interventions by such scholars as Joyce Hill and Gillian Overing have posited a more dialectical relationship between the poem's treatment of heroism and royal women. Hill analyzes the stock figure of the *geomuru ides,* "sad woman," in Old English heroic poetry, and suggests that her laments at once register women's victimization under the heroic ethos, and point to its larger costs to the culture as a whole.[6] Overing, whose *Language, Sign and Gender in Beowulf* remains to date one of the most insightful readings of the poem's gender dynamics, contends that female figures in *Beowulf* "embody the unsettling presence of ambiguity and paradox," and thus serve as agents for "deflecting or redirecting . . . death-centered masculine desire."[7] For Overing, the discomfiting confrontations with ambiguity and paradox that queens present extend beyond the intratextual world of the poem to the interpretive practices of modern readers. Contemporary readings of *Beowulf,* she suggests, ought to mirror the non-linear and digressive nature of the poem's linguistic and thematic structures, exemplified in its female figures, whose strong associations with weaving urge that interpretive closure and resolution be resisted in favor of a more open-ended hermeneutics of process.[8]

For all of the poem's emphasis on reflection, process, and the multiplicity of interpretive possibility, one nevertheless cannot escape the strong sense that at the same time, *Beowulf* urges its readers to adopt strong critical positions that move toward interpretive closure. The narrator's continuous reliance on maxims, the characters' constant recourse to heartfelt boasts and promises that represent attempts to stabilize an unknown future, the sincere and highly partisan speeches of Hrothgar and the Last Survivor, and most notably, Beowulf's single-minded vision of an astonishingly beautiful heroic world that provides the matter for the Christian narrator's critique of that world, all stake a strong claim for interpretive control. Female characters in *Beowulf* do, as Overing contends, call into question the unequivocal win-or-die logic that undergirds the heroic world.[9] Yet they do not simply introduce ambiguity and disorder into this world and then abandon it in a kind of chaotic state of choric confusion. What the feminine voices of the poem do is to gesture toward the possibility of a new model of heroism that redefines, and incorporates the energies of, preconversion Germanic heroism so as to bring it more closely in line with the Christian worldview of the poem's readers.

Anglo-Saxonists have often remarked on Old English poetry's powerful synthetic capacities and on Christian poets' extraordinary abilities to harmonize concepts that hail from very different ideological arenas. Commenting on the creative synthesis between religious and heroic idealism found in such poems as *Beowulf,* Roberta Frank, for example, argues that "between *Bede's Death Song* [ca. 735] and *Maldon* [ca. 991] something happened to Old English poetry"—a "something" that Frank identifies as the "rebarbarization [of Old English poetry]," or the newfound sense among Anglo-Saxon writers that such apparently incompatible ideals as piety and heroic life could be brought together into a productive and organic whole.[10] Yet as Christian poets found a place in their writings for heroic tropes, these tropes did not emerge intact. To move a figure, image, or idea into a new textual arena is necessarily to transform it. As the *Beowulf* poet mobilizes feminine voices to prescribe a new model of heroism premised on turning the violent energies of heroic self-assertion inward and waging battles against one's inner vices rather than against human foes, the very nature of such entrenched heroic ideas as "battle," "enemy," and "hero" undergo significant shifts to the point where the "heroic," as either generic category or cultural code, becomes almost unrecognizable.[11] Indeed this is precisely the point. By asking readers to embrace a vision of heroism that so powerfully deviates from conventional representations of the heroic ethos as encoded in such texts as *Cynewulf and Cyneheard* or the self-consciously archaic *Battle of Maldon,* the *Beowulf* poet urges readers, both medieval and modern, to challenge rigid definitions of the "heroic" and to expand their understandings of this concept.

In suggesting that heroism is redefined through the poem's "feminine voices," I invoke a broad understanding of both terms, and view the phrase as inclusive not simply of Wealhtheow's words, but also all of the actions, gestures, and utterances of the other women in the poem whose words are not reported, and also the words and actions of the aged king Hrothgar. Carol Clover argues that within Old Norse literature, old age asserts a feminizing influence, or a kind of gender degradation, on men, placing them in a social partnership with "most women, children, slaves, and . . . disabled, or otherwise disenfranchised men."[12] The feminizing effects of old age are similarly apparent in Hrothgar, who was once "an cyning / æghwæs orleahtre, oþ þæt hine yldo benam / mægenes wynnum" (a king blameless in everything until old age deprived him of the joys of strength; 1885b–87a). Unable to protect his people or to avenge their sufferings, Hrothgar absents himself, both literally and figuratively, from the masculine world of heroic action, exhibiting a notable preference for female company (664–65a) as well as a tendency to disappear quietly when battle is at hand.[13] Having ceded any direct participation in the masculine world of heroic action, Hrothgar takes on a variety of roles typically associated in Anglo-Saxon literature with women, namely, mourning battle losses and encouraging others to exact revenge for them. Moreover, Hrothgar's exclusion from activities deemed central to male heroic life appears to be long-standing in nature. Marked as he is by ongoing impotence in battle against the Grendelkin as well as a comparative dearth of past heroic exploits, it is as if, in Edward Irving's words, "[Hrothgar] is not only old now, but was always old."[14] While Hrothgar's loss of masculine potency is depicted as a lamentable (albeit normative) aspect of heroic life (1887b), it is nevertheless this social demotion to a position akin to those occupied by the poem's female figures that enables Hrothgar's voice, at various moments, to join theirs in positing new models of heroic masculinity.

Indeed it should come as no surpise that the *Beowulf* poet would look to an aged king to critique and redefine heroism. Within Anglo-Saxon culture, old age was strongly associated with wisdom, as evidenced by the dual meanings of the term *frod* as both "old" and "wise." Wisdom occupies a central position in early medieval definitions of heroism, such as that famously advanced by Isidore of Seville in his widely circulated *Etymologiae:* "For men are called 'heroes' as if to say that they are 'aerial' and worthy of heaven on account of wisdom and fortitude."[15] Isidore's identification of heroism as composed of *sapientia* and *fortitudo* was a crucial catalyst for R. E. Kaske's foundational study of these characteristics as intrinsic to the Anglo-Saxon heroic ideal and as the "controlling theme of *Beowulf.*"[16] Yet if, as Kaske claims, "*fortitudo* implies physical might and courage consistently enough . . . with regard to *sapientia,* we seem to have in *Beowulf* a [more] . . . eclectic concept," poised somewhere between pagan Germanic and Christian ideology, and a concept that was undergoing redefinition as Christianity gained a firmer hold on the Anglo-Saxons.[17] Like the aged Hrothgar, the women in *Beowulf* are especially well positioned to participate in such redefinitions—or to prescribe a new kind of *sapientia* that might act as both the mate and the necessary counterpoint to *fortitudo*—for like age, femaleness was an attribute that was thought to be accompanied by mental prowess and the ability to provide sound advice, particularly in matters requiring foresight. The strong association between women and wisdom is felt throughout the Anglo-Saxon corpus and quite powerfully in *Beowulf:* Wealhtheow is both "mode geþungen" (accomplished in mind; 624a) and "wisfæst wordum" (wise in words; 626a), and Hygd is both onomastically associated with "mind" and described as "wis welþungen" (wise, well-accomplished; 1927a).[18] The poet's belief in an association between age and wisdom is similarly apparent: the narrator evinces great surprise that Hygd is so wise, in spite of her youth (1926b–28), and the aged Hrothgar is consistently marked by such epithets as *wis,* "wise," *snotor,* "wise," and *frod,* "wise" or "old."[19] As *Beowulf* critiques and calls into question a heroic ethos of violence and vengeance, it does so through the voices of those members of Anglo-Saxon society who were believed to be most capable of providing sound guidance and least capable of participating in the acts of militancy that were intrinsic to that ethos.

A second major factor that makes representations of queens particularly rich sites for investigating cultural redefinitions of heroic masculinity centers on queens' status as women. All of the named female figures in *Beowulf* are queens. Royal women in the poem thus stand as representative of "woman," and as figures around whom accrue anxieties, questions, and issues regarding sexual difference. Attempts to redefine heroism will be especially visible in textual attempts to address concerns that arise around the topic of sexual difference because both heroism and sexual difference in Anglo-Saxon culture were constituted through the same social criteria: namely, one's participation in various forms of war and militancy. That is, heroism was in part an effect produced by one's performance on the battlefield; similarly, maleness and femaleness were effects produced by the assumption of particular social roles in relation to war and militancy.

That idea that maleness and femaleness were neither hard nor fixed entities determined solely through biology but were, instead, conditions of being in the world that could be assumed through acts of militancy is most vividly borne out in the homiletic and hagiographic tradition, which features numerous women transcending their feminine natures and taking on more masculine ones. We will consider these texts in more detail shortly, yet for now it might suffice to recall Cynewulf's *Elene,* in which Elene's militant Christianity reverses the normative gendered distribution of power between her and the Jewish, hence temporarily feminized, Judas. Similarly, we might also look to the spiritually authentic transvestism of such female saints as Perpetua, Eugenia, and Euphrosyne, which suggests that the Anglo-Saxons believed that spiritual fortitude was a force capable of transcending sexual difference, with militant Christianity offering a route to becoming *geworht werlice,* "made male," and both idol-worship and Judaism presenting potentially dangerous paths to effeminacy. In a path-breaking essay published in 1990, Carol Clover argues that for the early Scandinavians, the crucial distinction between "male" and "female" was not grounded in the body but in power.[20] Through close analysis of both lexical evidence and literary tropes, Clover makes a compelling case that the early Scandinavians viewed sexual difference less as a biological given than as a product of cultural assumptions about the body based on social rank and gendered social roles. The particular social roles that produced sexual difference, she maintains, were acts conveying the sense that one had power and status both within and beyond one's own community.[21]

While power and status in early Scandinavia and Anglo-Saxon England were signaled through the possession of a wide range of assets, including movable wealth, property, marital ties, and distinguished genealogies, within Anglo-Saxon England, the acquisition and enactment of power and status tended to cluster around a very specific social phenomenon, namely, war. War was a primary means of augmenting one's movable wealth and property; the implements for waging war were at once objects of wealth and markers of social status; and tales of military victory both established and testified to distinguished genealogies, and also served as a means of augmenting one's power by making it widely known. For the Anglo-Saxons, I want to argue, sexual difference did not simply reside in power but in a highly specific form of power, namely, military power as it was manifested in the roles both men and women played in the constant aggression that was intrinsic to Anglo-Saxon culture, even during times of relative peace. This is not to say that the Anglo-Saxons were unaware of physiological differences between men and women. Rather, these physiological differences were not the primary factors distinguishing men and women from one another. The more important dividing line between members of Anglo-Saxon society was the particular relationship to militancy a person took up in his or her behavior and thoughts—an idea that is most clearly expressed in the Anglo-Saxons' use of the term *wæpnedmann,* "weaponed-person," as a common means of designating a male person.

As Judith Butler has famously argued, the fact that sexual difference is not a bodily given but an effect of givenness produced through the performance of gender norms necessitates the continual reiteration of those norms in order to sustain cultural belief in the fixity of sexual difference.[22] In societies in which sexual difference is understood as a heightened form of gender difference, and in which maleness and femaleness are viewed as differences of degree rather than kind, it is likely that the performance of such roles was even more crucial for producing the illusion of that fixity, or for maintaining clear distinctions between men and women. The desire to maintain such distinctions is felt as a crucial component of the traditional heroic ethos of vengeance and physical violence depicted in *Beowulf,* an ethos that demands adherence to normative gender roles, and which strives to enforce strict divisions between men's and women's spheres of action. Yet adherence to this heroic ethos is also shown to foreclose women's ability to enact such prescribed feminine roles as peaceweaving, and to produce women's transgression of gender norms. By contrast, the new heroism articulated by both Hrothgar and the poem's queens—a heroism invested less in tribal warfare than in battles against one's inner vices—suggests the possibility of softening rigid boundaries of sexual difference, and allowing for a greater fluidity around gender roles and a more expansive definition of heroic masculinity. One way to conceptualize heroism is to view it as an amplification of cultural norms that are generally considered to be exemplary. Textual attempts to redefine heroic masculinity thus do not simply result in the creation of new kinds of literary heroes or figures for social reverence. Rather, new definitions of heroism result in new models of masculinity for a broad range of men.

Inexhaustible Militancy and Impotent Peaceweaving

Perhaps nowhere in *Beowulf* does a queen more sharply call into question the heroic ethos than in the "Finnsburg episode." Told by a scop in Hrothgar's hall immediately after Beowulf's defeat of Grendel, the episode narrates the whole of Hildeburh's life, from its glorious beginning at the Frisian court, where the queen "mæste heold / worolde wynne" (held the greatest of world's joy; 1079b–80a), to its unfortunate end in a ship bound for Denmark, upon which the bereaved queen is ferried back to her people, having been deprived of her closest male relations by Danish-Frisian feuding. Hildeburh's unsuccessful career as a peace-pledge culminates in the central scene of the Finnsburg episode, in which the queen presides over a funeral pyre whose grisly contents stand as a microcosm of life governed by an ethos of heroism:

> hafelan multon,
> bengeato burston,   ðonne blod ætspranc,
> laðbite lices.   Lig ealle forswealg,
> gæsta gifrost,   þara ðe þær guð fornam
> bega folces;   wæs hira blæd scacen.
>
> (1120b–24)[23]

─────

> Heads melted, wound-openings burst as blood sprang forth, hostile bites of the body. Fire swallowed them, the greediest of ghosts, all of those whom war had taken away from both people. Their glory had departed.

These images of male corpses in ongoing, involuntary states of action remind us that even death is no rest for warriors whose lives are ruled by a heroic code that is rooted in the exchange of violence. The springing blood and bursting flesh that continues to ensue from their dead bodies signals an ongoing cycle of death-driven action: blood shed in war will be avenged with additional bloodshed. That the mutilated bodies in the fire are not named but described simply as generic heads and flesh suggests their status as metonyms for numerous other bodies to be destroyed in similar battles. The melting heads, so securely trapped within the grasp of the fire and so clearly removed from their possible functions as trophies for signifying a clear battle-victor, emphasize that the winner in blood feud is neither Dane nor Frisian, but the fire itself, symbol of an ethos of insatiable violence that feeds on the destruction of men and their treasures. The point is more clearly conveyed in the poet's characterization of the fire as a spirit that consumes all with nondiscriminatory tastes: it is the "greediest of ghosts," content to prey on the bodies of Danes and Frisians alike, and to exact a hefty compensation "from both people." The fire's consumption of "heads," evoking both the warriors' boar helmets and the human heads that once resided beneath them, signals the disappearance of the war-gear commonly used to memorialize the glories of battle, and at the same time forecasts that future Danish-Frisian feuding will be undertaken in the absence of wisdom, with the body's main site of reason no longer operative but simply melting away.[24]

Although we are told quite clearly that Hildeburh "geomrode giddum" (sorrowed with songs; 1118a) over the funeral pyre, the contents of her songs are not revealed and their meaning is far from clear. John Hill argues that Hildeburh's laments register an implicit call to arms that is ultimately taken up by her kinsman Hengest in his brutal attack on Finn and the reddening of the Frisian hall.[25] While Hill's interpretation of Hildeburh as a kind of Germanic whetting woman offers an interesting alternative to the more common view of the queen as a passive victim of Danish-Frisian feuding, his argument ultimately cannot be sustained.[26] Hengest's attack on Finn is explicitly identified as proceeding from the sword laid in his lap by the aggrieved son of the dead Hunlaf, and from tales of Frisian treachery recounted by two warriors, Guthlaf and Oslaf, incensed over their brother's death. It is not women's words but the sword and its stories that are here depicted as the catalysts of war. A more convincing analysis of Hildeburh's role is offered by Joyce Hill, who points out that the narrator's application to Hildeburh of the highly formulaic phrase "Þæt wæs geomuru ides!" (That was a mournful woman!; 1075b) signals her function as a "stereotype of the sorrowing woman" found throughout Old English heroic poetry, and most notably, at Beowulf's funeral.[27] Hildeburh's transformation over the course of the Finnsburg episode from a named character to an unnamed wailing woman further allies her laments with those voiced by the anonymous woman who mourns Beowulf's death:[28]

swylce giomorgyd   (s)io g(eo)meowle
(æfter Biowulfe   b)undenheorde
(song) sorgcearig,   sæde geneahhe
þæt hio hyre (hearmda)gas   hearde (ondre)de,
wælfylla worn,   (wigen) egesan,
hy[n]ðo (ond) h(æftny)d.

(3150–55a)[29]

_____

Likewise, the woman with bound locks sang a tale of mourning about Beowulf, one weighed down by sorrowful cares said again and again that she sorely feared for herself days of lamentation, a great number of slaughters, the terror of invading troops, humiliation and captivity.

In both cases, the woman's function is, as Joyce Hill suggests, to "define the essentials of heroic tragedy."[30] And if Hildeburh's onomastic association with "battle-city" marks her tears as emblems of the inevitable tragedy awaiting a culture that takes battle as the primary component of its identity, the increased age of the Geatish woman suggests that her laments enunciate the more advanced stages in the life of such a culture.[31] Significantly, the Geatish woman's projections for the future awaiting her community are wholly lacking in any mention of heroic glory or honor and are composed solely of a litany of anticipated torments. The truth of the Geatish woman's forecast is underwritten by her age, which allies her with the stock literary figure of the old Germanic wise woman.[32]

The funeral pyres over which the two women preside are marked by striking similarities that further gloss the meaning of their laments. The leaping flames that swallow up the bodies of Hildeburh's brother and son, and the gold and precious weaponry of the Danes, prefigure the flames at Beowulf's cremation, which devour both the hero's literal body and its symbolic equivalent: the dragon's treasure-hoard, figured repeatedly as a purchase for which Beowulf has exchanged his life (2799–2800a, 2842b–43, 3011b–14a). The designation of the treasure-hoard after burial as a hoard "eldum swa unnyt, swa hi(t æro)r wæs" (as useless to men as it was before; 3168) highlights the uselessness of a commodity removed from the economy of exchange and the uselessness of earthly treasure in comparison with the true treasures of the heavenly kingdom. Yet the role that the treasure plays in outlining both the logic and the relative merits of earthly and spiritual economies ought not to obscure its crucial function as an index of the effects of the heroic code on human life: the equation of Beowulf's life with a treasure that is ultimately deemed useless indicts his adherence to a heroic ethos of vengeance and violence which is shown, in the end, to reduce the value of the warrior's life to nothing.

The debilitating effects of this code are depicted as extending far beyond the life of the individual warrior. Although Beowulf confidently asserts that the treasure for which he has given his life will ultimately provide for the needs of the people after he is gone (2747–51, 2794–2801a), his words fail to convince some of his listeners, ringing hollowly as mere distractions from his actual inability to secure his people's future safety through the provision of an heir. It is this sentiment that undergirds the Messenger's pronouncement of the treasure's ultimate fate, as well as that of the Geats:

> þa sceall brond fretan,
> æled þeccean, — nalles eorl wegan
> maððum to gemyndum, ne mægð scyne
> habban on healse hringweorðunge,
> ac sceal geormormod, golde bereafod
> oft nalles æne elland tredan.
>
> (3014b–19)

These shall the fire devour, flames enfold. No earl shall wear ornament in remembrance, nor any beautiful maiden have ring-adornment on her neck; but mournful-hearted, stripped of gold, she shall walk, often, not once, in a strange land.

Part of the horror in the Messenger's prediction is the ongoing nature of the torment that he describes. While Beowulf's death indeed presages the demise of the Geats, what the Messenger isolates is the fact that this demise will be neither immediate nor clean, but a painfully drawn-out, seemingly endless expanse of suffering, a prophecy that is echoed in both the content and the rhetorical style of the nameless woman's lament, which articulates a future of invasion, humiliation, and captivity, and names these terrors *geneahhe*, "repeatedly" (3152b). Yet the more implicit horror that resides in the Messenger's vision is how closely it allies the remaining Geats with the left-over kin of Cain. Much as Grendel and his mother are condemned to tread mournfully as exiles through strange lands, so too is this remaining Geatish couple consigned to a similar fate. Critics have long noted the eerie familiarity of the monsters, their humanlike appendages, emotions, and dwellings that resonate so closely with those of the warriors in the poem.[33] The very thin line demarcating the boundary between militancy and monstrosity is especially evident in the poet's description of the Jutes at Finnsburg as *Eotena* (1072a, 1088a, 1141a; "Eotenum," 1145a), a term whose semantic indeterminacy as the genitive plural of both *Eotan*, "Jutes," and *eoten*, "giant," allies the participants in the blood feud with nonhumans.[34] That the poet asserts a future for the Geats which so closely resembles that prescribed for the descendents of a race defined by the twin characteristics of death-directed violence and monstrosity effectually suggests that life within a cultural group ruled by the logic of the sword's edge is ultimately dehumanizing.

The dehumanizing effects exacted upon the members of heroic society are vividly borne out in Hildeburh's fate. The final scene of the Finnsburg episode, in which the Danes plunder Frisian treasure-hoards and carry both the treasure and Hildeburh back to Denmark, has been rightly seen as evidence of Hildeburh's passivity and victimization—in the end, she is reduced to a kind of war booty. Yet to read the equation between queen and treasure in this scene as indicative only of female victimization and objectification is to overlook how much it deviates from the typical relationship between queen and treasure in heroic poetry and historical writings.[35] All of the good queens in *Beowulf* are depicted as wearing, distributing, or receiving treasure: Wealhtheow appears "under gyldnum beage" (under a gold crown; 1163a), both she and Freawaru are "goldhroden" (gold-adorned; 614a, 640b, 2025a) or "beaghroden" (ring-adorned; 623b), and Wealhtheow, Freawaru, and Hygd all distribute or receive arm ornaments, neck rings, or twisted gold (1216–18a, 2018b–19, 2172–76, 2369–70a). These very positive images of queens and treasure—echoed in such texts as *Maxims I, Widsith,* and the *Encomium Emmae*—remind us that the figuration of queens as at once symbols of treasure and agents of its circulation was not simply a poetic trope or a historical fact but a strategy mobilized by Anglo-Saxon writers to signal heroic life at its best.[36] In the case of Hildeburh, however, Danish-Frisian feuding collapses the distinction between queen and treasure. Unable to wear or, more importantly, to participate in the circulation of treasure, Hildeburh is reduced to no more than a symbol of treasure—a transformation that signals the perversion of normative queenly roles and the toxic effects of heroic life.

Nevertheless, the Danes' delight at hearing the tale raises the possibility of interpreting its concluding verses in a very different light. In response to the idea of a ship laden with queen and treasure and bound for Denmark, "gamen eft astah, / beorhtode bencsweg, byrelas sealdon / win of wunderfatum" (joy rose up afterwards, conversation at the benches resounded brightly, cupbearers poured wine from wonderful vessels; 1160b–62a). Such wholesale merriment within Hrothgar's court, augmented by Wealhtheow's generous dispensing of treasure, suggests that the Danes have not read Hildeburh and her treasure-laden ship as a sign of the costs of heroism, but as a sign of Danish triumph which presages such pleasures as the sharing of treasures, song, conversation, and wine—in both their own court and that of the tale. Yet the unsettling familiarity of the ship and its cargo seriously calls into question the advisability of reading the tale in such a positive light. Those who would view the ship as a prelude to hall-joys marked by the liberal distribution of war spoils, as do the Danes, risk overlooking the fact that the last time we saw a ship laden with treasure, it did not alight upon shore to take up a life of circulation as an index of royal largesse but simply floated off as the grim companion to a dead king on a voyage to regions unknown (34–52). Much as that image of Scyld is the last we see of the king and his treasures, so too is this our last glimpse of Hildeburh, whose final epithet as *drihtlic wif,* "noble wife" (1158a), evokes the "dryhtlic iren" (noble iron; 892a) used in Sigemund's dragon fight, thus suggesting her objectification and also the next, less successful dragon fight that will give rise to her reincarnation in the form of the nameless wailing woman.

In much Old English poetry, narrators assume that female lament is inevitable. In *Deor,* for example, Beadohild mourns her impregnation by Weland, who has raped her as revenge against her father, yet the poem's stanzaic refrain, "Þæs ofereode, þisses swa mæg" (that passed; so can this), suggests that Beadohild's sorrow is part of the inevitable course of human life.[37] *The Fortunes of Men* presents female mourning in a similar fashion: one woman mourns her young son's death and consumption by wolves, and another keens as the red tongues of flame swathe her son on the funeral pyre.[38] Yet the laments of both women occur in the context of a long list of hardships used to remind readers that "ne bið swylc monnes geweald!" (such is not in man's control; 14b), but in the hands of the "weoroda nergend" (Savior of Hosts; 93b), who simply ought to be thanked for all that he allots to human kind.[39] Although the ongoing nature of Hildeburh's laments and the ongoing restlessness within the funeral pyre over which they are voiced evoke a similar sense of female sorrow as part of life's course, the actions that accompany those laments suggest that the queen's role is more complex than simply that of a female mourner of the vicissitudes of heroic life. As Hildeburh commands the body of her Danish brother to be placed alongside the shoulder of her Frisian son—thus creating the "shoulder-companions" in death that she was unable to make in life—she orchestrates a grim parody of her designated queenly role as peaceweaver. To refuse outright a social role is to suggest one's personal dissatisfaction or lack of fit with that role. To parody a social role, however, is to expose its flaws or to reveal contradictions in its logic. Gillian Overing argues that one such contradiction is produced by the cultural context in which the peaceweaver attempts her work. "Peace-weavers," she argues, "are assigned the role of creating peace, in fact, embodying peace, in a culture where war and death are privileged values."[40]

Yet contradictions in the logic of peaceweaving are produced not only by the Anglo-Saxons' respective valuations of war and peace but also by their fundamental understandings of these concepts. As J. M. Wallace-Hadrill argues, within both Roman and Germanic culture, war and peace were not conceptualized as discrete entities but as "two poles of a single concept."[41] Pointing to the existence of a separate class of *bellatores* and the concept of peaceweaving as evidence for cultural belief, Wallace-Hadrill suggests that "peace, then, was not merely absence of war; it was a condition that in practice resulted from war, and which would always demand a warlike stance."[42] Wallace-Hadrill's wide-ranging study of Roman and Germanic ideologies of war usefully extends the earlier work of Vilhelm Grønbech, who argues for the martial component of peace as a more strictly Anglo-Saxon idea.[43] Contrasting the semantic nuances of Old English *frið*, "peace," with its Latin counterpart, *pax*, Grønbech argues that *frið* contains an element of militancy and a sense of aggressive readiness for action that in *pax* is far more attenuated.[44] If *frið* in Germanic culture was indeed believed to proceed from war, the failure of female peaceweaving in the Finnsburg episode and in Beowulf's projected future for Freawaru is perhaps not all that surprising. In a society in which peace is only effected through war and war is defined as the rightful domain of men, weaving peace through female bodies would seem to be theoretically impossible. Within such a culture, the female peaceweaver can only symbolize a peace that has been effected through the actions of men, which may partly explain why, as Jane Chance notes, Wealhtheow always appears after a battle has been concluded.[45]

Within such a social system, participation in the inexorable dialectic of failed peaceweaving is not limited to women. When Hildeburh proves unable to allay fighting between the Danes and Frisians by marrying Finn, the men themselves step in to try their hand, using deeply sworn oaths and verbal declarations of truce in the hopes of settling deadly murder-hatred.

Yet *friðowær,* "verbal peace-agreement," ultimately proves as ineffective as *friðusibb,* "peace-pledge through marriage," establishing only a fragile and fleeting truce that merely delays Hengest's war-hostilities. The power of both female bodies and male words is shown to pale in comparison with that of the sword, whose dual capacity to invoke memories of past conflicts and to inflict deadly cuts makes it at once the catalyst for inspiring war and the machinery for waging it.

What unites Hildeburh's body and the men's truce-oaths is that both exemplify models of peacemaking which rely on the assumption that representation can produce reality. In the case of the marriage as peace-pledge, the bride is intended to represent one people, her husband another, and their union and its literal fruits are to symbolize, and to produce, a new generation of peace between two formerly or potentially hostile tribes. In the case of the men's truce-oaths, imaginary projections of a peaceful future, in the form of pledges and promises, are believed to be capable of ensuring that such a future will indeed come to pass. Yet as the Finnsburg episode so strongly suggests, both textual and verbal representation—either symbols carved into the ancient work of giants or words spoken by an old whetting warrior—possess enough strength to generate war but not enough to effect peace. In the final hour of conflict resolution, words will ultimately give way to battle, or as Finn puts it: "gyf þonne Frysna hwylc frecnan spræce / ðæs morþorhetes myndgiend wære, / þonne hit sweordes ecg seðan scolde" (if with rash speech any of the Frisians should insist upon reminding of deadly murder-hatred, then the sword's edge must settle it; 1104–6).

While the scop's tragic tale of Finnsburg seems to offer a definitive statement on the futility of peace efforts within a culture of violence, Hrothgar appears reluctant to succumb to such overarching pessimism. Refusing to interpret heroic legends of failed peace-marriage within the Danish past as cautionary exemplars, Hrothgar remains firmly convinced that a diplomatic marriage of his daughter, Freawaru, to Ingeld will settle deadly feuds between the Danes and Heathobards. It is, rather, Beowulf who seems to have most profoundly taken the scop's tale to heart, perhaps because it accords so well with his own worldview. Upon returning to Geatland, Beowulf assumes a scop-like persona, recounting stories that he has heard in Heorot, as well as his own heroic feats within the Danish court. And as Beowulf regales Hygelac with stories drawn from both legend and life, the distinction between the two begins to blur. Transforming his own life into the stuff of legend, he concomitantly transforms Freawaru's life into a re-enactment of Hildeburh's, predicting that like Hildeburh, Freawaru will also marry a king outside of her own tribe, be unable to weave peace between the two tribes, be separated from her husband by emotional (rather than physical) distance, and be absolved of any guilt for her failed peace-weaving. Freawaru's future, as Beowulf imagines it, is simply the re-enactment of a tragic heroic tale, and one that encapsulates all of the formal and thematic elements that are typically found in Anglo-Saxon heroic legend. Few scholars would disagree with Friedrich Klaeber's assertion that "none of the Anglo-Saxon poems equals the 'Finn tale' in its thorough Germanic and heroic character," and except for perhaps *The Battle of Maldon* there is no Old English text whose characters more clearly exemplify such ideals as undying loyalty, death-defying bravery, and death-directed vengeance—all of which signal their residence in the world of heroic legend.[46] Nor is the poet unaware of the highly stylized legendary quality of the tale and its characters. As Joyce Hill points out, "The poet . . . knew that in Hildeburh he was presenting and defining a stereotype," and both the tale's highly allusive nature and the narrator's prefatory claim that "gid oft wrecen" (tale [was] often told; 1065b) mark the song of Finnsburg as an exemplar of numerous other legends encapsulating similar ethics and ideals.[47]

As much as we might attribute the untenability of female peaceweaving to such Germanic ideologies of war as those outlined by Wallace-Hadrill and Grønbech, we must nevertheless recognize that in *Beowulf,* the failure of female peaceweaving and the uncontrollable energies of the sword are not depicted as inevitable aspects of Germanic life. Rather they are located within the deepest recesses of heroic legend and the mind of its staunchest defender, Beowulf, who sees his own life and the lives of those around him as conforming to the entrenched stereotypes and nonnegotiable codes of a bygone heroic past epitomized in songs like the Finnsburg episode. Not surprisingly, Beowulf characterizes what he has heard sung in Heorot as "soð ond sarlic, . . . syllic . . . rehte æfter rihte" (true and tragic . . . remarkable [and] rightfully recounted; 2109–10a). His emphasis on the formal qualities of legendary tales and his inclination to rewrite those tales by retaining their basic plot structures and inserting contemporary names testify to his firm belief that stories "feorran" (from a time long ago; 2106b) encapsulate generic truths capable of eliciting similar responses from, and being played out by, people across time.[48]

Back in the "real world," or the poem's narrative present, however, the timeless and transcultural exemplarity of heroic legends is called into question, and Beowulf's "true" tales are revealed as more historically contingent than he believes them to be. Although there are no overtly successful images of female peace-pledges in the text, the poet repeatedly hints at the possibility: Wealhtheow's name as "foreign servant" and her designation as *friðusibb folca,* "peace-pledge of the people" (2017a), suggest her potential success as a peace-pledge between the Danes and another kingdom; Hrothgar's sister is described as the *healsgebedda,* "close bed-fellow" (63b), of the Swedish king, Onela; and Hygd is associated with peaceweaving when the poet invokes the epithet *freoðuwebbe,* "peaceweaver" (1942a), to describe a role befitting a good queen.[49] Hints of a possible dichotomy between legend and life come into clearer view when we broaden our gaze and consider the dual audiences of the Finnsburg episode. In ways that Fred Robinson has illustrated, the episode highlights a sharp divide between the knowledge of the Danes within Heorot and that of the poem's audience: the Danes view the tale as *healgamen,* "hall-entertainment" (1066a), or as a celebration of Danish victory, and thus as a fitting historical parallel for their own triumph over Grendel; yet the audience—aware of both the imminent attack of Grendel's mother and the ultimate demise of the Danes when Heorot is set afire by hostile tribes—knows that neither the immediate nor the long-term future for the Danes is to be celebrated.[50] To read the Finnsburg episode as encapsulating ethics or events that might be re-enacted in contemporary life is to take the same, very limited view of the characters in that doomed court. What the tale so clearly reveals, by contrast, is the deeply misguided nature of believing, as do both the Danes and Beowulf, that legends provide accurate mirrors or models of life. If the tale does suggest itself as fitting in the immediate narrative moment, the highly occasional nature of that fit only serves to drive home the point that any apparent accordance between legend and life is temporally limited. Put another way, the fleeting nature of the tale's appropriateness for the Danes in Heorot serves to suggest that the ethics contained within heroic legend have, at best, an extremely limited applicability: for the Danes in Heorot, that moment is the time immediately following Grendel's defeat; for the poem's audience, it is the moment occupied by the pre-Christian heroic past on the timeline of Anglo-Saxon culture. If the urge to vengeance exhibited when Hengest takes up the sword is indeed characterized as a *woroldrædenne,* "world custom" (1142b), both the self-conscious legendary quality of the

Finnsburg episode and Beowulf's staunch belief in the possibility of its continual re-enactment reveal that the parameters of that "world" enclose a realm composed less of skies and seas than of heroic legends and the fantasies of those who love them.[51]

The poet's location of failed peaceweaving within the deep recesses of a heroic past offers a strong impetus for rethinking common modern views of peaceweaving as a misogynist trafficking in women, with female bodies pressed into the service of creating national harmony, and valued mainly for their capacity to ground relations between men.[52] To believe in the efficacy of peaceweaving is to award a position of primacy to the world of domesticity, with intertribal political relations, long-standing tensions between men, and the necessity for waging war all dictated by the status of *wifluf*, "wife-love." Peaceweaving proceeds according to a logic that demands that one redefine the place traditionally allotted to the domestic world within a heroic ethos—in which home and hall typically provide the rationale for battle (one fights to protect women), the impetus to battle (one is impelled to battle by whetting women), or the audience for battle (women celebrate victory or mourn failure)—and recognize women as central forces, rather than marginal supports, in the production of social order. It is thus not surprising that Beowulf so fiercely clings to the belief that conflicts between men cannot be ameliorated by intertribal marriage, and that attempts to weave peace through women are inexorably doomed to failure. To believe otherwise would be to acknowledge the energies of battle as deeply imbricated in women and domestic life, and thus to erode a crucial principle undergirding the worldview to which he subscribes: that the realms of domesticity and war are deeply incompatible, or, as he puts it, "oft seldan hwær / æfter leodhryre lytle hwile / bongar bugeð, þeah seo bryd duge" (seldom does the spear rest but for a little while although the bride is good; 2029b–31). Beowulf's maximlike statement regarding the autonomy of domestic life and war, as well as the "spear's" ability to function in only one of these realms at a time, finds a more particularized expression in his subsequent claim that the emergence of Ingeld's deadly hatred for the Danes will be accompanied by a subsiding of his love for Freawaru (2064b–66). For Beowulf, the heat of *wifluf* and that of battle cannot effectively coexist, and Freawaru's exogamous marriage thus consigns her, in his view, not only to a future of failed peaceweaving but also to the eventual emotional distancing of her husband.[53]

If adherence to an ethos of heroism is shown to foreclose women's ability to weave peace successfully and to interfere with marital affection, these are only some of its minor demands. The broken bodies of Hildeburh's male kin and Beowulf, and the female mourners who preside over their funeral pyres dramatize the more significant costs of a heroic code in which earthly glory and masculine identity are predicated on acts of violence. The characters in the poem of course do not fully recognize this, any more than they recognize who might have received Scyld's body and its gold-laden ship. Yet as races, treasures, and glory disappear, leaving in their wake a collective of wailing women, impoverished exiles, and skeletal remains, the poem systematically tallies the extravagant price of adherence to an old Germanic ethos of heroism, and ultimately poses the possibility that the bargain might not be a good one.

Female Militancy

While Hildeburh's critique of the heroic ethos is enacted through her assumption of the stock female role of the *geomuru ides,* the challenges offered by both Grendel's mother and Thryth are grounded in their attempts to invert stock female roles and to assume masculine ones. Both female figures refuse the role of hostess, creating halls that are hostile rather than welcoming to male retainers. Similarly, both invert the role of peaceweaver: Grendel's mother seeks to destroy bonds between men in Heorot, as well as the woven nets of Beowulf's mailcoat, while Thryth weaves "wælbende . . . handgewriþene" (deadly bonds . . . twisted by hand; 1936a, 1937a), and her marriage does not weave peace between men but rather peace between herself and male retainers. As both female figures refuse normative feminine roles, each takes on a role that is typically reserved, both within Anglo-Saxon heroic poetry and law codes, for men: they assume the role of agent of retaliatory violence. In the case of Grendel's mother, her battles in Heorot and the mere are almost obsessively designated as attempts to equal the score for past wrongs done to her kin: both the narrator and Beowulf stipulate vengeance as her primary motive (1256b, 1278b, 2118a), and Hrothgar asserts mantrically that Grendel's mother "þa fæhðe wræc" (avenged the feud; 1333b), "wolde hyre mæg wrecan" (wanted to avenge her kinsman; 1339b), and "fæhðe gestæled" (avenged enmity; 1340b). In the case of Thryth, retaliatory violence is exemplified by her prescriptions of death as punishment for retainers who commit *ligetorne*, "pretended injury," by daring to cast their eyes upon her.[54]

Two different textual traditions offer images of female militancy akin to those of Grendel's mother and Thryth. The first is Old Norse poetry, in which appears the valkyrie figure, a battle-maid created by the fusion of mortal and supernatural elements, who may assume the form of either a baleful war-spirit of men's destruction, or a benevolent war-guardian and protector of heroes. Helen Damico has explored the possibility that the valkyrie and her accompanying energies can be found in Old English literature, and has identified several attributes shared by both Grendel's mother and Thryth and these warriorlike valkyrie brides.[55] Nevertheless, the cultural ramifications of Damico's argument are restricted by the obscure nature of the relationship between Old Norse and Old English poetry. Resemblances between characters who reside in either corpus may indeed derive from a shared oral tradition between Icelandic and Anglo-Saxon culture, but in the end the identification of analogues offers limited possibilities for understanding the cultural work performed by textual depictions of female militancy in a specific historical context.

The second is the Anglo-Saxon homiletic and hagiographic tradition, in which is found the female warrior-saint or *miles Christi*. Exemplified by such figures as Elene, Judith, and Juliana, the *miles Christi* marshals spiritual weapons of mental, emotional, and verbal fortitude, directing barbed arrows of faith against such figures as the stubborn Jew, the heathen persecutor, and the devil or personified vices. The most extreme manifestation of the *miles Christi* theme is found in the numerous Anglo-Saxon texts that dramatize spiritual militancy and devoted service within God's army as forms of social and psychological discipline that enable women to transcend female birth sex and to "become male." In his prose *De virginitate*, Aldhelm urges the nuns of Barking, for example, to "struggle zealously with the arrows of spiritual armament and the iron-tipped spears of the virtues" so as never to be accused of confronting their spiritual enemies "after the fashion of timid soldiers effeminately fearing the horror of war and the battle-calls of the trumpeter."[56] The motif of women becoming male serves as a thematic focus in the "transvestite saints legends," in which women's assumption of masculine dress and comportment typically offers escape from both marriage and the spiritual weakness associated with femininity. The classic example is the *Life of Perpetua*, briefly recounted in the anonymous *Old English Martyrology,* in which "Perpetuan mætte þa heo wæs on mædenhade þæt heo wære on wæres hiwe ond þæt heo hæfde sweord on handa ond þæt heo stranglice fuhte mid þy" (Perpetua dreamed that when she was in her girlhood she had the appearance of a man and that she had a sword in her hand and that she fought with it strongly)—a dream that is afterward "eall eft on hire martyrdome gefylled, þa heo mid werlice geþohte deofol oferswiðde ond þa hæðnan ehteras" (completely fulfilled in her martyrdom when she overcame the devil and the heathen persecutors with manly thought).[57] More developed accounts of transvestite saints are found in Ælfric's *Life of Eugenia* and the anonymous *Life of Euphrosyne,* in which female saints cloak themselves in the dress of monks and live under the "pretense" of being male monks for most of their lives; their extreme piety and the great respect they command within these communities suggest that the mimicry of maleness has the capacity to result in more substantive transformations, or that spiritual maleness can effectually eclipse biological femaleness.[58]

The phenomenon of women-becoming-male can be traced back to the first century of Christianity, and specifically to the familiar theological premise that sexual difference is indicative of man's fallen state, and ultimately to be undone by Christian redemption.[59] Nevertheless, the fact that some Anglo-Saxon writers were willing to engage this trope stands as evidence not simply of their immersion in early Christian ideology but also of their openness to envisioning sexual difference as a fluid spectrum across which women, at least, could move. Moreover, various aspects of these narratives—for example, Aldhelm's strong encouragement for the Barking nuns to shun feminine behavior, the delight exhibited by Eugenia and Euphrosyne when they "become men," and the use of these texts as exemplary narratives—figure such movement as desirable. This is not to deny that these narratives also encode a complex set of anxieties generated by women's assumption of masculine dress and comportment, but simply to suggest that they portray cross-gendered women as ultimately sympathetic figures, and women's assumption of militant masculinity as a laudable achievement.[60] As Ælfric approvingly puts it in his homily for Midlent Sunday: "Þeah gif wifman bið werlice geworht 7 strang to godes willan, heo bið þonne geteald to ðam werum þe æt godes mysan sittað" (Yet if a woman is made manfully and strong in accordance with God's will, she will be counted among the men who sit at God's table).[61]

Such is not, however, the case in *Beowulf,* which exhibits a profound lack of tolerance for female militancy and women's transgression of normative gender roles. Unlike the nuns of Barking or the transvestite saints, for whom the adoption of militant masculinity enables the transcendence of biological femaleness, Grendel's mother is not made fully or laudably male by her acts of vengeance, but rather a persona of confused gender identity. She is marked as female by such nouns as "ides aglæcwif" (monster-wife of a woman; 1259a) and "merewif" (sea-woman; 1519a) and by her description as "idese onlicnes" (in the likeness of a woman; 1351a), but also as male by such nouns as "secg" (man, or warrior; 1379a), and more often simply by masculine pronouns (1260a, 1392b, 1394b, 1497b).[62] Far from giving rise to a more perfect being, the conflation of masculinity and femininity in one persona results in a creature who is marked as both monstrous and also as a caricature of male identity, via its reduction to generic linguistic markers (i.e., pronouns). Given the premium that the Anglo-Saxons placed on naming and lineage, this generic maleness is coded as suspect at best and highly undesirable at worst.

In the case of Thryth, female insurrection leads to even more direct assertions of its undesirability: her attempts to counter the unsolicited attentions of men with violence give rise to the narrator's condemnatory remark that "ne bið swylc cwenlic þeaw / idese to efnanne" (such is not a queenly custom for a woman to perform; 1940b–41a), followed by an immediate attempt to reassert normative gender roles by invoking the more acceptable custom of peaceweaving (1942a). Both female figures are also formally contained by being sandwiched in the poem between women who enact more normative gender roles: Grendel's mother is positioned between Wealhtheow and the unnamed woman (most likely Wealhtheow) who gazes upon Grendel's severed head, while Thryth appears between Hygd and Freawaru.[63] Nor is either female figure permitted to persist in her transgression of gender boundaries: Thryth is repatriated into conventional femininity by her marriage to Offa, and Grendel's mother is quite spectacularly killed.

The poem's efforts to contain Grendel's mother and Thryth have often been read as symptomatic of anxiety generated by the "dangers of uncontrolled feminine power."[64] Yet to posit "gender anxiety" as the dominant explanation for the poet's refusal to countenance these transgressive female figures is to obscure the fact that their transgression is almost obsessively localized on retaliatory violence—the very act that is central to male heroic aggression. We have seen that Anglo-Saxon homilists and hagiographers offer broad sanction for women's assumption of masculine militancy. Female saints are all shown to be enhanced rather than abased by performative enactments of maleness that entail adopting a virulent militancy of the spirit, suggesting that this is a kind of masculinity worthy of emulation. That both Grendel's mother and Thryth are fiercely prohibited from particular forms of masculine behavior that involve retributive violence stands as a thinly veiled assertion on the part of the poet that this is a kind of masculinity that should, perhaps, not be replicated.[65]

For all the *Beowulf* poet's apparent rejection of gender transgression, the narrative nevertheless requires just such transgression in order to consolidate male heroism. Masculinized women might indeed be monstrous, in other words, but that monstrosity is strangely constitutive of properly masculinized heroic men. In order to achieve true heroic stature, Beowulf must combat and conquer Grendel's mother, a point that is signaled by the poet's description of their encounter through all of the stock tropes of heroic battle: the hero is challenged to enact feats never before accomplished; boasts of glory are followed by elaborate accounts of arms donned; grave anxiety arises regarding the battle's outcome; a narrow victory establishes the opponent's worthiness; and a celebration ensues, complete with the display of the enemy's head and songs in praise of the hero. If the battle between Beowulf and Grendel's mother suggests that acts of female transgression are necessary for male heroism, it positions the blurred boundaries of sexual difference occasioned through such acts as similarly essential. The narrator's claim that the challenge presented by Grendel's mother was one in which "wæs se gryre læssa / efne swa micle, swa bið mægþa cræft, / wiggryre wifes be wæpnedmen" (the terror was indeed less by just so much as is the strength of a woman, the war-terror of a wife, in comparison with that of an armed man's; 1282b–84) implicitly identifies military strength as a primary means of differentiating between men and women. Nevertheless the ambiguity of the statement, as well as the difficulty of Beowulf's battle and the failure of the arms that he has brought to it, raises the possibility that the battle-strength of the armed man might be outstripped by the war-terror of the crazed female, thus calling into question the reliability of martial strength as a criterion for determining sexual difference. The battle between Beowulf and Grendel's mother becomes at once a means of policing gender transgression, and of reinscribing clear boundaries of sexual difference and reliable criteria for its determination. Beowulf's triumphant emergence from the mere signals that the threat of female transgression is vanquished, and it proves, at the same time, that the comparative war-terror of the *wæpnedmon* is definitively superior to that of the *wif.* Physical warfare is restored as the rightful provenance of men (in concert with God), as is the reliability of martial strength as a determinant of sexual difference. Nevertheless, it is those very acts of restoration that are shown to be constitutive of Beowulf's heroism.

Offa's taming of Thryth reveals male heroism as similarly premised on female transgression. As Dorothy Whitelock points out, of all the kings in the poem, Offa is the only one who is described in an unequivocally positive manner: he is "þone selestan bi sæm tweonum, / eormencynnes" (the best between the two seas of all mankind; 1956–57a).[66] The poet's evident regard for Offa leads Whitelock to read the Thryth digression primarily as a kind of segue to him: "when he [the poet] had once launched on the story of Thryth, he left her very rapidly to sing the praises of Offa, as if that had been his real purpose in introducing the digression."[67] Yet if the poet did view the Thryth digression mainly as a device for incorporating songs in praise of Offa, it is quite puzzling as to why—aside from a brief description of Offa as "geofum ond guðum, garcene man" (a man [who was] brave with gifts and in battles; 1958)—we are given so little information about either his military exploits or his political accomplishments. While it is reasonable to suppose, as Whitelock points out, that "the audience which listened to this eulogy knew something of the deeds of Offa," the poet nevertheless seems wholly uninterested in recalling them.[68] Unlike the *Widsith* poet, for example, who delights in recounting how Offa "geslog . . . cnihtwesende, cynerica mæst" (gained through fighting the greatest of kingdoms, while still a youth; 38a, 39), and how he "[a]ne sweorde / merce gemærde wið Myrgingum / bi Fifeldore" (with a single sword fixed the boundary against the Myrgings at Fifeldor; 41b–43a), the *Beowulf* poet gives us almost no specifics regarding Offa's military and political achievements, and instead lavishes the bulk of his energies on recounting how Offa tamed his wife.[69] The resultant narrative imbalance creates the sense that Offa's ability to bring a violent woman more into line with normative female behavior constitutes a significant part of the rationale for his being "wide geweorðod" (widely honored; 1959a). The point is underscored by the various scop figures who appear in this passage: it is neither Offa's generosity nor his battles that they feel compelled to make known, but rather his wife's profound behavioral changes upon her arrival at his court. Once the "ealodrincende oðer sædan" (aledrinkers [have] told [this] other story; 1945), the narrator

again reveals his perception of Offa's exemplary kingship as inextricably intertwined with his success in creating an exemplary wife: the narrator's assertion that Offa was the "hæleþa brego, / ealles moncynnes mine gefræge /
þone selestan" (the best lord of warriors of all mankind, as I have heard tell;
1954b–56a) is both grammatically intertwined with, and also immediately
follows upon, the account of Thryth's having "hiold heahlufan wið hæleþa
brego" (held high-love toward the lord of warriors; 1954), as if the queen's
esteem for Offa were a model for how others ought to regard him, or as if
his worthiness of honor were predicated on his being worthy of her—that
is, "man enough" to control her. Far from serving merely as a transition into
praise for Offa, the Thryth digression reveals a crucial aspect of the king's
character which renders him worthy of such praise.

If part of Hildeburh's function is to suggest that a social system that
entails adherence to old models of Germanic heroism forecloses women's
ability to enact such prescribed gender roles as peaceweaving, what both
Grendel's mother and Thryth dramatize is the extent to which women's
transgression of gender roles is intrinsic to that system. In a culture in which
heroic masculinity is predicated on violence, women's enactment of violence
must be fiercely curtailed in order to maintain clear boundaries of sexual
difference. At the same time, because the making of male heroes in the
poem is premised in part on the hero's ability to overcome, with no small
difficulty, an almost-equal female antagonist, female insurrection must be
perpetually reproduced in order to allow the creation of the male hero.

Revisioning Heroism

Perhaps nowhere in *Beowulf* is a new model of heroism more suggestively
expressed than in Hrothgar's famous speech. Numerous Christian affinities
in the diction and imagery of the speech, or "sermon," as some would argue,
have proved a critical touchstone for ongoing debates over the relative
strengths of paganism and Christianity as worldviews informing the
poem.[70] My interest lies less in entering those debates than in isolating a
central idea in Hrothgar's speech that stands as a defining feature of the
new heroic masculinity and which is deeply compatible with a Christian
worldview: the interiorization of violence in the interests of reshaping the
self. When Hrothgar warns Beowulf to guard against the corrupting forces
of pride and avarice, urging him to "bebeorh þe ðone bealonið" (keep

yourself against that wickedness; 1758a) and "oferhyda ne gym" (have no care for pride; 1760b), he articulates a model of heroism that is underwritten by the idea that aggression needs to be directed inward rather than outward. According to the wise and aged king, Beowulf ought to adopt a fiercely defensive militancy not against other men, as does the bloodthirsty Heremod, but against the "biteran stræle" (bitter arrows; 1746a) and "wom wundorbebodum wergan gastes" (perverse mysterious commands of the accursed spirit; 1747) that assault the man who allows his "sawele hyrde" (soul's guardian; 1742a) to go off duty and luxuriate in a "slæp to fæst" (too sound sleep; 1742b). Various parallels in Scripture and commentary have led some to suggest that Hrothgar's allegory derives from Christian sources, while others maintain that its Christian resonances simply point to instances of convergence between the conceptual and lexical registers of pre- and postconversion Germanic piety.[71] Although the sources for the sermon remain unknown, we can be fairly certain that at least some of the poem's readers would have recognized the spiritual valences of Hrothgar's depiction of inner life as a battleground—familiar from Ephesians 6:11–17 and Psalm 11:2, and popularized in the *Psychomachia* tradition.[72] We can also be fairly sure that readers would have recognized the easy ideological accord between the interiorized spiritual combat that Hrothgar outlines and the exteriorized physical violence that was so much a part of the Anglo-Saxon world.[73] Hrothgar's insistence on the slayer's martial prowess and his ability to render defenseless even a man so powerful that "him eal worold / wendeð on willan" (the whole world turns to his will; 1738b–39a) effectively constructs the accursed spirit as a worthy foe and, by extension, spiritual battle as a sufficiently challenging enterprise for even the "secg betsta" (best of warriors; 1759a), all the while redirecting the sword's edge away from human foes and toward the devil's temptations, identified as the real threat to the hypothetical ruler. As it discovers a new place for the energies of violence, Hrothgar's speech also finds a new function for the material agents of violence. When Hrothgar gazes upon the snake-ornamented battle-hilt and subsequently produces a speech designed to reshape the inner self, he radically revises an older mnemonics of weaponry. Unlike the aged Heathobard ash-warrior for whom the sight of weapons produces memories of a violent past that demands redress through recourse to further violence (2041–56), Hrothgar's gaze upon the hilt produces memories of a no less vexed past, but one that demands redress through transformation of the self. Hrothgar's demonstration of revisionist remembrance suggests that weapons ought not to inspire unthinking replication of the violence encoded in their histories, but a more thoughtful cultivation of the self, guided by the positive and negative exemplars evoked by an ancient heirloom.

The gendered implications of Hrothgar's interiorized model of heroism become clearer when placed in relation to the numerous Anglo-Saxon homilies and saints' lives that exhibit a similar sensibility. All of the transvestite female saints, for example, become male not by taking up a fiercely aggressive militancy directed outward against others but through a militancy that is directed inward against the self. Even when this aggression seems to be directed outward, as in the case of the Barking nuns, who fight against personified vices, or as in the cases of Perpetua and Eugenia, who fight against flesh and blood heathen persecutors who threaten their chastity, a woman's becoming male is strongly associated with her assumption of a new and different interiority, most notably her assumption of a "masculine mind." Perpetua "mid werlice geþohte deofol oferswiðde ond þa hæðnan ehteras" (overcame the devil and heathen persecutors with manlike thought); similarly, Eugenia "wunode on þam mynstre mid wærlicum mode" (lived in the minster with a manlike mind), as evidenced by the fact that she "heold on hyre þeawum halige drohtnunge ðurh modes liþnesse and mycelre eadmodnesse" (observed in her conduct the holy service with gentleness of mind and great humility).[74] Maleness within these texts is shown to be contingent not on physical strength but on strength of mind, fortitude of will, and virility of faith and righteous conduct. Such claims for the exercise of interior strength as capable of "making men" sharply contrast with conventional Anglo-Saxon thought: both strength of mind—as indicated in a capacity for wisdom, foresight, or good counsel—and fortitude of will were attributes that were strongly associated with women.[75] Anglo-Saxon homilists' and hagiographers' evident interest in translating and circulating texts that depict these inner traits as capable of making women male is, I would suggest, motivated in part by a desire to dislodge the strong ideological link in Anglo-Saxon thought between mental fortitude and femininity, and to redefine strength of mind, inner fortitude, and inwardly directed battle as fittingly male pursuits—thus discouraging violence between men and valorizing the nonmilitary life. These texts, then, function much like both Hrothgar's sermon and the *Beowulf* poet's evident refusal to countenance female militancy: as textual moments that point to a culture's attempts to find its way toward a new model of masculine heroism, one rooted less in external proficiency in war than in cultivation of the inner self.

Dangerous Refusals

Beowulf appears to have little interest in adopting either new models of masculinity or an interiorized heroism proffered by an aged king. Prior to Hrothgar's speech, Beowulf has articulated his own model of heroism, one that sharply diverges from Hrothgar's and which indeed arises as a corrective to the king's tearful response to the loss of his most beloved retainer, Æschere:

> Ne sorga, snotor guma! Selre bið æghwæm,
> þæt he his freond wrece, þonne he fela murne.
> (1384–85)

> ———

> Do not sorrow, wise man. It is better for a man to avenge his friend than to mourn much.

In keeping with his tendency to divide the world into strict binaries, Beowulf outlines two possible responses to violence—the one interiorized and associated with femininity and military loss (mourning), and the other exteriorized and associated with masculinity and military glory (seeking vengeance)—and the choice for Beowulf is quite clear. Much as the unlocking of Hengest's breast-hoard—symbolized in the melting of the ice-locked wintry sea-roads—gives way to a springtime of vengeance, the unlocking of the male breast-hoard, according to Beowulf, ought not to give way to the public expression of its sorrowful contents but to the transformation of those contents into action. To adopt the former mode of behavior, in Beowulf's eyes, is to place oneself in the symbolic company of women, such as the mournful Hildeburh or the wailing Geatish woman, or of aged and impotent men, such as the sorrowing Hrothgar or the grieving *gamol ceorl*, "old man" (2444–62a), immobilized by his son's death and his own inability to avenge it.

Beowulf's evident desire to distance himself from the symbolic company of women is further felt in his efforts to dissociate himself from women in a very literal sense. As many scholars have noted, Beowulf never engages in any kind of romantic or sexual relationship with a woman. Fred Robinson attempts to explain the poem's silence on this issue by suggesting that the *Beowulf* poet may have considered that "Beowulf's marital status was of insufficient interest to warrant mention in the poem."[76] Yet Robinson's explanation remains problematic in light of the fact that the poet appears deeply interested in the marital status of so many other male characters in the poem. Far from suggesting a lack of interest on the part of the poet, the silence around his marital status reflects Beowulf's desire to maintain a strict division between the worlds of battle and domestic life and to direct the bulk of his energies toward forming close relationships with men— desires that are severely criticized as the poem unfolds their grave effects.

If Beowulf's decision not to take a queen reflects a worldview that privileges male-male relations and the world of battle in which those relations were typically formed, his lack of a queen, in fact, interferes with his ability to produce the very relationships between men on which military success so heavily depended, namely, the bonds between a lord and his retainers. As the ritualized cup-passing of Wealhtheow and Hygd remind us, one of the queen's chief roles was to cement relations of loyalty between the king and his retainers. By passing the cup first to her husband, and subsequently offering drinks to the rest of the men, the queen reiterated social hierarchies within the hall, thus staving off potential challenges to royal leadership.[77] Her gold-adorned presence within the hall functioned as a mnemonic for the *morgengifu*, "morning-gift," given to her by her lord on the morning after their first night of marriage, thus reminding retainers of the royal treasure-stores and the king's willingness to distribute them to those whom he loved. Moreover, as a woman who very likely hailed from a different kingdom, the queen signaled her lord's capacity not only to love but also to love a person who was distanced from him by such factors as tribal affiliation or geography, thus suggesting the king's capacity to love his retainers, who were similarly distanced from their lord by such factors as birth and wealth. In refusing to take a queen, Beowulf cuts off a crucial channel for producing loyalty among his retainers. It is little wonder that all but one of his troop of eleven "æðelinga bearn" (sons of nobles; 2597a) desert him in the final hour, fleeing to the woods in order to protect their own lives rather than that of their lord.

The more systemic problem signaled by Beowulf's refusal to take a queen is that it disrupts genealogical continuity in the construction of both individual and cultural identity. Personal identity in Anglo-Saxon culture was determined not solely by one's own actions, but also by the deeds of one's father and sons. By not marrying and reproducing, Beowulf short-circuits this normative model of identity formation, implicitly demanding that he be judged solely for his own deeds rather than those of his descendants, whose actions might be interpreted as glosses on his own life. In refusing to participate in a cultural system that would construct his identity as an ac-cretion of past and future generations, Beowulf challenges the importance of genealogical continuity, and the need to attend to the work of maintain-ing a vital and ongoing relationship between the past and future.

Beowulf's failure to marry and to reproduce also disrupts genealogical continuity at a larger cultural level. When Beowulf dies without leaving a son to serve as his successor, he sets in motion grave anxiety about the Geatish future. The Messenger predicts that Beowulf's fall will invite fatal attacks from the Franks, Frisians, and Swedes, and Beowulf's last thoughts are for the son he never had. These final scenes, in which Beowulf laments his lack of a son and ultimately bequeaths his war-gear and treasure to Wig-laf, have elicited significant scholarly attention, much of which centers on identifying Beowulf's precise genealogical ties to both Wiglaf and the Waegmundings, in the hope of shedding some light on the complexities of Anglo-Saxon kinship structures and succession practices.[78]

Yet it is worth recalling that succession is a cultural practice that raises issues far broader than the particularities of kin relations, genealogies, or inheritance patterns. For what succession does is to focus the eyes of a peo-ple on questions of transition, or on the desired relationship between past, present, and future. A new king will, ideally, replicate and build on the achievements of his predecessor, or, conversely, offer a welcome change from social problems instantiated by his failures. The close ideological links between succession and cultural transition help to explain the *Beowulf* poet's obsessive interest in the former. Much as the poem's numerous his-torical digressions, reaching far back into the Germanic past, may be seen as a narrative strategy designed to encourage readers to contemplate the complex relationships between past and present, the poem's sustained at-tention to succession may be seen as a thematic strategy geared toward this same goal. The heated debates, uncertainty, and confusion generated within the Danish and Geatish kingdoms by the question of how best to fill an empty throne are, in effect, attempts to offer possible solutions to the cen-tral problem posed by the poem: how or what sort of relationship might Anglo-Saxon Christian readers maintain to their Germanic ancestors de-picted within the poem?

Indeed Beowulf gives relatively little thought to succession, and by extension, little thought to the desired mode of linking past and future. It is only very late in his life—indeed when he is dying—that Beowulf attends to the question of who might lead his people once he has gone.[79] The ultimate demise prophesied for the Geats because of Beowulf's belief that succession considerations might be deferred until the final hour stands as a lesson to English readers on the dangers of believing genealogical continuity to be a dispensable concern. To adhere to this belief, as Beowulf does, is shown to portend doom for both the individual and his culture and to foreclose the possibility of maintaining a vital link between past and future, thus admonishing readers about the importance of forging a productive relation to their own vexed cultural past.

It is precisely this work to which the queens in the poem direct the bulk of their energies. What is striking about the two central queenly figures in *Beowulf,* Wealhtheow and Hygd, is how fully their identities and energies are invested in the issue of succession. Of Wealhtheow's two speeches, one is almost entirely devoted to advising Hrothgar to ensure her sons' claims to the throne. Similarly, Hygd's most memorable act is when she offers Beowulf the Geatish kingdom. Although the two queens appear to endorse very different models of succession—Wealhtheow seems to favor genealogical continuity, namely, the succession of the most direct blood heir, while Hygd seems to endorse *comitatus* values, namely, the succession of the strongest man—on closer inspection, their views converge on a number of crucial points.

Each queen seriously considers endorsing her own son as king, a position that is consistent with stances taken by historical queens, most famously Emma, who refused to marry Cnut until he affirmed by oath that only a son of theirs should succeed to the throne.[80] Yet neither Wealhtheow nor Hygd offers unconditional support for the succession of her own sons. Although Wealhtheow urges Hrothgar to leave the kingdom to their sons, she also acknowledges their youth as a potential hindrance to their immediate succession and thus seeks assistance from her nephew Hrothulf. Likewise, Hygd carefully considers her own son, preferring Beowulf's candidacy only after recognizing that her son might not be able to protect their kingdom. The succession practice endorsed by both queens is neither wholesale acceptance nor wholesale rejection of the idea that the new king must be the most direct blood heir. Rather, what each queen urges is careful consideration of the possibility of maintaining an unbroken genealogical line between past, present, and future, but the need ultimately to recognize that these cultural moments ought not to be linked in such a direct fashion. In so doing, these queens model how contemporary Anglo-Saxon readers might approach their own relationship to their preconversion Germanic past and its guiding ethos of heroism: neither to adopt it wholesale nor to reject it outright, but to reflect upon it and thereby find a way to acknowledge the heated claims of Germanic blood, tempered by the cooler voice of Christian reason.

The Feminization of Heroism

If Beowulf has little interest in taking on roles associated with femininity, the poem nevertheless repeatedly thrusts such roles upon him—insisting that to enact feminine roles does not turn one into a woman but instead offers a viable path to heroic glory. As Robert Morey has forcefully argued, Beowulf successfully takes on the role of peaceweaver by putting an end to old strife between the Danes and the Geats, thus rising to the status of hero by assuming a social role typically associated with women.[81] To be sure, Beowulf does not weave peace through the usual feminine methods of intertribal marriage or cup-passing within the mead hall. Nevertheless, Beowulf's sustained efforts to create *sib gemæne*, "shared peace" (1857a), between the Danes and the Geats, his commitment to restraining the violent forces of heroic self-assertion, evidenced by such figures as Unferth and Onela, and his pride in having lived a life in which he "ne sohte searoniðas" (sought no treacherous quarrels; 2738a) all work to create an inextricable link between Beowulf's heroism and his capacity to wage peace. For all his evident skill in battle, Beowulf is nevertheless, as Roberta Frank puts it, a "pagan prince of peace."[82] By casting the poem's undeniable hero in the customarily feminine role of peaceweaver, the *Beowulf* poet urges readers to reconceive the creation of amity, social cohesion, and harmonious relations between men as properly masculine work, and to endorse a more expansive definition of heroic male conduct.

The boundaries of heroic action are further broadened by the fact that Beowulf's quest for heroism entails a series of battles that are fought against not people but monsters. Although Beowulf actively resists the interiorized model of heroism offered to him by the aged, and thus feminized, Hrothgar, the poet suggests that in battling with monsters, Beowulf ultimately enacts precisely what Hrothgar prescribes, and in so doing becomes a hero.

The exact nature of the monsters that Beowulf battles in his quest for heroism has occasioned much debate. Some critics view the monsters as allegorical representations of flaws in the inner self (e.g., Grendel as jealousy, Grendel's mother as vengeance, the dragon as avarice), while others read them as literal threats to the two kingdoms.[83] Yet neither a strictly allegorical nor a strictly literal reading of the monsters can adequately account for these ambiguous beings, who, as Tolkien pointed out, "become 'adversaries of God' and so begin to symbolize (and ultimately to become identified with) the powers of evil, even while they remain . . . mortal denizens of the material world."[84] As Beowulf battles monsters who may be read as both actual exterior threats to the Danes and Geats and also as interior threats to the human soul or psyche, he is positioned in a space somewhere between two different models of heroism: an exteriorized model based on channeling aggression outward to exact retribution for past wrongs, and an interiorized model based on turning aggression inward and battling one's own personal weaknesses, a model prescribed to him by Hrothgar.

As Hrothgar focuses on redirecting the warrior's violence so as to reform the masculine self, Wealhtheow enjoins the reorganization of the warrior's personal qualities so as to produce men who might be most beneficial to the Danish kingdom: his concern is the making of the individual hero; her concern is how that hero might affect the entire hall.[85] While Wealhtheow's prescriptions for male thought and behavior diverge slightly from Hrothgar's in their greater concern for the immediate community, they nevertheless share his insistence on grounding heroism in factors other than the exhibition of physical might. Two key qualities surface repeatedly in Wealhtheow's prescriptions for exemplary behavior, namely, mildness and gentleness, which she prescribes as desirable traits for men, regardless of age or social station. When advising the aged Hrothgar on fostering diplomatic relations between the Danes and Geats, she urges him to "to Geatum spræc / mildum wordum" (speak to the Geats with mild words; 1171b–72a). The maximlike nature of the queen's subsequent claim, "swa sceal man don" (so should a man do; 1172b), enlarges the scope of her prescriptions, preparing for her subsequent vision of each young retainer in Heorot as "modes milde, mandrihtne hol[d]" (mild of mind, loyal to his lord; 1229). If the queen asserts that both her husband and her retainers will be mild, implicit in the ordering of her assertions is the idea that the king's behavior ought to function as an exemplar for the rest of the court, and that a man's "loyal[ty] to his lord" consists not simply of marching behind his battle-standards on the field but in upholding standards of behavior set by him within the hall.

Closely related to Wealhtheow's prescriptions for mildness are her efforts to create a court in which men are demonstrably *liðe*, "gentle," as is evident when she urges Beowulf to "wes / lara liðe" (be gentle of counsel; 1219b–20a) to her sons. Wealhtheow's verbal efforts to promote more harmonious relations among the men in her court is underscored by her passing of the peace-cup, an object that is later described, when it re-emerges in Hygd's hands, as a *liðwæge* (1982b), a hapax legomenon whose usual translation as "cup with strong drink" may obscure the sense of *lið* as the first half of the compound, which suggests that the queen bears a drink whose potency resides less in its capacity to fortify battle-strength than in its ability to facilitate more harmonious and gentler relations between men.

It is tempting to interpret Wealhtheow's prescriptions for heroic masculinity as occasioned by her perceptions of Heorot's newfound safety, with mildness and gentleness permissible, and indeed desirable, characteristics for men within her hall only after it has been cleansed of immediate threats. Yet it is not immediately after Beowulf's defeat of Grendel but after the scop's tale of Hildeburh's sorrows that Wealhtheow expresses her views on heroic masculinity—views that represent a considerable departure from her earlier position. When Wealhtheow first appears in the poem, she is closely allied with the figure of the Germanic whetting woman: her ritualized cup-passing within the court is quickly followed by Beowulf's boasts that he will either kill Grendel or die trying, and her response to his *gilpcwide*, "boasting speech," although not reported, is clearly sufficiently approving to give rise to the narrator's remark that "ðam wife þa word wel licodon" (these words were well pleasing to the woman; 639). Yet the heavy costs exacted by both battle and the pursuit of heroism through acts of retaliatory violence which are so clearly revealed in the song of Finnsburg appear to have transformed the nature of the queen's prescriptions for appropriate masculine behavior. No longer an advocate for militant heroism, she now urges gentleness and mildness, and if battles are to be fought, that they be approached "mid cræfte" (with skill; 1219a), a term whose strong association with thought and reflection effectually suggests a form of violence that is tempered by reason.[86]

There are those who might argue that the trustworthiness of Wealhtheow's voice and, by extension, her prescriptions for male behavior are called into question by her gravely mistaken prognosis regarding Hrothulf's future treatment of her sons. If one believes, as do many scholars, that the poet points to a future in which Hrothulf did not in fact remain loyal to Hrethric and Hrothmund but ultimately usurped the throne (1017b–19 and 1162b–65a), Wealhtheow's claim that she "can / glædne Hroþulf, þæt he þa geogoðe wile / arum healdan" (knows that gracious Hrothulf will hold the young warriors in honor; 1180b–82a) stands, at best, as an ironic assertion of a future inexorably marked by masculine discord and an admission of her own inability to sway its course, and at worst, as a naïve projection of a future that exists only in her imagination and which is pathetically out of touch with reality.[87] Seen in a different light, however, the truth content of Wealhtheow's words is undeniable, and the credibility of both her voice and prescriptions for heroic masculinity remains unquestioned. For writers like Bede and Asser, truth was synonymous with the truth of Christian faith, and with the construction of events in a manner that upheld the righteousness of its values and the rightful treatment of its proponents.[88] For Wealhtheow, truth is synonymous with the truth of a rightfully ordered heroic world and the personal qualities that would be upheld within such a world: mildness, gentleness, and honor between men.

While the factual truth of Wealhtheow's predictions regarding Hrothulf's honorable treatment of her sons is never made clear, what is brought into the light unequivocally is the truth of her alternative model of heroic masculinity. Early in the poem, Wealhtheow forecasts to Beowulf that "hafast þu gefered, þæt ðe feor ond neah / ealne wideferhþ weras ehtigað" (you have brought it about that men near and far will forever praise you; 1221–22), and indeed he is not forgotten. Yet as the Geats mourn the death of their lord, what they remember about him is not the superlative strength of his handgrip but his unmatched capacities for mildness, gentleness, and kindness.[89]

Swa begnornodon   Geata leode
hlafordes (hry)re,   heorðgeneatas;
cwædon þæt he wære   wyruldcyning[a]
manna mildust   ond mon(ðw)ærust,
leodum liðost   ond lofgeornost.
                                        (3178–82)

> Thus the Geatish people, his hearth-companions, mourned the death of their lord, said that among earthly kings he was the mildest of men and gentlest, kindest to his people and most eager for fame.

If earlier on in the poem, the will of the queen is shown to embody the will of the Danish people,[90] the clear echo of Wealhtheow's voice that is evident in the Geats' commemorative remarks for their dead lord further establishes a simultaneity between the voice of a *ðeodcwen*, "people-queen," and that of a larger community. Yet the simultaneity of those wishes converges not, as Beowulf believes, on a shared appreciation for violence, but on a mutual recognition of the inherent worth of very different qualities. As Beowulf enters the annals of Germanic legend by being *milde* and *liðe*, Wealhtheow's alternative vision of heroic masculinity is shown to have moved beyond the confines of an individual woman's mind and taken root in the collective consciousness of the Geats. The fact that Beowulf dies without an heir offers an ever greater ray of hope that the new heroism will take hold. While Beowulf's lack of progeny indeed suggests that there will never be another warrior of comparable heroic stature, it nevertheless also signals that he is himself an anachronism.[91] As Beowulf dies, so too will the exemplum of heroism that he so fiercely defends. If separating oneself from women and reproduction is marked in *Beowulf* as a defining feature of the old heroic ethos, it is also shown to portend its death.

To be sure, *Beowulf* does not wholeheartedly endorse a masculine heroism grounded in mildness, gentleness, or kindness. The poem's final, much-debated characterization of Beowulf as *lofgeornost*, "most eager for fame," stands as a sobering reminder of the relentless hold that fantasies of immortalization tend to exert within any heroic ethos, and of the Anglo-Saxons' deep-seated belief that the pursuit of battle-blood offered the most direct route to securing long-standing remembrance. Yet by presenting heroic quests through Hildeburh's eyes rather than through the eyes of such warriors as Finn or Hengest, the *Beowulf* poet effectively forces contemporary audiences to disengage temporarily from identification with these male heroes and their investments in heroic violence, and to become more critical readers of both the text and the ancient, outmoded heroic age that it so vividly portrays. As the poem depicts Beowulf achieving heroism through peaceweaving and through enacting roles prescribed for him by an aged king and a woman, it shifts the grounds for fame toward battles that are waged against the self rather than others. By broadening the roles through which men are shown to acquire heroic glory and prohibiting women from emulating behavior traditionally associated with heroic masculinity, the *Beowulf* poet gestures toward the possibility of redefining both heroism and masculinity. Through the thicket of different viewpoints, digressions, and flashbacks, the poem's feminine voices allow us to discern a thin but strong line of argument that critiques the old and gestures toward the new. In this, *Beowulf* is typical of Old English poetry, whose great power resides in its ability to suggest things without really saying them.[92]

Chapter 4

Queenship and Royal Counsel in the Age of the *Unræd*

Anglo-Saxon writers seldom provide sustained discussions of the intimacies of royal marriage, tending to focus instead on queens as vehicles for exploring more public sociopolitical problems. As we have seen in the cases of Bede, Cynewulf, and the *Beowulf* poet, Anglo-Saxon writers were less inclined to use queens for modeling such concerns as domestic harmony, marital fidelity, or even sexual rectitude, than for addressing more wide-ranging and non-gender-specific issues such as conversion, social hierarchy, and heroism. Ælfric's adaptation of the Old Testament book of Kings (992–1002) is thus highly unusual, offering as it does a rare glimpse into the private life of the Israelite king Ahab and his queen, Jezebel.[1] Yet as Ælfric dramatizes the powerful trust and personal closeness that characterize Ahab and Jezebel's relationship, he reveals a tendency similar to that of other Anglo-Saxon writers to mobilize queens for the purposes of social critique. Transforming spousal confidences and bedroom exchanges into an occasion for social and political commentary, Ælfric uses the royal marriage and its accompanying intimacies to figure such contemporary political issues as queenly authority and kingly counsel, as well as more long-standing monastic anxieties about idolatry and the reception of demonically inspired advice.

For all of its apparent richness in terms of immediate political topicality and ongoing monastic concerns, *Kings* has nevertheless received little attention from modern critics, an oversight that may be explained as the last vestige of an outdated critical sensibility that would dismiss vernacular biblical translations as non-English, derivative, and artistically lacking. We might consider, for example, one of the first and only critical responses to *Kings,* namely, Walter Skeat's 1881 characterization of the text as a "mere epitome of passages from the Book of Kings; [with] extracts relat[ing] to Saul, David, Ahab, Jehu, Hezekiah, Manasses, and Josiah."[2] Skeat's view of *Kings* as a rather uninspired list of extracts relating to male rulers reveals how very little excitement *Kings* and its female protagonist have generated among modern critics, a lack of interest that is particularly striking when contrasted with Ælfric's own fascination with Kings and with Jezebel.[3] Although *Kings* is an extremely condensed version of the biblical narrative, Ælfric nevertheless carefully relates, and at times expands upon, all of the discussions of Jezebel found in his Latin sources, offering a comparatively detailed account of Jezebel's tyrannical and idolatrous practices, her marriage to the evil Israelite king Ahab, and her efforts to murder God's prophets and to defend the absolute power of the monarchy. The attention Ælfric lavishes upon Jezebel represents a marked departure from his treatment of the other characters in the biblical narrative, whose roles are either cut or dramatically condensed. It is striking that Ælfric devotes so much of *Kings* to Jezebel. It is even more striking that this protracted depiction of abhorrent queenship, with its dual emphases on the queen as chief political agent and as adviser to the king, appears in a collection intended for two of King Æthelred's closest advisers.

My study of Jezebel begins from the assumption that vernacular versions of the Bible were not poor imitations of their Latin precursors but cultural artifacts in their own right, and valuable sources of insight into Anglo-Saxon culture. As Malcolm Godden argues: "For the Anglo-Saxons the Old Testament was a veiled way of talking about their own situation . . . a means of considering and articulating the ways in which kingship, politics and warfare related to the rule of God."[4] New understanding of biblical translations in recent years has been accompanied by a revised understanding of Ælfric. Once viewed as a cloistered monk invested primarily in matters of doctrine and theology, Ælfric is now increasingly recognized for his deep concern for England's national and political welfare, for his strong connections to court through his primary patrons Æthelmær and Æthelweard, and for his use of Old Testament translations to offer contemporary social and political critique.[5]

Yet as Ælfric famously remarked in his "Preface to Genesis," translating the Old Testament was a problematic enterprise, fraught by a constant tension between the desire to preserve the word of God faithfully and the urge to transform the Old Law so that it would not be misinterpreted—a danger that he saw as especially keen for lay audiences, less experienced with figural reading.[6] This tension between preservation and transformation is underwritten by a further dialectic, namely, the fear that biblical characters might function as dangerous exemplars, and the knowledge that exemplarity was precisely the lens through which these characters could be received, thus making them a potentially powerful means of influencing contemporary politics, patterns of thought, and social practice. Perhaps nowhere in Ælfric's writings is this dialectic more richly revealed than in *Kings*. In spite of Ælfric's expressed anxieties over transforming the divine Word, his queenly protagonist, Jezebel, proved remarkably protean when translated from Latin into Old English.[7] This chapter traces key differences between Ælfric's Jezebel and her biblical counterpart to reveal the cultural work that she performed for both Ælfric and for late tenth-century audiences.

Any attempt to use source study to understand the cultural work that a biblical character might have performed for contemporary readers, however, is beset with difficulties.[8] Determining the precise Latin text(s) that served as source material for a vernacular translation is always a challenging enterprise, and especially so in the case of *Kings,* which consists of very brief summaries of particular episodes in Kings rather than a full translation of the entire biblical book. Scholars have generally assumed that Ælfric relied mainly on the Vulgate for all of his vernacular biblical adaptations, and the Ælfrician portions of the Old English *Heptateuch* confirm this theory since they are essentially faithful to the Latin of the Vulgate.[9] Nevertheless, recent studies by such scholars as Richard Marsden and Stewart Brookes have urged us to broaden our consideration of the possible sources for Ælfric's biblical adaptations; indeed Brookes makes the compelling case that Ælfric may have relied on Old Latin texts rather than, or in addition to, the Vulgate.[10]

The difficulties of identifying the exact textual sources for *Kings* are compounded by the fact that Ælfric was very likely also working with "memorial sources," that is, remembered versions of Kings and/or biblical commentaries which he had heard read aloud. As Allen Frantzen and Nicholas Howe have shown, the highly oral/aural nature of Anglo-Saxon literary culture meant that one could know a text quite well without ever having encountered it in written form.[11] Aural reception was especially widespread in the case of such texts as biblical narratives, which composed the bulk of daily public readings in Anglo-Saxon monasteries, and which also formed the basis for patristic commentaries that were much studied and discussed. Indeed, an Old Testament figure such as Jezebel was not a single character, but rather a web of ideas produced by communal readings, commentaries, and discussions—much as, for example, Frankenstein is not a discrete product of Mary Shelley's imagination but a conglomeration of ideas that have accrued to the monster by virtue of its translation into various modern media.

In spite of the grave difficulties attendant upon the identification and recovery of both textual and memorial sources, source study remains a vibrant and revealing critical activity, and particularly when used in conjunction with such approaches as reception study and cultural analysis. While it is not clear precisely which texts served as source material for *Kings,* what is clear is that it is deeply invested in contemporary political concerns. As Ælfric translates Jezebel out of an imagined Old Testament past and into his own time, he uses the legendary biblical queen to offer a veiled critique of both queenly authority and royal counsel—two especially tense issues during the latter decades of the tenth century, in the light of contemporary changes in queenship and Æthelred's notorious difficulties in securing good counsel. By localizing unwise counsel in the female figure Jezebel and relying on the entrenched Anglo-Saxon association between women and counsel, Ælfric constructs a portrait of royal counsel that both critiques and humanizes the transgressions of the adolescent Æthelred which took place immediately prior to Ælfric's composing of *Kings.* Yet as Ælfric's use of Jezebel broadens beyond the articulation of local political critique to encompass larger concerns about idolatry and demonically inspired advice, he reveals a desire to disrupt the long-standing Anglo-Saxon association between women and counsel and to relocate the capacity for good counsel in pious habits of living rather than biological sex. Ælfric's threading of both immediate political troubles and ever-present spiritual dangers through the figure of Jezebel attests to Anglo-Saxon writers' strong sense of the Old Testament as vitally and dialectically engaged with their own culture: their belief that biblical characters were not to be narrowly allegorized and viewed merely as typological shadows of the New Law, but as textual exemplars who could be transported out of the past and mobilized and refigured to address contemporary cultural problems.

Reception

Ælfric's *Kings* survives in two manuscripts: London, British Library, Cotton Julius E. vii (s. xi in.), and Oxford, Bodleian Library, Hatton 115 (s. xi², xii. med.).[12] The former is written mainly in one hand, and contains Latin and Old English prefaces and a contemporary Latin table of contents in which the scribe lists *Kings* as "XVII . . . De libro regnum." *Kings* is the seventeenth out of a total of thirty-nine items, consisting mainly of Ælfrician saints' lives, as well as four non-Ælfrician lives and seven non-hagiographical pieces. The collection contains three Old Testament paraphrases: *Kings, Maccabees,* and a self-contained item (which uses the story of Absalom and Achitophel and is tacked onto the Passion of Saint Alban), and *Kings* is the only one of these three items not assigned to a specific day for reading. *Kings* appears between *De Auguriis* (a sermon that warns strongly against prophecy and witchcraft) and the Passion of Saint Alban. Hatton 115 is a more eclectic collection of ecclesiastical materials: it contains homilies, saints' lives, hortatory sermons, and a number of Old Testament pieces, including a homily on Exodus and Numbers, a translation of Judges, and material from Genesis. In Hatton 115, *Kings* appears close to the end of the manuscript, between the *Interrogationes Sigewulfi* and a sermon containing descriptions of hell.[13]

Julius E. vii opens with a Latin and an Old English preface, neither of which is contained in any other manuscript of Ælfric's *Lives of Saints*. Both prefaces state that the items contained in the *Lives of Saints* were translated from Latin at the request of the ealdorman Æthelweard and his son Æthelmær, who were personal officials and chief advisers of Æthelred. Æthelweard, ealdorman of the Western Provinces and kinsman to Æthelred, served as senior ealdorman from 993 until his death ca. 998 and was responsible for the military defense of the southwest against the Vikings.[14] His son Æthelmær, described in the vernacular version of charter S 914 as "mines hlafordes discðen" (my lord's thegn), lived in the king's household and had charge over a number of royal lands, which he used as sites for Cerne Abbey (in which Ælfric wrote the *Lives of Saints*) and for the abbey of Eynsham, over which Æthelmær appointed Ælfric as abbot in 1005.[15] Both Æthelweard and Æthelmær consistently appear in prominent positions on witness lists to late tenth-century charters; such lists, as Simon Keynes argues, "serve as an invaluable guide to the composition of a group of laymen who would have been in frequent and intimate attendance on the king, and who as his personal officials may have exerted considerable influence on his deci-sions."[16] Ælfric offers the *Lives* to his two noble patrons, with the accompa-nying remark that it should edify "quibus cumque placuerit huic operi operam dare, siue legendo, seu audiendo" (as many, namely, as are pleased to study this work, either by reading or hearing it read), a statement that points to Ælfric's belief that his collection would reach a broader audience.[17] Ælfric's claims in the prefaces to have translated passions and lives that were formerly unknown to the laity on account of their being available only in Latin, and to have written about saints who were formerly honored only by *mynstermenn*, "people in monasteries," suggest that his anticipated audi-ence was composed largely of laypeople.[18]

The precise contexts in which laypeople might have had access to *Kings* is a vexed issue. Peter Clemoes argues that the items in the *Lives* were not intended for liturgical use but for pious reading at any time, a view sup-ported by the fact that, unlike most liturgical pieces, the items in the *Lives* do not announce themselves as such through oral markers or through refer-ences to the particular occasions and days on which they are to be read.[19] Yet we know that what actually happened to the items contained in the *Lives* was very different from what Ælfric intended. Although Ælfric vehe-mently protested against dividing up, miscopying, and adding to his collec-tions, even during his own lifetime his works were nonetheless taken out of their original contexts, miscopied, and inserted into new and diverse collec-tions of ecclesiastical materials.[20] It is possible that at some point *Kings* was inserted into a collection intended for liturgical use, a possibility that is fur-ther supported by Milton McC. Gatch's suggestion that the Night Office— part of the daily round of nonsacramental, monastic services to be celebrated or recited at intervals over the course of the day and night—would have been a likely setting for the public reading of such Old Testament narratives as Kings. Gatch identifies Kings as a "summer history" that would have been read between the second Sunday after Pentecost and the beginning of August.[21] The reading of Old Testament narratives during the Night Office was part of the general monastic goal of reading the entire Bible aloud dur-ing the course of one year.[22] Those readings that could not be completed during the Office were then continued in the refectory.[23] Although removal to the refectory would certainly have eliminated a lay audience, it is possible that laypeople were present to hear the Night Office, especially in light of the fact that monastic churches often served local communities as well as monks and nuns.[24] Whether or not laypeople ever heard portions of the

Night Office—and the late night hours during which the Night Office took place may well have deterred lay attendance—the Office nevertheless provides a useful model for understanding how laypeople may have used *Kings*. If Ælfric's Old Testament translations were indeed adaptations of materials from the monastic devotional life for pious laymen and nonmonastic clergy seeking to emulate monastic religious practices, Ælfric's lay patrons may well have read the text aloud on Sundays, at mealtimes, or during other periods of the day allotted to devotion, in imitation of such monastic practices as the Night Office.[25]

Jezebel's Past

There are only two extant Old English discussions of Jezebel: Ælfric's *Kings* and his homily on the beheading of Saint John the Baptist. However, Jezebel was invoked in numerous patristic writings and Anglo-Latin texts, all of which would have helped to shape the production and reception of Ælfric's Jezebel.[26] Ambrose (ca. 340–97) interpreted Jezebel as a typological figure for Synagogue, a symbol of false belief and heretical practice that was especially evident in her disdain for and misunderstanding of Scripture. As he asks in *Epistula* 14: "Who is Jezebel when engaged in persecution, if not Synagoga, flowing vainly, abounding vainly in the Scriptures, which she neither cares for nor understands?"[27] Ambrose also viewed Jezebel as a symbol of worldly temptations, and he thus saw the good prophet Elijah's flight from her and escape to the desert not as indicative of cowardice or fear of women, but as evidence of rightful resistance to the seductions of earthly pleasures.[28] Yet if Ambrose saw Jezebel as a symbol of such enduring cultural problems as heresy and worldly temptations, he also viewed her as a means of exploring more immediate cultural concerns, drawing parallels between Jezebel's persecution of righteous prophets and the Arian tormenters of his own time.[29] Ambrose's belief in Jezebel as a timeless and transcultural exemplar is evident in his *De Nabuthae*, in which he claims that "haec est Iezabel non una, sed multiplex, non unius temporis, sed temporum plurimorum" (this Jezebel is not single but multiple; she does not belong to one time but to many times).[30]

Aldhelm (ca. 639–710) invokes Jezebel and Ahab toward the end of his verse *De virginitate* in a section detailing the allegorical confrontation of vices and virtues which does not appear in his prose version of this text.

The torments prescribed for the royal couple are intended to exemplify the just due allotted to the followers of Avarice, a figure that is, here, allegorically gendered female and depicted as an armed leader of combat with powerful backing:

> Next, a third Vice, Avarice, foments a battle, a Vice which is, perhaps, best explained as "greed." A dense army surrounds this leader of combat; she does not walk as a lone pedestrian through public roads. . . . Hear also of the greedy king of the Hebrew nation, Ahab, by whom the blooming vineyard belonging to Naboth was taken by fraud, when Ahab's cruel wife forged a heinous document (in Ahab's name). The Avenger, looking down from the high heavens, punished this crime brought about by their fraudulent sin. For dogs licked up the flowing blood of the tyrant, where Naboth, the innocent leader who had harmed no-one with weapons, lay buried under a shower of rocks. The savage dogs, however, fiercely tore Jezabel to pieces with their teeth and crushed her limbs, drenched with purple gore, into the ground—Jezebel who had written the letter to the town and had cruelly punished the righteous followers of the Lord.[31]

What is most striking about this depiction of Jezebel and Ahab is the relative emphases that Aldhelm places on their respective punishments: he radically condenses the Old Testament's lengthy account of Ahab's suffering, but recounts all the details that are provided about Jezebel's torment.[32] Aldhelm's efforts to highlight Jezebel's suffering may be partly explained by the fact that he was most likely writing for a female audience: the nuns of Barking Abbey.[33] Perhaps Aldhelm believed that emphasizing the severe punishment allotted to a female practitioner of avarice would serve as a more effective deterrent for women readers. Given that the prologue to the prose De virginitate envisions the nuns' struggles against their inner vices as permitting them to conquer the "womanly" aspects of their natures, it is also fitting that Aldhelm portrays the nuns' foes as vices that are allegorically gendered female and exemplified through such female figures as Jezebel.[34] Like Ambrose, Aldhelm also invokes Jezebel's disdain for written texts; yet he focuses not on her misunderstanding of Scripture but on her misuse of written documents in order to validate the fraudulent acquisition of property and to persecute the righteous followers of God.

Unlike Aldhelm's discussion of Jezebel, which is based upon her depiction in the Old Testament, most of Bede's references to Jezebel are taken from the New Testament (Apoc. 2:20–23), in which she symbolizes the seductions of sexual and spiritual fornication that threaten to lead God's servants astray. In his *Explanatio Apocalypsis*, Bede explores the etymology of the name Jezebel, stating that "nomen Jezabel, quod fluxum sanguinis sonat, convenit hæreticis" (the name Jezebel, which means the flow of blood, is fitting for heretics).[35] Like Ambrose, Bede emphasizes Jezebel's capacity to signify across geographic and temporal boundaries, referring to her as a *figura* to be found *per orbem* (throughout the world).[36] Bede never mentions Jezebel in his commentary on Kings.[37] His only reference to the Old Testament Jezebel occurs in his homily on Saint John the Baptist, in which Jezebel and Ahab exemplify types of the wicked who torment true believers.[38]

The Old Testament representation of Jezebel as a persecutor of righteous churchmen greatly appealed to such writers as the seventh-century Italian hagiographer Jonas of Bobbio and the eighth-century English hagiographer Eddius Stephanus, who used hagiography to explore contemporary historical events and cultural concerns. Both men invoked the name Jezebel as a condemnatory epithet for queens who tormented bishops and holy men. Writing of the late sixth-century Merovingian queen Brunhild's supposed role in the stoning of the bishop Desiderius of Vienne, Jonas states that "mentem Brunichildis . . . secundae ut erat Zezabelis" (Brunhild's mind became like that of a second Jezebel).[39] Similarly, Eddius, in his *Life of Wilfrid*, repeatedly invokes Jezebel to discuss queens who persecuted bishops or convinced their husbands to do so:

> Nam illo tempore malivola regina nomine Baldhild ecclesiam Dei persecuta est; sicut olim pessima regina Iezabel, quae prophetas Dei occidit, ita ista, exceptis sacerdotibus ac diaconibus, novem episcopos occidere iussit, ex quibus unus est iste Dalfinus episcopus.[40]

———

> For at that time there was an evil-hearted queen named Baldhild who persecuted the church of God. Even as of old the wicked Queen Jezebel slew the prophets of God, so she, though sparing

the priests and deacons, gave command to slay nine bishops, one of whom was this Bishop Dalfinus.[41]

Later on in the *Life of Wilfrid,* Eddius draws on Jezebel's association with worldly temptations to discuss Queen Iurminburg's capacities to incite in her husband an overvaluation of earthly glories and a disdain for holy men:

> Iamiamque de faretra sua venenatas sagittas venifica in cor regis, quasi impiissima Gezabel prophetas Dei occidens et Heliam persequens, per auditum verborum emisit, enumerans ei eloquenter sancti Wilfrithi episcopi omnem gloriam eius secularem et divitias necnon coenobiorum multitudinem et aedificiorum magnitudinem innumerumque exercitum sodalium regalibus vestimentis et armis ornatum. Talibus itaque iaculis cor regis vulneratum, ambo callide quaerentes sanctum caput ecclesiae in suum interitum contempnere.[42]

———

> Forthwith this sorceress [Queen Iurminburg] shot poisoned arrows of speech from her quiver into the heart of the king, as the wicked Jezebel did when she slew the prophets of the Lord and persecuted Elijah. She eloquently described to him all the temporal glories of St Wilfrid, his riches, the number of his monasteries, the greatness of his buildings, his countless army of followers arrayed in royal vestments and arms. With such shafts as these the king's heart was wounded. They both sought skillfully to humiliate the holy head of the Church to their own destruction.[43]

By Ælfric's time, then, the term "Jezebel" conveyed a range of meanings. It was used to refer to heretics and idolaters, to invoke the misuse of written language, either the misreading of Scripture or the creation of fraudulent documents, and to describe strife between queens and churchmen, particularly strife that involved queenly counsel that incited kings to a love of worldly pleasures and a hatred for bishops and for other representatives of Church authority. While patristic and early medieval writers vary widely in their particular views on Jezebel, they nevertheless exhibit a shared sense of the biblical queen as a malleable and enduring figure who could be used to address both contemporary political concerns and more long-standing social problems.

Narrative Strategies

In spite of the commonly held belief that Jezebel's exemplarity was timeless and transcultural, the fact remained that she and her Old Testament companions inhabited a world that was very different from early medieval England. In order to create exemplars who might not seem so foreign to Anglo-Saxon audiences, Ælfric employs many of the same narrative strategies in *Kings* as he does in his saints' lives, most notably, a tendency to transform characters into generic figures that were seemingly unanchored to particular cultural contexts.[44] Ælfric greatly simplifies the complicated genealogies and difficult proper names attached to the characters in the biblical book of Kings, typically limiting their genealogies to one generation or omitting them altogether, and often dispensing with biblical figures' proper names in favor of more generalized epithets such as *seo cwen*, "the queen," *se cyning*, "the king," or *his cyne-hlaford*, "his lord." Ælfric further dislocates the biblical characters from their ancient and unfamiliar historical contexts by excising almost all of the place names in the Old Testament book. Although he does locate the text in Israel, all of the detailed descriptions of Middle Eastern land and water masses are removed and replaced by such generic phrases as "his earde" (his country; 73), "þam lande" (that land; 58), or "anre dune" (a hill; 142), resulting in a rather hazy sense of geography and a sense that *Kings* could be set anywhere in Christendom.[45] In keeping with his attempts to universalize Kings, Ælfric does not translate many of the cultural practices depicted in the biblical book which would have seemed foreign to Anglo-Saxon readers, such as the use of eunuchs for royal advisers, or the practice of appointing judges to rule under theocracy. In the interest of offering readers unambiguous exemplars of good and evil, Ælfric describes the biblical characters through highly moralistic epithets, referring to Jezebel, for example, as "þæt fracode wif" (that wicked woman; 160) or "þæt hetelice wif" (that hateful woman; 194), and to the pious Hezechiah as "se geleaffulla cynincg" (the faithful king; 388).

Yet if Ælfric simplifies the moral dimensions of the biblical characters, he nevertheless grants them a kind of rudimentary interiority by adding frequent references to their mental and emotional states. Readers are told, for example, that Jezebel was "hetelice gemodod" (violently minded; 50), and that she "swor þurh hire godas mid syrwigendum mode" (swore through her gods with a plotting mind; 157), while David is said ever to have obeyed God "mid ealre heortan" (with all of his heart; 34). In spite of their utter simplicity, characters' inner lives are often given precedence over their actions, particularly in the last third of *Kings,* which devolves into a series of skeletal accounts of the reigns of such kings as Hezekiah, Manasses, Ammon, and Josias. Ælfric provides only the sketchiest of plot details concerning these kings' actions, describing Manasses, for example, simply as a king who "mid manegum yfelum dædum þone ælmihtigan god gegremode" (provoked the Almighty God with many evil deeds; 436). What Ælfric is most intent on stressing is these kings' interior states: he claims that Hezekiah turned to God "mid ealre heortan" (with all of his heart; 389) and cried to Him "anmodlice" (with a single mind; 400), and that Josiah turned to God "geornlice / mid ealre heortan" (zealously, with his whole heart; 466–67).

Ælfric's efforts to convey a strong sense of biblical characters' inner states and his apparent lack of interest in relating the Bible's detailed descriptions of their battles and journeys remind us that *Kings* and indeed all of Ælfric's Old Testament translations were designed less to teach biblical history than to effect moral and spiritual reform. Rather than encouraging reform through direct preaching, *Kings* offers a set of exemplars whose interior lives provide emotional scripts or blueprints for readers to use in reforming their own inner lives. Intratextual examples offer further instruction on the art of emulation as a means of spiritual reform: Ahaziah becomes a "swyðe yfel-dæda" (very evil-doer; 228) by imitating his parents, Jezebel and Ahab, who "him yfele gebysnodon" (had set for him an evil example; 230), while Josiah "rixode þrymlice" (reigned gloriously; 470) on account of his having "ge-efenlæhte dauide / on ealre godnysse" (imitated David in all goodness; 459–60). Creating biblical characters with active interior lives enables Ælfric to offer his readers accessible exemplars. Anglo-Saxon readers might not, for example, be able to match David's heroic bravery in battling a lion or a giant, but they might nevertheless be able to emulate his whole-hearted devotion to God. By stressing the interior lives of his characters, Ælfric also takes the focus off their morally dubious cultural practices, thus encouraging readers to emulate Solomon's wisdom or Elijah's love for the Creator, for example, rather than the former's marital practices or the latter's animal sacrifices.

The rewards for adopting an inner life similar to those of the pious biblical kings are set forth toward the opening of *Kings*, in which Ælfric outlines one of the text's major purposes: to use biblical kings as historical justification for the belief that both devotion to God and the lack thereof would receive their just due—not in the hereafter but within one's own lifetime:

> and þa ðe god wurðodon wurdon gemærsode.
> and sige-fæste wæron Symle on gefeohte.
> þa ðe fram gode bugon to bysmor-fullum hæðenscype
> þa wurdon gescynde. and a unsigefæste.
>
> (41–44)

Those who worshiped God were exalted and were always victorious in battle, and those who turned from God to shameful idolatry were ever put to shame and always unsuccessful.

To further convince readers that worldly success was a product of pious living, Ælfric excises the various occasions in the biblical narrative in which impious characters are rewarded by good fate, such as when the idolatrous king Ahab wins two major battles against the Syrian army (3 Kings 20).

Ælfric's transformations of the biblical book of Kings all work to create a sense of its characters and events as universal phenomena—generic, transcultural, and symbolic rather than particular, rooted, or individual. It is, paradoxically, this very drive toward universalism that allows *Kings* to address particularized cultural concerns effectively. Once dehistoricized and removed from their ancient and unfamiliar cultural contexts, Old Testament characters and events could then more easily resonate with contemporary Anglo-Saxon concerns. This drive toward the generic is evident in Ælfric's transformations of Jezebel throughout *Kings,* and it is what enables her to speak to such social and political issues as the increasing authority of late tenth-century queens, kingly counsel, and idolatry.

Kings: Ælfric's Commentary on Queenship

Throughout *Kings,* Ælfric enhances Jezebel's authority, a tendency that is immediately apparent in his practice of naming her. Unlike the Bible, which tends to refer to Jezebel either by her proper name or as the *regis uxor,* "wife of the king," and almost never as *regina,* Ælfric most often refers to Jezebel as *cwen.*[46] Ælfric's practice of naming Jezebel must be, in part, attributed to the formal constraints of alliterative prose. It is also possible that Ælfric refers to Jezebel as *cwen* in order to make it seem as if she were Ahab's only wife, thus avoiding the potential problems of discussing polygamy, which figures quite clearly in the biblical text (3 Kings 20:7).[47] However, Ælfric's practice of naming Jezebel must also be seen in the light of his tendency to departicularize biblical characters in the interest of creating generic exemplars that would more closely resemble the political figures within Anglo-Saxon culture. And as we have seen in the case of Elene, the term *cwen* would have borne very particular cultural implications for late tenth-century readers in light of the new titling practices emerging at this time for queens and queen mothers. Both Ælfric and his readers would probably have understood the term *cwen* as a title serving to heighten and call attention to Jezebel's official status as a queen and to the power deriving from her regal position.

Ælfric's efforts to foreground Jezebel's authority are also felt in his emphasis on her ability to incite her husband to sin. The Vulgate's introduction to Ahab makes only a very oblique connection between Ahab's sins and Jezebel:

> Nec suffecit ei ut ambularet in peccatis Hieroboam filii Nabath insuper duxit uxorem Hiezabel filiam Ethbaal regis Sidoniorum et abiit et servivit Baal et adoravit eum. (*Biblia Sacra,* 489)

———

> Nor was it enough for him to walk in the sins of Jeroboam the son of Nabat: but he also took to wife Jezabel daughter of Ethbaal king of the Sidonians. And he went, and served Baal, and adored him. (3 Kings 16:31)

Ahab's decision to marry Jezebel and to worship her god, Baal, is thus figured in the Bible as merely another one of the king's many sins, and it is only much later on in the biblical book that we are explicitly told of the role that Jezebel plays in instigating his crimes (3 Kings 21:25). By contrast, Ælfric foregrounds Jezebel as the chief force behind her husband's cruel works:

immediately after introducing Ahab, Ælfric designates the king's provocation of God as a joint endeavor that is orchestrated largely by his wife:

þyses cyninges cwen wæs forcuþost wifa
Gezabel gehaten hetelice gemodod.
Seo tihte hyre wer to ælcere wælhreownysse.
and hi tyrgdon god mid gramlicum weorcum.

(49–52)

———

This king's queen was the most infamous of women, called Jezebel, fiercely minded. She incited her husband to every cruelty and they provoked God with cruel works.

The ramifications of Jezebel's influence extend far beyond the corruption of the king: we are told that "seo *tihte* hyre wer to ælcere wælhreownysse" (she incited her husband to every cruelty), and Ahab is then later condemned by God for having "min folc *mistihtest*" (misled my people; 212). The repetition of the verb *teon* suggests a chain of command in which Jezebel urges the king to sin, and he both follows his wife's behavioral prescriptions and extends them to his people. The king's subservience to Jezebel is further suggested by his reduction to "hyre wer" (her husband; 51), an epithet that is never applied to Ahab in the Bible.

In addition to stressing Jezebel's personal influence over her husband, Ælfric also heightens her political autonomy and her capacity to function as an independent royal agent. Unlike the biblical Jezebel, who is only able to give written orders after stealing the king's writing implements and forging his name and seal, Ælfric's Jezebel does not act under the auspices of the king but writes directly to the king's chief men on her own authority. And if the biblical Jezebel is only able to implement her orders after sending multiple letters to the chief men, Ælfric's Jezebel elicits an instant response from them after dispatching a single letter:

Þa sende gezabel sona anne pistol.
to naboðes neh-geburum mid þisum ge-banne.
. . . .

Þa dydon þa heafod-menn swa swa þæt hetelice wif
him on gewrite bebead.

(187–88, 194–95)

––––––––

Then Jezebel immediately sent a letter to Naboth's neighbors with
this message. . . . Then the chief men did just as that hateful woman
had commanded them in the letter.

Not surprisingly, Ælfric's emphasis on Jezebel's dangerous authority is accompanied by a similar stress on the punishment decreed for her by God. In the Vulgate, Jezebel's death and subsequent consumption by dogs is simply one in a long list of retributive acts that God allots for the house of Ahab:

Et percuties domum Ahab domini tui ut ulciscar sanguinem servorum meorum prophetarum et sanguinem omnium servorum Domini de manu Hiezabel perdamque omnem domum Ahab et interficiam de Ahab mingentem ad parietem et clausum et novissimum in Israhel et dabo domum Ahab sicut domum Hieroboam filii Nabath et sicut domum Baasa filii Ahia Hiezabel quoque comedent canes in agro Hiezrahel nec erit qui sepeliat eam. (*Biblia Sacra*, 516)

––––––––

And thou [the newly anointed king Jehu] shalt cut off the house of
Achab thy master, and I will revenge the blood of my servants the
prophets, and the blood of all the servants of the Lord at the hand
of Jezabel. And I will destroy all the house of Achab, and I will cut
off from Achab him that pisseth against the wall, and him that is
shut up, and the meanest in Israel. And I will make the house of
Achab like the house of Jeroboam the son of Nabat, and like the
house of Baasa the son of Ahias. And the dogs shall eat Jezabel in
the field of Jezrahel, and there shall be no one to bury her. (4 Kings
9:7–10)

The corresponding passage in Ælfric's text is, characteristically, much
shorter and focuses less on retribution against the house of Ahab than on
that against its mistress, Jezebel:

God ælmihtig cwæð be þe. ic ðe to cynincge gesmyrode.
ofer israhela folc. þæt þu eall adilegie
achabes ofsprincg ðæs arleasan cynincges.
þæt ic beo gewrecen on þære awyrigendan (sic) gezabel.
Heo bið hundum to mete na bebyrged on eorðan.

(321–25)

God almighty has said about you, "I have anointed you as king over
the people of Israel so that you may exterminate the offspring of
the wicked king Ahab so that I might be avenged on the accursed
Jezebel. She should be as meat for hounds, not at all buried in the
earth."

Ælfric further highlights the punishment given to Jezebel by intruding frequent reminders throughout the text that her trangressions against God
would receive their just due: at one point, Elijah prophesies that "gezabel
sceolan etan ælegrædige hundas" (greedy dogs shall eat Jezebel; 213), and
shortly afterward Ælfric makes it clear that Elijah's prophecies were fulfilled:

And his modor gezabel manfullice leofode
on fulum forligere and on ælcere fracodnysse.
oþþæt godes wracu hire wælhreownysse geendode.

(270–72)

And his mother Jezebel lived wickedly in foul fornication and in
every wickedness until God's vengeance ended her cruelty.

If Ælfric's portrayal of Jezebel points to anxieties about unchecked queenly
authority, there is, nevertheless, little reason to suspect that these anxieties
were motivated by any particular Anglo-Saxon queen. It is unclear exactly
who served as queen, or whether there even was a queen, when Ælfric was
writing *Kings*.[48] As Joyce Hill points out, the collection in which *Kings* is
contained was worked on over a period of time—between 992 and 1002.[49]

Over the course of this decade, Ælfric would have witnessed three royal women serving in close connection to Æthelred: Ælfthryth, wife to Edgar and mother to Æthelred (965–ca. 999), Ælfgifu, Æthelred's first wife (985–ca. 1000), and Ælfgifu-Emma, Æthelred's second wife and the daughter of Richard, Duke of Normandy (1002–52).[50] Historical sources offer little information about Æthelred's first queen, Ælfgifu, except that she bore ten children, a silence that, when considered along with the fact that Ælfgifu does not appear on witness lists to contemporary charters, suggests she was not considered an important presence in Æthelred's political life.[51] Æthelred's mother, Ælfthryth, by contrast, exercised significant influence over her son's public and private affairs: she acted as regent for Æthelred, who was most likely not more than twelve years old when he became king; she raised Æthelred's son Æthelstan, whose will refers to Ælfthryth as "minre ealdemodor þe me afedde" (my grandmother who brought me up);[52] she served as a frequent witness to royal charters; and she founded female monasteries at Winchester, Wiltshire, and Ramsey.[53] Toward the beginning of the period when Ælfric most likely began *Kings*, Ælfthryth seems to have regained a certain amount of public authority: after a brief hiatus during which she did not serve as a charter witness (984–93), Ælfthryth apparently renewed her attendance at the king's council and once again witnessed charters until ca. 999, at which point she may have either become ill or died.[54]

Yet far from using her authority as queen mother to hinder monastic interests, Ælfthryth was known for using her royal position to advance them. Around 970, Ælfthryth was appointed the "protectress and fearless guardian of the communities of nuns"; she was a close friend of Æthelwold, the reformist bishop of Winchester and teacher of Ælfric; and she was an avid supporter of the Winchester monastery in which Ælfric spent much of the early part of his life.[55] Given that the queens who served during Ælfric's lifetime would have given him every reason to believe that queenly power would be used to benefit the Church, why, then, does Ælfric so strongly insist in *Kings* upon a link between the authoritative and the abhorrent queen? What particular social climate led him to voice such anxieties over the power of the royal consort?

Ælfric's efforts in *Kings* to foreground the dangers of queenly power and authority are correctly understood, I would suggest, not by looking to any particular West Saxon queen but rather by broadening our gaze and considering changing ideals of queenship over the course of Ælfric's life-time (ca. 955–ca. 1010). As we have seen, the late tenth century witnessed a series of changes in the formal authority of queens: the use of new titling practices for queens and queen mothers, the increased use of queenly anoint-ing, the frequent enlisting of queens as witnesses to royal charters and thus as participants in royal council meetings, and the formal appointment of a queen as the official patron of female monasteries. Many of these changes gave the queen more autonomy from the king, granting her the authority to act not simply as the "king's wife" but as a political agent in her own right, with specific roles and responsibilities. The formalization of queenly au-thority, in effect, resulted in the creation of another independent royal agent, and thus an extension of the royal power base. Given the overtly roy-alist sentiments underpinning such documents as the *Regularis Concordia* and the *Benedictional of Æthelwold*, we can be fairly sure that the first gen-eration of reformers enthusiastically promoted the increased power of the royal family, a stance that is not surprising, considering that the reigning king and queen, Edgar and Ælfthryth, were well known for their piety and for their willingness to support monastic life.[56] Yet by the time Ælfric began *Kings*, Edgar had long since died and had been replaced by Æthelred, whose failure to protect his people from Danish invasions and lack of support for monastic life apparently failed to sustain Ælfric's confidence in royal au-thority. As Mary Clayton points out, in all of his works Ælfric only ever names Æthelred twice, and then only for the purposes of dating an event, a silence that, as she argues, is especially telling when contrasted with Ælf-ric's lavish praise for Edgar, as well as for such earlier kings as Alfred and Æthelstan.[57] There is much evidence to suggest that in the latter years of the tenth century, Ælfric had become disillusioned with the royal-monastic partnership championed by earlier reformers, and rather wary of the pos-sible ill-effects of royal power.[58] If this is indeed the case, it is not difficult to see that for Ælfric, the increased formalization of queenly authority would have posed a very real threat. Ælfric's efforts to highlight the dangers of authoritative queenship in *Kings* probably do not reflect his anxieties over the power of any individual West Saxon queen, but rather his anxieties that queenly power was becoming institutionalized, and, by extension, that the power of the royal family was expanding beyond desirable limits. Moreover, Jezebel was a particularly fitting image to use for expressing concerns about the potential dangers of burgeoning royal authority because she was strongly associated in biblical exegesis with a conception of monarchy centered on the absolute power of the king and on his exemption from the imperatives of godly authority or covenant law.[59]

Queenly Counsel and the Theft of a Vineyard

If Ælfric uses Jezebel to voice his anxieties over the public institutionalization of queens' power, he also draws on her story to explore one of the least institutionalized aspects of queenly authority: the queen's personal influence over her husband and her ability to sway his decisions through informal counsel. And it is in his construction of Jezebel as a royal counselor that Ælfric most radically departs from his sources. All the Latin versions of Kings depict Jezebel's husband as a king who seeks counsel frequently, and from an array of different sources, including Jewish prophets, pagan prophets, and the ancients of his land. This counsel has diverse results— sometimes positive, sometimes negative. On one occasion, following the advice of the local ancients leads to Ahab's triumphant victory over the Syrian army (3 Kings 20). On another occasion, following the advice of his prophets leads to Ahab's being stabbed and dying a slow and painful death (3 Kings 22). Ælfric's sources depict Ahab not as an uncounseled king but as one who is simply unable to distinguish between good and bad counsel, a king who is willing to follow almost anyone's advice, especially if it coincides with his own ideas. Yet Ælfric excises all the scenes in the biblical narrative in which Ahab seeks counsel from his male advisers, incorporating into Kings only those scenes in which he seeks counsel from Jezebel. In Ælfric's Kings, Jezebel appears to be Ahab's only counselor, and each time he seeks counsel from her the results are disastrous: their first meeting results in Jezebel's sending out a posse of men to kill the righteous prophet Elijah (156–59), and their second meeting leads to Jezebel's ordering the chief men to kill the God-fearing thane Naboth so that she might steal his property (184–86).

What is most striking about these "counsel scenes" is how radically they refigure the idea of counsel. One way of understanding counsel is to view it as an entity generated by the self-perception of a lack in one's knowledge, and by the subsequent desire to fill that lack with the knowledge stores of another. The urge to seek counsel might be characterized as a kind of adult version of Lacan's mirror stage: the recognition not of the self as other but of the other as a necessary supplement to the self. Put another way, to seek counsel is to relinquish the fantasy of the self as intellectually autonomous and to acknowledge the potential benefits of intellectual collaboration. Yet when Ahab seeks advice from Jezebel, it is not his store of knowledge that is augmented but hers. Moreover, Jezebel's advice does not enable Ahab but further debilitates him: their meetings always lead to his inaction and to her assumption of full control over royal affairs. Ælfric's depiction of Jezebel as a royal counselor conveys the sense that she has not only replaced the king's counselors but also perverted the fundamental idea of counsel as the provision of enabling information.

It is tempting to view Ælfric's emphasis on Jezebel's destructive counsel as motivated by a generalized misogyny that finds voice in anxieties about female speech. Overtly antifeminist diatribes against female speech are more characteristic of post-Conquest literature, but similar sensibilities do occasionally emerge in Anglo-Saxon texts, as in *Genesis B,* which underscores Eve's verbal capacities as cause of the Fall ("Hio spræce him þicce to and speon hine ealne dæg / on þa dimman dæd," 684–85a; "Heo spræc ða to Adame idesa sceonost / ful þiclice," 704–5a),[60] and also in the "Acerbot Charm," in which the speaker concludes a charm designed to ward against unfruitful land with the following plea to God:

Nu ic bidde ðone waldend,   se ðe ðas woruld gesceop,
þæt ne sy nan to þæs cwidol wif   ne to þæs cræftig man
þæt awendan ne mæge   word þus gecwedene.[61]

Now I ask the ruler, he who created this world, that there might not be any woman so eloquent nor any man so skilled so as to be able to change the words that I have thus spoken.

Moreover, the Benedictine reforms brought into England increased anxieties about female autonomy and women's sexuality, creating a social milieu more open to misogynist rhetoric, such as that found in Ælfric's homily on the beheading of Saint John the Baptist. In a fairly straightforward translation of an antifeminist homiletic tirade associated with Saint

John Chrysostom, Ælfric remarks on Jezebel as the betrayer of Naboth and places her in the company of such women as Delilah and Herodias:[62]

> Ac se wisa salomon cwæð þæt selre wære to wunienne. mid leon. 7 dracan. þonne mid yfelum wife 7 oferspecum; witodlice iohannes on westene wunode betwux eallum deorcynne. ungederod. 7 betwux dracan. 7 aspidum. 7 eallum | wurmcynne. 7 hi hine ondredon: soðlice seo awyrigede herodias mid beheafdunge hine acwealde: 7 swa mæres mannes dead to gyfe hire dehter hleapunge underfeng; danihel se witega læg seofon niht betwux seofon leonum on anum seaðe ungewemmed. ac þæt awyrigede wif gezabel. beswac þone rihtwisan naboð to his feore. þurh lease gewitnysse; Se witega ionas wæs gehealden unformolten on þæs hweles innoðe þreo niht: 7 seo swicole dalila þone strangan samson mid olæcunge bepæhte. 7 bescornum feaxe his feondum belæwde; Eornostlice nis nan wyrmcynn. ne wildeora cyn. on yfelnysse gelic yfelum wife.[63]

But the wise Solomon said that it would be better to dwell with the lion and the dragon than with an evil and talkative woman. Now John had lived in the waste unhurt among all the animal-kind, and among serpents, and asps, and all the worm-kind, and they dreaded him. But the accursed Herodias slew him by beheading, and received the death of so great a man as a gift for her daughter's dancing. Daniel the prophet lay seven nights with seven lions in one den, uninjured, but the accursed woman Jezebel betrayed the righteous Naboth to his death by false witness. The prophet Jonah was preserved unconsumed in the belly of a whale for three nights, and the treacherous Delilah deceived the strong Samson with flattery and, his locks being shorn, betrayed him to his foes. Truly there is no family of worms nor of wild beasts that is like in evilness to an evil woman.

Although this homily establishes that Jezebel could at times serve as a means for Ælfric to voice anxieties about the dangers of female speech, I would nevertheless argue against assuming that it is indicative of any kind of overarching opposition on Ælfric's part to female speech or to reliance on women for counsel. Indeed, tracing images of female counsel throughout the Ælfrician corpus reveals numerous very positive depictions of women advisers—figures such as Lucy, Judith, and Esther, all of whom are shown providing valuable advice on a wide range of subjects.[64] When Ælfric does express disapproval of female counsel, it tends to be focused quite specifically on instances in which women direct their counsel toward inciting men to violence, one of the traditional roles assigned to women in various Germanic literatures.[65] In his homily on the beheading of Saint John the Baptist, for example, Ælfric writes disapprovingly of Herodias's dancing daughter, whose request for the head of John the Baptist offers Herod a ready pretext for following through with his plans of murder.[66] The dancing daughter's harmful counsel is immediately contrasted with the "þingunge þæs snoteran wifes abigail" (intercession of the wise wife Abigail), who, in a kind of inverted image of the Germanic whetting woman, dissuaded her husband, David, from committing murder, so that he ultimately "awende his swurd into þære scæðe 7 herode þæs wifes snotornysse þe him forwyrnde þone pleolican mansliht" (returned his sword to his sheath, and praised the wisdom of the woman who forbade him that perilous murder).[67]

Ælfric's *Esther* reveals similar anxieties regarding the use of female counsel to incite men to violence. His version of Esther omits chapters 9 and 10 of the biblical book, in which Esther advises her husband to embark on a series of retaliatory battles against those who had formerly conspired to eradicate her people.[68] Likewise, Ælfric's rendition of Judges does not include the wise prophetess Deborah, a figure who is known for advising the Israelite Barak to lead an army of ten thousand men against the Canaanites (Judges 4–5).[69] Like Herodias's dancing daughter, Esther, and Deborah, Jezebel is instrumental in urging men to violence—and violence that Ælfric would have seen as particularly lamentable in that it was targeted against God's prophets. If Ælfric's efforts to highlight Jezebel's dangerous counsel are motivated by gender concerns, those concerns do not, I would argue, center on a wholesale opposition to female counsel but rather on opposition to the belief that female counsel was rightly used for inciting men to violence.

Moreover, it is worth recalling that in the latter years of the tenth century, it was probably not *female* counsel that was foremost in Ælfric's mind. As Simon Keynes points out, the early part of Æthelred's reign

(984–ca. 993) was a period during which the king was misled by corrupt counselors, who took advantage of the king's youth and inexperience to embark on a host of wrongdoings for their own profit.[70] These wrongdoings included "the maltreatment of certain churches, the reduction of their privileges and the appropriation of their property," and were enabled by Æthelred's authorization of royal diplomas that reallocated formerly monastic properties to various laymen, including the king's own counselors.[71] Keynes characterizes Æthelred's reign from 984 to ca. 993 as "the period of youthful indiscretions," a time of unjust rule that, in later years, the king would openly acknowledge and attempt to explain as having taken place "partly on account of the ignorance of my youth . . . and partly on account of the abhorrent greed of certain of those men who ought to administer to my interest."[72] Ælfric never directly addresses Æthelred's propensity for succumbing to the *unræd*, "mis-counsel," that gave rise to the king's youthful indiscretions as well as the memorable epithet assigned to him by twelfth-century writers.[73] Yet Ælfric's writings nevertheless exhibit an obsessive interest in highlighting both the reception and the provision of counsel as ready pitfalls for kings, with potentially dire consequences for their people. In his homily for Monday in Rogationtide, for example, Ælfric writes that "þæt folc bið gesælig þurh snoterne cyning. . . . And hi beoð geyrmede ðurh unwisne cyning. on manegum ungelimpum. for his misræde" (the people will be happy by means of a wise king . . . and they will be afflicted by means of an unwise king, by many misfortunes because of his mis-counsel).[74] In his *Letter to Sigeweard* (1005–6), Ælfric urges:

> Witan sceoldan smeagan mid wislicum geþeahte, þonne on mancinne to micel yfel bið, hwilc þæra stelenna þæs cinestoles wære tobrocen, 7 betan þone sona.[75]

> Counselors ought to consider with wise thought, in times when there is too much evil against mankind, which pillar of the royal throne is broken and amend it immediately.

The topic of counsel also arises in Ælfric's Old English rendition of the *De duodecim abusiuis* in a section on the *unrihtwis cyning*, "unjust king." Ælfric urges that for a king to rule justly, witan hym sceolan rædan 7 . . . He sceal soðfæste menn settan hym to gerefan . . . 7 beon on earfoðnysse anræde. . . . Wite eac se cyning hu hyt is gecweden on bocum gif he rihtwisnysse ne hylt þæt swa swa he ahafan is on his cynesetle toforan oþrum mannum. swa he bið eft genyþerad on þam nyþemestan witum under þam unrihtwisum. þe he unrædlice geheold.[76]

––––––––

counselors must advise him and . . . he must appoint honest men as his reeves . . . and be resolute in times of trouble. . . . Let the king know also that it is said in books that, if he does not uphold justice, just as he is raised up on his throne above other people so will he be brought low by the lowest punishments under the unjust whom he unadvisedly supported.

The term *boc* that appears in this passage is Ælfric's standard term for referring to the various books of the Old Testament. His claim here that books exemplify the punishments to be meted out to those kings who fail to uphold justice is nowhere better illustrated than in the biblical book of Kings, which contains numerous examples of ill-advised kings who ignore God's counsel and are subsequently "brought low by the lowest punishments." Ælfric's *Kings* heightens the sense of just due given to such kings by shortening the temporal span between a king's sinful deeds and his punishment, thus creating a stronger sense of an immediate causal relation between bad fate and disregard for God's counsel, and also by excising any occasion in the biblical text in which a good fate befalls kings who fail to heed God's counsel. Moreover, throughout *Kings*, Ælfric repeatedly invokes the term *ræd*, "counsel," opening the text with a reference to Saul, whose rise to kingship did not proceed in accordance with *godes ræd*, "God's counsel" (3), subsequently remarking on the pious Elijah and Jehu as having invoked God's word *anrædlice*, "resolutely" (247, 320), and moving finally to the idolatrous king Ammon, who *rixode unrædfastlice*, "ruled rashly" (456), for two years and was then killed by his own thanes. It is hard not to detect—or to believe that Æthelred's former counselors would not have detected—a hint of criticism directed at Æthelred in these references, particularly when they are read in the light of the so-called vineyard scene, in which Ælfric's critique of kingly *unræd* finds its fullest expression.

The vineyard scene is one of the most dramatic episodes in the biblical book of Kings. Focusing on Ahab's obsessive desire to possess the vineyard of the God-fearing thane Naboth, Naboth's staunch refusal to grant the king his ancestral lands, and Jezebel's fierce intent to defend the absolute power of the king, the episode turns on an intensely private moment of consultation between Jezebel and Ahab, which results in the king's unknowingly authorizing the production of fraudulent documents, in the stoning of Naboth, and in the royal couple's ultimate acquisition of the vineyard. Ælfric appears to have been preoccupied with the vineyard scene, writing about it in three different works: in a homily on the beheading of Saint John the Baptist, in *Admonitio ad Filium Spiritualem* (a letter intended for monks and nuns), and in *Kings*. As we have seen, in his homily on Saint John the Baptist, Ælfric never mentions Ahab, presenting Jezebel as solely responsible for the vineyard theft and subsequent death of Naboth. By contrast, in his *Admonitio ad Filium Spiritualem,* Ælfric focuses solely on Ahab, who appears in a section "De Avaritia Fugiendum" (On Avoiding Avarice):[77]

Ahab eac se kining yfele wearð beswicen for Naboðes winearde ðe he wolice genam. and he for ðam hraðe feoll on gefeohte ofslagen. ðæt swa wurde on him gewreken Naboð ðe ær wæs ofslagen for his agenum winearde.[78]

———

The king Ahab also was evilly deceived on account of Naboth's vineyard, which he wrongfully took, and on account of this he quickly fell, being killed in the fight so that Naboth, who was formerly killed for the vineyard he possessed, was avenged.

Although Ælfric does not explicitly discuss Jezebel, he does implicitly invoke her when he states that "se kining yfele wearð beswicen," a phrase that is not present in Ælfric's Latin source, and which effectively reminds readers that Ahab was not solely responsible for stealing Naboth's vineyard.[79] The different emphases that Ælfric places on Jezebel in these two texts may be in part a function of their intended audiences. Ælfric's homily on the beheading of Saint John the Baptist was written primarily for laypeople, who may not have been all that familiar with Kings, whereas his *Admonitio ad*

Filium Spiritualem was intended for monks and nuns, who would have known the Old Testament book quite well. Ælfric may have thus thought it necessary in his homily to spell out clearly Jezebel's role in the theft of Naboth's vineyard, but not in the *Admonitio ad Filium Spiritualem,* in which he could simply suggest that Ahab was deceived by avarice and expect that his monastic audiences would know of Jezebel's role in the theft and, also, of her typological association with avarice.

Ælfric's most developed account of the vineyard scene occurs in *Kings.* Unlike so many of the other scenes from the biblical text, which he radically condenses, Ælfric carefully relates even very small details of the vineyard episode, lingering on Ahab's willingness to approve Jezebel's rather nebulous plans to acquire Naboth's property, on her production of the fraudulent letter that leads to Naboth's stoning, and on her lamentable success in stealing Naboth's ancestral lands. With its emphasis on bad counsel provided by a typological figure of worldly greed, on the production of fraudulent documents, and on the theft of lands from a God-fearing man, the vineyard scene in *Kings* almost uncannily mirrors events that had transpired during the early years of Æthelred's reign when the counsel of greedy advisers resulted in the king's unknowing authorization of royal charters depriving monks of their land.[80] It is, I would argue, no accident that when Ahab has finished consulting with Jezebel, Ælfric frames the queen's parting comments to her husband as an order to "aris . . . mid rædfæstum mode" (arise with a mind firm in counsel; 185), a phrase that notably departs from the Vulgate's "aequo esto animo" (be calm in spirit; *Biblia Sacra,* 498) and which must be read as deeply ironic in light of the fact that Jezebel has offered the king no counsel at all but simply a large dose of *oleccung,* "flattery," and a promise to rectify matters with Naboth. This bizarre, almost parodic, counsel scene is also striking in that it dramatizes the very kind of counsel that Ælfric feared and repeatedly warned against, namely, counsel that was carried out in secret and never made known to the kingdom at large. In his homily for the Sunday after the Ascension of the Lord, Ælfric urges that, according to Christ's example,

> þæt witan sceolan cyðan heora word openlice,
> and þa ðe manegum rædaþ, na mid runungum,
> for ðan þe manega magon maran ræd findan
> þonne ænlypige magon mid agenum gewille.[81]

counselors and those who advise many must declare their words
openly, not with whisperings, because many people are able to find
greater advice than individuals can through their own will.

Later on in this homily, Ælfric insists: "And þæs behofað se cyning þæt he
clypige to his witum, / and be heora ræde, na be rununge fare" (And it is
advisable for the king that he should call upon his counselors and proceed
according to their advice, not according to whisperings).[82] Jezebel's counsel,
which is carried out in the privacy of the royal bedchambers and never made
known to anyone except the king, is precisely the kind of counsel that Ælfric's homilies warn against. It is also precisely the kind of counsel that
would have been likely to lead to the "youthful indiscretions" of the adolescent Æthelred and to allow those indiscretions to go unchecked for almost
a decade.

For all of *Kings*'s remarkable resemblance to the early years of Æthelred's reign, Ælfric's text nevertheless diverges from contemporary history
on one very crucial topic: kingly repentance. Several royal charters make it
clear that by the year 993, Æthelred had come to regret his youthful indiscretions—that he openly admitted his misdeeds and, in an attempt to make
amends, returned many of the monastic lands that he and his men had
wrongly appropriated.[83] In these acts of atonement, Æthelred once again
finds a strong parallel in his biblical counterpart, Ahab, who, after being
apprised of his misdeeds and the punishment that they have merited him,
repents—tearing his clothes, donning a hairshirt, casting down his head,
fasting, and sleeping in sackcloth—and is thus granted partial forgiveness
by the Lord (3 Kings 21:27–29). Yet Ælfric's *Kings* excludes all of Ahab's
acts of atonement, and thus portrays the king as beyond either repentance
or forgiveness. One explanation for Ælfric's omission of Ahab's atonement
is that it was composed of acts that would have seemed unusual to Anglo-
Saxon laypeople (e.g., tearing one's garments or sleeping in sackcloth); Ælfric's typical practice of translation was either to exclude unfamiliar cultural
practices or to explain them. Moreover, Ælfric usually tried to provide his
readers with clear, uncomplicated exemplars, and he may have thought that
including Ahab's repentance and God's subsequent softening of the king's
punishment would have interfered with readers' ability to understand Ahab
as a straightforward exemplar of immoral behavior that would receive its
just due. Yet when Ælfric's omission of Ahab's atonement and partial abso-
lution are considered in the light of the strong parallels between Ahab and

Æthelred, it also implies a sharp critique of Æthelred—a kind of unwillingness on Ælfric's part to acknowledge his own king's admissions of wrongdoing and requests for pardon.

Ælfric's harshness toward Æthelred may be in part explained as an attempt to uphold basic ideals of just kingship, two important components of which were the king's duty to seek counsel and his duty to protect his people from theft. These obligations must have been common knowledge among the Anglo-Saxons, as they were clearly spelled out by the bishop during the king's coronation ceremony, and in one of the few parts of the ceremony conducted in the vernacular:

> Gehalgodes cynges riht is, þæt he nænig ne man ne fordeme, and þæt he wuduwan and steopcild, and æltheodige werige and amundige, and stala forebeode . . . and ealde and wise and syfre him to getheahtorum hæbbe, and rightwise mæn him to wicnerum sette.[84]

> The duty of a hallowed king is that he judge no man unrighteously, and that he defend and protect widows and orphans and strangers, that he forbid thefts . . . and have old and wise men as counselors and set righteous men as stewards for himself.

Similarly, *Maxims I* dictates that the ideal king is one who distributes property to his people as opposed to claiming it for himself:

> Cyning biþ anwealdes georn;
> lað se þe londes monað,   leof se þe mare beodeð.[85]

> A king is eager for territory. Hateful is he who claims lands; beloved is he who gives more.

Æthelred's failure to seek good counsel and to protect his people from theft constituted a serious breach of his royal responsibilities. By refusing to acknowledge God's partial forgiveness of Ahab, Ælfric's *Kings* depicts failure to uphold the responsibilities of royal office as a grave offense that would not be treated lightly or forgotten easily. Ælfric's harsh attitude toward irresponsible kingship may have been partly motivated by personal grudges, for some of the properties that Æthelred appropriated were lands belonging to Ælfric's own monastery—the Old Minster, Winchester, where Ælfric was educated and spent perhaps as much as two decades of his life.[86]

Yet if *Kings* stands as a harsh critique of royal counsel during the early years of Æthelred's reign, it is nevertheless a critique that proceeds with great caution—and necessarily so. It is worth recalling that *Kings* was composed for Æthelweard and Æthelmær, who had for many years served as both Ælfric's chief patrons and Æthelred's chief counselors. Judging from their frequent requests for pious and meditative texts, both men were avid and careful readers, and men for whom even the subtlest intimations of royal counsel gone awry would have certainly struck a powerful chord. Any attempt on Ælfric's part to criticize royal counsel thus called for the greatest tact and delicacy so as not to offend the two men responsible for his own professional advancement, as well as the financial well-being of Cerne and Eynsham, the monasteries in which Ælfric spent the later portion of his life and composed the bulk of his writings.

For all that *Kings* voices a sharp critique of Æthelred's propensities for succumbing to unwise counsel, it also exhibits signs of latitude toward the king's youthful foibles. Although Ælfric's depiction of Ahab clearly conveys the idea that an ill-counseled king who fails to uphold the duties of his office will be severely punished, the fact that Ælfric so thoroughly localizes bad counsel in the female figure Jezebel effectively softens the king's responsibility for his actions, suggesting that when a king falls prey to bad counsel, it may not always be his fault. Within Anglo-Saxon culture, women were strongly associated with the provision of good counsel and wise advice.[87] The sententious collection known as *Maxims I* states that it is a wife's duty to counsel her husband and a husband's duty to solicit his wife's advice.[88] The association between wives and counsel is further borne out, as we have seen, in the examples of Wealhtheow, who counsels Hrothgar on the future well-being of their sons and on royal succession; Judith, who counsels her nation's army on war with the Assyrians; and Edith, who is praised for being a "consilio efficax ex prompta" (skilful and ready counsellor).[89] Given the powerful link in Anglo-Saxon thought between wives and counsel, both Ælfric and his readers would probably have seen a kind of inevitability in Ahab's decision to rely on Jezebel's counsel, and thus a kind of inevitability in his having been led astray. What *Kings* does, then, is to dramatize the problem of a king who falls prey to bad counsel, but understandably so, thus partially excusing the misdeeds of Ahab, and by extension those of his modern incarnation, Æthelred, who, like his biblical counterpart, was led astray by the very people in whom he was supposed to be able to put his firmest trust. The final lines of *Kings*, in which Ælfric claims that "he who obeys sins and despises God's commands now in the time of the gospel is like the kings who chose idolatry and despised their Creator" further humanizes kingly misdeeds by reminding readers that immoral behavior is equally available to, and indeed a force capable of leveling differences between, men of diverse social stations.[90] Yet if Ælfric suggests that any man might replicate the sins of, and thus be like, a bad king, he never invokes that idea's logical corollary: that obedience to God might make an ordinary man akin to a good king. The parallel that Ælfric draws between the sinful man and the bad king effectively situates kingly immorality in the more human or ordinary aspects of the king's person, while preserving the more admirable aspects of his person as that which renders him special and different from ordinary men, and indeed fit to serve as Christ's earthly representative.

Indeed we ought not be surprised that *Kings* sets forth a critique of royal counsel which at the same time exhibits strains of sympathy for Æthelred and casts his youthful misdeeds in a slightly gentler light. For if Ælfric's efforts to humanize royal transgressions were in part motivated by his desire to avoid offending his patrons, it is also true that by the time Ælfric came to compose *Kings* (ca. 992–1002), he could well afford to be generous: Æthelred had returned the wrongfully appropriated monastic lands, including those lands belonging to the Old Minster at Winchester, and had surrounded himself with wise and trusted counselors. At this point, Æthelred's youthful indiscretions were all but a fairly dim memory, almost a decade old. Whether he continued to harbor resentment and mistrust toward Æthelred—as his works suggest—by locating bad counsel in the figure of the evil wife, Jezebel, Ælfric is able to construct a critique of royal counsel that not only humanizes royal transgressions but also safely distances the idea of bad counsel from men, thus preventing any risk of offending or alienating his patrons.

For the Love of Idols

Yet if Ælfric used Jezebel to express his views on immediate political issues, he also drew on her to explore more enduring social problems, namely, *deofolgild*, "idolatry," a term that was commonly used by the Anglo-Saxons to describe both the literal practice of idol worship, as well as any social practice that entailed turning away from God's commands and toward sin. As Ælfric puts it:

> Deofol-gild bið þæt man his drihten forlæte. and his cristendom.
> and to deofollicum hæðenscype gebuge. bysmrigende his scyppend.
> Oðer deofolgild is derigendlic þære sawle.
> ðonne se man forsihð his scyppendes beboda.
> and þa sceandlican leahtras begæð. þe se sceocca hine lærð.[91]

_____

> Idolatry is when a man forsakes his Lord and his Christianity and yields to diabolical heathenism, dishonoring his Creator. There is another idolatry, hurtful to the soul, when a man despises his Creator's commands and practices the shameful sins which the devil teaches him.

These comments on *deofolgild* occur in Ælfric's homily *De Auguriis*—the text immediately preceding *Kings* in Julius E. vii—and they resonate strongly with the final lines of *Kings*, in which Ælfric urges readers to view the sinful kings in his text as exemplars of *deofolgild:*

> ac we cweðað to soðum se þe synnum gehyrsumað.
> and godes beboda forsyhð nu on þæs godspelles timan.
> þæt he bið þam cynincgum gelic ðe gecuron deofolgild.
> and heora scyppend forsawon.
>
> (476–79)

_____

> But we say in truth that he who obeys sins and despises God's bidding now in the time of the gospel is like the kings who chose idolatry and despised their Creator.

The thematic echoes between *De Auguriis* and *Kings* suggest that either Ælfric or a later compiler placed the two texts next to one another as fitting companion pieces—with the former offering general warnings that one ought not to engage in prophecy, witchcraft, or idolatry, and the latter providing specific, and rather frightening, examples of Old Testament figures who failed to heed such warnings.[92] Indeed another very pragmatic reason for placing *De Auguriis* before *Kings* was to remind readers that they ought not to engage in any modern forms of prophecy, or believe in fortune-telling or divination, so that when they encountered these practices in *Kings,* they would not be tempted to view them as biblical precedents for contemporary behavior.

The resonances between *Kings* and *De Auguriis* are further felt in Ælfric's use of the same terms to describe the "wicked women" who appear in both texts. In *Kings* Ælfric refers to Jezebel as a *hæts* (350), a term that appears only twice in the corpus, and which either Ælfric or a later scribe glossed in Julius E. vii with the phrase *vel sceande* (or shameful one). In *De Auguriis* Ælfric invokes the term *hæts* to describe women engaged in such practices as adultery, self-induced abortion, and the concocting of love potions, warning that "cristene men sceolan . . . forhogian þa hætsan . and ðyllice hæðengyld (Christian men must . . . shun those *hætsan* and such idolatry; 162–64). Similarly, Ælfric describes Jezebel as engaged in the practice of *unlybba,* "witchcraft" (333), the same word that he uses in *De Auguriis* (25) in a fairly straightforward rendition of Paul's discussion of *veneficia,* "sorcery," as one of the manifest works of the flesh (Gal. 5:20).

Where Jezebel and the witches in *De Auguriis* most closely resemble each other, however, is in their provision of potentially destructive counsel. Much as Jezebel's counsel leads her husband to provoke God and to thus be consigned to death, the witches in *De Auguriis* provide counsel that gravely endangers those who inquire after it:

> Ne sceal se cristena befrinan þa fulan wiccan
> be his gesundfulnysse. þeahðe heo secgan cunne
> sum ðincg þurh deofol. forðan þe hit bið derigendlic.
> and eall hit bið ættrig þæt him of cymð
>
> (124–27)

The Christian man must not inquire of the foul witch concerning his health though she may be able to tell something through the devil, for it will be harmful and all will be poisonous which comes from it.

Ælfric claims further that female diviners are given information by the devil for the very purpose of destroying those who seek out sorcery:

Nu cwyð sum wiglere þæt wiccan oft secgað
swa swa hit agæð mid soðum ðincge.
Nu secge we to soðan þæt se ungesewenlica deofol
þe flyhð geond þas woruld. and fela ðincg gesihð
geswutelað þæra wiccan hwæt heo secge mannum.
þæt þa beon fordone þe ðæne dry-cræft secað.

(108–13)

———

Now a certain sorcerer may say that witches often declare just as something may happen, with a true result. Now we say as a truth that the invisible devil who flies throughout the world and sees many things often reveals to the witch what she should say to men so that they may be destroyed who seek this sorcery.

Ælfric's comments reveal two broad strains of thought: first, an acknowledgment of the potential draw to seeking out female diviners for information about one's health or future; and second, a warning that such counsel must be avoided at all costs because it derives from the devil. Ælfric admits that witches "may be able to tell something" or even, as sorcerers say, to "declare just as something may happen, with a true result." Yet the diabolical nature of the sources from which witches' counsel hails ultimately renders it false, whether or not the witch's prophecy is objectively confirmed by events. For Ælfric, true counsel appears to be less a function of verifiable accuracy than of divine origins, an idea that is more clearly expressed in his homily for the eighth Sunday after Pentecost, in which he reminds readers that counsel is one of the sevenfold gifts of the Holy Spirit:

An is se halga gast þe sylð gecorenum mannum ða seofonfealdan gife. þæt is wisdom. and andgit. ræd. and strengð. ingehyd. and arfæstnys. godes ege is seo seofoðe.[93]

———

It is the Holy Ghost alone who gives to chosen people the seven-fold graces, that is, wisdom and understanding, counsel and strength, knowledge and piety; awe of God is the seventh.

Ælfric makes this point in numerous homilies, most often (as above) through various renditions of Isaiah 11:2–3,[94] although occasionally through 1 Corinthians 12:8–10, as in his homily for the Holy Day of Pentecost, in which he claims: "Sumum men he forgifð wisdom. 7 spræce . . . sumum witegunge" (To some he [the Holy Spirit] gives wisdom and eloquence . . . to some prophetic power).[95]

Ælfric's injunctions that counsel ought to be understood as a gift that is granted by the Holy Spirit to a select group of people points to a subtle distinction between modern and Anglo-Saxon understandings of counsel. Within modern culture, counsel tends to be conceptualized as the provision of knowledge that one has acquired through one's own efforts (e.g., study or experience); it is thus knowledge that the counselor will tend to claim as his or her own. However, for Ælfric, counsel seems to have been closer to what we might think of as intercession or prophecy: the transmission of wisdom that is not one's own intellectual property but ultimately belongs to another, and higher, source. Ælfric's efforts to highlight the dangers of Jezebel's counsel, I would argue, point less to his fear of specifically female counsel than to his fear of counsel that derives from false sources. The point is not to warn against the counsel of women but to warn against the seductions of idolatry. Yet because Ælfric was writing during a period in which anxieties about female sexuality were escalating and because sexual and spiritual fornication were so closely linked in the minds of medieval churchmen, the female counselor becomes a ready figure for absorbing anxieties about the seductions of idolatry, which are in turn figured through the image of the female counselor who seduces people to sin through her false speech.[96]

It is crucial to recognize that although Ælfric uses the image of the evil female counselor to warn against the seductions of idolatry, he does not seem to have been generally opposed to women serving as counselors or prophets. Indeed Ælfric's discussion of Anna in his homily on the Purification of the Virgin suggests a desire to frame biological sex as wholly irrelevant in determining a person's right to provide advice or to prophesy:

> Đa ða se simeon hæfde gewitegod þas witegunge be criste: þa com þær sum wuduwe seo wæs anna gehaten; Seo lyfode mid hire were seofon gear: 7 syððan heo wæs wuduwe. feower 7 hundeahtati geara: 7 þeowude gode on fæstenum 7 on gebedum. 7 on clæn-nysse . . . Rihtlice swa halig wif wæs þæs wyrðe þæt heo moste witighgean embe crist: þa ða heo swa lange on clænnysse gode þeowude; Behealde ge wif 7 understandað hu be hyre awriten is.[97]

> When Simeon had prophesied this prophecy about Christ, then a certain widow came there who was called Anna. She had lived with her husband for seven years and afterwards was a widow until the age of eighty-four and she served God in fasting and in prayers and in chastity . . . It was rightful that so holy a woman was worthy to prophesy about Christ since she had served God so long in chastity. Behold you women and understand how it is written about her.

By linking Anna's prophetic abilities with her chastity, Ælfric effectively dislodges any association between counsel and biological sex, suggesting that the capacity to provide good counsel derives, instead, from exemplary habits of living that render the counselor's body and mind fit to mediate information from divine sources.[98] Exemplary living was equally accessible to men and women, and Ælfric's views thus render the role of counselor equally available to either sex.[99] The idea that women who live "mid fullum ge-leafan" (with full belief) might indeed be chosen to transmit God's Word is clearly set forth in Ælfric's account of the Sibylls in his *Letter to Sigeweard:*

> Tyn mædena wæron on mislicre tide on hæþenum leodum, þa man het Sibillas, þæt synd "witegestran," 7 hi witegodon ealle be þam

Hælende Criste, 7 heora bec setton swiðe swutelice ðurh þone
soþan God be ealre his fare mid fullum geleafan, for ðan þe God
wolde him gewitan habban of hæðenum leodum 7 of geleafullum;
ac heora bec ne synd na on ure gesetnissum on þære biblioþecan
swa swa þas oðre beoð.[100]

———

There were ten maidens in various times among the heathen people whom people called Sibylls, that is to say, prophetesses, and
they prophesied all about the Saviour Christ and undoubtedly
composed their books through [the assistance of] the true God,
concerning his passage, with full belief. For God wanted to have
witnesses for him among both heathen and believing people, yet
their books are not set in our Bible as are the others.

If in *Kings,* then, Ælfric mobilizes the entrenched Anglo-Saxon association
between women and counsel to advance a sympathetic political critique of
Æthelred, in his homilies he seeks to disrupt that association and to relocate the capacity to provide good counsel in exemplary habits of living and
belief.

Writing circa 540 about the fall of Roman Britain to Germanic invad-
ers, the monk Gildas remarked, "I gazed on these things and many others
in the Old Testament as though on a mirror reflecting our own life."[101] Like
Gildas, Ælfric also turned to the Old Testament during a period of cultural
crisis to find possible explanations and solutions for the problems facing his
society. However, unlike Gildas, Ælfric did not view the Old Testament as
a clear reflection of contemporary life but rather as a group of stories that, if
carefully molded and shaped, could be used to express his views on such
difficult contemporary issues as changing ideals of queenship, royal counsel, and idolatry. As the Israelite king Ahab's torturous death and the fall of
his people demonstrated, to leave such problems unresolved would have disastrous consequences. That Ælfric translated and sent this version of Kings
to two of Æthelred's chief counselors suggests that he believed England did
not need to suffer a similar fate.

Chapter 5

Queenship and Social Reform
in Ælfric's *Esther*

seo cwen hæfde getacnunge þære halgan gelaðunge ealles cristenes
folces. . . . Be þissere gelaðunge cwæð se witega to gode; Adstitit
regina a dextris tuis. in uestitu deaurato. circumdata uarietate; Þæt
is. Seo cwen stent æt ðinre swyðran. on ofergyldum gyrlan. ymbscryd mid menigfealdre fahnysse.[1]

The queen was a type of the holy Church of all Christian folk. . . .
Of this Church the prophet said to God, "Adstitit regina a dextris
tuis, in vestitu deaurato, circumdata varietate"; that is, "The queen
stands at thy right, in gilded apparel, clothed in manifold variety."

This quotation from Ælfric's homily "On the Dedication of a Church" lucidly illustrates one of the most culturally enduring metaphors of queenship: the queen as Church united to Christ in marriage. Yet even as Ælfric
attempts to stabilize the symbolic significance of the queen, he continually
highlights her imaginative potential: draped in the elaborate garments
befitting Christ's spouse and glossed in both Latin and the vernacular, she

is literally, figurally, and even lexically "ymbscryd mid menigfealdre fahnysse" (clothed in manifold variety). This chapter further investigates
queens' imaginative potential for Ælfric by considering the two royal
women, Vashti and Esther, who appear in his adaptation of the Old Testament book of Esther.[2] Like *Kings*, *Esther* is deeply engaged with the social
and political issues of Ælfric's own time—perhaps even more so, as *Esther*
belongs to the later phase of Ælfric's career, during which he became increasingly outspoken on contemporary cultural problems. When considering the more socially and politically engaged nature of Ælfric's later writings,
it is useful to recall that Ælfric composed all of his major works after leaving
the Old Minster, Winchester—a monastery situated in the town that was
both home to the royal family and the intellectual center of the Benedictine
reforms—and taking up residence at two fairly secluded monasteries: first
at Cerne Abbas, in Dorset, where he lived from ca. 987–1005, and then at
Eynsham, where he served as abbot from 1005 until his death, ca. 1010. It is
as though the more cloistered Ælfric became, and the more physically distanced from the court and the key political figures in lay society, the more
he relied on texts as a proxy for his physical presence and as a means of
maintaining a voice in the social and political issues of his time. Ælfric's
Esther was most likely composed between 1002 and 1005, and it exhibits the
strong engagement with contemporary politics characteristic of Ælfric's
later works.[3] In spite of an increased interest in understanding Ælfric's writings as cultural artifacts, however, *Esther* has received little attention.[4]

Focusing on points in *Esther* where he departs from his Latin sources, I
argue that Ælfric uses the Old Testament queens Vashti and Esther to create an exemplar for contemporary queenship during a historical moment
that witnessed significant changes in the social and symbolic roles available
to Anglo-Saxon queens.[5] However, in the process of modeling roles for
royal women, Ælfric encounters a series of problems around larger and more
culturally pervasive issues, such as communal faith, marriage, and female
beauty and sexual practice. Through selective translation of his sources and
adoption of a complex set of lexical and symbolic strategies, Ælfric negoti-
ates these problems so as to transform the two Old Testament queens into
exemplars who might more effectively convey the ethical and social direc-
tives of the late tenth- and early eleventh-century Benedictine reformers.
The biblical story of a queen who saves her people from a royal mandate of
genocide becomes, for Ælfric, an occasion to propagate reformist ideologies
of gender, marriage, and lay spirituality, and thus becomes a way to en-

hance our understanding of the role that literature played in the Benedictine reforms. While Ælfric's portrayal of the two queens varies in the extent to which it reproduces the views and representational strategies that were characteristic of reformist thought, it nevertheless consistently points to his firm belief that characters of extreme wealth and social privilege could serve as models across boundaries of both rank and social station and exert a cultural impact that extended far beyond the royal palace. Tracing Ælfric's treatment of the two biblical queens offers additional evidence of his belief that Old Testament characters were vibrant and malleable figures who could be metaphorically resurrected from the past and mobilized and refigured to create textual exemplars for addressing contemporary cultural concerns. In the case of *Esther*, Ælfric's queenly exemplars serve as a means of promoting stricter ideals of faith and domestic social order in a nation that found itself increasingly destabilized in the face of ever-encroaching Danish forces.

Esther and Lay Belief

Esther was frequently presented to early medieval queens as an exemplar of piety and, more specifically, as a model of how a queen might strengthen the faith of her husband and her people. Hrabanus Maurus, bishop of Fulda, dedicated his commentaries on Judith (A.D. 834) and Esther (836) to the empress Judith, the second wife of Louis the Pious, urging her to "always place Esther, a queen like you, before the eyes of your heart, as someone to be imitated in every act of piety and sanctity."[6] Less than a decade later (841–51), Hrabanus rededicated both commentaries to the empress Ermengard, wife of Louis's son Lothar I.[7] In 876 Pope John VIII sent a letter to the empress Richildis, wife of Charles the Bald, begging her to act as an advocate of the Christian Church, claiming that "you will be for the Church of Christ near [your] pious husband in the way of that holy Esther who was near her husband on behalf of the Israelite people."[8] Similarly, the 856 coronation *ordo* for the marriage of Judith to Æthelwulf, the father of Alfred the Great, twice invokes Esther as a model for the new queen. She is mentioned once in a list along with several other Old Testament women: "I pledge you, a chaste and modest virgin, to one man, as a future wife, just as these holy women were to their husbands: Sarah, Rebecca, Rachel, Esther, Judith, Anna, Naomi."[9] Esther then appears again, after the anointing, in a description of her effects upon the king: "That you [God], by means of her [Esther's] prayers, inclined the savage heart of the king toward mercy and salvation for those believing in you."[10]

In spite of these apparent precedents, there is no direct evidence that Ælfric composed *Esther* for any particular queen, or indeed for any specific audience. The text survives only in a transcription made by the antiquarian William L'Isle (1569?–1637), whose obsession with preserving Old English biblical text was, unfortunately, matched by an equally profound lack of interest in preserving Anglo-Saxon authorial commentary, which may explain why *Esther*—unlike Ælfric's adaptations of other biblical texts such as Kings, Judith, and portions of Genesis—contains no prefatory remarks or other commentary that might point to an intended audience.[11] Ælfric's interest in using Esther as an exemplar of queenship is, however, suggested by the way he names her throughout his translation. Whereas the Latin sources tend to refer to Esther by her proper name, Ælfric rarely does so, referring to her most often simply as *cwen*, "queen"—much as he does in the case of Jezebel.[12] While Ælfric's practice of naming Esther may be in part due to the formal constraints of alliterative prose, it also points to a desire to dissociate the Jewish queen from her status as a particular historical personage so as to create a more generic exemplar of queenship for Anglo-Saxon readers.

Ælfric's only surviving remark on *Esther* appears in his *Letter to Sigeweard* (1005), in which he asserts:

> Hester seo cwen, þe hire kynn ahredde, hæfð eac ane boc on þisum getele, for ðan þe Godes lof ys gelogod þæron; ða ic awende on Englisc on ure wisan sceortlice.

———

> Esther the queen, who saved her people, also has one book in this number because the praise of God is contained therein, which I have briefly translated into English in our idiom.[13]

Although this statement occurs as part of a long list of explanatory remarks that Ælfric provides on other Old Testament books, it is nevertheless distinguished from them by a slightly stronger tone of defensiveness, or the perceived need not only to explain but also to justify Esther's inclusion among these other books. This tonal difference suggests Ælfric's tacit acknowledgment of the heated debates that Esther had provoked among his intellectual predecessors. Such debates tended to center on the text's lack of overt piety and, by extension, its deserved canonical status; far from containing "Godes lof" (praise of God) in abundance, the Hebrew original of the book of Esther contains no references to God at all, nor to any religious practices except for fasting. Although the various translations of Esther into Greek were augmented with a series of lengthy additions that heightened the religious tenor of the text (hereafter, the Additions), Esther was not given a secure place in Christian Scripture until the Council of Carthage in 397 and remained unpopular among Christian commentators for quite some time.[14] For Ælfric, such problems were somewhat mitigated by the Latin sources with which he was most likely working. The Vulgate, for instance, contains numerous references to both God and prayer, all of which are taken from the Greek Additions: when Jerome translated the Hebrew text into Latin, he appended these Greek-based verses mainly to the end of the text, with prefatory remarks signaling that these were passages "nec in Hebraeo nec apud ullum fertur Interpretum" (not found in the Hebrew or in any of the commentaries).[15] Like Jerome, Ælfric also places his most detailed discussions of piety at the end of Esther, but rather than offering strict translations of the Additions he treats them quite freely. Most notably, he consistently heightens Esther's faith, crediting the queen not only with a profound personal piety but also with a capacity for proselytizing, as, for example, in the case of her husband. While the Vulgate does offer a rather oblique suggestion that the king converted (16:15–16), Ælfric makes the point far more clearly, and also directly attributes the king's emergent belief in God and pursuit of righteous works to his wife Esther:[16]

> *And se cyning wearð gerihtlæht þurh þære cwene geleafan*
> *gode to wurðmynte, þe ealle þing gewylt.*
> *And he herode god, þe hine geuferode*
> *and to cyninge geceas ofer swilcne anweald.*
> *And he wæs rihtwis and rædfast on weorcum.*
> And he hæfde oþerne naman Artarxerses.
>
> (323–28)

And the king was corrected through the belief of the queen to worship God who controls all things. And he praised God who honored him and chose him as a king over such a realm. And he was righteous and resolute in works. And he had another name, Artaxerxes.

The concluding reference to Ahasuerus's other name as "Artarxerses" is most likely intended to introduce readers to the Greek-based form of the king's name, which is often used in patristic commentaries, Old Latin versions of Esther, and the final chapters of the Vulgate.[17] However, because Ælfric invokes this supplementary name immediately after mentioning the king's newfound acknowledgment of God, audiences familiar with accounts of conversion in such texts as Bede's *Historia Ecclesiastica* and Cynewulf's *Elene,* in which religious converts receive a new name, may have read the reference accordingly, and thus been further convinced of Esther's ability to effect her husband's wholesale spiritual transformation.

As well as an ability to promote religious belief within her immediate home, Ælfric also credits Esther with similar capabilities within her community:

Þis wearð þa geforþod and hi on friþe wunedon
þurh þære cwene þingunge, þe him þa geheolp
and fram deaþe ahredde þurh hire drihtnes fultum,
þe heo on gelyfde on Abrahames wisan.
Þa Iudeiscan eac wundorlice blissodon,
þæt hi swilcne forespræcan him afunden hæfdon,
and heoldon þa godes æ þæs þe glædlicor
æfter Moyses wissunge, þæs mæran heretogan.

(312–19)

This was then carried out and they lived in peace through the intercession of the queen who helped them and saved them from death through the help of her Lord, whom she believed in according to the way of Abraham. Moreover, the Jews rejoiced wonderfully *that they had found such an intercessor for themselves and held the law of God the more gladly according to the instruction of Moses, the great commander.*

What is most striking about these lines is not simply that they establish the idea of the queen as an intercessor between God and her people, but how clearly they reveal Ælfric's intent to highlight spiritual intercession as a crucial, if not the most important, role that the queen plays in the text as a whole. The opening remarks seem designed to summarize the queen's political maneuverings to convince the king that her people should be allowed to live in peace and should be spared from bodily harm; by the end of the passage, however, political intercession has undergone a noticeable transformation and taken on a far more spiritual gloss. The juxtaposition of the Jewish people's joy in Esther-as-intercessor, and their renewed zeal for God's law, effectively works to suggest that Esther's intercession was primarily responsible for promoting the spiritual rather than the political welfare of her community, thus lending a very different sense to the phrase that the queen "saved [her people] from death," namely, that the death from which Esther saved them was more than simply physical.

This movement away from the political and toward the spiritual is characteristic of the way that Ælfric treats Esther throughout the text: he consistently enhances and celebrates her efficacy in spiritual matters, but tends to overlook or downplay her participation in secular, political affairs. This tendency is lucidly illustrated toward the end of *Esther* when the king distributes rewards to both Esther and her uncle Mordecai. The Vulgate clearly denotes three exchanges of wealth: to Esther the king gives Haman's *domus*, a term that here suggests both an actual residence and its surrounding lands (8:1, 8:7); to Mordecai he gives his personal ring (8:2); and then Esther gives Mordecai jurisdiction over her *domus* (8:2). In Ælfric's version, these exchanges are changed only slightly, but the difference is striking: Esther is depicted as not having any part in the transference of jurisdiction over royal property to her kinsman Mordecai.

Lacking the power to grant control over royal lands, Ælfric's Esther is similarly restricted in her capacity to serve as a royal counselor, again reducing the sense that she wields any direct political influence. Instead it is Esther's role as an intercessor that Ælfric places at center stage, building upon the biblical account's depiction of Esther pleading with her husband and closing his narrative, as we have seen, by adding several lines that call attention to the queen's intercessory functions (312–13, 316–17). We might recall that Ælfric's treatment of counsel in his homilies, *Kings*, and *De Auguriis* suggests that, for him, counsel was indeed intercessory in nature: to provide counsel was to serve as a channel for either God's Word or that of the devil.

However, it also worth acknowledging that when considered less in relation to their divine or demonic sources and more in terms of their political influence, counsel and intercession are two very different practices: in the former, external input is sought as part of the process of deciding upon a future course of action, while in the latter, external input is recognized only for the purposes of modifying decisions that have already been made. Throughout *Esther*, Ælfric carefully differentiates between these two practices through a series of lexical choices that clearly define the king's men as counselors and the king's wife as an intercessor. Ælfric's descriptions of the king's thanes rely heavily on Old English words that clearly mean that these men have been formally designated as members of the royal counsel: he refers to them twice as the *witan*, "royal council" (46, 106), and frequently claims that these men provide *ræd*, "counsel" (47, 48, 106). By contrast, Ælfric never describes Esther either as a member of the *witan* or as a provider of *ræd*, referring to her only as a *forespræca*, "intercessor" (317), or as one who provides *þingung*, "mediation" (313).

What is most striking about Ælfric's depiction of the queen Esther—his emphasis on her power in spiritual affairs and lack of power in more secular matters, such as land administration or formal political counsel—is how selectively this portrait of queenship engages with the actual roles of contemporary Anglo-Saxon queens. While late tenth- and early eleventh-century queens such as Ælfthryth and Emma were indeed considered valuable patrons of churches and monasteries and strong supporters of the faith, documentary evidence suggests that these queens were also active participants in more secular affairs.[18] Tenth-century land-grant charters reveal that Ælfthryth exercised significant influence over her son Æthelred's political life: she acted as regent for Æthelred, who was not more than twelve when he became king, and was often present at meetings of the royal council to make decisions regarding the distribution of royal lands.[19] Similarly, the frequency with which Emma's signature appears on royal land-grant charters suggests that she too attended meetings of the royal council and had a voice in the distribution of royal lands.[20] Considered historically, Ælfric's depiction of queenship in *Esther* raises a difficult question: if late Anglo-Saxon documentary evidence verifies that contemporary queens served as active participants in such secular political affairs as land administration and the provision of formal royal counsel, why then does Ælfric create an exemplar of queenship that minimizes these roles and instead channels the queen's energy into spiritual edification, intercession, and the exercise of a type of political power that is conspicuously marked as informal and personal in nature?

One possible response to this question is offered by Mary Clayton, who reads *Esther* as a reaction to the Saint Brice's Day massacre, and as Ælfric's attempt to forestall future bloodshed of the order that ensued on November 13, 1002, when Æthelred commanded the slaughter of all of the Danes in England. Focusing on parallels between the contemporary Danes and the biblical Jews, Clayton suggests that "Ælfric's *Esther* may . . . have been deliberately written with Emma in mind . . . as a model of how Emma should or could have acted," namely, as a peacemaking intercessor who might have effectively restrained her husband from ordering a Danish holocaust, just as Esther was able to prevent Ahasuerus from killing the Jews.[21]

While a desire to influence the behavior of an individual queen may well partly account for Ælfric's depiction of queenship in *Esther*, it is nevertheless worth remembering that Ælfric intended at least some of his Old Testament translations to reach numerous readers from a diverse spectrum of social classes.[22] Even when writing for an individual patron, as in his *Letter to Sigeweard*, Ælfric openly acknowledges that texts were often received by audiences far broader than an author's immediate patron.[23] Moreover Ælfric's repeated injunctions that later writers not reorder or miscopy his texts suggest that he envisioned them not simply for short-term consumption but for more enduring use.[24] Given the fairly expansive scope of his imagined audiences, it is less likely that Ælfric intended Esther to serve as a behavioral model for a particular Anglo-Saxon queen than as an exemplar who might effectively create a series of broader public expectations regarding the social roles that ought to be assumed by both contemporary and future queens.

Indeed, there was perhaps no more opportune time than the early eleventh century for Ælfric to initiate attempts to construct cultural ideals of queenship. As Pauline Stafford argues, late tenth- and early eleventh-century England witnessed a host of significant changes in the social and symbolic power of queens: the establishment of new titles for queens and queen mothers, the increased use of public anointing ceremonies for queens, the formal appointment of a queen as the official patron of female monasteries, and the regular appearance of queens' signatures on royal charters.[25] Ælfric's depiction of Esther as a queen who lacked the ability to transfer property freely and whose agency was confined to the roles of intercessor and spiritual counselor is thus somewhat removed from the actual roles of such contemporary queens as Ælfthryth and Emma. His portrait of Esther as an arbiter of lay piety and agent of conversion bears a marked resemblance instead to seventh- and eighth-century queens as depicted in the letters of such popes as Gregory the Great and Boniface V, in which queens are portrayed as strong supporters of the faith and as potential catalysts for the conversion of their husbands and people.[26] Far from representing the realities of late Anglo-Saxon queenship, Ælfric's *Esther* is thus an attempt to create an exemplar that would thrust the function of the queen back in time, confining her to the traditional roles of intercessor and spiritual adviser—familiar, readily available models of Anglo-Saxon queenship that Ælfric would have known well through earlier works.

In an important study of late medieval queenship, Paul Strohm reminds us that the celebration of queenly intercession in a wide range of late twelfth- and thirteenth-century literary and historical writings corresponded with a decline and deinstitutionalization of queens' actual social power.[27] This inverse relationship between textual representations and social formations leads Strohm to suggest that the warmth with which clerics and chroniclers promoted intercessory queenship is "cause for added suspicion," and that intercession may have been "more likely to dupe women than to empower them" by promising women a form of power that was in fact "power premised on exceptional vulnerability . . . [and] on an exclusion from the centers of mundane authority."[28] It is tempting, then, to follow Strohm's logic and to view Ælfric's celebration of queenly intercession in *Esther* as indicative of veiled resistance to the increasing participation of contemporary queens in formal political affairs, and as an attempt to limit queens' power both by consigning it to the margins and by reifying a Pauline spousal dynamic premised on the idea of the submissive wife's subordinating herself to an all-powerful but indulgent husband.

Yet had Ælfric seen Esther as an opportunity to promote female subservience within marriage, it seems rather odd that he overlooked some fairly obvious opportunities offered by his source texts to do so. The Vulgate makes much of the disobedient queen Vashti's punishment as a lesson in humility to wives of all social classes: after Vashti is exiled, one of the king's counselors presses for an edict to be published throughout the entire empire that would state, "Let all wives, as well of the greater as of the lesser, give honour to their husbands" (1:20), an idea that "pleased the king" (1:21), who immediately sends out letters so that "every nation could hear and read, in divers languages and characters, that the husbands should be rulers and

masters in their houses" (1:22). Given that Ælfric was writing during a period often characterized as one during which gender boundaries were hardening and women's autonomy increasingly restricted—with the writings of
both Ælfric and his contemporaries often seen as the strongest evidence for
the increased misogyny of the period—one might expect that Ælfric's *Esther* would actively engage with these biblical discussions of a national program designed to encourage wifely subservience at all social levels.[29] But
Ælfric omits these injunctions for wifely subservience found in his sources
and, in fact, seems uninterested in any of the episodes in the biblical text
that openly advocate the subordination of women, either royal or otherwise.
In light of this apparent disinterest, Ælfric's treatment of queenship in
Esther—his attempts to confine Esther to the role of spiritual mediator and
to underscore the informal and personal nature of her political power—is
not, I would argue, an attempt to limit the power of royal women *qua*
women. However, precisely what it was is slightly more difficult to say.

A first clue to Ælfric's depiction of queenship in *Esther* may be found in
his evolving views on royal power during Æthelred's reign. We have seen
that by the 990s, Ælfric had become somewhat disillusioned with Æthelred's politics and thus wary of any political or social changes that might
sanction increases in royal power. Christopher Jones convincingly argues
that Ælfric's *Letter to the Monks of Eynsham* (ca. 1005) is marked by a retreat
from the overt royalism that was so much a part of earlier reformist ideologies, suggesting that Ælfric's views of Æthelred had not improved after the
king's attempts to make amends for his youthful indiscretions, and that, if
anything, by the new millennium Ælfric had become even more wary of
royal power.[30] In *Kings,* Ælfric's distrust of royal power manifests itself in a
negative exemplar of queenship that seeks to highlight the dangers of autonomous queenly authority as exhibited in the figure of Jezebel. In *Esther,*
Ælfric's distrust of royal power manifests itself in a positive exemplar of
queenship that seeks to highlight the national benefits of queenly authority
that is confined within the royal household. Yet both texts, I would argue,
reflect anxieties that center less on individual queens or on female power
than they do on royal power and the possibility of its extension through the
formal sanctioning of queenly authority. This line of reasoning finds further support in Ælfric's treatment of queenship in his *Letter to the Monks of
Eynsham,* which, though based largely on the *Regularis concordia,* quietly
omits the *Concordia's* clear prescription that the monks' so-called *psalmi
familiares* or *psalmi pro benefactoribus* should include psalms specifically

devoted to the queen.[31] Stating only that psalms should be sung "pro rege et pro benefactoribus" (for the king and benefactors), Ælfric effaces the idea of the queen as a royal agent to whom the monks might appeal in her own right, independent of the king.

Yet even as Ælfric's treatment of queenship in both *Esther* and the *Letter to the Monks of Eynsham* suggests a departure from the royalist leanings of earlier reformers, his emphasis on spiritual queenship in *Esther* concomitantly reveals a distinct indebtedness to them, offering as it does a consummate example of their tendency to portray the royal family as spiritual guardians of the nation. Motivated largely by a desire to extricate monasteries from aristocratic control, reformers cultivated—or at least professed to cultivate—royal patronage over that of the local nobility, attempting to forge a sense of England as one people united under the spiritual guardianship of a tightly knit Church and royal family. Symbolic attempts to express the union of reformed monastic and royal interests are apparent in the period's art, which placed a heightened emphasis upon the idea of the king and queen as both earthly representatives of the heavenly court and as intercessors for the people's spiritual welfare.[32] So too written texts from the period advanced a notion of the royal family as spiritual guardians of the nation. The *Regularis concordia* celebrates an ideal of harmonious relations between the Church and the royal family, claiming that the monasteries are forbidden to acknowledge the overlordship of any secular persons, while commanding them to draw freely on the sovereign power of the king and queen and to have access to both when desired. In accordance with this, the *Concordia* prescribes extensive prayers for the king, queen, and royal family, positioning both the king and queen as protectors of monastic life, with Edgar responsible for guiding and protecting male monasteries, and his queen, Ælfthryth, assuming a similar role with respect to female communities.[33] The royal family's new responsibilities for national spirituality as outlined in the *Concordia* are features of the reform program which are specific to England, with no precedents in similar Continental customaries.[34] Ælfric's portrait of spiritual queenship in *Esther* thus suggests a possible route to renewing communal faith that had been marked as uniquely English in nature.

Ælfric's depiction of queenship in *Esther* embraces not only an earlier thematics of "spiritual queenship" but also the more general rhetoric of the reform movement, which was similarly specific to England, in that it entailed a celebration of its own cultural past. As such scholars as Antonia Gransden, Patrick Wormald, and Christopher Jones have argued, the reforms were characterized by a rather complicated sense of nostalgia, a desire to return to two different pasts: a faraway Anglo-Saxon golden age, with its firmly entrenched monastic episcopacy; and the more immediate past of Edgar's reign, in which monasteries flourished, Danish invasions were minimal, and the monastic orders were able to depend on wholesale support from the royal family.[35] Ælfric's emphasis in *Esther* on the queen as spiritual protector of the nation captures both of these senses of the past: a desire to return both to the seventh and early eighth centuries, in which queens were strongly associated with England's conversion, and also to the reign of Edgar, whose queen, Ælfthryth, was well known for her support of monastic life and communal faith.

That Ælfric's *Esther* might suggest a desire to return to the past is perhaps not all that surprising, for the period in which he composed the text was a deeply troubled one. By the start of the eleventh century, several decades of renewed Danish incursions had left the English forces significantly weakened, and, as Malcolm Godden has shown, Ælfric frequently looked to the Old Testament for paradigms that might provide possible explanations for England's current political crises.[36] While Ælfric explored a variety of different paradigms for comprehending the invasions—viewing them as the age-old conflict between the forces of the devil and followers of God, or as tribulations that were part of a final and inevitable apocalypse— his writings often reflect an adherence to the belief that the Danish attacks were a divine punishment occasioned by England's dual failure in the realms of both monastic and lay life, and that increased prayer and attention to righteous living among both communities offered a possible remedy for these national political ills.[37] This belief is forcefully articulated in his homily "De oratione Moysi" (On the Prayer of Moses), in which Ælfric depicts Joshua's military success as a direct result of Moses' prayers and urges readers to understand this relationship between prayer and political well-being as an exemplar for contemporary life:

> Be þisum we magon tocnawen þæt we cristene sceolan
> on ælcere earfoðnisse æfre to gode clypian.
> and his fultumes biddan mid fullum geleafan.
> gif he ðonne nele his fultum us don

ne ure bene gehyran. þonne bið hit swutol
Þæt we mid yfelum dædum hine ær gegremedon.[38]

————

From this we can recognize that we Christians should in every distress call to God and ask for his help; if he will not give us help nor hear our petition it will be clear that we have angered him previously with our evil deeds.

The sense that there exists an underlying causal relation between the nation's faith and its political health is less overtly articulated, but nevertheless very much present, in *Esther*, which repeatedly portrays the queen turning to her faith, and encouraging her people to do likewise, during moments of intense national crisis. For example, immediately after Esther has learned of the plot to destroy her people, she commands that "hire cynn eall sceolde fæstan þreo dagas on an *and godes fultum biddan*" (all of her people should fast continually for three days *and pray for God's help;* 173–74), a passage in which Ælfric has redirected the focus of the people's prayers away from Esther and toward God: in the Vulgate, Esther does not command her people to pray to God but rather to "orate pro me" (pray for me; 4:16). Similarly, Ælfric frames Esther's own response to her people's imminent danger as a program of fasting and prayer: "And heo sylf eall swa eac swylce fæste, *biddende æt gode, þæt he geburge þam folce and eallum þam manncynne on swa micelre frecednysse*" (And likewise she herself would also fast, *praying to God that he might save the people and all of mankind in such great danger;* 175–77). And when Esther begs her husband to prepare an edict ensuring peace for the Jews, Ælfric adds that her request for national salvation was "*mid godes ege onbryrd*" (*inspired with the fear of God;* 296).

The overall effect of Ælfric's added references to prayer and faith in *Esther* is to create a much more direct link than does the biblical text between public faith and national salvation. Although Ælfric never spells out the topical implications of the Esther narrative, the parallels between the Jews and the English, between Ælfric's construction of the believing queen and his vision of a faithful Anglo-Saxon populace, are fairly obvious: just as Esther brought about the salvation of her people through increased faith, so too, Ælfric seems to be suggesting, could a more faithful populace bring about England's salvation, a united and victorious nation free from the grasp of the diabolical Danes.[39] In Ælfric's translation, then, the queen functions as a metaphor for an impeccably faithful English people, an idea supported by the fairly standard interpretation of the queen by commentators and homilists as a symbol for the communal body of the Church, or the congregation of Christian believers.[40] Given Ælfric's concerns about the rapidly splintering faith of the English people, as well as the material realities of Danish divisiveness, the queen acts as a vehicle for Ælfric to envision a wholeness of people and place very different from what actually existed in early eleventh-century England, a wholeness that, *Esther* suggests, might be effected through prayer and communal faith, championed by a queen wholly devoted to these matters, such as could be found in the form of an Old Testament queen filtered through nostalgic remembrance of the queens found in Ælfric's own cultural past. Yet if Ælfric's backward-looking portrait of queenship in *Esther* exhibits a similar tendency to glorify the past as is found in modes of remembrance that would be categorized within modern Western culture under the broad rubric of "nostalgia," it also strongly resists such categorization by virtue of its underlying goals. Within modern Western culture, nostalgia tends to be characterized as a kind of temporal pathology, an inability to fully acknowledge the present which thus occasions psychic return to a fictionalized past.[41] However, Ælfric's resurrection of an imagined spiritual queenship from days past is marked less by a yearning to return to a bygone Anglo-Saxon golden age of spiritual queenship than by a desire to harness the energies of that age for addressing the problems of his own time and effecting social change. Queenship in *Esther*, then, is perhaps less accurately characterized as nostalgic than as visionary: an attempt to mobilize the rhetoric of retrospection in order to end the miseries of the present and, it is hoped, to recapture the future.

The End of the Royal Marriage

Within early medieval culture, queens symbolized not only the perfect union between Christ and the Church but also the more secular union between husband and wife. In his *De rectoribus christianis,* the ninth-century Irishman Sedulius Scottus—whose writings influenced Anglo-Saxon ideologies of rulership[42]—invokes Esther to explain the symbolic complexities of the royal marriage.

As Christ united the Church to him with a chaste love,
so a wife should cleave to her husband;
in her heart gentle simplicity like the beauty of a dove
should always abound.
Piety, prudence, and sacred authority should adorn her,
just as gracious Esther shone.
A king and queen should cherish the bonds of peace;
in both there should be agreement and concord . . .
if a ruler and his wife are to rule the people justly,
let them first rule their own family.[43]

While Sedulius focuses upon a celebration of nuptial harmony, presenting Esther as the exemplary royal wife, the biblical narrative opens with a very different example: that of Ahasuerus's first wife, Vashti. Far from "cleav[ing] to her husband" and "cherish[ing] the bonds of peace . . . agreement and concord," Vashti separates herself from her husband and incites his wrath by defying his command that she appear at his banquet and display her beauty to his guests. Fearing that this very public show of marital insurrection within the palace would set a precedent for wifely disobedience and usher in social anarchy within their own homes (1:15–21), Ahasuerus's counselors advise him to cast aside Vashti and find another wife. Indeed it is this spectacular "divorce" that initiates the process that leads to Esther's becoming queen.

For Ælfric, however, this plot would have raised some quite serious problems: while wifely repudiation and serial monogamy were indeed common practices among Anglo-Saxon kings, such acts were also strictly regulated by both secular and ecclesiastical law-codes, and increasingly so in the late tenth and eleventh centuries, when reformers strove to redefine and more strictly regulate a range of marital practices including spousal continence, observance of approved times for sexual relations, and, most notably, wifely repudiation.[44] While late tenth- and early eleventh-century vernacular penitentials do indeed outline numerous conditions legitimating spousal separation and subsequent remarriage—including differences of religion, female adultery, one partner's desire to enter monastic life, and male impotence[45]—Ælfric's homilies and pastoral letters reveal that his own position on spousal repudiation and remarriage was far more strict. In his homily

"Monday. On the Greater Litany," for example, Ælfric emphasizes the indissolubility of marriage, warning that

> Ure drihten forbead. mid his agenum muðe. ða yfelan twæmincge
> betwux æwum ðus; Swa hwa swa his æwe forlæt. and oðer genimð.
> he við þonne eawbræce. and eac forligr;[46]

———

> Our Lord forbade with his own mouth the evil separation between
> two married people thus: "Whoever abandons his lawful wife and
> takes another is then an adulterer and also a fornicator."

Ælfric's Latin and Old English letters to Wulfstan express similarly negative sentiments toward remarriage: the letters give no approved reasons for remarriage except the death of a spouse; they include prohibitions against the attendance of priests and their blessing of second marriages; and they prescribe strict penances for those who do remarry. Ælfric's opposition to remarriage is also evident in his Old English letter to his diocesan bishop, Wulfsige of Sherborne (ca. 992–1002), in which he grudgingly admits that "se læweda mot swa-þeah be þæs apostoles leafe oðre siðe wifigan, gif his wif him ætfylð" (the layman might, however, with the apostle's permission [Paul], marry a second time if he loses his wife), but prefaces his remark with the assertion that "ne nan preost ne mot beon æt þam bryd-lacum ahwær þær man æft wifað, oððe wif eft ceorlað, ne hy togædere bletsian. Swylce man bycnige him, swa-þæt him selre wære, þæt hy wunodon on clænnysse" (no priest may be at the marriage anywhere where a man takes another wife or a woman takes another husband, nor bless them together. One may thus indicate to them that it would be better for them if they lived in chastity).[47] Given Ælfric's fierce opposition to spousal repudiation and remarriage, as well as his grave concerns—most famously expressed in his "Preface to Genesis"—that laypeople might understand Old Testament figures as exemplars of marriage and sexual practices, Esther must have presented Ælfric with a fairly serious problem: how was he to present her as an exemplary queen, when her queenship was contingent on the king's repudiation of his first wife, Vashti, an act that boldly flouted the same ecclesiastical laws that Ælfric was struggling to uphold?[48]

One way in which Ælfric attempts to deal with this problem is by increasing the contrast between Vashti and Esther. Whereas the Latin versions of Esther contain three named women—Vashti, Esther, and Zares (Haman's wife)—Ælfric excises Zares from the narrative, thus enhancing the sense of Vashti and Esther as foils for one another, as positive and negative exemplars of queenship. So too Ælfric enhances Esther's piety and humility, while concomitantly blackening Vashti's character, presenting her as self-aggrandizing and disrespectful to her husband. For example, the Latin sources simply state that "Vasthi quoque regina fecit convivium feminarum" (Also Vashti the queen made a feast for the women; 1:9), but Ælfric creates a rather incriminating rationale behind Vashti's feast through his claim that it was one "heo wolde habban to hire mærþe" (she wanted to have for her [own] glory; 30–31).

But it is the particular model of marriage that Ælfric draws upon which most forcefully legitimates Ahasuerus's repudiation of his first wife. Throughout the text, Ælfric depicts the king's two marriages not according to the Christian scheme of marriage as the inviolable union between Christ and the Church, but according to the Anglo-Saxon model of marriage as a bond between lord and retainer.[49] The term *cynehlaford*, "liege-lord," is used seven times throughout the text, invoked interchangeably to describe the relationship between the king and his wives, Vashti and Esther, as well as the bond between the king and his thanes. However, Ælfric most often refers to the king simply as "se cyning," reserving the term *cynehlaford* to call attention to moments during which the strength of these bonds of faith is called into question (56, 112, 185, 220, 279, 288, 297). For example, when describing the disloyal thanes who are plotting to kill the king, Ælfric claims that these men "woldon berædan swiðe unrihtlice heora cynehlaford" (desired, very unrighteously, to betray their liege-lord; 111–12). It is thus significant that in discussing Vashti's refusal to appear at the banquet, the king's counselors claim that "seo cwen forseah hire cynehlaford" (the queen scorned her liege-lord; 56), a departure from the Latin, which simply states that Vashti refused "rex Asuerus" (King Assuerus; 1:17). By describing Vashti's behavior in the same terms as that of a king's disloyal thanes, Ælfric constructs her disobedience not as a private dispute between husband and wife but as a public violation of one of the most fundamental social bonds operative in Anglo-Saxon culture: the bond of loyalty between lord and retainer. Ahasuerus's repudiation of Vashti is thus figured not as a husband's personal decision to dismiss an unsuitable wife, but as a king's social obligation to discipline an unruly subject. A common punishment for breaking a pledge of loyalty was exile, and this is precisely how Ælfric depicts Vashti's punishment.[50] Whereas in the Latin sources, it is decided that "nequaquam ultra Vasthi ingrediatur ad regem" (Vasthi come in no more to the king; 1:19), in Ælfric's text the queen is not only prohibited from future contact with the king, but also exiled from the entire community of privilege in which she had previously moved: "þæt seo cwen Vasthi ne cume næfre heononforð into þinum pallente betwux þinum gebeorum" (that the queen Vashti should never come henceforth into your palace among your guests; 63–64).

If Ælfric depicts the marriage of King Ahasuerus and his first wife, Vashti, as the bond between lord and retainer gone awry, he portrays the king's second marriage to Esther as an idealization of this bond, an exemplar of absolute love between husband and wife figured as the reciprocal love between sovereign and subject. Ælfric's Latin source texts depict Esther as a queen who despises her royal status, hates her husband, and claims never to have either eaten at his table or rejoiced in anything except God since arriving at the royal court (14:15–18). In marked contrast, Ælfric's Esther appears genuinely to love and respect the king. Throughout the narrative, she refers to him as *leof*, "dear one" or "sir" (187, 252), the same term used by his thanes (53, 60), thus calling attention to the queen's dual status as loving wife and dutiful subject. Although the term *leof* is also used by the treacherous Haman (152), thus reminding that pronouncements of regard may at times be disingenuous, Ælfric never suggests that Esther's devotion to her husband is anything but real. By manipulating his source texts, then, and placing the king's two marriages into the familiar, readily available Anglo-Saxon model of marriage as a bond between lord and retainer, Ælfric transforms a biblical narrative whose plot depends on a transgression of ecclesiastical marital law into a model of the exemplary union between husband and wife.

The Two Queens' Bodies

The attempts of late Anglo-Saxon reformers to regulate lay marriage were part of their more general efforts during this period to heighten standards of sexual morality. While many of their discussions centered on priestly celibacy and strictness within the cloister, the monastic standards of chastity came, over time, to be urged on the laity in somewhat softened form. As such issues as monastic chastity, priestly celibacy, kingly monogamy, and sexual abstinence among the laity came increasingly to the fore, women's bodies and the desire they were thought to provoke tended to be seen as hindrances to promoting stricter ideals of sexual conduct.[51] Reformers' anxieties about the female body are evident in their efforts to eradicate mixed-sex devotional arrangements (i.e., double monasteries), to promote the increased cloistering of women religious, and to redefine cultural attitudes toward such formerly accepted social practices as concubinage.[52] These anxieties also find voice in Ælfric's discussions of the beautiful bodies of the two queens, Vashti and Esther.

All of the different versions of Esther remark on the queen's supreme beauty, and throughout his adaptation, Ælfric enhances the sense of Esther as extremely beautiful, often adding references to her beauty at points where there are none explicitly given in the Vulgate, as for example, when he remarks on Esther's "fægra nebwlite" (fair face; 89) or describes her as "on wæstme cyrten" (beautiful in form; 99). That Ælfric emphasizes Esther's beauty is not surprising, for such a move is indeed consistent both with his depictions of other pious heroines as extremely beautiful—Eugenia, Agnes, Agatha, Cecilia, Judith—as well as with ideologies of beauty in Anglo-Saxon texts: Anglo-Saxon writers, for the most part, tended to equate physical beauty with good and ugliness with evil.[53] This ideological link between beauty and virtue is particularly apparent in Old English biblical translations and saints' lives, and Ælfric could thus have reasonably expected his emphasis on Esther's beauty to serve as a shorthand means of calling attention to her virtue. Complicating such easy associations, however, is the fact that Esther's is not the only beautiful body in the narrative. The disobedient and self-aggrandizing queen Vashti is also described in Ælfric's Latin sources as extremely beautiful, a point that is central to the plot of the biblical narrative, for it explains why the king wants her to appear at his banquet in a public display. Vashti's beauty would have thus presented a very real problem for Ælfric: simply to eliminate it from his translation would have resulted in a confusing text; yet, to present Vashti as beautiful was to run the risk of his audiences' misreading such a representation and readily assuming that Vashti's beauty, like Esther's, was a sign of inner virtue. How, then, to disrupt the automatic cultural association between physical perfection and inner virtue? How to prevent his readers from interpreting all beautiful bodies in the same way?

One way Ælfric does so is through highly selective Old English translations of the terminology of beauty in his Latin sources. The Vulgate, for example, employs various forms of the adjective *pulchra*, "beautiful," or the noun *pulchritudo*, "beauty," as a means of interchangeably denoting the physical beauty of Esther, Vashti, and the multitude of unnamed virgins presented to King Ahasuerus. Esther is described as "pulchra nimis" (very beautiful; 2:7) or as being pleasing "incredibili pulchritudine" (on account of her incredible beauty; 2:15), Vashti is "pulchra valde" (very beautiful; 1:11), and the unnamed virgins are "virgines pulchrae" (beautiful virgins; 2:8).[54] The Vulgate's indiscriminate use of the adjective *pulchra* as a term equally applicable to almost all of the women in the text masks any sense of Esther's beauty as unique or in any way linked to inner virtue. Likewise, the Vulgate describes Esther as "decora facie" (beautiful in appearance; 2:7) and "formonsa [*sic*] valde" (very beautiful in form; 2:15), or through adjectives of exteriority that locate Esther's beauty alongside that of all the other women in the narrative: squarely in the realm of the senses. However, Ælfric is far more selective in translating these terms. In the case of Vashti, for example, he only uses the adjective *wlitig*, "beautiful," or the substantive *wlite*, "beauty," to describe her. When introducing Vashti, Ælfric simply states that "seo wæs swiðe wlitig" (she was very beautiful; 28), a phrase echoed twelve lines later when he describes her as "swiðe wlitig on hiwe" (very beautiful in appearance; 40), a translation of the Vulgate's "pulchra valde" (1:11). The pairing of the adjective *wlitig* with the additional phrase *on hiwe* suggests an attempt on Ælfric's part to link *wlitig* with physical or sensual beauty, a denotative move that would have found support in numerous other vernacular texts that use the term *wlitig* to invoke beauty that appeals mainly to the senses: the earth in *Phoenix* (l. 7a), the aroma of the panther in *Panther* (l. 65a), and the beautiful, ancient sword in Grendel's cave (*Beowulf*, 1662b).[55] While Esther is in fact described twice as *wlitig*, the adjective is always accompanied by reference to her *fægernysse*: she is either "wlitig mædenmann on wundorlicre fægernysse" (beautiful maiden of wonderful fairness; 82) or "swiðe wlitig on wundorlicre gefægernysse" (very beautiful of wonderful fairness; 97).

The adjective *fæger*, as a term for beauty in Anglo-Saxon culture, was laden with religious significance and resonated with a multiplicity of meanings.[56] As a description of the Phoenix symbolizing Christ's resurrection (*Phoenix*, 291a), Eve before the Fall (*Genesis*, 457a), the angels in *Genesis* (79a), and Christ's body in *The Dream of the Rood* (73a), the term frequently suggested physical beauty that was linked to unblemished character and righteous belief.[57] Ælfric capitalizes on the term's associative richness in his first description of Esther. While the Vulgate, when introducing Esther, focuses solely on her physical beauty, Ælfric adds a brief description of the pious environment in which she was raised, forging an immediate and inextricable bond between the queen's physical beauty and her piety by describing both as *fæger*:

> and he mid him hæfde
> his broðor dohter, seo hatte Hester,
> wlitig mædenmann on wundorlicre fægernysse.
> *And he hi geforðode on fægerum þeawum*
> *æfter godes æ and his ege symle*
>
> (80–84)

---

and he [Mordecai] had with him his brother's daughter, who was named Esther, a beautiful maiden of wonderful fairness. *And he raised her in fair customs, always according to God's law, and in His continual awe.*

Having established this link between Esther's fair body and character, Ælfric repeatedly invokes the term *fæger* in relation to Esther: he refers to "hire fægra nebwlite" (her fair face; 89), a phrase that is not present in his Latin sources; he describes her as "swiðe wlitig on wuldorlicre gefægernysse" (very beautiful in wonderful fairness; 97), a translation from the Latin "formonsa valde et incredibili pulchritudine" (very beautiful and on account of her incredible beauty; 2:15); and where the Latin has Esther adorning herself in royal apparel (5:1), Ælfric simply claims that the queen is "swiðe fægeres hiwes" (very fair in appearance; 179). Significantly, neither Vashti nor anyone else in the text except Esther is ever described as *fæger*. Thus while Ælfric showcases the two queens' beautiful bodies, he also distinguishes between them through a carefully chosen set of Old English terms, which create the sense that Vashti's beauty is merely physical, unlike Esther's, which is the embodiment of her inner virtue.

Still, Ælfric, known for his tendency to construct hagiographic exemplars as clear and unambiguously moral figures, may have worried that his
careful terminological distinctions between the two queens' beauty could
be lost on readers inadequately attuned to such linguistic subtleties. He
thus further differentiates between the two queens by advancing a new and
carefully structured set of criteria for an ideal queen, in which physical
beauty is only one of several qualifying factors. These factors are clearly set
out as part of the plan to be undertaken immediately after the king has ban-
ished his first queen and is looking for a new one:

Hit wearþ þa gecweden þurh þæs cyninges witan,
þæt man ofaxode on eallum his rice,
gif ænig mæden ahwær mihte beon afunden
swa wlitiges hiwes, *þe him wurðe wære;*
and swilcere gebyrde, þe his gebedda wære;
and seo þænne fenge to Vasthies wurðmynte.

(70–75)

It was then said by the king's counselors that it should be asked
throughout the kingdom if there might anywhere be found any
maiden so beautiful in appearance *who would be worthy to him and
of such birth* that she might be his consort, and attain Vashti's
honor.

The criteria that Ælfric sets up to guide Ahasuerus's choice of a new
queen are strikingly different from the Vulgate, in which the only qualifica-
tions for queenship are physical beauty, feminine adornments, youth, virginity, and the ability to please the eyes of the king (2:3–4). While Ælfric
concurs that the ideal queen should be a beautiful virgin, he omits any mention of the fact that physical beauty should be heightened by outward adornments and adds that the ideal wife for King Ahasuerus would be a woman
who was not only beautiful but also *wurð,* "worthy," of the king and de-
scended from a suitable family. Moreover, by presenting physical beauty before mentioning the additional attributes of worth and birth, Ælfric creates

a structural system of reception in which the reader is coerced into looking beyond the queen's beauty and considering whether it is matched by a similarly fine character. This structural scheme is apparent throughout the text, as Ælfric repeatedly appends discussions of both Vashti's and Esther's characters immediately after his references to their beauty, thus forcing his readers to view physical beauty as only an initial qualification for an ideal queen, a surface that may or may not prove a reliable guide to what lies beneath. In the case of Vashti, for example, Ælfric introduces the queen through the statement that "his cwen hatte Vasthi, seo wæs swiðe wlitig" (his queen was named Vashti; she was very beautiful; 28). But, as we have seen, he immediately undermines Vashti's beauty by calling attention to her self-aggrandizement with the claim that the queen desired a banquet *"for her own glory"* (*to hire mærþe;* 31). Eight lines later, Ælfric again invokes Vashti's beauty, only to follow it with dismissive remarks about the queen's willfulness and wifely disobedience: *"Ac heo hit forsoc and nolde gehyrsumian him to his willan"* (*And she scorned it [the king's command] and did not want to be obedient to his will;* 42–43). By contrast, Ælfric's discussions of Esther's beauty are always buttressed by positive references to her character, as, for example, when he claims that Esther was "swiðe wlitig on wundorlicre gefægernysse and swiþe lufigendlic eallum onlociendum" (very beautiful in wonderful fairness and very lovely for all those observing her; 97–98) and then immediately afterward that she was *"wislice geþeawod"* (*wisely mannered;* 99).

Yet even as Ælfric encourages his readers to probe beneath beautiful female surfaces, he also capitalizes on Esther's immediate visual appeal, using it as a welcome substitute for the more problematic rationale that his Latin sources offer in explanation of Ahasuerus's choice of Esther as his new queen. Ælfric's sources depict Esther as one of numerous women who take part in an extensive series of queenship auditions: the women are first subjected to a one-year regimen of oiling and perfuming, each is then brought individually to the palace for one night and, if found to be "pleasing to the king," subsequently invited back for further consideration. Given Ælfric's consistently outspoken opposition to premarital sex, it is not surprising that he deletes all references to the royal harem, the preparation of female bodies, and Esther's overnight stay in the palace, replacing this material with a somewhat different explanation for why the king chooses Esther as his new queen:

Seo wearð þa gebroht and besæd þam cyninge.
And he hi sceawode and him sona gelicode
hire fægra nebwlite and lufode hi swiðe
ofer ealle þa oðre, þe he ær gesceawode.

(87–90)

She was then brought and placed near the king. And he observed her, and her fair face was immediately pleasing to him and he loved her greatly over all the others whom he had observed before.

The idea that sexual pleasure might provide an acceptable motive for choosing a royal wife has no place in Ælfric's text, which instead authorizes the incitement of the king's desire through recourse to verbs of spectatorship (*sceawode, gesceawode*) that are notably absent from the analogous scene in the biblical account (2:17). Ælfric configures sovereign love as solely a product of visual pleasure, thus transforming the royal marriage in *Esther* into one undertaken in strict accord with contemporary ecclesiastical prohibitions against premarital sex—for until the king marries Esther, he is just looking.

While maintaining the fiction of Esther's sexual integrity is of evident concern to Ælfric throughout *Esther,* occasionally even the subject of female chastity—a matter of such obsessive interest to Ælfric and his contemporaries—appears to be somewhat overshadowed by his intent to model roles for royal women. This competition between social morality and royal exemplarity is perhaps nowhere more evident than in the "garden scene," in which the king returns from his garden to find Esther and his counselor Haman in a rather problematic pose of intimacy:

Qui cum reversus esset de horto nemoribus consito et intrasset convivii locum repperit Aman super lectulum corruisse in quo iacebat Hester et ait etiam reginam vult opprimere me praesente in domo mea. (7:8)

And when the king came back out of the garden set with trees, and entered into the place of the banquet, he found Aman was fallen upon the bed on which Esther lay, and he said: He will force the queen also in my presence, in my own house.

Given Ælfric's characteristic reticence about explicit depictions of sexual matters, it is not surprising that he glosses over the more overtly sexual aspects of this scene. In Ælfric's text, there are no beds, the queen is upright rather than lying down, Haman's motives for lying at the queen's *feet* are clearly spelled out; and there is only the faintest suggestion of sexual impropriety:

Ac he hraþe sona
eft eode him inn. And efne Aman
þa niþer afeallen to þære cwene fotum,
þæt heo him gefultumode to his agenum feore.
Þa oflicode þam cyninge, þæt he læg hire swa gehende.

(270–74)

———

But he [the king] quickly afterwards came inside. And Haman merely fell down at the queen's feet, so that she might help him save his own life. This was displeasing to the king that he lay so near to her.

Yet to read this scene only as further indication of Ælfric's bowdlerizing tendencies is to miss the crucial point that, even in Ælfric's sources, this scene is in fact not about sex at all. That Haman's physical proximity to Esther bespeaks an imminent sexual violation is merely Ahasuerus's misreading of Haman's intentions. What Haman really wants from Esther is intercession—not for her to provide him with sexual pleasure but for her to use her influence with the king in order that she might, as Ælfric so bluntly puts it, "help him [Haman] save his own life." Enacted in the absence of the king, Haman's appeal is indeed a slimy one, but the sliminess has nothing to do with illicit sex and everything to do with the traduction of royal patronage through private appeals to a queen whose husband has absented himself and is engaged in what Ælfric describes as a pretense of counsel:

"eode him sona ut binnon his æppeltun *swilce for rædinge*" (he went out then, immediately to his apple orchard *as if for counsel;* 269–70). This phrase has no apparent source in the Latin texts but serves as a fitting description for a king who has recently been exposed as the dupe of his closest counselor and who has throughout the text tended to maintain a level of political awareness just barely sufficient for him to ward off the potentially disastrous plottings of his own subjects. Yet while Ahasuerus lacks the capacity for reaching beyond the murkiest understanding of Haman's real intentions, Ælfric ensures that his readers do not fall prey to the king's rather crude social hermeneutics—by spelling out precisely why Haman has come to Esther and what he really wants. The resulting scene, having been stripped of any overtly sexual discussion regarding the potential violation of the queen's body, is one that sharply focuses the reader's gaze on what Ælfric seems to identify as the true conundrum at hand here: the potential violation of the queen's intercessory function. While much of *Esther,* then, bespeaks Ælfric's efforts to celebrate the potential benefits of queenly intercession, this scene registers his anxieties regarding its potential misuse.

Relying on the possibilities offered by biblical translation to create a past peopled with characters radically different from those present in his Latin sources, and capitalizing on the metaphorical potential of the queen, Ælfric uses the biblical queens Vashti and Esther to construct an exemplar of queenship that might effectively promote social ideals and practices that had become highly charged in the context of the reforms. His attempts to effect social change were not merely a part of ongoing ecclesiastical efforts to regulate communal faith, lay marriage, and sexual practice. Rather, Ælfric deeply believed that these social changes would appease an angry God who might then deliver the English from Danish forces—just as He saved the Israelites in the biblical Esther-narrative. This fantasy would, of course, never come true. Roughly fifteen years after Ælfric completed *Esther,* England fell to the Danes, and the conquering king Cnut took Emma, queen of the English, as his new bride. Yet Ælfric's staunch attempts to create vernacular exemplary narratives such as *Esther* attest to his firm belief that such a fate could be averted and that, for him, as a leader of the Benedictine reforms, such prevention was a part of his job.

Conclusion

So why queens? Why invest so much energy in tracing how such a small and elite class of women is depicted within the literature of a particular period? The simplest answer is that for the period under consideration, queens are essentially all we've got. Across a spectrum of Anglo-Saxon texts, royal women stand out as the dominant female figures; their presence is felt with far greater force than that of any other group of women. Indeed, my book grew from a desire to write about women in Anglo-Saxon texts, but the women who appear in those texts dictated that it would ultimately be a book about queens. Even so, it is striking how little *Ruling Women* really centers on either queens or women. To be sure, all of my chapters investigate queens as they are depicted by various authors and in different texts. And in each chapter, I have shown that Anglo-Saxon writers used legendary royal wives to model cultural ideals of queenship during a time when that institution was changing, and to construct ideologies of gender for women of lesser social status. Yet when Anglo-Saxon writers turned to legendary queens, they did so in order to express their views on cultural problems that range far beyond such issues as either queenship or gender. For Bede, queens figure the painful process of conversion and the transformation of cultural attitudes toward earthly wealth; for Cynewulf, queens image the maintenance of ever-precarious social hierarchies in postconversion society; for the *Beowulf* poet, queens reveal the tensions between competing models of heroism and the possibility of redefining the criteria for cultural memorialization; and for Ælfric, queens dramatize the immediate political troubles and spiritual deviance that both he and his fellow reformers believed could destroy England. For all these writers, queens serve as mediatory figures; they evoke the bridging of differences or, conversely, the destruction of existing unities, between groups of people, social structures, and systems of belief. However, the cultural concerns that are most insistently mediated through legendary royal women center less on queenship or gender than they do on issues that cut across boundaries of both social rank and gender. Hence this book's rather lengthy forays into such topics as conversion, hierarchy, community, heroism, counsel, idolatry, and the Benedictine reforms.

For a while these thematic "digressions" worried me, as if the book's refusal to stay on course reflected a lack of interest on my own part in Anglo-Saxon royal women and the worlds of privilege in which they moved. On further reflection, it has become clear to me that these digressions are the places where we stand to learn the most. Representations of legendary queens in Anglo-Saxon writings do tell us about both queenship and gender—and they tell us a lot. Part of what they tell us has to do with cultural attitudes and social roles attendant upon queens and women in Anglo-Saxon society. For example, when Ælfric explains that the Old Testament queen Vashti's refusal to wear her crown at a public banquet was an act that was contrary to "heora seode" (their custom; *Esther*, l. 32), we learn that queens in Anglo-Saxon England, unlike their counterparts in the ancient Mediterranean world, were probably not expected to wear crowns at formal banquets. Similarly, when Cynewulf endorses the subservience of a Jewish (and thus spiritually feminized) man to a Christian (and thus spiritually masculinized) woman, we learn that for some Anglo-Saxon writers, spiritual gender took precedence over biological sex in the determination of social hierarchies. Representations of legendary queens offer a valuable means to continue the work of recovering a literary history of both queens and women and of reconstructing what life might have been like—or at least what Anglo-Saxon writers might have wanted life to be like—for Anglo-Saxon queens and for women of lesser social status.

But what is most interesting about Anglo-Saxon depictions of legendary queens is not so much their ability to shed light on the lives of a few very privileged women or even on more culturally pervasive gender norms as their capacity to help us rethink the most problematic issues of Anglo-Saxon literature and culture, as well as the critical assumptions that have long guided our efforts to understand such issues. A case in point is the new understanding of Bede that emerges from considering his account of queens as agents of Christian conversion in conjunction with that of Ælfric. We have seen that Ælfric's depiction of queenship in his early eleventh-century *Esther* translation is driven by a desire to recreate a bygone Anglo-Saxon golden age and that this desire finds voice in Ælfric's re-envisioning of the exemplary queen Esther as one whose energies are directed toward the conversion of her husband and her people. Yet as Ælfric recreates Esther in the image of the seventh- and eighth-century Anglo-Saxon queen-proselytizer, his retrospective account of queenship bears far less resemblance to the kind of queenship depicted in Bede's *Historia Ecclesiastica* (A.D. 731)—a text that, as we have seen, actively works to distance queens from the process of royal conversion—than to the kind of queenship that is found in the letters of Bede's near contemporaries, Pope Gregory the Great and Pope Boniface V. The fact that Ælfric's nostalgic recreation of an Anglo-Saxon past filled with queen-proselytizers so sharply diverges from Bede's account of that past and so closely resembles the accounts offered by such writers as Gregory and Boniface V urges us to rethink the central place that we have awarded both Bede and his writings for so many years within Anglo-Saxon studies. To acknowledge how very much Ælfric's vision of seventh- and eighth-century Anglo-Saxon queenship differs from Bede's is to be reminded that although our own understanding of the early Anglo-Saxon period is largely reliant on representations given to us by Bede, his was nevertheless only one voice of this period, and his works, however influential, cannot be taken as representative. In short, examining queens in both Bede and Ælfric teaches us that the early Middle Ages ought not to be viewed—as it so consistently is by Anglo-Saxonists—as the "Age of Bede" or "Bede's World."[1]

If studying representations of queens in Anglo-Saxon writings can shed light on issues other than gender, the converse is also true: studying issues other than queenship and gender can lead to a stronger understanding of both. This point is nicely expressed by the author of the *Encomium Emmae Reginae* (1041–42), who insists that his lengthy discussions of Swein Forkbeard (Emma's Danish father-in-law) and sociopolitical relations between the Danes and English ought not to be seen as indicative of a lack of interest in Emma but as forms of praise for her:

> Perchance, O Reader, you will wonder, and will accuse me of error
> or incompetence because at the beginning of this book I bring to

attention the deeds and glory of Sveinn, that most active king, since in the above epistle, I pledge myself to devote this book to the praise of the Queen. But you will admit that this is the case, and allow that I nowhere deviate from her praises, if you wisely compare the beginning with the middle, and the end with the beginning.[2]

It would be tempting to attribute the Encomiast's belief that praising Emma was rightfully done through praising her father-in-law, Swein, to a latent misogyny in which women are viewed less as individuals in their own right than as extensions of their male relations. Yet the Encomiast strongly urges against such a reading by reminding us that male figures have long been celebrated through praise of their families. Presenting the *Encomium* as akin to the *Aeneid* and Emma as a kind of Octavian figure, he claims:

Who can deny that the Aeneid, written by Virgil, is everywhere devoted to the praises of Octavian, although practically no mention of him by name, or clearly very little, is seen to be introduced? Note, therefore, that the praise accorded to his family everywhere celebrates the glory of their fame and renown to his own honour. Who can deny that this book is entirely devoted to the praise of the Queen, since it is not only written to her glory, but since that subject occupies the greatest part of it?[3]

The Encomiast's belief that writing a text in praise of a queen might serve as a means for him to express his views on Anglo-Danish relations, warfare, and men's heroic pursuits, and, conversely, that such topics were all perfectly legitimate ways of praising a woman, encapsulates one of the major arguments of my book: that Anglo-Saxon writers saw gender as inextricably intertwined with broader cultural concerns, and that critical studies that take early medieval women and gender relations as their major focus must investigate these topics within the broader cultural matrix within which Anglo-Saxon writers so insistently place them.

Unlike their later medieval counterparts, Anglo-Saxon writers did not position legendary royal women within misogynist diatribes; nor did they place these female figures within gender debates akin to say, the fourteenth- and fifteenth-century *querelle des femmes*. Rather, Anglo-Saxon writers positioned legendary royal women in the midst of texts that were designed to express their authors' views on the most difficult and contentious issues of Anglo-Saxon society. And they did so, I would argue, because these authors saw women as deeply affected by and able to affect those issues. This is not to perpetuate the Golden Age hypothesis—that Anglo-Saxon England was a kind of paradise for women. Rather it is to counter a persistent assumption among medievalists that textual representations of women are shaped mainly by gender norms—either current norms or ones in the making—and that such representations are thus rightfully studied mainly by scholars who take gender as their primary topic of investigation.

To cling to the idea that representations of queens are only about establishing cultural ideals of queenship or gender, or to explain legendary queens' entanglement in a very broad matrix of social issues as solely indicative of the shifting and insidious faces of a misogyny that refuses to announce itself as such, are critical positions that can, at times, be productive. We still know very little about roles available to Anglo-Saxon women, either literary or social, or about the workings of early medieval misogyny, and studies that isolate female figures in literary and historical writings in order to close these critical gaps are certainly valuable. At the same time, to contextualize representations of women in Anglo-Saxon texts solely within discourses of gender is to overlook the contexts in which Anglo-Saxon writers placed these female figures and thus to lose sight of the cultural attitudes toward gender that those contexts suggest. Anglo-Saxon writers' insistence on situating royal women in the midst of cultural debates over non-gender-specific issues speaks to these writers' belief that gender, however central to identity, was not the only, or even the major, force that made people the way they were. And it speaks further to these writers' belief that other kinds of differences, such as differences between paganism and Christianity, or between active participation in and exclusion from physical warfare, loomed larger than did differences between men and women.

One of the long-standing goals of feminist literary study has been to change not only what scholars study but also the methods by which such study is practiced—that is, to integrate rather than simply to add gender into existent scholarship. My account of queenship in Anglo-Saxon literature demonstrates that the most central issues in Anglo-Saxon literature and culture, namely conversion, hierarchy, heroism, counsel, idolatry, and lay spirituality, cannot be understood accurately without serious consideration of the role that legendary queens play in pre-Conquest writings. For it was through legendary queens that Anglo-Saxon writers sought to explore the problems that they saw as most pressing within their own culture.

Why? This is the most difficult question, and indeed it has a number of answers. Anglo-Saxon writers drew on legendary queens to express their views on a range of cultural issues, in part, because queens carried familiar typological and symbolic meanings that were vested with the authority of tradition. Moreover, because queens' roles, unlike those of their male counterparts, were not yet fully codified, writers could feel free to experiment in their depictions of these female figures. And Anglo-Saxon writers were also attracted to legendary queens because queens moved within the circles of power and privilege from which Anglo-Saxon cultural norms most often emerged. Yet as central as royal women were to the workings of these circles, they also stood outside those structures, and thus offered a way of imagining alternatives to them. A good example is the case of *Beowulf,* in which queens serve as a means for the *Beowulf* poet to redefine an old and outdated model of heroism. By placing the grief of the female figure Hildeburh (rather than, say, the bravery of the male warriors Finn or Hengest) at the center of the Finnsburg episode, the poem urges readers to focus on the costs rather than the glories of the traditional heroic code of violent action and to adopt the view of those members of society, such as women and aged men, who were unable to participate fully in that code. By encouraging readers to see the Finnsburg episode through Hildeburh's eyes, the *Beowulf* poet urges readers to question the traditional heroic code and to consider possible alternatives to it. Writing about women or encouraging readers to view social formations through the eyes of women was a powerful tool, and one that Anglo-Saxon writers drew on consistently, for social critique.

Queens have retained their capacity to urge social critique, yet the ways in which they do so has changed. In modern culture, queenship has become the stuff of irony, as evidenced in such phrases as "welfare queen," "queen bee," or "drag queen"—images that encode social critiques, yet critiques that are reliant on an evocation of cynicism, archness, and ironic distance which is largely absent from Anglo-Saxon writers' discussions of royal women. Yet if we consider irony in its broadest dimensions, and allow that it need not entail any of the bite or edge that are its usual companions within modern culture but only a distinction between utterance and meaning—a definition that moves irony closer to the idea of deconstruction—it becomes evident that Anglo-Saxon representations of queens do share a sense of irony similar to that which accompanies the evocation of queens in modern culture. As Anglo-Saxon writers use queens either to shore up or to pose alternatives to existing social formations, these writers inevitably expose the constructedness of those formations, and in so doing, inadvertently invite revisionist thinking that is ultimately at odds with their own intentions. One example is Bede's *Historia Ecclesiastica,* in which Bede seeks to write women out of the history of England's conversion, and in so doing ultimately reveals the very real power that the model of conversion-by-marriage must have held within early Anglo-Saxon culture. Another example is Cynewulf's *Elene,* which mobilizes a queen in order to shore up highly traditional and conservative hierarchies of rank and gender, but which ultimately exposes both the fluidity of tradition and the highly constructed nature of those hierarchies.

My title, *Ruling Women,* seeks to capture these dual operations at work in Anglo-Saxon depictions of legendary queens. The queens who appear in my study were indeed rulers; they exerted significant power within their fictive communities, and, more importantly, they wielded significant control over the imaginative energies of Anglo-Saxons authors, often refusing to stay within prescribed boundaries and conveying ideas that deviated considerably from their author's intentions. At the same time, legendary queens were a means of ruling over women, since textual representations of royal women modeled cultural ideals of queenship and femininity. Yet for medievalists, the term "rule" also carries a third meaning, and one that is specific to medieval textual culture: to rule is to create the lines on a piece of parchment that will ultimately serve as a framework for a scribe's writing. Whether as the faint lines created by drypoint impressions or the more visible lines drawn with the ink of crushed berries or insects, ruling was crucial as it provided Anglo-Saxon writers with a basic structure upon which to compose. It is this third sense of ruling, as the creation of a structure or series of guiding lines, that best captures the major goal of my book. Examining a range of representations of legendary queens from Bede to Ælfric, *Ruling Women* does not provide a comprehensive account of these pervasive female figures. Instead, it posits a methodological framework within which we can more easily comprehend the ways in which queenship was culturally contested ground, at once offering an ahistorical iconic and typological consistency and inviting a resituating of that consistency within a contemporary Anglo-Saxon framework that challenged its putative immutability. Typological criticism has successfully focused on the former, and, more recently, feminist criticism has successfully exposed the often gendered terms of the latter. *Ruling Women*, however, brings together these historically antagonistic critical paradigms to show how legendary royal women illuminate the shifting terrain of early medieval queenship, and in so doing, reveal the ideological fissures and cultural stakes of Anglo-Saxon literary praxis.

Abbreviations

ASPR   Anglo-Saxon Poetic Records

CCSL   Corpus Christianorum Series Latina

CSEL   Corpus Scriptorum Ecclesiasticorum Latinorum

EEMF   Early English Manuscripts in Facsimile

EETS   Early English Text Society
            o.s., Original Series
            s.s., Supplemental Series

MGH   Monumenta Germaniae Historica, cited by subseries and volume

NPNF   A Select Library of Nicene and Post-Nicene Fathers of the Christian
            Church

PL   *Patrologia Latina,* edited by J.-P. Migne. 221 vols. Paris, 1844–64. Cited
            by volume and column

PMLA   Publications of the Modern Language Association of America

Notes

Introduction

1. Robert Deshman, "*Benedictus Monarcha et Monachus:* Early Medieval Ruler Theology and the Anglo-Saxon Reform," *Frühmittelalterliche Studien* 22 (1988): 223.

2. I have adopted the dating proposed by Simon Keynes: *The Liber Vitae of the New Minster and Hyde Abbey Winchester: British Library Stowe 944,* ed. Simon Keynes, EEMF 26 (Copenhagen: Rosenkilde and Bagger, 1996), 37–38, 69, 99.

3. The second drawing of an Anglo-Saxon queen appears as the frontispiece of the earliest surviving copy of the *Encomium Emmae Reginae* (London, British Library, Additional 33241, fol. 1ᵛ). Emma is depicted enthroned and in the company of her two surviving sons, Harthacnut and Edward, with the Encomiast presenting her the text. In addition to these two portraits proper, there are several other images worth mentioning. The eighth-century Mercian queen Cynethryth, wife of Offa, appears on Anglo-Saxon coinage, and the seventh-century royal abbess and former Northumbrian queen Æthelthryth appears twice in the *Benedictional of Æthelwold.*

4. To be sure, Ælfgifu's clothing differs from the Virgin Mary's in certain respects: Ælfgifu wears a decorated diadem or fillet around her head, she receives a second veil, and her hood has two streamers, decorated and ending in tags, emerging from underneath. Yet as Gale Owen notes, these differences are minimal in comparison with those between Cnut on the one hand and Christ and Saint Peter on the other, and the drawing clearly reflects Anglo-Saxon artists' tendency to distinguish between the garments worn by secular men and those worn by angels,

Christ, and the Evangelists, and to blur those distinctions in depictions of women: Gale R. Owen, "Wynflæd's Wardrobe," *Anglo-Saxon England* 8 (1979): 195–222, esp. 196.

5. J. M. Wallace-Hadrill, *Early Germanic Kingship in England and on the Continent* (Oxford: Clarendon Press, 1971), 92–93.

6. On Cnut's strategic use of piety and Church patronage to strengthen and legitimize his rule, see M. K. Lawson, *Cnut: The Danes in England in the Early Eleventh Century* (London: Longman, 1993), 133–60; and Jan Gerchow, "Prayers for King Cnut: The Liturgical Commemoration of a Conqueror," in *England in the Eleventh Century: Proceedings of the 1990 Harlaxton Symposium*, ed. Carola Hicks (Stamford: Paul Watkins, 1992), 219–38. Gerchow usefully reminds us that the image of Cnut in the *Liber Vitae* portrait closely resembles, and is perhaps deliberately modeled on, the depiction of Edgar in the New Minster Charter frontispiece (London, British Library, Cotton Vespasian A. viii, fol. 2v), and that Cnut thus appears as a kind of "Edgar *redivivus*," forging a sense of spiritual continuity between the two reigns (234). On Cnut's use of marriage to establish his position, see Simon Keynes, "The Æthelings in Normandy," *Anglo-Norman Studies* 13 (1990): 173–205.

7. Cnut's reasons for marrying Emma are complicated, and probably center on his desire to shore up his claims to the throne through a number of strategies: by securing Emma's support against her sons' claims to the throne, by fostering a sense of continuity between the current regime and the previous one under Æthelred and Emma, and by gaining the support of those in court circles who were already loyal to her. In any case, the marriage effectively alienated Emma from her sons by Æthelred (Alfred and Edward), for upon marrying Cnut, she cut off their claims to the throne in favor of those of a son by herself and Cnut. For the duration of Cnut's reign, the æthelings remained in exile in Normandy, apparently in accordance with his wishes. *Anglo-Saxon Chronicle* entries reveal that even after Cnut's death in 1035 and Edward's return to England, relations between Emma and her sons, or at least between Edward and Emma—Alfred died in 1037—remained quite strained: in 1037, after Emma had been driven into exile in Flanders and sought help from Edward, he refused her request. Relations between mother and son appear to have declined further in subsequent years: soon after Edward became king in 1042, he confiscated her lands and wealth, an act that the 1043 entry to the D text of the *Anglo-Saxon Chronicle* explains as a result of the fact that Emma had been "æror þam cynge hire suna swiðe heard, þæt heo him læsse dyde þonne he wolde, ær þam þe he cyng wære 7 eac syððan" (previously very hard to the king, her son, in that she did less for him than he wished both before he became king and afterwards as well, *The Anglo-Saxon Chronicle: A Collaborative Edition*, vol. 6, MS D, ed. G. P. Cubbin [Cambridge: D. S. Brewer, 1996], 67). For further discussion of the family politics, see Keynes, "The Æthelings in Normandy."

8. *Encomium Emmae Reginae,* ed. and trans. Alistair Campbell, with a supplementary introduction by Simon Keynes (Cambridge: Cambridge University Press, 1998); *The Life of King Edward Who Rests at Westminster, Attributed to a Monk of Saint-Bertin,* 2nd ed., ed. and trans. Frank Barlow (Oxford: Clarendon Press, 1992). Emma was born in Normandy in the 980s and her Norman name, Emma, has strong Frankish dynastic connotations. At the time of her marriage to Æthelred II in 1002, she either took or was given the English name *Ælfgifu* (the name of Æthelred's first wife, and of his grandmother). Although *Ælfgifu* served as the queen's official name, she was still popularly known as Emma (Imme), particularly in non-English sources such as the *Encomium Emmae Reginae.* For further discussion of these names, see Campbell, *Encomium Emmae,* xvii, 55–61, and also Pauline Stafford, *Queen Emma and Queen Edith: Queenship and Women's Power in Eleventh-Century England* (Oxford: Blackwell, 1997), 7–11.

9. Barlow, *The Life of King Edward,* xx–xxiii.

10. On Anglo-Saxon attitudes toward the past, see Malcolm Godden, "Biblical Literature: The Old Testament," in *The Cambridge Companion to Old English Literature,* ed. Malcolm Godden and Michael Lapidge (Cambridge: Cambridge University Press, 1991), 206–26; Nicholas Howe, *Migration and Mythmaking in Anglo-Saxon England* (New Haven: Yale University Press, 1989); and Michael Hunter, "Germanic and Roman Antiquity and the Sense of the Past in Anglo-Saxon England," *Anglo-Saxon England* 3 (1974): 29–50.

11. The classic discussion is Caroline Walker Bynum, *Jesus as Mother: Studies in the Spirituality of the High Middle Ages* (Berkeley: University of California Press, 1982), 110–69.

12. As Janet L. Nelson argues, "Episcopacy, aristocracy, [and] kingship can be said to have existed as institutions, but it is much harder to identify anything that could be called 'queenship'": "Queens as Jezebels: The Careers of Brunhild and Balthild in Merovingian History," in *Medieval Women: Dedicated and Presented to Professor Rosalind M. T. Hill,* ed. Derek Baker, Studies in Church History, Subsidia 1 (Oxford: Basil Blackwell, 1978), 31–77, quotation at 39; repr. as "Queens as Jezebels: Brunhild and Balthild in Merovingian History," in *Politics and Ritual in Early Medieval Europe,* ed. Janet L. Nelson (London: Hambledon Press, 1986), 1–48, at 9.

13. Barbara Raw, *Anglo-Saxon Crucifixion Iconography and the Art of the Monastic Revival* (Cambridge: Cambridge University Press, 1990), 8, 14, 27, 31, 35, 38.

14. *Bede's Ecclesiastical History of the English People,* ed. Bertram Colgrave and R. A. B. Mynors (Oxford: Clarendon Press, 1969), 2.

15. Ibid., 3.

16. There have, however, been a number of important historicist readings of *Judith,* the *Chronicle* poems, and *The Battle of Maldon.* See, respectively, David Chamberlain, "*Judith*: A Fragmentary and Political Poem," in *Anglo-Saxon Poetry: Essays in Appreciation for John C. McGalliard,* ed. Lewis E. Nicholson and Dolores

Warwick Frese (Notre Dame, Ind.: University of Notre Dame Press, 1975), 135–59; Katherine O'Brien O'Keeffe, "Body and Law in Late Anglo-Saxon England," *Anglo-Saxon England* 27 (1998): 209–32; and W. G. Busse and R. Holtei, "*The Battle of Maldon:* A Historical, Heroic and Political Poem," *Neophilologus* 65 (1981): 614–21. For a stimulating account of historicist criticism in Anglo-Saxon studies, see Nicholas Howe, "Historicist Approaches," in *Reading Old English Texts,* ed. Katherine O'Brien O'Keeffe (Cambridge: Cambridge University Press, 1997), 79–100.

17. The one major exception is Susan J. Ridyard's valuable study of Anglo-Saxon royal saints—both male and female—in Anglo-Latin hagiography: *The Royal Saints of Anglo-Saxon England: A Study of West Saxon and East Anglian Cults* (Cambridge: Cambridge University Press, 1988).

18. Classic typological readings of female figures in Old English literature include Thomas Hill, "Sapiential Structure and Figural Narrative in the Old English 'Elene,'" *Traditio* 27 (1971): 159–77; and Joseph Wittig, "Figural Narrative in Cynewulf's *Juliana,*" *Anglo-Saxon England* 4 (1974): 37–55. Both articles are reprinted, Hill's essay with revisions, in *Cynewulf: Basic Readings,* ed. Robert E. Bjork (New York: Garland, 1996): Hill, 207–28; Wittig, 147–69. Jane Chance exhibits similar sensibilities: "There were thus two archetypes of women that ordered the Anglo-Saxon social world . . . their depiction was colored by Germanic heroic imagery and values" (*Woman as Hero in Old English Literature* [Syracuse: Syracuse University Press, 1986], xvii).

19. For a provocative discussion of how studies of medieval queenship might contribute to broader feminist analyses of women and power, see *Women and Sovereignty,* ed. Louise Olga Fradenburg, *Cosmos* 7 (Edinburgh: Edinburgh University Press, 1992), 1–13. On the theoretical dimensions and social effects of royal marriage and the sovereign's love for his wife, see Fradenburg's *City, Marriage, Tournament: Arts of Rule in Late Medieval Scotland* (Madison: University of Wisconsin Press, 1991), esp. 67–149. Peggy McCracken, *The Romance of Adultery: Queenship and Sexual Transgression in Old French Literature* (Philadelphia: University of Pennsylvania Press, 1998), 1–24, is also excellent, particularly on intersections between literary and historical queens.

20. *The Anglo-Saxon Chronicle: A Collaborative Edition,* vol. 5, MS C, ed. Katherine O'Brien O'Keeffe (Cambridge: D. S. Brewer, 2001), 44.

21. Riddle 80 in *The Exeter Book,* ed. George Philip Krapp and Elliott Van Kirk Dobbie, ASPR 3 (New York: Columbia University Press, 1936), 235, ll. 3b–5.

22. Both *cwen* and *cwene* are vexed terms, whose multiple meanings encapsulate the extremely ill defined nature of Anglo-Saxon queenship. The Toronto-based *Dictionary of Old English* gives seven main definitions for *cwen,* some with subdivisions: "1. woman; noblewoman, lady, 1.a. glossing *anilis = ealdra cwena* 'of old women'"; "2. *cwena geliger* 'fornication with women', perhaps specifically 'adultery'"; "3. wife, consort"; "4. queen, female ruler, wife or consort of a king, emperor, patri-

arch or other Old Testament figure, 4.a. as a title, regularly placed immediately after personal name, occasionally before"; "5. as an epithet for the Virgin Mary, either with the specific sense 'woman, maiden' . . . or 'queen'"; "6.a. figurative: *seo gastlice cwen* 'the spiritual queen,' 6.b. figurative: *ealra mægna cwen* 'queen of all virtues' (a metaphor for virginity, maidenhood and here applied to the Virgin Mary), 6.c. figurative: *cwen ealra yfla / ealdorlicra leahtra cwen* 'queen of all sins / mortal sins' (a metaphor for *oferhygd, ofermodignes* 'pride, presumption')"; and "7. as an element in personal names, e.g. *Cwen-burh, -gyth, -thryth.*" The weak feminine *cwene* has a similarly broad range of meanings; the *Dictionary* gives five main definitions, some with subdivisions: "1. woman"; "2. wife, 2.a. [possibly] mistress, concubine"; "3. queen, empress; princess, 3.a. as a title placed immediately after personal name"; "4. as an epithet of the Virgin Mary"; and "5. as a place-name element." Moreover, as the *Dictionary* reminds us, "the morphological forms of *cwen* and *cwene* cannot be clearly distinguished, nor is the sense division between them always certain": *Dictionary of Old English: A to F on CD-ROM* (Toronto: Pontifical Institute of Mediaeval Studies, 2003).

23. Joseph T. Shipley, *The Origins of English Words: A Discursive Dictionary of Indo-European Roots* (Baltimore: Johns Hopkins University Press, 1984), 139.

24. Claude Lévi-Strauss, *Structural Anthropology,* trans. C. Jacobsen and B. Grundfest Shoepf (Harmondsworth: Penguin, 1977), 61–62. Quoted in Janet L. Nelson, "Women and the Word in the Earlier Middle Ages," in *Women in the Church: Papers Read at the 1989 Summer Meeting and the 1990 Winter Meeting of the Ecclesiastical Historical Society,* ed. W. J. Sheils and Diana Wood (Oxford: Basil Blackwell, 1990), 58.

25. On these debates, see Christine Fell, *Women in Anglo-Saxon England* (London: British Museum Publications, 1984); Stephanie Hollis, *Anglo-Saxon Women and the Church: Sharing a Common Fate* (Woodbridge, Suffolk: Boydell Press, 1992); and Anne L. Klinck, "Anglo-Saxon Women and the Law," *Journal of Medieval History* 8 (1982): 107–21. Fell argues that the position of women declined greatly after the Norman Conquest, while Hollis argues against viewing the Conquest as a watershed in women's history, and maintains that the position of women had begun to decline well before the Conquest, perhaps as early as the eighth century. Klinck, by contrast, argues that the position of women gradually improved from the eighth through eleventh centuries, an argument that has been challenged by Fell on the grounds that Klinck draws conclusions from the absence of source materials and fails to attend to post-Conquest canon law. In recent years, feminist Anglo-Saxonists have begun to complicate the "Golden Age debates" by shifting focus away from the issue of female power itself and toward the institutional structures— both modern and Anglo-Saxon—that have prevented scholars from understanding fully women's roles in Anglo-Saxon literature and culture. See, for example, Clare A. Lees and Gillian R. Overing, *Double Agents: Women and Clerical Culture*

in Anglo-Saxon England (Philadelphia: University of Pennsylvania Press, 2001); and also Josephine Bloomfield, "Diminished by Kindness: Frederick Klaeber's Rewriting of Wealhtheow," *Journal of English and Germanic Philology* 93 (1994): 183–203.

26. For an indispensable account of the social roles available to Anglo-Saxon queens, see Stafford's *Queen Emma and Queen Edith*. Also useful is Stafford, *Queens, Concubines, and Dowagers: The King's Wife in the Early Middle Ages* (Athens: University of Georgia Press, 1983). On early medieval queens' coronation ceremonies and other royal rituals, see Nelson, *Politics and Ritual*. Another useful collection is *Queens and Queenship in Medieval Europe: Proceedings of a Conference Held at King's College London, April 1995*, ed. Anne J. Duggan (Woodbridge, Suffolk: Boydell Press, 1997).

27. For the relevant annals, see *English Historical Documents*, vol. 1, *c. 500–1042*, ed. Dorothy Whitelock, 2nd ed. (London: Eyre Methuen, 1979), 166, 210–17. That the Mercians may have preferred Ælfwynn over Edward as their next ruler is suggested by annal 919 of the *Mercian Register*, which recounts in a rather resentful tone how Ælfwynn was deprived of her former authority in Mercia ("ælces anwealdes on Myrcum benumen"): *The Anglo-Saxon Chronicle*, vol. 5, MS C, ed. O'Keeffe, 76. This annal does not, however, offer conclusive evidence that Ælfwynn was either serving as the ruler of Mercia after her mother's death or that she would have done so had not Edward assumed this position by force. See also F. T. Wainwright, "Æthelflæd, Lady of the Mercians," in *New Readings on Women in Old English Literature*, ed. Helen Damico and Alexandra Hennessey Olsen (Bloomington: Indiana University Press, 1990), 44–55, esp. 53.

28. Stafford, *Queen Emma and Queen Edith*, 188.

29. Fred C. Robinson, "The Prescient Woman in Old English Literature," in *Philologia Anglica: Essays Presented to Professor Yoshio Terasawa on the Occasion of His Sixtieth Birthday*, ed. Kinshiro Oshitari et al. (Tokyo: Kenkyusha, 1988), 241–50; reprinted in *The Tomb of Beowulf and Other Essays on Old English* (Oxford: Blackwell, 1993), 155–63.

30. "They even believe that there is in women a certain holiness and power of prophecy, and they do not neglect to seek their advice nor do they disregard their replies": *Germania*, book 8; cited in Robinson, "The Prescient Woman," 155.

31. *The Exeter Book*, ed. Krapp and Dobbie, 159–60, ll. 86a, 91b–92.

32. See Boniface's letters to Queen Æthelburh and King Edwin, which were reproduced in Bede's *Historia Ecclesiastica: Bede's Ecclesiastical History of the English People*, ed. Colgrave and Mynors, ii. 10–11, 167–74; and also Gregory's letter to Bertha: "Epistle 29," trans. James Barmby, in *Gregory the Great, Ephraim Syrus, Aphrahat*, NPNF, 2nd ser., vol. 13, pt. 2, ed. Philip Schaff and Henry Wace (New York: Christian Literature Co., 1898), 56–57. See also Jane Tibbetts Schulenburg, *Forgetful of Their Sex: Female Sanctity and Society, ca. 500–1100* (Chicago: University of Chicago Press, 1998), 176–209.

33. On women's roles in the establishment of the conversion-age Church, see Susan J. Ridyard, "Anglo-Saxon Women and the Church in the Age of Conversion," in *Monks, Nuns, and Friars in Mediaeval Society*, ed. Edward B. King, Jacqueline T. Schaefer, and William B. Wadley, Sewanee Mediaeval Studies 4 (Sewanee, Tenn.: Press of the University of the South, 1989), 105–32.

34. For an important discussion of Anglo-Saxon concubinage, see Margaret Clunies Ross, "Concubinage in Anglo-Saxon England," *Past and Present* 108 (1985): 3–34.

35. My interpretation of the queens discussed in the *Life of Alfred* proceeds according to the fairly standard view of the *Life* as a contemporary biography composed by Asser. Yet questions regarding the authenticity of the text's dating and authorship have been raised, most recently by Alfred Smyth, who argues that the *Life* is a late tenth- or early eleventh-century forgery: Alfred P. Smyth, *King Alfred the Great* (Oxford: Oxford University Press, 1995), esp. 271–324.

36. *Asser's Life of King Alfred Together with the Annals of St. Neot's*, ed. William Henry Stevenson (Oxford: Clarendon Press, 1904), 11–12.

37. *Alfred the Great: Asser's Life of King Alfred and Other Contemporary Sources*, ed. and trans. Simon Keynes and Michael Lapidge (London: Penguin Books, 1983), 71.

38. On the high regard for queens in early medieval Wales, see the Laws of Hywel Dda (*Ancient Laws and Institutes of Wales*, ed. and trans. Aneurin Owen [London: Record Commissioners, 1841]), which stipulate numerous important arenas in which Welsh queens exercised power: the queen was attended by eight of the twenty-four royal officers (*Ancient Laws*, 5); she was the only person besides the king with the authority to convey safely a legal offender beyond Wales without pursuit or obstruction (Gwentian Code, *Ancient Laws*, 629); the queen was entitled to one-third of the produce of the king's landed property (*Ancient Laws*, 7) and the right to give away without the king's permission one-third of the domestic goods that came into his possession (*Ancient Laws*, 95); she retained the right to her daughter's *gobyr*, a fee paid upon the girl's marriage (Gwentian Code, *Ancient Laws*, 747); both the queen and her horses were honored with an annual "progress" or ceremonial journey, during which goods, land, and money were bestowed on the processors (Gwentian Code, *Ancient Laws*, 771; Dimetian Code, *Ancient Laws*, 487); the queen had significant responsibility for the court's clothing, and her sewing needle (along with the mediciner's and chief huntsman's) was valued as one of the three legal needles of the court (Dimetian Code, *Ancient Laws*, 451); and the queen (along with the priest and the mediciner) was one of three people with whom the king was permitted to consult privately, without the presence of his judge (Dimetian Code, *Ancient Laws*, 449). It is worth noting, by contrast, that queens are never mentioned in the Anglo-Saxon law codes.

39. For a discussion of Anglo-Saxon queens and royal women as witnesses to charters, see Stafford, *Queen Emma and Queen Edith*, 91, 182, 183 n. 106, 193–206,

231–32, 265–66; Keynes and Lapidge, ed. and trans., *Alfred the Great,* 235; and Simon Keynes, *The Diplomas of Æthelred "The Unready" 978–1016* (Cambridge: Cambridge University Press, 1980), 187.

40. Pauline Stafford, "The King's Wife in Wessex, 800–1066," *Past and Present* 91 (1981): 3–27; reprinted in *New Readings on Women,* ed. Damico and Olsen, 56–78. The issues that are raised in this essay are further taken up in Stafford, *Queen Emma and Queen Edith.*

41. Paul Strohm, *Hochon's Arrow: The Social Imagination of Fourteenth-Century Texts* (Princeton: Princeton University Press, 1992), 95–96.

Chapter 1   The Costs of Queenship

1. For a balanced and comprehensive discussion of early medieval women as agents of conversion, see Jane Tibbetts Schulenburg, *Forgetful of Their Sex: Female Sanctity and Society, ca. 500–1100* (Chicago: University of Chicago Press, 1998), 176–209.

2. *Liber historiae Francorum,* ed. and trans. Bernard S. Bachrach (Lawrence, Kans.: Coronado Press, 1973), chap. 12, 39–40. For more on Clotild, see Schulenburg, *Forgetful of Their Sex,* 180–87.

3. Schulenburg, *Forgetful of Their Sex,* 180–91.

4. There is an extensive literature on the conversion of Anglo-Saxon England. For an excellent bibliography, see Simon Keynes, *Anglo-Saxon History: A Select Bibliography,* 3rd rev. ed., *Old English Newsletter, Subsidia* 13 (Kalamazoo, Mich.: Medieval Institute, 1998); rev. and updated for second online publication at http://www.wmich.edu/medieval/research/rawl/keynesbib/home.htm. Among the listed texts, good starting points are Henry Mayr-Harting, *The Coming of Christianity to Anglo-Saxon England,* 3rd ed. (1972; University Park: Pennsylvania State University Press, 1991); and James Campbell, "The First Century of Christianity in England," *Ampleforth Journal* 76 (1971): 12–29, reprinted in James Campbell, *Essays in Anglo-Saxon History* (London: Hambledon Press, 1986), 49–67. Other useful studies include N. J. Higham, *An English Empire: Bede and the Early Anglo-Saxon Kings* (Manchester: Manchester University Press, 1995), and *The Convert Kings: Power and Religious Affiliation in Early Anglo-Saxon England* (Manchester: Manchester University Press, 1997), which consider conversion from the different perspectives of Bede and the convert kings. Also indispensable is *St Augustine and the Conversion of England,* ed. Richard Gameson (Stroud, Gloucestershire: Sutton, 1999). For a provocative account of the theoretical difficulties attendant upon historicist studies of conversion, with particular emphasis on the twelfth century, see Karl F. Morrison, *Understanding Conversion* (Charlottesville: University Press of Virginia, 1992). A classic account of conversion is A. D. Nock, *Conversion: The Old*

and the New in Religion from Alexander the Great to Augustine of Hippo (1933; repr., Oxford: Oxford University Press, 1961).

5. Morrison, *Understanding Conversion*, xii.

6. Cordula Nolte and Ruth Mazo Karras have identified a similar absence of female conversion narratives in their respective studies of Merovingian and Scandinavian writings. Nolte attributes this absence to a general lack of interest among medieval authors in the conversion experiences of women and girls, as well as to the collective nature of medieval conversion, in which a king typically converts "together with his entire family." Mazo Karras argues that women are generally absent from accounts of the conversion of Scandinavia—which took place in the tenth and eleventh centuries but is mainly recorded in later thirteenth-century writings—because thirteenth-century writers tended to remember conversion not as an inner transformation but as a shifting of political allegiances, in which women, historically, played little part. See, respectively, Cordula Nolte, "Gender and Conversion in the Merovingian Era," in *Varieties of Religious Conversion in the Middle Ages*, ed. James Muldoon (Gainesville: University Press of Florida, 1997), 81–99, quotation at 84; and, in this same collection, Ruth Mazo Karras, "God and Man in Medieval Scandinavia: Writing—and Gendering—the Conversion," 100–114.

7. J. M. Wallace-Hadrill, for example, writes that "[Bede's] pages are packed with material on royal ladies whose contribution to the slow process of national conversion was vital": *Early Germanic Kingship in England and on the Continent* (Oxford: Clarendon Press, 1971), 91. James Campbell takes a similar position on queens as agents of Christian conversion, describing Æthelberht's marriage to Bertha as "the first link in a chain of events which was to lead to the conversion of Kent": *The Anglo-Saxons*, ed. James Campbell et al. (Oxford: Phaidon, 1982; London: Penguin, 1991), 44, 52, quotation at 44. D. J. V. Fisher's introduction to Anglo-Saxon culture refrains from offering strong opinions on queens and conversion but deals briefly with Bertha and Æthelburh: *The Anglo-Saxon Age c. 400–1042* (London: Longman, 1973), 57, 58, 73–74, 114.

8. See Stephanie Hollis, *Anglo-Saxon Women and the Church: Sharing a Common Fate* (Woodbridge, Suffolk: Boydell Press, 1992), 208–42. Dorsey Armstrong, "Holy Queens as Agents of Christianization in Bede's *Ecclesiastical History:* A Reconsideration," *Medieval Encounters* 4 (1998): 228–41, argues that Bede works to present the conversion by marriage model as unviable. Armstrong's analysis is brief but nevertheless cogent, and I largely agree with her findings.

9. Clare A. Lees and Gillian R. Overing's "Birthing Bishops and Fathering Poets: Bede, Hild, and the Relations of Cultural Production," *Exemplaria* 6 (1994): 35–65, offers a groundbreaking analysis of the *HE*'s representations of women as a product of Bede's biases, and as a microcosm of the larger biases attendant upon women within the Anglo-Saxon historical record. These arguments are extended in Clare A. Lees and Gillian R. Overing, *Double Agents: Women and Clerical Culture*

in Anglo-Saxon England (Philadelphia: University of Pennsylvania Press, 2001), which theorizes the relationship between women's material contributions to Anglo-Saxon culture and women's elusive presence within the texts that are our only record of that culture. For a lucid discussion of Bede's biases as a historian, see Walter Goffart, "The *Historia Ecclesiastica:* Bede's Agenda and Ours," *Haskins Society Journal: Studies in Medieval History* 2 (1990): 29–45.

10. Schulenburg defines "domestic proselytization" as the "special evangelizing or apostolic role which women were encouraged to exercise within the confines of the 'home' and family": *Forgetful of Their Sex,* 469.

11. All Latin citations to Bede's *Historia Ecclesiastica* refer to *Bede's Ecclesiastical History of the English People,* ed. Bertram Colgrave and R. A. B. Mynors (Oxford: Clarendon Press, 1969), and are cited parenthetically by book, chapter, and page number. Unless otherwise noted, all translations are from this edition as well.

12. H. M. Chadwick, *Early Scotland: The Picts, the Scots, & the Welsh of Southern Scotland* (Cambridge: Cambridge University Press, 1949), 89, argues that Bede is describing matrilinear succession. Alfred P. Smyth, *Warlords and Holy Men: Scotland AD 80–1000* (Edinburgh: Edinburgh University Press, 1984), 60, refutes the matrilinear thesis and contends that Bede is not describing matrilinear succession but rather actual female succession as practiced under exceptional circumstances by the Picts of his own day.

13. H. M. Chadwick, *Early Scotland,* 89; see also 81–98, which offers further discussion of both the Irish *Cruithnig* myths and Pictish succession practices. Nora Chadwick, "Pictish and Celtic Marriage in Early Literary Tradition," *Scottish Gaelic Studies* 8 (1955): 56–115, at 68–71, is also useful.

14. Finding a vocabulary that might adequately capture the complex dynamics of women's exchange in medieval society is a difficult task. Because the Irish women are part of a system of exchange in which they elicit longstanding obligations of reciprocity and sociability rather than immediate monetary payment, they more closely resemble the definition of "gift" as famously proposed by Marcel Mauss, than the common understandings of "commodity" as bequeathed to us from Marx; see, respectively, Marcel Mauss, *The Gift: The Form and Reason for Exchange in Archaic Societies,* trans. W. D. Halls (New York: Norton, 1990; originally publ. as "Essai sur le don. Forme et raison de l'échange dans le societés archaïques" (1923–24), reprinted in Marcel Mauss, *Sociologie et Anthropologie* (Paris: Presses Universitaires de France, 1968), 145–79; and Karl Marx, *Capital,* vol. 1., *A Critical Analysis of Capitalist Production,* trans. from the 3rd German ed. by Samuel Moore and Edward Aveling, ed. Frederick Engels (1887; Moscow: Progress Publishers, 1971). Throughout this chapter, however, I refer to the Irish women not only as "gifts" but also as "commodities," in part because recent anthropological work urging a less rigid distinction between the two terms seems right to me, particularly when considering precapitalist societies; and in part because the term "commodity" helps to

capture the larger sociopolitical implications of the Irish women's exchange which are not sufficiently invoked by "gift," because of the latter term's modern associations with reciprocity, holidays, and altruism. For a thought-provoking study of these issues, see Arjun Appadurai, "Introduction: Commodities and the Politics of Value," in *The Social Life of Things: Commodities in Cultural Perspective*, ed. Arjun Appadurai (Cambridge: Cambridge University Press, 1986), 3–63; my definition of commodity follows Appadurai's, 7.

15. See Annette B. Weiner, *Inalienable Possessions: The Paradox of Keeping-While-Giving* (Berkeley: University of California Press, 1992), 66–97; cited and discussed with respect to marriage alliances in the later Middle Ages in Susan Crane, *The Performance of Self: Ritual, Clothing, and Identity During the Hundred Years War* (Philadelphia: University of Pennsylvania Press, 2002), 28.

16. For an important study of royal female sanctity, see Susan Ridyard, *The Royal Saints of Anglo-Saxon England: A Study of West Saxon and East Anglian Cults* (Cambridge: Cambridge University Press, 1988).

17. This is not to say that queens never suffer in the *HE*—Osthryth, for example, is assassinated by Mercian nobles, and Æthelburh is forced to flee from Northumbria to Kent when her husband is killed—but simply that they almost never suffer in defense of Christianity. Nor are queens ever threatened with suffering that is at all related to their spiritual lives, for the defilement to which they are vulnerable always remains at the abstract level of potential spiritual corruption through contact with their pagan husbands and people, never escalating into actual physical danger or sexual threats. Æthelthryth stands as the sole exception: a queen who is willing to toil in defense of her virginity, to work hard to extricate herself from the marriages that hinder her entrance to monastic life, and to suffer after entering monastic life, as a penance for her former life of wealth and ease. Æthelthryth's virginity, as well as her overt renunciation of such markers of queenship as elaborate clothing, lavish meals, and royal jewels, further differentiates her from the rest of the queens in the *HE*, and her toils as an earthly queen serve mainly to emphasize the inherently superior queenship to be enjoyed as Christ's spouse.

18. The Augustinian missionaries, for example, are depicted as "orationibus uidelicet assiduis uigiliis ac ieiuniis ser / uiendo, uerbum uitae quibus poterant praedicando. . . . secundum ea quae docebant ipsi per omnia uiuendo, et paratum ad patiendum aduersa quaeque uel etiam moriendum pro ea quam praedicabant ueritate animum habendo" (constantly engaged in prayers, in vigils, and fasts, they preached the word of life to as many as they could. . . . in all things they practised what they preached and kept themselves prepared to endure adversities, even to the point of dying for the truths they proclaimed; *HE*, i.25, 76, 77). Paulinus is also shown toiling on behalf of Christianity: "Laborauit multum. . . . multo tempore illo laborante in uerbo" (He set vigorously to work. . . . he toiled hard and long in preaching the word; *HE*, ii.9, 164, 165).

19. Ian Wood characterizes this scene as odd and most likely embroidered either by Canterbury tradition or by Bede's narrative craft: "The Mission of Augustine of Canterbury to the English," *Speculum* 69 (1994): 1–17, at 3.

20. Gregory's letter to Bertha is contained in *Councils and Ecclesiastical Documents Relating to Great Britain and Ireland*, ed. Arthur West Haddan and William Stubbs, 3 vols. (1871; repr., Oxford: Clarendon Press, 1964), 3:17–18. The letter is translated as "Epistle 29" by James Barmby, in *Gregory the Great, Ephraim Syrus, Aphrahat*, NPNF, 2nd ser., vol. 13, pt. 2, ed. Philip Schaff and Henry Wace (New York: Christian Literature Co., 1898), 56–57.

21. As argued by Wood, "The Mission of Augustine," 6–7, 10.

22. The fact that Gregory's letter does not appear in the *HE* has occasioned much debate, and it is indeed possible that Bede simply did not know of the letter. For a lucid discussion of possible reasons why the letter does not appear in the *HE*, see Schulenburg, *Forgetful of Their Sex*, 191–95.

23. Hollis, *Anglo-Saxon Women and the Church*, 179–270.

24. Lees and Overing, "Birthing Bishops and Fathering Poets."

25. Mayr-Harting, *The Coming of Christianity*, 63; and Wallace-Hadrill, *Early Germanic Kingship*, 29, 45.

26. Wood, "The Mission of Augustine," 9–10.

27. Wood points out that Bede places Æthelberht's conversion at 595, despite depicting him as a pagan upon Augustine's arrival in 597, and suggests that Æthelberht may have already converted in or around 595, before Augustine ever reached Kent: *The Merovingian Kingdoms, 450–751* (London: Longman, 1994), 178. Higham argues against the possibility of such an early date for Æthelberht's conversion on the grounds that Gregory's correspondence assumes both that Æthelberht was non-Christian when Augustine arrived and that the latter was responsible for his conversion: *The Convert Kings*, 57, and 121 n. 24.

28. On evidence for the existence of British Christianity in England, and particularly in Kent, during the sixth and seventh centuries, see Clare Stancliffe, "The British Church and the Mission of Augustine," in *St Augustine and the Conversion of England*, ed. Gameson, 107–51, esp. 115–22.

29. *HE*, i.14, i.22, ii.2, v.23. For more on Bede's treatment of the British, see Stancliffe, "The British Church," and Higham, *An English Empire*, 16–46.

30. Mayr-Harting, *The Coming of Christianity*, 63–67.

31. The extent to which Æthelberht was in fact subordinate to the Franks remains unclear. Historians have noted Gregory's correspondence as offering possible evidence that Kent was a satellite of the Frankish kingdom, or at least that Gregory seemed to think it was when, in July 596, he wrote to the Frankish kings Theuderic and Theudebert, asserting: "I have every reason to think that you heartily wish your subjects [*subiectos vestros*] to be converted to the same faith as yourselves, their kings and lords"; cited in Wallace-Hadrill, *Early Germanic Kingship*, 25. Higham

argues that Gregory's letter may simply reflect his knowledge of the Merovingians' view of England as their dependent, and be part of a strategy to persuade the Frankish kings to support missionary efforts in England: *The Convert Kings*, 80–82.

32. Argued by Higham, *An English Empire*, 50–52.

33. Judith Butler, *The Psychic Life of Power: Theories in Subjection* (Stanford: Stanford University Press, 1997).

34. Ibid., 2.

35. Ibid., 15.

36. See D. P. Kirby, *The Earliest English Kings* (London: Unwin Hyman, 1991), 34–35; and Higham, *The Convert Kings*, 53–132, with quotation at 116–17.

37. On Frankish influence in sixth- and seventh-century Kent, see Barbara Yorke, "The Reception of Christianity at the Anglo-Saxon Royal Courts," in *St Augustine and the Conversion of England*, ed. Gameson, 152–73, esp. 157–58; and, in this same volume, Stéphane Lebecq, "England and the Continent in the Sixth and Seventh Centuries: The Question of Logistics," 50–67. Also helpful are Campbell, "The First Century of Christianity," 53–67; and Higham, *The Convert Kings*, 82–90.

38. Argued by Higham, *The Convert Kings*, 82–86.

39. On Bede's efforts to justify English claims to the island via spiritual inheritance from the Romans, see Higham, *An English Empire*, 16–46. Nicholas Howe offers another useful perspective on this question by showing that Bede narrates the native Britons' loss of the island and the Germanic migration as manifestations of divine justice, with "British darkness giv[ing] way to Anglo-Saxon light": *Migration and Mythmaking in Anglo-Saxon England* (New Haven: Yale University Press, 1989), 47–71, 108–11, quotation at 47.

40. Saint Martin was, of course, extremely popular throughout all of Western Europe, perhaps even, as Wallace-Hadrill suggests, the greatest patron saint except for Saint Peter. In spite of his pervasive appeal, Martin was strongly associated with patronage of the Merovingian dynasty since its beginnings under Clovis, and hence of the Franks as a new people: Wallace-Hadrill, "Bede and Plummer," in *Early Medieval History* (Oxford: Basil Blackwell, 1975), 76–95; reprinted in Wallace-Hadrill, *Bede's Ecclesiastical History of the English People: A Historical Commentary* (Oxford: Clarendon Press, 1988), xv–xxxv, with discussion of Martin at xxxii–xxxiii. However, Bede emphasizes the church's connection not to Frankia but to Rome, claiming that it was an "ecclesia in honorem sancti Martini antiquitus facta, dum adhuc Romani Brittaniam incolerent" (church built in ancient times in honour of Saint Martin, while the Romans were still in Britain; *HE*, i.26, pp. 76, 77). Colgrave and Mynors note the ambiguity of the phrasing but assert that Bede seems to be implying that the church was both built and dedicated to Martin during Roman times: *HE*, pp. 76–77 n. 2. If such is the case, Bede may well be attempting to dissociate Martin from Frankia by stressing his appeal among the Romans.

41. It is not clear where Æthelberht was baptized. Charles Plummer notes Saint Martin's as a strong possibility: *Venerabilis Baedae opera historica*, ed. C. Plummer, 2 vols. (1896; repr., Oxford: Oxford University Press, 1946), 2:44, 494.

42. Mayr-Harting, *The Coming of Christianity*, 66. Mayr-Harting attributes Edwin's reluctance to convert to a fear of offending his pagan overlord, Rædwald: 66–68.

43. Armstrong, "Holy Queens as Agents of Christianization," 235.

44. I have adopted the dating proposed by Peter Hunter Blair, "The Letters of Pope Boniface V and the Mission of Paulinus to Northumbria," in *England Before the Conquest: Studies in Primary Sources Presented to Dorothy Whitelock*, ed. Peter Clemoes and Kathleen Hughes (Cambridge: Cambridge University Press, 1971), 5–13, at 9. For more on the dating of Pope Boniface V's letters to both Æthelburh and Edwin, see D. P. Kirby, "Bede and Northumbrian Chronology," *English Historical Review* 78 (1963): 514–27.

45. Colgrave and Mynors translate *virgine* as "princess's"; I have changed it to "virgin's" so as to illustrate more clearly the comparison between the virgin queen and the virginal body of the Northumbrians, both of which are rendered through the noun *virgo*.

46. There is an extensive body of scholarship on the complex relationships between surface and identity. I cite here only a few particularly thought-provoking studies. Eve Kosofsky Sedgwick, "The Character in the Veil: Imagery of the Surface in the Gothic Novel," *PMLA* 96 (1981): 255–70, offers a critique of the tendency in criticism of the Gothic to link sexuality with depth and repression with surface, arguing that Gothic convention links such surfaces as the veil, flesh, and physiognomy with sexuality and uses the marking of these surfaces as a means of establishing personal identity. Judith Butler's theory of gender as constructed through the reiterated performance of social norms is famously articulated in *Gender Trouble: Feminism and the Subversion of Identity* (New York: Routledge, 1990), and further elaborated and defended in the light of critiques of its failure to account for the materiality of the gendered body in *Bodies That Matter: On the Discursive Limits of "Sex"* (London: Routledge, 1993). Susan Crane's *The Performance of Self* considers how material and rhetorical performances, such as clothing, heraldic signs, and Maying ceremonies, produced identity as conceptualized in late medieval literature and courtly culture.

47. Anglo-Saxon literature is so saturated with stock depictions of such material and rhetorical performances as weaponry and boasting, and references interiority so thoroughly via recourse to such externals as weather, geography, and clothing that—the tenuous and ill-understood relationship that Anglo-Saxon literature bears to culture notwithstanding—it seems likely that the self in Anglo-Saxon society was at least in part constituted through material and rhetorical performances.

48. See Fred C. Robinson, "The Prescient Woman in Old English Literature," in *Philologia Anglica: Essays Presented to Professor Yoshio Terasawa on the Occasion of His Sixtieth Birthday*, ed. Kinshiro Oshitari et al. (Tokyo: Kenkyusha, 1988), 241–50; reprinted in *The Tomb of Beowulf and Other Essays on Old English* (Oxford: Blackwell, 1993), 155–63.

49. Hollis, *Anglo-Saxon Women and the Church*, 227; and Armstrong, "Holy Queens as Agents of Christianization," 239.

50. Hollis, *Anglo-Saxon Women and the Church*, 230.

51. Wallace-Hadrill points out that "the passage sounds more in conformity with Bede's own thinking . . . than with what may actually have occurred": *Bede's Ecclesiastical History*, 37.

52. Wallace-Hadrill, *Early Medieval History*, 84–85; and Campbell, "Bede I," in Campbell, *Essays in Anglo-Saxon History*, 1–27, at 26.

53. "Gregorius Berthæ Reginæ Anglorum," in *Councils and Ecclesiastical Documents*, ed. Haddan and Stubbs, 18; my trans.

54. Although Bede refers to Eadbald as *perfidus* (*HE*, ii.5, p. 150), it is worth noting, as Colgrave and Mynors point out, that to call Eadbald an apostate is unfair, as he had in fact never been a Christian: *HE*, ii.5, p. 151 n. 5.

55. Marriage between a son and stepmother was a regular rule among some Anglo-Saxon tribes: Plummer, *Venerabilis Baedae opera historica*, 2:88. The practice makes particularly good sense among wealthy families, for it permits the consolidation of familial wealth that would become diffused if a widow were to remarry outside her husband's family.

56. Higham claims that one of the political implications of Rædwald's baptism was to confirm his subjection to Æthelberht: *The Convert Kings*, 102–3. Hollis argues that the opposition Rædwald's wife demonstrates toward her husband's conversion can be traced to this implication: *Anglo-Saxon Women and the Church*, 234.

57. See, for example, Ps. 105:38–39, Jer. 3:8–9, Ezek. 23:30–31, and Hos. chaps. 1–3, and also Defensor's *Liber scintillarum:* "Isidorus dixit. Fornicatio carnis adulterium est. fornicatio animę séruitus idolorum est" (Isidore said: "Fornication of the body is adultery; fornication of the spirit is the service of idols"). The Old English gloss stands as follows: "sæde forligr flæsces unrihthæmed ys forligr sawle þeowdom deofulgylda ys": *Defensor's Liber Scintillarum with an Interlinear Anglo-Saxon Version*, ed. E. W. Rhodes, EETS o.s. 93 (London: N. Trübner, 1889; repr. Millwood, N.Y.: Krauss Reprint, 1987), Latin and Old English at 87.

58. During the fourth and fifth centuries, conversion became increasingly identified with asceticism and monasticism, so much so, that unless otherwise defined in context, the term *conversio* came to mean entrance into monastic life: Morrison, *Understanding Conversion*, 14. For more on early medieval kings who renounced their kingdoms to adopt the religious life, and on Bede's attitude toward this practice, see Clare Stancliffe, "Kings Who Opted Out," in *Ideal and Reality in*

Frankish and Anglo-Saxon Society: Studies Presented to J. M. Wallace-Hadrill, ed. Patrick Wormald et al. (Oxford: Basil Blackwell, 1983), 154–76; and Wallace-Hadrill, *Early Germanic Kingship*, 87–91.

59. Stancliffe, "Kings Who Opted Out," 160–61, 175–76.

60. The Bible contains numerous injunctions regarding the indissolubility of marriage; see, for example, 1 Cor. 7, and Luke 16:18. The idea that one must obtain spousal consent before embarking on a life of continence is a recurrent theme in patristic writings; a typical formulation appears in the first book of Saint Augustine's *De adulterinis coniugiis*, in which he claims: "Ubi dominus nec continentiam uoluit suscipi nisi pari concordia atque consensu" (The Lord's will has been that no one undertake to practice the virtue of continence without mutual agreement and consent): Augustine, *De adulterinis coniugiis*, ed. Joseph Zycha, CSEL 41 (Vienna: F. Tempsky, 1900), bk. 1, chap. 3, p. 350; cited translation is from *Adulterous Marriages*, trans. Charles T. Heugelmeyer, in *Saint Augustine: Treatises on Marriage and Other Subjects*, The Fathers of the Church 27, ed. Roy J. Deferrari (1955; repr., with corrections, Washington, D.C.: Catholic University of America Press, 1969), 65. Similar sentiments are forcefully expressed in the correspondence of Pope Gregory the Great, as in his letter to Adrian, notary of Panormus, in which he responds to Agathosa's complaint that her husband had entered a monastery without her consent: "Quia, etsi mundana lex praecipit conversionis gratia utrolibet invito solvi posse coniugium, divina haec lex fieri non permittit" (For, although mundane law declares that marriage may be dissolved for the sake of conversion against the will of either party, yet divine law does not permit this to be done): Gregory the Great, *Gregorii I Papae registrum epistolarum* 11.30, ed. Paul Ewald and Ludo M. Hartmann, MGH Epistolae 1 and 2 (Berlin: Weidmann, 1887–99); cited translation is from "Epistle 50," trans. Barmby, in *Gregory the Great, Ephraim Syrus, Aphrahat*, 69. *Registrum epistolarum* 11.27 is also relevant.

61. The Anglo-Saxons placed a high premium on communal celebration and feasting. Bede's depiction of spiritual difference between husband and wife as a hindrance to these forms of sociability would very likely have augmented its sense of reprehensibility among his readers.

62. Hollis points out that the *HE*'s depiction of gender segregation as an organizing principle for the double monasteries at Barking, Faremoutiers, and Ely may be less a reflection of actual social practice than of Bede's aversion to mixed religious communities: *Anglo-Saxon Women and the Church*, 245.

63. Hollis, *Anglo-Saxon Women and the Church*, 230.

64. Joan Nicholson, for example, when discussing the early kings' belief that "daughters might gainfully be used as propitiatory offerings," claims that "parents were readier to part with daughters [than sons]" and questions whether Edwin might "have been less eager in the case of a son": *"Feminae Gloriosiae:* Women in the Age of Bede," in *Medieval Women: Dedicated and Presented to Professor Rosalind*

M. T. Hill on the Occasion of Her Seventieth Birthday, ed. Derek Baker, Studies in Church History, Subsidia 1 (Oxford: Basil Blackwell, 1978), 15–29, quotations at 22, 16, and 22. Similar sentiments are expressed in Eileen Power's study of late medieval nuns. Power argues that some male relatives "use[d] the nunnery as a 'dumping ground' for unwanted and often unwilling girls, whom it was desirable to put out of the world" in order to claim possession of their inheritance: *Medieval English Nunneries (ca. 1275–1535)* (Cambridge: Cambridge University Press, 1922), 29.

65. See, for example, Susan J. Ridyard, "Anglo-Saxon Women and the Church in the Age of Conversion," in *Monks, Nuns, and Friars in Mediaeval Society*, ed. Edward B. King, Jacqueline T. Schaefer, and William B. Wadley, Sewanee Mediaeval Studies 4 (Sewanee, Tenn.: Press of the University of the South, 1989), 105–32.

66. Mayke de Jong, *In Samuel's Image: Child Oblation in the Early Medieval West* (Leiden: E. J. Brill, 1996), 1. For a lucid discussion of child oblation as practiced in Anglo-Saxon England and in Continental monasteries of Anglo-Saxon inspiration, see 46–55, 137–38, 169–70, 212–13.

67. See *HE*, v.24, pp. 566–67. Whether Bede's early life is more accurately described as child oblation proper or as fosterage by monastic parents is a vexed issue. For more on the intersections between oblation and fosterage, see de Jong, *In Samuel's Image*, 205–19, with discussion of Bede at 212–13.

68. My understanding of child oblation and its symbolic implications is much indebted to de Jong's *In Samuel's Image*, esp. 267–89.

69. Ridyard, "Anglo-Saxon Women and the Church," 105–6.

70. De Jong points out that complaints about parents off-loading superfluous and disabled children on monasteries did not become widespread until the twelfth century, and even then, such complaints were all concerned with boys, not girls: *In Samuel's Image*, 300–301.

71. Ridyard, "Anglo-Saxon Women and the Church."

72. Susan Ridyard argues convincingly that the renunciation of royal status and its material trappings was a far more important criterion for royal female saints than for their male counterparts. For men, Ridyard maintains, it was not the renunciation of royal status but rather the fulfillment of royal duty upon which sanctity was founded: *The Royal Saints of Anglo-Saxon England*, 82–92.

73. For more on Bede's treatment of Hild, see Lees and Overing, "Birthing Bishops and Fathering Poets." On Hild's royal connections, see the *HE* (iv.23, p. 406), which reports that Hild was the daughter of Hereric, Edwin's nephew, and also that her sister, Hereswith, was the mother of Ealdwulf, king of the East Angles.

74. Bede's objections to these monasteries are twofold: first, he believes that laymen are establishing them merely to evade taxation and military obligations; and second, he is opposed to monasteries that are run by abbots and abbesses appointed on the basis of their familial connections, and believes that spiritual leaders

ought to be chosen instead on the basis of such qualities as virtue and chastity: *Epistola Bede ad Ecgbertum Episcopum*, ed. C. Plummer, in *Venerabilis Baedae opera historica*, 1: 405–23, esp. 415–18; trans. D. H. Farmer, in *Ecclesiastical History of the English People with Bede's Letter to Egbert and Cuthbert's Letter on the Death of Bede* (1955; rev. and repr., London: Penguin, 1990), 337–51, esp. 345–47.

75. A few additional occasions in the *HE* in which Bede alludes to queens and royal women as potential advocates for the Church are: Eanflæd's request to her cousin, King Eorcenberht of Kent, to provide assistance with Wilfrid's pilgrimage to Rome (*HE*, v.19); Osthryth's transference of her uncle's relics to Bardney monastery (*HE*, iii.11); and Bliththryth's (Plectrudis's) request to her husband, Pippin of Heristal, ruler of the Franks, to endow a monastery for the bishop Swithberht (*HE*, v.11).

76. Such churchmen include, as we have seen, Pope Gregory the Great, Pope Boniface V, and Bishop Paulinus of York. It is worth recalling that Gregory's letters consistently recognize queens as crucial forces in promoting Christianity; see Wood, "The Mission of Augustine," 6–7.

77. Robert A. Markus, *Conversion and Disenchantment in Augustine's Spiritual Career* (Villanova, Pa.: Villanova University Press, 1989).

78. The evidence for queens' dowries is quite slim and tends to derive from fairly late sources. See Pauline Stafford, *Queen Emma and Queen Edith: Queenship and Women's Power in Eleventh-Century England* (Oxford: Blackwell Publishers, 1997), 130 n. 173, 134–35, 139, 218, 251.

Chapter 2   Crossing Queens, Pleasing Hierarchies

1. Gregory's letter to Bertha is dated to 601. In that same year, Gregory also sent a letter to Æthelberht, urging the king to make conversion of his people a primary concern and invoking Constantine as a worthy exemplar in this project. The letter to Æthelberht is cited in full in Bede's *Historia Ecclesiastica* (i.32), yet the letter to Bertha is absent. Stephanie Hollis argues that Bede's failure to include the letter to Bertha is indicative of his general hostility to female influence, particularly in ecclesiastical affairs. See Hollis, *Anglo-Saxon Women and the Church: Sharing a Common Fate* (Woodbridge, Suffolk: Boydell Press, 1992), 220–27 and 225 n. 104. For more on the letter, see Jane Tibbetts Schulenburg, *Forgetful of Their Sex: Female Sanctity and Society, ca. 500–1100* (Chicago: Chicago University Press, 1998), 191–95.

2. *Councils and Ecclesiastical Documents Relating to Great Britain and Ireland*, ed. Arthur West Haddan and William Stubbs, 3 vols. (1871; repr., Oxford: Clarendon Press, 1964), 3:17.

3. "Epistle 29," trans. James Barmby, in *Gregory the Great, Ephraim Syrus, Aphrahat*, NPNF, 2nd ser., vol. 13, pt. 2, ed. Philip Schaff and Henry Wace (New York: Christian Literature Co. 1898), 56–57, at 57.

4. Kenneth G. Holum, *Theodosian Empresses: Women and Imperial Dominion in Late Antiquity* (Berkeley: University of California Press, 1982), 25–26 and 26 n. 77.

5. Cited in Holum, *Theodosian Empresses*, 216.

6. Gregory of Tours, *Glory of the Martyrs*, trans. Raymond Van Dam (Liverpool: Liverpool University Press, 1988), 22.

7. A modern English translation of Baudonivia's *Vita Radegundis* appears in *Sainted Women of the Dark Ages*, ed. and trans. Jo Ann McNamara and John E. Halborg, with E. Gordon Whatley (Durham, N.C.: Duke University Press, 1992), 86–105, quotation at 97.

8. The letter was presented and read at the Second Council of Nice in 787. For the Latin letter, see PL 96:1217. The letter is translated in *The Seven Ecumenical Councils of the Undivided Church*, ed. Henry R. Percival, NPNF, 2nd ser., vol. 14, ed. Philip Schaff and Henry Wace (New York: Charles Scribner's Sons, 1900), 536–37.

9. In his *De obitu Theodosii oratio*, Ambrose draws an explicit comparison between Helena and Mary, claiming that "visitata est Maria ut Evam liberaret; visitata est Helena ut imperatores redimerentur" (Mary was visited to liberate Eve; Helen was visited so that emperors might be redeemed): Sister Mary Dolorosa Mannix, *Sancti Ambrosii oratio de obitu Theodosii: Text, Translation, Introduction, and Commentary*, Patristic Studies, vol. 9 (Washington, D.C.: Catholic University of America, 1925), 61 (Latin), 80 (trans.). For more on the association between queenship and Mary, see Pauline Stafford, *Queen Emma and Queen Edith: Queenship and Women's Power in Eleventh-Century England* (Oxford: Blackwell, 1997), 163, 166–68, 172–74, 178, and passim; and Mary Clayton, *The Cult of the Virgin Mary in Anglo-Saxon England* (Cambridge: Cambridge University Press, 1990), 59, 146, 164–65, 171–72, 273, and passim.

10. The term *inventio* (literally "finding" or "discovery") refers to a hagiographic subgenre that deals with the finding of a saint's relics. *Inventio* narratives may appear as discrete texts or as episodes embedded in longer histories, sermons, or letters. Early *inventio* narratives survive from the fifth century, and the genre was most popular in England during the late eleventh and twelfth centuries. *Inventio* narratives formed a crucial part of a monastery's history, and were typically written to authenticate particular relics and to justify a house's claim to them. For a thought-provoking account of the intersections between *inventiones* and fictionality, with a focus on twelfth-century English historical writing, see Monika Otter, *Inventiones: Fiction and Referentiality in Twelfth-Century English Historical Writing* (Chapel Hill: University of North Carolina Press, 1996).

11. For useful bibliographies, see P. O. E. Gradon, ed., *Cynewulf's "Elene,"* rev. ed. (London: University of Exeter Press, 1977), 76–80; Gordon Whatley, "The Figure of Constantine the Great in Cynewulf's 'Elene,'" *Traditio* 37 (1981): 161–202, at

162–63 n. 7; and *Cynewulf: Basic Readings,* ed. Robert E. Bjork (New York: Garland, 1996), which contains landmark essays on Cynewulf, and suggestions for further reading at xv.

12. See Helen Damico, *Beowulf's Wealhtheow and the Valkyrie Tradition* (Madison: University of Wisconsin Press, 1984), 25–32, 35–39, 49–50; Alexandra Hennessey Olsen, "Cynewulf's Autonomous Women: A Reconsideration of Elene and Juliana," in *New Readings on Women in Old English Literature,* ed. Helen Damico and Alexandra Hennessey Olsen (Bloomington: Indiana University Press, 1990), 222–32; and Jane Chance, *Woman as Hero in Old English Literature* (Syracuse: Syracuse University Press, 1986), 31–38, 46–52.

13. The first critic to read Elene as a figure for *Ecclesia* was Thomas Hill, although it should be noted that Hill's typological reading maintains a profound sensitivity to the literal and historical levels of the poem: Thomas Hill, "Sapiential Structure and Figural Narrative in the Old English *Elene,*" *Traditio* 27 (1971): 159–77; rev. and repr. in *Cynewulf: Basic Readings,* ed. Bjork, 207–28, esp. 213–14. Other critics who read Elene as a type of *Ecclesia* or the New Law include Jackson Campbell, "Cynewulf's Multiple Revelations," in *Cynewulf: Basic Readings,* ed. Bjork, 229–50, esp. 234–36 (first published in *Medievalia et Humanistica* 3 [1972]: 257–77); Catharine A. Regan, "Evangelicalism as the Informing Principle of Cynewulf's *Elene,*" in *Cynewulf: Basic Readings,* ed. Bjork, 251–80, esp. 253–55 (first published in *Traditio* 29 [1973]: 27–52); Whatley, "Figure of Constantine the Great," 200; Earl Anderson, "Cynewulf's *Elene*: Manuscript Division and Structural Symmetry," *Modern Philology* 72 (1974): 111–22, esp. 113; and John P. Hermann, *Allegories of War: Language and Violence in Old English Poetry* (Ann Arbor: University of Michigan Press, 1989), 99–100.

14. Whatley, "Figure of Constantine the Great"; Clare A. Lees, "At a Crossroads: Old English and Feminist Criticism," in *Reading Old English Texts,* ed. Katherine O'Brien O'Keeffe (Cambridge: Cambridge University Press, 1997), 146–69, esp. 159–67; and Joyce Tally Lionarons, "Cultural Syncretism and the Construction of Gender in Cynewulf's *Elene,*" *Exemplaria* 10 (1998): 51–68.

15. R. D. Fulk, "Cynewulf: Canon, Dialect, and Date," in *Cynewulf: Basic Readings,* ed. Bjork, 3–21, at 16. For a more extensive discussion of date and locale for Cynewulf's works, see R. D. Fulk, *A History of Old English Meter* (Philadelphia: University of Pennsylvania Press, 1992), 351–68, and passim.

16. Patrick W. Conner, "On Dating Cynewulf," in *Cynewulf: Basic Readings,* ed. Bjork, 23–55. Conner's argument rests on three contentions: a reconsideration of Cynewulf's habit of spelling his name as both CYNWULF and CYNEWULF and refutation of former arguments that the different spellings reflect linguistic changes taking place in the eighth or possibly ninth centuries; a reconsideration of the West Saxon near-rhymes in the epilogue to *Elene* and refutation of received opinion that these near-rhymes represent what were once exact rhymes in an earlier Anglian dialect; and the contention that *Fates of the Apostles* takes as its source an

augmented version of the *Martyrologium* of Usuard, which, Conner contends, would not have been available in England until the tenth century. Conner's argument, particularly the portion that rests on source evidence, has been favorably received by Fulk, "Cynewulf: Canon, Dialect, and Date," 16–17. However, John M. McCulloh, "Did Cynewulf Use a Martyrology? Reconsidering the Sources of *The Fates of the Apostles*," *Anglo-Saxon England* 29 (2000): 67–83, challenges Conner's use of source evidence, arguing that the martyrology under question is neither the work of Usuard nor a likely source for *Fates*.

17. Scholars who do read Old English poetry through historicist and cultural paradigms are noted in my introduction, n. 16.

18. For more on the date, provenance, and compilation of the Vercelli Book, see *The Vercelli Book: A Late Tenth-Century Manuscript Containing Prose and Verse,* ed. Celia Sisam, EEMF 19 (Copenhagen: Rosenkilde and Bagger, 1976), 44, and 13–50; and also D. G. Scragg, "The Compilation of the Vercelli Book," *Anglo-Saxon England* 2 (1973): 189–207.

19. References to the *Inventio Sanctae Crucis* are to *Inventio Sanctae Crucis,* ed. Alfred Holder (Leipzig: B. G. Teubner, 1889), specifically, to Holder's transcription of the eighth-century manuscript from the Benedictine monastery of St. Gall, Switzerland, St. Gall 225, which Gradon, *Cynewulf's "Elene,"* 18–19, takes as representing the type of version Cynewulf used. The legend is also available in G. Henschen and E. Papebroch, eds., *Acta sanctorum, Maius I* (Antwerp, 1680), 445–48, and it is translated in *Sources and Analogues of Old English Poetry,* ed. Michael J. B. Allen and Daniel G. Calder (Cambridge: D. S. Brewer, 1976), 59–68. While the version contained in the *Acta sanctorum* is more accessible than Holder's transcription, it is a conflation of several different manuscripts and hence less reliable. Gordon Whatley contends that by the ninth century, the *Inventio* legend was circulating in England in manuscripts that show little variation from one another. He suggests further that the legend had early acquired a fixed form and that changes made between the seventh and tenth centuries were mainly editorial in nature: "Figure of Constantine the Great," 161–62 n. 2. Because the Latin legend has changed so little over the years, one feels justified in drawing tentative conclusions based on careful comparisons between *Elene* and the St. Gall manuscript.

20. Wulfstan's third homily on the Christian life offers a typical early medieval formulation of the idea of the Church as a mother: "Ealle we habbað ænne heofonlicne fæder 7 ane gastlice modor, seo is ecclesia genamod, þæt is Godes cyrice" (We all have a heavenly father and a spiritual mother who is called *Ecclesia,* that is, God's church): *The Homilies of Wulfstan,* ed. Dorothy Bethurum (Oxford: Clarendon Press, 1957), 202, ll. 41–43.

21. See Chance, *Woman as Hero,* 47; and Lionarons, "Cultural Syncretism," 68.

22. See Erich Auerbach, "Figura," in *Scenes from the Drama of European Literature* (1959; repr., Minneapolis: University of Minnesota Press, 1984), 40–41; and Hill, "Sapiential Structure and Figural Narrative," 165.

23. All citations from *Elene* are by line numbers and refer to Gradon, ed., *Cynewulf's "Elene."*

24. Auerbach, "Figura," 53.

25. For important discussions of conversion in *Elene*, see Robert Stepsis and Richard Rand, "Contrast and Conversion in Cynewulf's *Elene*," *Neuphilologische Mitteilungen* 70 (1969): 273–82; Daniel Calder, "Strife, Revelation, and Conversion: The Thematic Structure of *Elene*," *English Studies* 53 (1972): 201–10, which is reworked in Daniel G. Calder, *Cynewulf* (Boston: Twayne, 1981), 104–38; and Campbell, "Cynewulf's Multiple Revelations."

26. *Ælfric's Catholic Homilies: The Second Series, Text*, ed. Malcolm Godden, EETS s.s. 5 (London: Oxford University Press, 1979) (hereafter *CH II*), p. 340, ll. 175–76. *Cwen* and its closest Latin equivalent, *regina*, appear to have been the preferred terms for invoking the queen's typological significance as Church. The corpus contains no instances in which *hlæfdige* is unequivocally used to symbolize the Church. However, in his sermon on Christianity, Wulfstan states: "Ecclesia enim sponsa Cristi est et omnium domina" (The Church is the spouse of Christ and the lady of all things), and opposite these lines in Bodleian Library, Hatton MS 113, *domina* is glossed as *hlæfdige*: *The Homilies of Wulfstan*, p. 195, l. 33. While this gloss is, admittedly, in a later hand, *hlæfdige* was a standard gloss for *domina* (Stafford, *Queen Emma and Queen Edith*, 58); it thus seems likely that *hlæfdige* carried a typological resonance similar to that of *domina*.

27. Jackson Campbell, "Cynewulf's Multiple Revelations," 235, notes that *þeoden* in line 267 could equally well be referring to Constantine or to God.

28. The Latin is contained in *Asser's Life of King Alfred Together with the Annals of St. Neot's*, ed. William Henry Stevenson (Oxford: Clarendon Press, 1904), 11. For a modern English translation of the relevant passages, see *Alfred the Great: Asser's Life of King Alfred and Other Contemporary Sources*, ed. and trans. Simon Keynes and Michael Lapidge (London: Penguin, 1983), 71.

29. Stafford, *Queen Emma and Queen Edith*, 62; see also *Asser's Life of King Alfred*, ed. Stevenson, 202.

30. Stafford, *Queen Emma and Queen Edith*, 57–59.

31. Ibid., 57 n. 9.

32. Ælfric's homily for the Invention of the Cross is very brief. Other than a few remarks on Elene's piety, Ælfric takes little interest in her, and the text is focused mainly on Constantine's battle with the bloodthirsty general Maxentius and the emperor's resolve not to shed the blood of his own people: *CH II*, ed. Godden, pp. 174–76. Malcolm Godden, *Ælfric's Catholic Homilies: Introduction, Commentary and Glossary*, EETS s.s. 18 (Oxford: Oxford University Press, 2000), 513, argues that Ælfric was most likely aware of the more traditional version of the legend—which is what Cynewulf was retelling—but evidently preferred the account of the Invention given in the *Historia Ecclesiastica* of Eusebius and Rufinus (Ælfric's main source).

33. I am here following Gradon's suggestion that the phrase "wira gespon" refers to a type of gold filigree ornament on Elene's breast: *Cynewulf's "Elene,"* 67. However, it is worth noting that the phrase is ambiguous and may simply refer to the nails of Christ. Perhaps the most accurate reading of the phrase is to see it as encapsulating a sense of both royal wealth and spiritual riches, and thus reminding readers that the saintly queen is in possession of both.

34. *Maxims I*, in *The Exeter Book*, ed. George Philip Krapp and Elliott Van Kirk Dobbie, ASPR 3 (New York: Columbia University Press, 1936), 156–163, at 161, ll. 125–26. It is worth noting, however, that since *cwen* is here parallel with *guma*, the former may be translated simply as "noble woman" or "lady"; these lines are thus most likely intended to convey the sense that treasure is befitting any upper-class woman, and not only royal women or queens.

35. Ælfric's homily "On the Dedication of a Church," clearly formulates the idea of the elaborately adorned queen as a symbol for the Church: "Seo gastlice cwen godes geladung is geglencged mid deorwurðre frætewunge. and menigfealdum bleo goddra drohtnunga and mihta" (The spiritual queen, God's Church, is adorned with the precious ornament and manifold color of good habits and virtues): *CH II*, ed. Godden, p. 341, ll. 191–92. Scriptural passages that explore this idea include Ps. 44:9–14, much of the Song of Songs, and Apoc. 12:1 and 21:2.

36. Barbara C. Raw, *Anglo-Saxon Crucifixion Iconography and the Art of the Monastic Revival* (Cambridge: Cambridge University Press, 1990), 8–11.

37. *Ælfric's Catholic Homilies: The First Series, Text*, ed. Peter Clemoes, EETS s.s. 17 (Oxford: Oxford University Press, 1997), p. 490, ll. 122–26.

38. The Latin citations are from *Asser's Life of King Alfred*, ed. Stevenson, 11–12; the translations are from *Alfred the Great*, ed. and trans. Keynes and Lapidge, 71.

39. Stafford, *Queen Emma and Queen Edith*, 167.

40. *Encomium Emmae Reginae*, ed. and trans. Alistair Campbell, with a supplementary introduction by Simon Keynes (Cambridge: Cambridge University Press, 1998), xlii.

41. "Cui cum ex more et iure regia sedes assidue pararetur a regis latere, preter ecclesiam et regalem mensam malebat ad pedes ipsius sedere, nisi forte manum illi porrigeret, uel nutu dextere iuxta se ad sedendum inuitaret siue cogeret" (Although by custom and law a royal throne was always prepared for her at the king's side, she preferred, except in church and at the royal table, to sit at his feet, unless perchance he should reach out his hand to her, or with a gesture of the hand invite or command her to sit next to him): *The Life of King Edward Who Rests at Westminster, Attributed to a Monk of Saint-Bertin*, ed. and trans. Frank Barlow, 2nd ed. (Oxford: Oxford University Press, 1992), 64–65.

42. For a stimulating discussion of how allegory and typology generate spatial conceptions of temporality, see Magnus Ullén, "Dante in Paradise: The End of Allegorical Interpretation," *New Literary History* 32 (2001): 177–99.

43. While Elene does not undergo a spiritual shift of the same magnitude as those experienced by Constantine, Judas, or the poet, after receiving the nails with which Christ was crucified, she is filled with the gift of wisdom and inhabited by the Holy Spirit, an inner renewal that could be interpreted as a kind of conversion ("heo gefylled wæs / wisdomes gife 7 þa wic beheold / halig heofonlic gast, hreðer weardode, / æðelne innoð"; 1142b–45a). I am grateful to Dabney Anderson Bankert for this point.

44. Jan Willem Drijvers, *Helena Augusta: The Mother of Constantine the Great and the Legend of Her Finding of the True Cross* (Leiden: E. J. Brill, 1992), 65–67.

45. Ibid., 66–70.

46. For more on Anglo-Saxon attitudes toward "just war," see J. E. Cross, "The Ethic of War in Old English," in *England Before the Conquest: Studies in Primary Sources Presented to Dorothy Whitelock*, ed. Peter Clemoes and Kathleen Hughes (Cambridge: Cambridge University Press, 1971), 269–82; and J. M. Wallace-Hadrill, "War and Peace in the Earlier Middle Ages," *Transactions of the Royal Historical Society* 5th ser., 25 (1975): 157–74.

47. Whatley, "Figure of Constantine the Great," 171–72.

48. Early legends recounting the discovery of the Cross are mildly antipagan rather than virulently anti-Jewish, and it was not until the fifth and sixth centuries that the virulently anti-Jewish Judas Cyriacus legend became widely known across Europe: Drijvers, *Helena Augusta*, 183–88. Drijvers argues that "it was in all likelihood because of its anti-Jewish character that the legend featuring Judas Cyriacus ousted the original legend of Helena, at least in the West, and became in the Middle Ages the most popular version of the legend of the discovery of the Cross" (188). E. Gordon Whatley points out that the feast of the Invention was one of a small number of feasts that the Jews of Spain, under the aggressively anti-Judaic Visigothic kings, were required by law to observe: E. Gordon Whatley, "Constantine the Great, the Empress Helena, and the Relics of the Holy Cross," in *Medieval Hagiography: An Anthology*, ed. Thomas Head (New York: Garland, 2000), 80.

49. *The Claudius Pontificals*, ed. D. H. Turner, Henry Bradshaw Society, vol. 97 (Chicester: Regnum Press for the Henry Bradshaw Society, 1971), 95; discussed in Stafford, *Queen Emma and Queen Edith*, 166. The cited *ordo*, contained in Claudius Pontifical II (London, BL Cotton Claudius A. iii), belongs to a rescension known as the "Second English Ordo." It survives in multiple manuscripts (both English and Continental), which are discussed at length by Janet Nelson, "The Second English Ordo," in *Politics and Ritual in Early Medieval Europe*, ed. Janet Nelson (London: Hambledon Press, 1986), 361–74, who argues at 372–74 that a version of the *ordo* was composed for Ælfthryth's coronation in 973. For more on early medieval queens' coronations, see Nelson, "Early Medieval Rites of Queen-Making and the Shaping of Medieval Queenship," in *Queens and Queenship in Medieval Europe*, ed. Anne J. Duggan (Woodbridge, Suffolk: Boydell Press, 1997), 301–15; and also Julie Anne Smith, "The Earliest Queen-Making Rites," *Church History* 66 (1997): 18–35.

50. Karl F. Morrison, *Understanding Conversion* (Charlottesville: University Press of Virginia, 1992), xii–xiv.

51. It is worth noting that many of the Old English verbs used to denote the act of conversion (e.g., *gewendan, gebugan,* and *gecierran*) were frequently employed in a more general sense as well, conveying the idea of any type of change or turn.

52. *Regularis concordia Anglicae nationis monachorum sanctimonialiumque: The Monastic Agreement of the Monks and Nuns of the English Nation,* ed. and trans. Thomas Symons (London: Thomas Nelson and Sons, 1953), 2.

53. See Robert Deshman, "*Christus rex et magi reges*: Kingship and Christology in Ottonian and Anglo-Saxon Art," *Frühmittelalterliche Studien* 10 (1976): 367–405; and Deshman, "*Benedictus Monarcha et Monachus*: Early Medieval Ruler Theology and the Anglo-Saxon Reform," *Frühmittelalterliche Studien* 22 (1988): 204–40.

54. On the nostalgia driving the reforms, see Antonia Gransden, "Traditionalism and Continuity During the Last Century of Anglo-Saxon Monasticism," *Journal of Ecclesiastical History* 40 (1989): 159–207, esp. 161–64, 180; and Patrick Wormald, "Æthelwold and His Continental Counterparts: Contact, Comparison, Contrast," in *Bishop Æthelwold: His Career and Influence,* ed. Barbara Yorke (Woodbridge: Boydell Press, 1988), 13–42, esp. 38–41.

55. The extent to which Anglo-Saxon queens were actually able to effect royal conversion and attitudes toward the conversion by marriage model are vexed issues, particularly when considered with respect to Bede's depictions of queens in the *Historia Ecclesiastica.* See chapter 1 of this book.

56. Both of Boniface's letters are reproduced in Bede's *Historia Ecclesiastica,* 2:10–11.

57. "Ðonne wæs Sancte Eormenhild, Ercenbrihtes dohtor and Seaxburge, forgyfen Wulfhere, Pendan sunu Myrcena cinges, to cwene. And on hyra dagum Myrcena ðeod onfeng fulluht" (Eormenhild, daughter of Eorcenberht and Seaxburg, was given to Wulfhere, son of Penda, king of the Mercians, for his queen. And in their days the people of Mercia received baptism): M. J. Swanton, "A Fragmentary Life of St. Mildred and Other Kentish Royal Saints," *Archaeologia Cantiana* 91 (1975): 15–27, at 27. A nearly identical formulation occurs in the so-called *Þa Halgan* or "Kentish royal legend," an account of Kent's early Christian kings and their saintly families: *Die Heiligen Englands: Angelsächsisch und Lateinisch,* ed. Felix Liebermann (Hanover: Hahn, 1889), 7. For a detailed study of the Mildrith legend, see D. W. Rollason, *The Mildrith Legend: A Study in Early Medieval Hagiography in England* (Leicester: Leicester University Press, 1982). For more on Eormenhild and the sources in which she appears, see Susan Ridyard, *The Royal Saints of Anglo-Saxon England: A Study of West Saxon and East Anglian Cults* (Cambridge: Cambridge University Press, 1988), 50, 60, 89–92, 179–82.

58. William H. Sewell, Jr., "The Concept(s) of Culture," in *Beyond the Cultural Turn: New Directions in the Study of Society and Culture,* ed. Victoria E. Bonnell and Lynn Hunt (Berkeley: University of California Press, 1999), 51.

59. Elene is cited in two eleventh-century English calendars: Francis Wormald, ed., *English Kalendars Before A.D. 1100* (London: Henry Bradshaw Society, 1934; repr. Wolfeboro, N.H.: Boydell and Brewer, 1988), 37 and 261. She appears seven times in Anglo-Saxon litanies of the saints: *Anglo-Saxon Litanies of the Saints,* ed. Michael Lapidge, Henry Bradshaw Society 106 (London: Boydell Press, 1991), 118, 130, 200, 238, 242, 294, 298. A gold coin circulating in early seventh-century England bears Elene's portrait and the inscription HELENA on one side: Leslie Webster and Janet Backhouse, eds., *The Making of England: Anglo-Saxon Art and Culture, A.D. 600–900* (Toronto: University of Toronto Press, 1991), 37. The *Inventio* of the Cross was celebrated with an annual festival on 3 May when one or more versions of the *Inventio* legend were read. The four extant vernacular versions of the legend are Cynewulf's *Elene,* Ælfric's homily entitled *Inventio Sanctae Crucis* (992), an anonymous mid- to late eleventh-century homily contained in the *Classbook of Saint Dunstan,* and a very brief account of the *Inventio* in the anonymous ninth-century *Old English Martyrology*: see, respectively, *Cynewulf's "Elene,"* ed. Gradon; *CH II,* ed. Godden, pp. 174–76; *The Old English Finding of the True Cross,* ed. and trans. Mary-Catherine Bodden (Cambridge: D. S. Brewer, 1987); *An Old English Martyrology,* ed. George Herzfeld, EETS o.s. 116 (London: Kegan Paul, Trench, Trübner, 1900), 72–73. Elene was also invoked at the annual Exaltation of the Cross festival on 14 September. The only surviving homily for the day is Ælfric's *Exaltatio Sancte Crucis*: *Ælfric's Lives of Saints,* ed. W. W. Skeat, EETS o.s. 76, 82, 94, 114 (London: Trübner, 1881–1900); repr. in 2 vols. (London: Oxford University Press, 1966), 2:144–58. An additional legend, commonly referred to as *The History of the Holy Rood* and dated to the eleventh century, does not indicate a specific occasion for its use: Allan Phillipson Robb, "The History of the Holy Rood-Tree: Four Anglo-Saxon Homilies" (Ph.D. diss., University of Illinois at Urbana-Champaign, 1975), 14–110.

60. Drijvers, *Helena Augusta,* 18.

61. Ibid., 15.

62. Ibid., 15–16.

63. Ibid., 15.

64. Ibid., 16.

65. It is possible that this information was conveyed through Eutropius's *Breviarium historiae Romanae,* which circulated in Anglo-Saxon England and served as an important source for Bede's *Historia Ecclesiastica.* Ambrose is another possibility, as many of his works were known to the Anglo-Saxons, although there is no concrete evidence that either *De obitu Theodosii* or *Origo Constantini* were among these known texts.

66. The Latin text is from *Aldhelmi Malmesbiriensis prosa de virginitate cum glosa latina atque anglosaxonica,* ed. Scott Gwara, 2 vols., CCSL 124A (Turnhout: Brepols, 2001), 655. Gwara's edition of the *Prosa de virginitate* is a revised version of Rudolf Ehwald's in *Aldhelmi opera,* MGH Auctores Antiquissimi (Berlin: Weidmann, 1919; repr., Berlin-Charlottenburg: Weidmann, 1961). The translation is from

Aldhelm: The Prose Works, trans. Michael Lapidge and Michael Herren (Cambridge: D. S. Brewer, 1979), 115.

67. *Bede's Ecclesiastical History of the English People,* ed. Bertram Colgrave and R. A. B. Mynors (Oxford: Clarendon Press, 1969), 36; trans. on 37.

68. PL 90:556A.

69. *The Old English Orosius,* ed. Janet Bately, EETS s.s. 6 (London: Oxford University Press, 1980), 148.

70. For a thorough discussion of these terms, see Margaret Clunies Ross, "Concubinage in Anglo-Saxon England," *Past and Present* 108 (1985): 3–34, esp. 16–18.

71. Although concubinage was considered an acceptable practice for Roman emperors, the hereditary rights of their children were not automatic, and the fact that Constantine's parents were never legally married was cause for controversy in the early fourth century. See Drijvers, *Helena Augusta,* 18–19.

72. Clunies Ross, "Concubinage in Anglo-Saxon England," 13–18 and 24–27. Given Bede's generally strict stance on sexual morality, it is likely that he supported the Church's efforts to eradicate royal concubinage, and hence somewhat surprising that the *Historia Ecclesiastica* so openly acknowledges Constantine's descent from a concubine. Thomas Tipton, "Inventing the Cross: A Study of Medieval *Inventio Crucis* Legends" (Ph.D. diss., Northwestern University, 1997), 95–101, argues that the *HE* reflects a general desire to dismiss Constantine's achievements, indicated by Bede's failure to mention Constantine's well-known role in putting down Arianism and his suggestion that it was under Constantine's rule that Arianism in fact arose: Tipton's logic thus offers another possible explanation for Bede's frank reference to Helena as a concubine: an attempt to downplay Constantine's heroism by invoking his lowly birth.

73. Clunies Ross, "Concubinage in Anglo-Saxon England," 18–33.

74. *English Historical Documents,* vol. 1, *c. 500–1042,* ed. Dorothy Whitelock, 2nd ed. (London: Eyre Methuen, 1979), 837–38; quoted in Clunies Ross, "Concubinage in Anglo-Saxon England," 27.

75. For more on these debates and on the increasing recourse to maternal genealogy as a means to back the accession of particular princes, see Barbara Yorke, "Æthelwold and the Politics of the Tenth Century," in *Bishop Æthelwold,* ed. Yorke, 65–88, esp. 69–73 and 81–84; and Pauline Stafford, "The King's Wife in Wessex, 800–1066," *Past and Present* 91 (1981): 3–27; repr. in *New Readings on Women,* ed. Damico and Olsen, 56–78, esp. 66–67.

76. Ibid.

77. Margaret Schlauch, "The Allegory of Church and Synagogue," *Speculum* 14 (1939): 448–64, esp. 453–55.

78. These points are clearly formulated in the New Testament; see Gal. 4:22–31. See also Schlauch, "Allegory of Church and Synagogue," 453–54.

79. Citations from Hrabanus Maurus are found in Schlauch, "Allegory of Church and Synagogue," 453–54. Isidore's discussion appears in his *In Genesin,* PL 83:268A.

80. The most well-known fiction about Helena's descent derives from Geoffrey of Monmouth's claim in his *Historia Regum Britanniae* that Helena was the daughter of Coel, king of the Britons. Tipton, "Inventing the Cross," 105–7, convincingly argues that Geoffrey's invention was motivated by a desire to establish a genealogical link between Rome and Britain, and hence a case for British imperialism.

81. *The Old English Version of Bede's Ecclesiastical History of the English People,* ed. and trans. Thomas Miller, EETS o.s. 95–96 (London: Trübner, 1890), 42. The translators further attempt to legitimize Constantine's claims to both Gaul and Britain by asserting that he was a "god casere" (good emperor), a phrase that is not present in the Latin, and that "Constantinus se casere wære on Breotone accened," a phrase that can only mean "the emperor Constantine was born in Britain" as opposed to the rather ambiguous Latin, "Constantinus in Brittania creatus imperator," which could mean either that Constantine was born in Britain or that he was elected as emperor in Britain.

82. That Cynewulf may have had some anxiety about Constantine being perceived as the rightful heir is also suggested by his reference very early in *Elene* to Constantine as "riht cyning" (13b).

83. Anderson, "Cynewulf's *Elene,*" 118, 120; Whatley, "Figure of Constantine the Great," 175–77.

84. Campbell, "Cynewulf's Multiple Revelations," 237 and 239–40.

85. See Hollis, *Anglo-Saxon Women and the Church,* 214–18.

86. See Pauline Stafford, "Queens, Nunneries and Reforming Churchmen: Gender, Religious Status and Reform in Tenth- and Eleventh-Century England," *Past and Present* 163 (1999): 3–35, esp. 6–10.

87. Clare A. Lees, *Tradition and Belief: Religious Writing in Late Anglo-Saxon England* (Minneapolis: University of Minnesota Press, 1999), 122–23.

88. For more on social hierarchy as depicted in homiletic literature, see M. R. Godden, "Money, Power, and Morality in Late Anglo-Saxon England," *Anglo-Saxon England* 19 (1990): 41–65, esp. 56–57.

89. For sensitive accounts of the reforms' gender implications, see Patricia Halpin, "Women Religious in Late Anglo-Saxon England," *Haskins Society Journal* 6 (1994): 97–110; Barbara Yorke, "'Sisters Under the Skin'? Anglo-Saxon Nuns and Nunneries in Southern England," *Reading Medieval Studies* 15 (1989): 95–117; and Stafford, "Queens, Nunneries and Reforming Churchmen." All three of these scholars productively complicate earlier, more simplistic understandings of the Benedictine reforms as a movement underwritten by wholesale misogyny and contributing to a general decline in women's autonomy. Stafford, for example, argues that the reformers' increased emphasis on chastity and celibacy rather than ordination created religious ideals that were (at least theoretically) possible for women to

achieve (7–12). Halpin and Yorke take up the issue of "lessened" opportunities for women religious during the tenth century, questioning the actual impact that the reforms had on women's houses, and raising the possibility that alternative, more informal opportunities for female religious practice may have developed during this period.

90. Stafford, "The King's Wife," 58–62.

91. Jane Tibbetts Schulenberg, "Women's Monastic Communities, 500–1100: Patterns of Expansion and Decline," *Signs: Journal of Women in Culture and Society* 14 (1989): 261–92, esp. 279–82.

92. Lionarons, "Cultural Syncretism," 56.

93. Ibid., 56 and 66.

94. Rosemary Woolf, "Saints' Lives," in *Continuations and Beginnings: Studies in Old English Literature,* ed. E. G. Stanley (London: Nelson, 1966), 47, first made the important observation that Elene's torturing of Judas might be read as an inverted passion, in which the ruler is the Christian and the prisoner the pagan.

95. Lionarons, "Cultural Syncretism," 62–64.

Chapter 3 *Beowulf* and the Gendering of Heroism

1. As pointed out by Gillian R. Overing, *Language, Sign and Gender in Beowulf* (Carbondale: Southern Illinois University Press, 1990), 73.

2. Hrothgar's claim that Beowulf's mother was honored by God in her childbearing echoes Luke 11:27, in which it is, interestingly, not a man but an unnamed woman in the crowd who calls out to Christ: "Blessed is the womb that bore thee and the paps that gave thee suck."

3. For a useful critical history of women and gender in *Beowulf,* see Alexandra Hennessey Olsen, "Gender Roles," in *A Beowulf Handbook,* ed. Robert E. Bjork and John D. Niles (Lincoln: University of Nebraska Press, 1997), 311–24.

4. Ibid., 313.

5. Seth Lerer, "*Beowulf* and Contemporary Critical Theory," in *A Beowulf Handbook,* ed. Bjork and Niles, 336.

6. Joyce Hill, "Þæt wæs geomuru ides! A Female Stereotype Examined," in *New Readings on Women in Old English Literature,* ed. Helen Damico and Alexandra Hennessey Olsen (Bloomington: Indiana University Press, 1990), 235–47.

7. Overing, *Language, Sign and Gender,* xxv and 111.

8. Ibid., xx–xxvi.

9. Ibid., xxiii.

10. Roberta Frank, "The *Beowulf* Poet's Sense of History," in *The Wisdom of Poetry: Essays in Early English Literature in Honor of Morton W. Bloomfield,* ed. Larry D. Benson and Siegfried Wenzel (Kalamazoo, Mich.: Medieval Institute Publications, 1982), 53–65, 271–77; repr. in *Beowulf: A Prose Translation,* 2nd ed., trans.

E. Talbot Donaldson and ed. Nicholas Howe (New York: W. W. Norton, 2002), 98–111, quotation at 109.

11. For an important overview of the Anglo-Saxon heroic ethos and its articulation in Old English poetry, see Katherine O'Brien O'Keeffe, "Heroic Values and Christian Ethics," in *The Cambridge Companion to Old English Literature*, ed. Malcolm Godden and Michael Lapidge (Cambridge: Cambridge University Press, 1991), 107–25.

12. Carol J. Clover, "Regardless of Sex: Men, Women, and Power in Early Northern Europe," *Speculum* 68 (1993): 363–87, at 380.

13. Edward B. Irving, Jr., "What to Do with Old Kings," in *Comparative Research on Oral Traditions: A Memorial for Milman Parry*, ed. John Miles Foley (Columbus, Ohio: Slavica, 1987), 259–68.

14. On the comparative thinness of Hrothgar's past as depicted in the poem, see Irving, "What to Do with Old Kings," 265–66. The quotation is also from Irving, at 266.

15. "Nam heroes appellantur viri quasi aerii et caelo digni propter sapientiam et fortitudinem": Isidore of Seville, *Etymologiarum sive originum*, ed. W. M. Lindsay (Oxford: Clarendon, 1911), vol. 1, bk. 39, 9; cited in R. E. Kaske, "*Sapientia et Fortitudo* as the Controlling Theme of *Beowulf*," *Studies in Philology* 55 (1958): 423–57; repr. in *An Anthology of Beowulf Criticism*, ed. Lewis E. Nicholson (Notre Dame, Ind.: University of Notre Dame Press, 1963), 269–310, at 270.

16. The quote is from the title of Kaske's essay.

17. Kaske, "*Sapientia et Fortitudo*," 272.

18. Kemp Malone makes the important point that Hygd is "consistently characterized in terms of her name": "Hygd," *Modern Language Notes* 56 (1941): 356–58, at 358. R. E. Kaske contends that Hygd's mental prowess is intended to mirror inversely Hygelac's lack of reflection: "'Hygelac' and 'Hygd,'" in *Studies in Old English Literature in Honor of Arthur G. Brodeur*, ed. Stanley B. Greenfield (1963; repr., Eugene: University of Oregon Press, 2001), 200–206. Fred C. Robinson offers broad support for Kaske's argument, but contends that the element *-lac* in *Hygelac* is correctly understood less as "lack" than as "play" or "strife," and that the name *Hygelac* thus connotes "instability of mind," "frivolity," or "perturbation": "The Significance of Names in Old English Literature," in *The Tomb of Beowulf and Other Essays on Old English* (Oxford: Blackwell, 1993), 185–223, at 213–17; originally printed in *Anglia* 86 (1968): 14–58.

19. Hrothgar is called "snotor hæleð" (wise man; 190b), "snotor guma" (wise man; 1384a), "snottra fengel" (wise lord, 1475a; "snotra fengel," 2156a), "se snotera" (the wise one, 1313b; "se snottra," 1786b), "frod" (wise or old; 279a, 1306b, 1724a, 2114a) and "þone wisan" (the wise one, 1318a; "se wisa," 1698b). These epithets are listed in Elaine Tuttle Hansen, "Hrothgar's 'Sermon' in *Beowulf* as Parental Wisdom," *Anglo-Saxon England* 10 (1982): 53–67, at 61 n. 23.

20. Clover, "Regardless of Sex," 377–81. Clover's study offers broad support for Thomas Laqueur's "one-sex" model of sexual difference, which centers on the idea that prior to the early eighteenth century the sexes were not viewed as essentially distinct categories but as positions on a continuum: Thomas Laqueur, *Making Sex: Body and Gender from the Greeks to Freud* (Cambridge: Harvard University Press, 1990). However, Clover importantly problematizes Laqueur's work by urging that the one-sex era ought to be seen as less monolithic and static than Laqueur would have it, and also by arguing that the "medievalization of the north"—i.e., Christianization and the adoption of European social forms that took place during the tenth and eleventh centuries—was accompanied by a shift to two-sex thinking much like the one that Laqueur posits as having taken place roughly eight hundred years later: 385–86.

21. Clover, "Regardless of Sex," 379–81.

22. *Bodies That Matter: On the Discursive Limits of "Sex"* (London: Routledge, 1993), 1–55. For Butler's more recent views on sexual difference, see "The End of Sexual Difference?" in *Feminist Consequences: Theory for a New Century*, ed. Elisabeth Bronfen and Misha Kavka (New York: Columbia University Press, 2001), 414–34.

23. All quotations from *Beowulf* are taken from Friedrich Klaeber, ed., *Beowulf and the Fight at Finnsburg*, 3rd ed., with 1st and 2nd supplements (Lexington, Mass.: D. C. Heath, 1950), and are cited by line number. Unless otherwise noted, all translations are my own.

24. Malcolm Godden offers the useful reminder that the Anglo-Saxons did not consider the head to be the only site for reason or thought. See M. R. Godden, "Anglo-Saxons on the Mind," in *Learning and Literature in Anglo-Saxon England*, ed. Michael Lapidge and Helmut Gneuss (Cambridge: Cambridge University Press, 1985), 271–98; repr. in *Old English Literature: Critical Essays*, ed. R. M. Liuzza (New Haven: Yale University Press, 2002), 284–314, at 302–8.

25. John M. Hill, *The Anglo-Saxon Warrior Ethic: Reconstructing Lordship in Early English Literature* (Gainesville: University Press of Florida, 2000), 64–67.

26. For a useful overview of the major critical positions on Hildeburh's agency, see John Hill, *The Anglo-Saxon Warrior Ethic*, 63–68. Overing, *Language, Sign and Gender*, 77–81, discusses the development of the widespread scholarly view of women in Old English poetry as passive and suffering victims.

27. Joyce Hill, "Þæt wæs geomuru ides!," 240–41.

28. As argued by Overing, *Language, Sign and Gender*, 86.

29. This passage occurs in a portion of the manuscript that is badly damaged. All observations regarding the unnamed woman are thus dependent on manuscript reconstructions and remain speculative. On the feminist implications of reconstructing this passage, see Helen Bennett, "The Female Mourner at Beowulf's Funeral: Filling in the Blanks/Hearing the Spaces," *Exemplaria* 4 (1992): 35–50.

30. Joyce Hill, "Þæt wæs geomuru ides!," 241.

31. I am here following the widely accepted view that the description of the Geatish woman as *bundenheorde*, "with locks bound up," indicates her advanced age; young Germanic women typically wore their hair loose and flowing: Klaeber, *Beowulf and the Fight at Finnsburg*, 311; *Beowulf: An Edition with Relevant Shorter Texts*, ed. Bruce Mitchell and Fred C. Robinson (1998; repr., Oxford: Blackwell Publishers, 2000), 160. Nevertheless, it is worth recalling that the *b* is uncertain in the manuscript, and even if the word is *bundenheorde*, it may simply mean that she is married.

32. On the wise woman in Germanic literature and culture, see Fred C. Robinson, "The Prescient Woman in Old English Literature," in *Philologia Anglica: Essays Presented to Professor Yoshio Terasawa on the Occasion of His Sixtieth Birthday*, ed. Kinshiro Oshitari et al. (Tokyo: Kenkyusha, 1988), 241–50; repr. in *The Tomb of Beowulf and Other Essays on Old English*, 155–63, esp. 156, 158; and also Kees Samplonius, "From Veleda to the Völva: Aspects of Female Divination in Germanic Europe," in *Sanctity and Motherhood: Essays on Holy Mothers in the Middle Ages*, ed. Anneke B. Mulder-Bakker (New York: Garland, 1995), 68–99.

33. See Andy Orchard, *Pride and Prodigies: Studies in the Monsters of the Beowulf Manuscript* (Cambridge: D. S. Brewer, 1995), 29–47; Katherine O'Brien O'Keeffe, "*Beowulf*, Lines 702b–836: Transformations and the Limits of the Human," *Texas Studies in Language and Literature* 23 (1981): 484–94; and Melinda J. Menzer's "*Aglæcwif* (*Beowulf* 1259a): Implications for -*wif* Compounds, Grendel's Mother, and Other *Aglæcan*," *English Language Notes* 34 (1996): 1–6, in which Menzer examines the term *aglæcwif* as applied to Grendel's mother and makes a strong case for *wif* as a marker of her humanity.

34. As Mitchell and Robinson point out, the dative plural of *Eotan*, "Jute," would be *Eotum* not *Eotenum*, but there is nevertheless confusion between "Jute" and "giant" at 1145a and also 902b, in which the phrase *mid Eotenum* is used to describe the final dwelling that is determined for the evil king Heremod: *Beowulf: An Edition with Relevant Shorter Texts*, 78. Whether the phrase means "among Jutes" or "among giants" has been much debated. R. E. Kaske argues that "throughout the Finn episode (and perhaps also in line 902) the term is to be understood as a hostile epithet for the Frisians": "The *Eotenas* in *Beowulf*," in *Old English Poetry: Fifteen Essays*, ed. Robert P. Creed (Providence: Brown University Press, 1967), 285–310, at 286; while Mitchell and Robinson (*Beowulf: An Edition with Relevant Shorter Texts*, 78) argue that the scribe confused the terms for "Jute" and "giant," as does R. W. Chambers: *Beowulf: An Introduction to the Study of the Poem with a Discussion of the Stories of Offa and Finn*, 3rd ed., with a supplement by C. L. Wrenn (Cambridge: Cambridge University Press, 1959), 261, 286.

35. For an insightful discussion of queens and treasure, see Pauline Stafford, "Queens and Treasure in the Early Middle Ages," in *Treasure in the Medieval West*, ed. Elizabeth M. Tyler (Woodbridge, Suffolk: York Medieval Press, 2000), 61–82.

36. *Maxims I*, for example, states, "Cyning sceal mid ceape cwene gebicgan, bunum ond beagum; bu sceolon ærest / geofum god wesan . . . ond wif . . . rumheort beon / mearum ond maþmum. . . . Gold geriseþ on guman sweorde, / sellic sigesceorp, sinc on cwene" (A king must obtain a queen with valuable goods, with drinking-vessels and rings. Both must, above all, be generous with gifts, and the woman shall be generous with horses and treasures. Gold is fitting on a man's sword, an excellent ornament of victory, treasure on a queen): *The Exeter Book*, ed. George Philip Krapp and Elliott Van Kirk Dobbie, ASPR 3 (New York: Columbia University Press, 1936), 159, ll. 81–87a; 161, ll. 125–26. The narrator of *Widsith* also links queens and treasure: "Ond me þa Ealhhild oþerne forgeaf, / dryhtcwen duguþe, dohtor Eadwines. Hyre lof lengde geond londa fela, / þonne ic be songe secgan sceolde / hwær ic under swegle selast wisse / goldhrodene cwen giefe bryttian" (And then Ealhhild, the daughter of Eadwine, a queen noble in dignity, gave me another [ring]. Her praise was spread throughout many lands, whenever I would tell in song where under the skies I best knew a gold-adorned queen distributing gifts): *The Exeter Book*, ed. Krapp and Dobbie, 152, ll. 97–102. The *Encomium Emmae Reginae* refers to Cnut sending Emma gifts prior to their marriage, and also to Emma as herself a treasure: "Mittuntur proci ad dominam, mittuntur dona regalia. . . . Leta<e>tur Gallia, letatur etiam Anglorum patria, dum tantum decus transuehitur per aequora" (Wooers were sent to the lady, royal gifts were sent. . . . Gaul rejoiced, the land of the English rejoiced likewise, when so great an ornament was conveyed over the seas): *Encomium Emmae Reginae*, ed. and trans. Alistair Campbell, with a supplementary introduction by Simon Keynes (Cambridge: Cambridge University Press, 1998), 32–33.

37. *Deor*, in *The Exeter Book*, ed. Krapp and Dobbie, 178–79.

38. "Sumum þæt gegongeð on geoguðfeore / þæt se endestæf earfeðmæcgum / wealic weorþeð. Sceal hine wulf etan, / har hæðstæpa; hinsiþ þonne / modor bimurneð. . . . Sumne on bæle sceal brond aswencan, / fretan frecne lig fægne monnan; / þær him lifgedal lungre weorðeð, / read reþe gled; reoteþ meowle, / seo hyre bearn gesihð brondas þeccan" (To one it happens that early in his life the end arrives, distressing to his family, sorrowful. The wolf, the hoary heath-stalker, will eat him. Then his mother will mourn his death. . . . Upon another one, the fire will inflict torment on the pyre, the terrible flames will devour the fated man. Death will come to him quickly, the fierce red flame. The woman will wail, she who sees the flames consume her child): *Fortunes of Men*, in *The Exeter Book*, ed. Krapp and Dobbie, 154–56, at ll. 10–14a, 43–47.

39. *Fortunes of Men*, in *The Exeter Book*, ed. Krapp and Dobbie, 154–56.

40. Overing, *Language, Sign and Gender*, 82. For a similar argument regarding the untenability of female peaceweaving, see Jane Chance, *Woman as Hero in Old English Literature* (Syracuse: Syracuse University Press, 1986), 100, 106–7.

41. J. M. Wallace-Hadrill, "War and Peace in the Earlier Middle Ages," *Transactions of the Royal Historical Society* 5th ser., 25 (1975), 157.

42. Ibid., 158.

43. Vilhelm Grønbech, *The Culture of the Teutons,* 2 vols., trans. William Worster, from *Vor Folkeæt i Oldtiden* I–IV (Copenhagen: Jespersen og Pios forlag, 1909–12; London: Humphrey Milford, 1931), 1:32–33, 59–61; cited in Damico, *Beowulf's Wealhtheow and the Valkyrie Tradition* (Madison: University of Wisconsin Press, 1984), 85. I am grateful to Professor Damico for reminding me that the concept of *frið* is an essentially martial one.

44. Grønbech, *Culture of the Teutons,* 1:59.

45. Chance, *Woman as Hero,* 99.

46. Klaeber, *Beowulf and the Fight at Finnsburg,* 235. For excellent overviews of the conventions of heroic legend, see Roberta Frank, "Germanic Legend in Old English Literature," in *The Cambridge Companion to Old English Literature,* ed. Godden and Lapidge, 88–106; and, in the same collection, Katherine O'Brien O'Keeffe, "Heroic Values and Christian Ethics," 107–25.

47. Joyce Hill, "Þæt wæs geomuru ides!," 241.

48. Seth Lerer makes a similar point about Beowulf as a reader, arguing that "what interests Beowulf are not the details of the songs performed at Heorot. . . . Instead, Beowulf focuses solely on form and quality": *Literacy and Power in Anglo-Saxon Literature* (Lincoln: University of Nebraska Press, 1991), 190.

49. John Hill makes a similar point: "Marriage alliances, despite a bride-queen's ambivalent place between two kin-groups, are not all doomed to failure": *The Anglo-Saxon Warrior Ethic,* 10. Hill points to the marriage of Beowulf's mother and Ecgtheow, and also to the marriage of Offa and Thryth as two other examples in which marriage may have successfully fostered dynastic alliances: 10, 52.

50. As Robinson puts it, "The Finn lay is appropriate on one level to the public occasion being celebrated in Heorot and on another to the tragic irony which poet and audience see in the future of the Danes": *Beowulf and the Appositive Style* (Knoxville: University of Tennessee Press, 1985), 26.

51. The MS *woroldrædenne* is a much disputed term. It is often translated as "way of the world," "world rule," or "universal custom," and understood as a reference to the obligation of revenge as a universal custom. However emendations to *woroldrædende,* "earthly ruler," or to *worodrædende* or *weorodrædende,* "ruler of the host," "king," have also been proposed. For more on *woroldrædenne* and on interpretations of line 1142, see *Beowulf and Judith,* ed. Elliott Van Kirk Dobbie, ASPR 4 (New York: Columbia University Press, 1953), 180–81.

52. The classic account of women as objects of exchange is Gayle Rubin, "The Traffic in Women: Notes on the 'Political Economy' of Sex," in *Toward an Anthropology of Women,* ed. Rayna R. Reiter (New York and London: Monthly Review Press, 1975), 157–210. Annette B. Weiner, *Inalienable Possessions: The Paradox of Keeping-While-Giving* (Berkeley: University of California Press, 1992), 13–15, offers a judicious summary of the development of the concept of trafficking in women, and

also problematizes early understandings of this kind of social exchange as a misogynist practice that necessarily contributes to the oppression of women.

53. That heterosexual romance and militancy are incompatible is adumbrated by such texts as *The Battle of Maldon* and *The Battle of Brunanburh,* whose heroes are notable for their lack of any romantic attachments to women. The idea is more strongly felt in such texts as *Cynewulf and Cyneheard* and the two Old English versions of *Judith,* in which military downfall follows closely on the heels of sexual surrender, and involving oneself with women presages the loss of heroic renown.

54. The term *ligetorn* is a hapax, and its interpretation thus merits caution. The standard translation of *ligetorn* as "pretended injury" might seem to mark Thryth's vengeful acts as unwarranted, and thus to distinguish them from those of such characters as Beowulf or Hengest. Nevertheless, I would argue that the fact that the "pretended injury" done to Thryth takes the form of a series of visual offenses suggests that her function is more complex than simply to highlight a strict division between warranted and unwarranted violence. The fact that Thryth's retaliatory violence arises as a response to being looked at by others forces readers to confront one of the most serious problems of retaliatory violence: that it arises as a response not to injury but to perceptions of injury, and perceptions that will very often be skewed. Thryth's violence is indeed marked as unwarranted, but the point is less to isolate her own mistaken judgment than to reveal mistaken judgment as the inexorable companion of a social system that endorses retaliatory violence.

55. Damico, *Beowulf's Wealhtheow and the Valkyrie Tradition,* 46–49.

56. "Spiritalis armaturae spiculis et ferratis uirtutum uenabulis nauiter certandum, ac nullatenus timidorum more militum horrorem belli et classica salpictae muliebriter metuentium": *Aldhelmi Malmesbiriensis prosa de virginitate cum glosa latina atque anglosaxonica,* ed. Scott Gwara, CCSL 124A (Turnhout: Brepols, 2001), pp. 131, 133, ll. 28–31; cited translation refers to *Aldhelm: The Prose Works,* trans. Michael Lapidge and Michael Herren (Cambridge: D. S. Brewer, 1979), 68.

57. *Life of Perpetua,* in *An Old English Martyrology,* ed. George Herzfeld, EETS, o.s. 116 (London: Kegan Paul, 1900), 34, 36.

58. For a sensitive reading of the performative elements in late medieval textual accounts of cross-gendered women, see Susan Crane, *The Performance of Self: Ritual, Clothing, and Identity During the Hundred Years War* (Philadelphia: University of Pennsylania Press, 2002), 73–106.

59. These ideas are famously encapsulated in Paul's claim that "for as many of you as have been baptized in Christ, have put on Christ. There is neither Jew nor Greek: there is neither bond nor free: there is neither male nor female. For you are all one in Christ Jesus" (Gal. 3:27–28); and in Jerome's assertion that "as long as a woman is for birth and children, she is different from man as body is from soul. But when she wishes to serve Christ more than the world, then she will cease to be a

woman, and will be called man"; cited in Barbara Newman, *From Virile Woman to WomanChrist: Studies in Medieval Religion and Literature* (Philadelphia: University of Pennsylvania Press, 1995), 4.

60. The transvestite saints' lives have generated extensive debate. Viewed generously, these legends endorse both gender fluidity and women's capacity for spiritual success; viewed less generously, they devalue womanhood and reify maleness. More recent studies have begun to consider how these texts may also construct ideals of masculinity. Useful readings on the lives include: Andrew P. Scheil, "Somatic Ambiguity and Masculine Desire in the Old English *Life of Euphrosyne*," *Exemplaria* 11 (1999): 345–61; John Anson, "The Female Transvestite in Early Monasticism: The Origin and Development of a Motif," *Viator* 5 (1974): 1–32; Vern L. Bullough, "Transvestism in the Middle Ages," in *Sexual Practices and the Medieval Church*, ed. Vern L. Bullough and James A. Brundage (Buffalo, N.Y.: Prometheus, 1982), 43–54. For insightful analyses of women's cross-gendering, see Elizabeth Castelli, "'I Will Make Mary Male': Pieties of the Body and Gender Transformation of Christian Women in Late Antiquity," in *Body Guards: The Cultural Politics of Gender Ambiguity*, ed. Julia Epstein and Kristina Straub (New York: Routledge, 1991), 29–49; and also Crane, *The Performance of Self*, 73–106.

61. *Ælfric's Catholic Homilies: The First Series, Text,* ed. Peter Clemoes, EETS s.s. 17 (Oxford: Oxford University Press, 1997), 279, ll. 115–17.

62. These are standard points; see, for example, Chance, *Woman as Hero*, 95, and Damico, *Beowulf's Wealhtheow and the Valkyrie Tradition*, 46.

63. The abrupt introduction of Thryth at line 1931b may point to a missing transition in the manuscript, thus rendering her exact position in the poem a matter for debate. For an overview of this problem and of other contested issues, such as Thryth's name and historical identity, see Klaeber, *Beowulf and the Fight at Finnsburg*, 195–200.

64. Shari Horner, *The Discourse of Enclosure: Representing Women in Old English Literature* (Albany: SUNY Press, 2001), 79.

65. My conclusions here are in agreement with those of Kevin S. Kiernan, who argues that the monstrosity of Grendel's mother functions as an "indictment of the kind of heroism that she represents," namely, a heroism that is vested in blood feud and the use of violence to right past wrongs: "Grendel's Heroic Mother," *In Geardagum* 6 (1984): 13–33, at 31. Our arguments, however, differ in their respective emphases: Kiernan views the monstrosity of Grendel's mother as the means by which the poem indicts retaliatory violence, whereas I locate this indictment in the poet's response to gender transgression.

66. Dorothy Whitelock, *The Audience of Beowulf* (1951; repr., Oxford: Clarendon Press, 1964), 60.

67. Ibid.

68. Ibid.

69. *Widsith,* in *The Exeter Book,* ed. Krapp and Dobbie, 150.

70. A useful starting point is Edward B. Irving, Jr., "Christian and Pagan Elements," in *A Beowulf Handbook,* ed. Bjork and Niles, 175–92, esp. 189. Irving observes that there are approximately four times as many Christian references in the first half of the poem as in the second; he attributes this imbalance, in part, to the fact that Hrothgar is absent from the second half of the poem: 185. For additional discussion, see Edward B. Irving, Jr., "The Nature of Christianity in *Beowulf,*" *Anglo-Saxon England* 13 (1984): 7–21; Margaret E. Goldsmith, *The Mode and Meaning of Beowulf* (London: Athlone, 1970), 183–209; and Hansen, "Hrothgar's 'Sermon.'"

71. Margaret E. Goldsmith, for example, contends that Hrothgar's speech is informed by "familiar homiletic material," possibly the writings of Ambrose, Augustine, and Gregory: *The Mode and Meaning of Beowulf,* 183–209, quotation at 185; while Fred C. Robinson argues that the numerous "Christian affinities" in Hrothgar's speech reflect pre-Christian vocabulary, phrasing, and concepts that were gradually expanded to convey new Christian meanings: *Beowulf and the Appositive Style,* 33–35. For a broader consideration of the intersections between the poem's Germanic and Christian registers, see Roberta Frank, "The *Beowulf* Poet's Sense of History."

72. Argued by John P. Hermann, *Allegories of War: Language and Violence in Old English Poetry* (Ann Arbor: University of Michigan Press, 1989), 7–36.

73. The ideological contiguities between physical and spiritual warfare are more fully discussed in Hermann, *Allegories of War.*

74. *Life of Perpetua,* in *An Old English Martyrology,* ed. Herzfeld, 36; *Life of Eugenia,* in *Ælfric's Lives of Saints,* ed. W. W. Skeat, EETS o.s. 76, 82, 94, 114 (London: Trübner, 1881–1900; London: Oxford University Press, 1966), 1:24–50, quotation at 30, ll. 93, 95–96.

75. Helen Damico, *Beowulf's Wealhtheow and the Valkyrie Tradition,* 49–50, points out that "an intemperate desire to have a wish fulfilled is a dominant emotional trait of the Anglo-Saxon epic heroines," and that this phenomenon is borne out in such female figures as Elene, Juliana, and Wealhtheow.

76. Fred C. Robinson, "Teaching the Backgrounds: History, Religion, Culture," in *Approaches to Teaching Beowulf,* ed. Jess B. Bessinger and Robert F. Yeager (New York: Modern Language Association of America, 1984), 119.

77. For further discussion of this ritual, see Michael J. Enright, "Lady with a Mead-Cup: Ritual, Group Cohesion and Hierarchy in the Germanic Warband," *Frühmittelalterliche Studien* 22 (1988): 170–203; repr. in his *Lady with a Mead Cup: Ritual Prophecy and Lordship in the European Warband from La Tène to the Viking Age* (Portland, Ore., and Dublin: Four Courts, 1996), 1–37.

78. Useful studies of these final scenes include, among others, Hill, *The Anglo-Saxon Warrior Ethic,* 19–46; Rolf H. Bremmer, Jr., "The Importance of Kinship:

Uncle and Nephew in *Beowulf*," *Amsterdamer Beiträge zur Älteren Germanistik* 15 (1980): 21–38; Stephen O. Glosecki, "*Beowulf* and the Wills: Traces of Totemism?" *Philological Quarterly* 78 (1999): 15–47; and Norman E. Eliason, "Beowulf, Wiglaf and the Wægmundings," *Anglo-Saxon England* 7 (1978): 95–105. For an indispensable attempt to sift out what we really know about Anglo-Saxon succession practices, see David N. Dumville, "The Ætheling: A Study in Anglo-Saxon Constitutional History," *Anglo-Saxon England* 8 (1979): 1–33.

79. Whether or not Beowulf intends to make Wiglaf his heir is a much-debated issue. Many scholars, including myself, believe that a transference of the kingdom is indeed suggested when Beowulf grants Wiglaf the dragon's treasure-hoard so as to provide him with the means to become the Geats' next ring-giver, when he leaves Wiglaf the arms that he would have otherwise left to his son, and when he asks Wiglaf to care for the Geats. For an important study of Beowulf's final words in the context of the early Germanic poetic genre of the "death song," see Joseph Harris, "Beowulf's Last Words," *Speculum* 67 (1992): 1–32. Harris points out that the theme of inheritance is commonly found in the Old Norse death song: 15–16.

80. "But she refused ever to become the bride of Knútr, unless he would affirm to her by oath, that he would never set up the son of any wife other than herself to rule after him, if it happened that God should give her a son by him. . . . Accordingly the king found what the lady said acceptable": *Encomium Emmae Reginae,* ed. Campbell, 33. Emma's views on the succession of her own sons are nevertheless complicated by the fact that in forcing Cnut to agree to make one of *their* sons heir to the throne, she effectively cut off the claims of Alfred and Edward, her two sons by Æthelred. For further discussion, see Simon Keynes, "The Æthelings in Normandy," *Anglo-Norman Studies* 13 (1990): 173–205, esp. 183–85.

81. Robert Morey, "Beowulf's Androgynous Heroism," *Journal of English and Germanic Philology* 95 (1996): 486–96.

82. Frank, "The *Beowulf* Poet's Sense of History," 108.

83. A worthwhile reading of the monsters' allegorical dimensions is offered by Arthur E. Du Bois, who characterizes both Beowulf and the monsters as "connotative creatures . . . [who] stand for an idea each. . . . Beowulf is national integrity, resulting from internal harmony. Grendel and his dam are the Danes' liability to punishment for weakness, pride, and treachery. The dragon is internal discord": "The Unity of *Beowulf*," *PMLA* 49 (1934): 374–405, quotation at 390–91. John D. Niles, by contrast, reads the monsters as more literal threats, arguing that "one cannot well account for the monsters by dismissing them as fairy-tale enemies or allegorical figures of no substance, for the poet presents both the naturalistic dragon and the strangely ambiguous Grendel creatures as inhabitants of the 'real' world": *Beowulf: The Poem and Its Tradition* (Cambridge: Harvard University Press, 1983), 28.

84. J. R. R. Tolkien, "*Beowulf:* The Monsters and the Critics," *Proceedings of the British Academy* 22 (1936): 245–95. Repr. in Nicholson, *An Anthology of Beowulf Criticism,* 51–103, quotation at 69.

85. I am grateful to Roy Liuzza for this point.

86. For a detailed discussion of the ways in which the term cræft, by the late ninth century, came to signify the unification of physical strength and spiritual or moral virtue, see Nicole Guenther Discenza, "Power, Skill and Virtue in the Old English *Boethius,*" *Anglo-Saxon England* 26 (1997): 81–108.

87. Hrothulf's supposed treachery and the implications of Wealhtheow's remarks regarding her future treatment of her sons are much-debated issues. Many scholars argue that Wealhtheow is aware of Hrothulf as a potential danger to her sons and that her speech is thus meant to be taken ironically, while others maintain that the textual references to Hrothulf's treachery are too inconclusive to support a reading of Hrothulf's future treachery and that Wealhtheow is sincere. Helen Damico, *Beowulf's Wealhtheow and the Valkyrie Tradition,* 122–32, offers a useful discussion of the problem; see also Mitchell and Robinson, *Beowulf,* 82, 87. For an attempt to reconstruct Hrothulf's actions, see Chambers, *Beowulf: An Introduction to the Study of the Poem,* 25–31. For a translation of the texts relevant to Hrothulf, see *Beowulf and Its Analogues,* trans. G. N. Garmonsway and Jacqueline Simpson (London: J. M. Dent and Sons, 1968), 155–206.

88. See J. M. Wallace-Hadrill, "Bede and Plummer," in *Early Medieval History* (Oxford: Basil Blackwell, 1975), 84–85; and James Campbell, "Bede I," in *Essays in Anglo-Saxon History,* ed. James Campbell (London: Hambledon Press, 1986), 26.

89. Mary P. Richards views the poem's closing lines as "a statement of his [Beowulf's] essential Christianity [and] . . . an affirmation of his spiritual excellence": "A Reexamination of Beowulf ll. 3180–3182," *English Language Notes* 10 (1973): 163–67, quotation at 167. Robert Morey argues that these lines associate Beowulf with the role of peaceweaver: "Beowulf's Androgynous Heroism," 493–96.

90. After Beowulf has defeated Grendel, Wealhtheow "Gode þancode / . . . þæs ðe hire se willa gelamp" (thanked God that her wish had come to pass; 625b, 626b), a statement that is immediately followed by Beowulf's claim that "Ic þæt hogode, . . . þæt ic anunga eowra leoda / willan geworhte" (I resolved . . . that I would altogether fulfill the will of your people; 632a, 634–35a). The poet's use of the term *willa* in this passage to describe both Wealhtheow's will and that of the Danes suggests that they are one and the same.

91. For more on the *Beowulf* poet's views on anachronism and historical chronology, see Frank, "The *Beowulf* Poet's Sense of History."

92. The suggestive power of Old English poetry derives from a number of different formal strategies, including allusive references to historical events and legendary figures, apposition, litotes, understatement, kennings, and comparisons and contrasts between characters.

Chapter 4 Queenship and Royal Counsel in the Age of the *Unræd*

1. I have adopted the dating proposed by Peter Clemoes, "The Chronology of Ælfric's Works," *Old English Newsletter, Subsidia* 5 (1980): 34; originally published in *The Anglo-Saxons: Studies in Some Aspects of Their History and Culture Presented to Bruce Dickins*, ed. Peter Clemoes (London: Bowes and Bowes, 1959), 212–47.

2. *Ælfric's Lives of Saints*, ed. W. W. Skeat, EETS o.s. 76, 82, 94, 114 (London: Trübner, 1881–1900; repr. in 2 vols., London: Oxford University Press, 1966), vol. 1 (hereafter *LS I*), 551. Throughout this chapter, italics are used to distinguish Ælfric's *Kings* from the biblical book of Kings.

3. A literature review for *Kings* unearths no full-length discussions of this text, merely Skeat's terse remark, Milton McC. Gatch's succinct overview of the dates and setting in which the biblical book of Kings might have been read, and Joyce Hill's brief consideration of *Kings*'s manuscript history. See, respectively, Milton McC. Gatch, "The Office in Late Anglo-Saxon Monasticism," *Learning and Literature in Anglo-Saxon England*, ed. Michael Lapidge and Helmut Gneuss (Cambridge: Cambridge University Press, 1985), 353–54; Joyce Hill, "The Dissemination of Ælfric's *Lives of Saints:* A Preliminary Survey," in *Holy Men and Holy Women: Old English Prose Saints' Lives and Their Contexts*, ed. Paul E. Szarmach (Albany: State University of New York Press, 1996), 235–59.

4. Malcolm Godden, "Biblical Literature: The Old Testament," in *The Cambridge Companion to Old English Literature*, ed. Malcolm Godden and Michael Lapidge (Cambridge: Cambridge University Press, 1991), 225.

5. Useful studies of Ælfric's theological views include: Milton McC. Gatch, *Preaching and Theology in Anglo-Saxon England: Ælfric and Wulfstan* (Toronto: University of Toronto Press, 1977); and Lynne Grundy, *Books and Grace: Ælfric's Theology* (London: King's College London, Centre for Late Antique and Medieval Studies, 1991). Essays that played a crucial role in establishing Ælfric as deeply engaged with contemporary social and political issues include Mary Clayton, "Of Mice and Men: Ælfric's Second Homily for the Feast of a Confessor," *Leeds Studies in English* 24 (1993): 1–26; and Malcolm Godden, "Apocalypse and Invasion in Late Anglo-Saxon England," in *From Anglo-Saxon to Early Middle English: Studies Presented to E. G. Stanley*, ed. Malcolm Godden, Douglas Gray, and Terry Hoad (Oxford: Clarendon Press, 1994), 130–62.

6. Ælfric's "Preface to Genesis" is contained in *Ælfric's Prefaces*, ed. Jonathan Wilcox, Durham Medieval Texts 9 (Durham: Durham Medieval Texts, 1994), 116–19. Wilcox provides insightful discussion of Ælfric's attitudes toward translation at 37–44, 63–65. See also Melinda J. Menzer, "The Preface as Admonition: Ælfric's Preface to Genesis," in *The Old English Hexateuch: Aspects and Approaches*, ed. Rebecca Barnhouse and Benjamin C. Withers (Kalamazoo, Mich.: Medieval Institute Publications, 2000), 15–39.

7. See Ælfric's "Preface to Genesis," in *Ælfric's Prefaces*, ed. Wilcox, p. 117, ll. 41–43.

8. Particularly thought-provoking critiques of the methods and problems of source study include Colin Chase, "Source Study as a Trick with Mirrors: Annihilation of Meaning in the Old English 'Mary of Egypt,'" in *Sources of Anglo-Saxon Culture*, ed. Paul E. Szarmach with Virginia Darrow Oggins, Studies in Medieval Culture 20 (Kalamazoo, Mich.: Medieval Institute Publications, 1986), 23–33; Clare A. Lees, "Working with Patristic Sources: Language and Context in Old English Homilies," in *Speaking Two Languages: Traditional Disciplines and Contemporary Theory in Medieval Studies*, ed. Allen J. Frantzen (Albany: State University of New York Press, 1991), 157–80; R. M. Liuzza, "What the Thunder Said: Anglo-Saxon Brontologies and the Problem of Sources," *Review of English Studies* 55 (2004): 1–23.

9. Richard Marsden, *The Text of the Old Testament in Anglo-Saxon England* (Cambridge: Cambridge University Press, 1995), 406, with useful discussion at 395–449.

10. Stewart Brookes, "Ælfric's Adaptation of the Book of Esther: A Source of Some Confusion," in *Essays on Anglo-Saxon and Related Themes in Memory of Lynne Grundy*, ed. Jane Roberts and Janet Nelson (London: King's College London, Centre for Late Antique and Medieval Studies, 2000), 37–63. Marsden too notes the possibility of Old Latin influence, and suggests that it was most likely transmitted through patristic commentaries: *The Text of the Old Testament*, 408–9. My own study of Ælfric's *Kings* proceeds on the cautious premise that Ælfric was working with the Vulgate—focusing mainly on differences between *Kings* and the Vulgate and checking those differences against the Old Latin version of Kings contained in *Bibliorum sacrorum Latinae versiones antiquae, seu Vetus Italica*, ed. Pierre Sabatier, 3 vols. (Rheims: Reginaldus Florentain, 1743; repr., Turnhout: Brepols, 1976), 1:475–628. References to the Vulgate are to *Biblia Sacra Iuxta Vulgatem Versionem*, ed. Robert Weber, 2 vols. (Stuttgart: Deutsche Bibelgesellschaft, 1983), 1:366–545; unless indicated otherwise, translations are from the Douay-Rheims.

11. Frantzen reminds us that to "know" a book in Anglo-Saxon England could mean to read, recite, listen to, copy, interpret, or remember it: *Desire for Origins: New Languages, Old English, and Teaching the Tradition* (New Brunswick, N.J.: Rutgers University Press, 1990), 86. Howe shows that the sense of reading as an oral, communal act was so ingrained in Anglo-Saxon culture as to inhere in the language itself, pointing out, for example, that the Old English *rædan* could mean "to read," "to give advice or counsel," or "to explain something obscure"; see "The Cultural Construction of Reading in Anglo-Saxon England," in *The Ethnography of Reading*, ed. Jonathan Boyarin (Berkeley: University of California Press, 1993), 58–79; repr. in *Old English Literature: Critical Essays*, ed. R. M. Liuzza (New Haven: Yale University Press, 2002), 1–22.

12. I have followed the dating proposed by N. R. Ker, *Catalogue of Manuscripts Containing Anglo-Saxon* (Oxford: Clarendon Press, 1957). Julius E. vii is item 162 and is discussed at pp. 206–10; Hatton 115 (Skeat's Junius 23) is item 332 and is discussed at pp. 399–403. Within Hatton 115, *Kings* appears in the portion of the manuscript composed in s. xi².

13. My discussion of the manuscript context for *Kings* is indebted to Joyce Hill, "The Dissemination of Ælfric's *Lives of Saints*," 237, 251.

14. The date of Æthelweard's death is uncertain. Simon Keynes suggests ca. 998, for it is in this year that Æthelweard ceases to witness charters: Keynes, *The Diplomas of King Æthelred "The Unready": 978–1016* (Cambridge: Cambridge University Press, 1980), 192 n. 139. Peter Clemoes suggests a later date, ca. 1002, although he acknowledges the uncertainty of his claim and reminds us that Kenneth Sisam worked on the basis of 998: Clemoes, "Chronology," 33. The date of Æthelweard's death is important for establishing a *terminus ad quem* for Ælfric's *Lives of Saints*, and thus for *Kings* as well.

15. Keynes notes that S 914 is spurious but that its witness list must derive from a genuine source: *The Diplomas of King Æthelred*, 161.

16. Keynes, *The Diplomas of King Æthelred*, 161. See also 190–93 and table 6.

17. *LS I*, 2–3. For additional discussion of Ælfric's intended audiences, see *Ælfric's Prefaces*, ed. Wilcox, 50–52; and for a fuller discussion, see Jonathan Wilcox, "The Audience of Ælfric's *Lives of Saints* and the Face of Cotton Caligula A. xiv, fols. 93–130," in *Beatus Vir: Studies in Honor of Phillip Pulsiano*, ed. A. N. Doane and Kirsten Wolf (Tempe, Ariz.: Medieval and Renaissance Texts and Studies, forthcoming).

18. *Ælfric's Prefaces*, ed. Wilcox, item 5a, p. 119, ll. 7–9; item 5b, p. 120, ll. 8–12.

19. Clemoes, "Chronology," 10. M. R. Godden offers further evidence for the nonliturgical nature of the items contained in the *Lives*, pointing out that they "do not refer to the feast day as the occasion for reading them, they are often very long, and they frequently include attached pieces on other issues": "Experiments in Genre: The Saints' Lives in Ælfric's *Catholic Homilies*," in *Holy Men, Holy Women*, ed. Szarmach, 261–87, at 261.

20. For further discussion, see Joyce Hill, "The Dissemination of Ælfric's *Lives of Saints*."

21. Gatch, "The Office in Late Anglo-Saxon Monasticism," 353–55.

22. Ibid., 355.

23. Ibid., 353–55.

24. Ibid., 355.

25. I am here again following Gatch, who argues that the *Lives* "ought to be understood . . . as an adaptation of materials from the monastic devotional life to the devotional life of laymen and non-monastic clergy": "The Office in Late Anglo-Saxon Monasticism," 362. See also Wilcox, *Ælfric's Prefaces*, 50.

26. My understanding of Jezebel's portrayal in patristic and medieval exegesis is much indebted to the comprehensive study by Jan M. Ziolkowski, *Jezebel: A Norman Latin Poem of the Early Eleventh Century* (New York: Peter Lang, 1989), 1–23. For an important study of Jezebel in relation to Merovingian queens, see Janet L. Nelson, "Queens as Jezebels: Brunhild and Balthild in Merovingian History," in *Medieval Women: Dedicated and Presented to Professor Rosalind M. T. Hill on the Occasion of Her Seventieth Birthday*, ed. Derek Baker, Studies in Church History, Subsidia 1 (Oxford: Basil Blackwell, 1978), 31–77. Repr. in Janet L. Nelson, *Politics and Ritual in Early Medieval Europe* (London: Hambledon Press, 1986), 1–49. Pauline Stafford's *Queens, Concubines, and Dowagers: The King's Wife in the Early Middle Ages* (Athens: University of Georgia Press, 1983), 13, 15, 19–20, 24–25, is also useful.

27. "Quae est Iezabel quae persequebatur, nisi synagoga vane fluens, vane abundans scriptures, quas neque custodit neque intellegit?": Ambrose, *Epistolae extra collectionem*, ed. Michaela Zelzer, *Sancti Ambrosii opera*, CSEL 82, pt. 10 (Vienna: Hoelder-Pichler-Tempsky, 1982), 277.

28. "Utique non mulierem fugiebat propheta tantus, sed hoc saeculum" (So great a prophet was by no means fleeing from a woman but rather from the world): Ambrose, *De fuga saeculi*, ed. Carolus Schenkl, *Sancti Ambrosii opera*, CSEL 32, pt. 2 (Vienna: F. Tempsky, 1897), 191.

29. See Ziolkowski, *Jezebel: A Norman Latin Poem*, 15.

30. *De Nabuthae*, ed. Carolus Schenkl, *Sancti Ambrosii opera*, CSEL 32, pt. 2 (Vienna: F. Tempsky, 1897), 491.

31. *Aldhelm: The Poetic Works*, trans. Michael Lapidge and James L. Rosier (Cambridge: D. S. Brewer, 1985), 159–60.

32. In the Vulgate, Ahab is grievously wounded by an arrow that strikes him between the lungs and the stomach; he is then forced to spend an entire day watching the remainder of the battle, as his blood seeps from his injured body onto the floor of the chariot in which he lies (3 Kings 22:34–35). Yet Aldhelm glosses over Ahab's extensive suffering, merely noting that "dogs licked up the flowing blood of the tyrant": *Aldhelm: The Poetic Works*, trans. Lapidge and Rosier, 160.

33. I am here following Lapidge and Rosier's suggestion that Aldhelm's promise in the prose *De virginitate* to provide the nuns with a hexameter version of the text offers enough evidence to conclude that the verse *De virginitate* was also intended for the nuns of Barking Abbey; the evidence is not, however, conclusive: *Aldhelm: The Poetic Works*, ed. Lapidge and Rosier, 97.

34. *Aldhelm: The Prose Works*, trans. Michael Lapidge and Michael Herren (Cambridge: D. S. Brewer, 1979), 68.

35. PL 93, 139C. For more on patristic and medieval etymologies of "Jezebel," see Ziolkowski, *Jezebel: A Norman Latin Poem*, 12–15.

36. "Et specialiter fuisse conjicitur mulier in supradicta Ecclesia docens memorata facinora, quae figura esset totius Jezabel per orbem, cui etiam manifestam

comminatur ultionem" (And particularly, it is conjectured that the woman teaching the crimes mentioned in the church discussed above is a figure of Jezebel who is found throughout the world, for whom it is here being threatened manifest revenge): PL 93, 139C.

37. *In Regum librum: XXX quaestiones,* ed. D. Hurst, CCSL 119 (Turnhout: Brepols, 1962), 293–322. Translated in *Bede: A Biblical Miscellany,* trans. W. Trent Foley and Arthur G. Holder (Liverpool: Liverpool University Press, 1999), 81–143.

38. *Homelia 23: In Decollatione Sancti Iohannis Baptistae,* ed. D. Hurst, CCSL 122 (Turnhout: Brepols, 1955), 349–57, at 350.

39. Jonas of Bobbio, *Vitae Columbani,* ed. Bruno Krusch, in *Ionae Vitae Sanctorum Columbani, Vedastis, Iohannis,* MGH, Scriptores Rerum Germanicarum in usum scholarum (Hanover: Hahn, 1905), chap. 18, 187.

40. *The Life of Bishop Wilfrid by Eddius Stephanus,* ed. and trans. Bertram Colgrave (1927; repr., Cambridge: Cambridge University Press, 1985), 14.

41. Ibid., 15.

42. Ibid., 48.

43. Ibid., 49.

44. For more on Ælfric's views on hagiography as a genre and on the stylistic tendencies characteristic of his saints' lives, see Godden, "Experiments in Genre," 261–87.

45. Citations to *Kings* are to *Ælfric's Lives of Saints,* ed. Skeat, 1:384–413, and are cited parenthetically by line number. Unless otherwise noted, all translations are my own.

46. The Vulgate refers to Jezebel as *regina* on only one occasion: long after Jezebel is dead, men of Judah come looking for the Israelite "sons of the king, and the sons of the queen" (4 Kings 10:13); this queen is undoubtedly Jezebel.

47. Ælfric's remarks in his "Preface to Genesis" reveal his anxieties that lay readers might interpret depictions of polygamy in Old Testament narratives as biblical sanction for such marital practices. See *Ælfric's Prefaces,* ed. Wilcox, 116–19.

48. If Æthelred's first wife died ca. 1000 and he married Emma in 1002, this would have left a period of approximately two years during which there was no queen. Moreover, it was during this same period that the queen mother Ælfthryth, who had so strongly supported the ecclesiastical reforms, either died or simply withdrew from her formerly active position in court. It is possible that Ælfric composed *Kings* during this interim period—a time when the queen mother was no longer a powerful presence in court and the future queen was unknown.

49. Joyce Hill, "The Dissemination of Ælfric's *Lives of Saints,*" 236.

50. The dates listed here are from the year that the woman became queen (i.e., the year that she married the king) to the date that is generally accepted for her death.

51. Keynes, *The Diplomas of King Æthelred,* 187.

52. *Anglo-Saxon Wills*, ed. and trans. Dorothy Whitelock (Cambridge: Cambridge University Press, 1930), item 20, 62; trans. on 63. Note that I have rendered Whitelock's *Ealdemodor* as *ealdemodor.*

53. For more on Ælfthryth's role in the monastic reform, see Marc Anthony Meyer, "Women and the Tenth-Century English Monastic Reform," *Revue Bénédictine* 87 (1977): 34–61.

54. See *Encomium Emmae Reginae*, ed. and trans. Alistair Campbell, with a supplementary introduction by Simon Keynes (Cambridge: Cambridge University Press, 1998), 55–65; and also Keynes, *The Diplomas of King Æthelred*, 187 n. 118. There is some uncertainty over the date of Ælfthryth's death. Keynes suggests that she died on 17 November 999, the year that she ceases to witness charters, or on that day in 1000 or 1001. See Keynes, *The Diplomas of King Æthelred*, 210 n. 203.

55. For this quotation, see *Regularis concordia Anglicae nationis monachorum sanctimonialiumque: The Monastic Agreement of the Monks and Nuns of the English Nation*, ed. and trans. Thomas Symons (London: Thomas Nelson and Sons, 1953), 2.

56. On Ælfthryth's role in ecclesiastical affairs, see Pauline Stafford, "The King's Wife in Wessex, 800–1066," in *New Readings on Women in Old English Literature*, ed. Helen Damico and Alexandra Hennessey Olsen (Bloomington: Indiana University Press, 1990), 66–67

57. Mary Clayton, "Ælfric and Æthelred," in *Essays on Anglo-Saxon and Related Themes in Memory of Lynne Grundy*, ed. Jane Roberts and Janet Nelson (London: King's College London, Centre for Late Antique and Medieval Studies, 2000), 65–88, at 66, 86–87.

58. See Clayton, "Ælfric and Æthelred"; Godden, "Apocalypse and Invasion," 134–36; and Christopher A. Jones, *Ælfric's Letter to the Monks of Eynsham*, Cambridge Studies in Anglo-Saxon England 24 (Cambridge: Cambridge University Press, 1998), 43–49.

59. Jezebel's efforts to uphold the absolute power of the monarchy are most apparent in the vineyard episode, in which she interprets Naboth's refusal to sell the vineyard to Ahab as a challenge to the monarchy's power and as an opportunity to prove that power as absolute (3 Kings 21:7).

60. *Genesis*, in *The Junius Manuscript*, ed. George Philip Krapp, ASPR 1 (New York: Columbia University Press, 1931), 24: "She spoke to him frequently and urged him on the entire day toward the dark deed"; "She, the most lovely of women, spoke then to Adam quite frequently."

61. *The Anglo-Saxon Minor Poems*, ed. Elliott Van Kirk Dobbie, ASPR 6 (New York: Columbia University Press, 1942), 118, ll. 64–66.

62. For the source of this passage, I have relied on Malcolm Godden, *Ælfric's Catholic Homilies: Introduction, Commentary and Glossary*, EETS s.s. 18 (Oxford: Oxford University Press, 2000), 273.

63. *Ælfric's Catholic Homilies: The First Series, Text,* ed. Peter Clemoes, EETS s.s. 17 (Oxford: Oxford University Press, 1992) (hereafter *CH I*), pp. 456–57, ll. 175–88.

64. See, for example, Lucy's valuable counsel to her mother on the transitory nature of earthly wealth: "Þa cwæð lucia. hlyst mines rædes / ne miht ðu naht lædan of þysum life mid þe." (Then Lucy said, "Hear my counsel; you cannot take anything with you from this life"; *LS I,* ed. Skeat, p. 212, ll. 46–47).

65. A classic example of the whetting woman is Hildegyth in *Waldere,* who reminds Waldere (the man to whom she is betrothed) to remember his past glories, to trust in his sword, and either to win renown or to die trying: *The Anglo-Saxon Minor Poems,* ed. Dobbie, pp. 4–5, ll. 2–32.

66. "Herodes hiwode hine sylfne unrotne þa seo dohtor hine þæs heafdes bæd: ac he blissode on his digelnyssum. for þan ðe heo ðæs mannes deað bæd þe he ær acwellan wolde gif he intingan hæfde" (Herod pretended to be sad when the daughter asked him for the head but he secretly rejoiced because she asked for the death of the man whom he previously would have killed, had he had a pretext; *CH I,* ed. Clemoes, p. 455, ll. 141–43).

67. *CH I,* ed. Clemoes, pp. 454–55, ll. 115–17.

68. Note, however, Stewart Brookes's point that the retaliatory battles are not present in the Old Latin versions of Esther. If Ælfric was working with an Old Latin text rather than the Vulgate, it is possible that he never cut these scenes at all: Stewart Brookes, "Ælfric's Adaptation of the Book of Esther," 51–52.

69. *The Old English Version of the Heptateuch, Ælfric's Treatise on the Old and New Testament and His Preface to Genesis,* ed. S. J. Crawford, EETS o.s. 160 (London: Oxford University Press, 1922), 403–6.

70. Keynes, *The Diplomas of King Æthelred,* 176–86.

71. Ibid., 177.

72. Ibid.

73. For more on the genealogy of Æthelred's epithet, see Simon Keynes, "The Declining Reputation of King Æthelred the Unready," in *Ethelred the Unready: Papers from the Millenary Conference,* ed. David Hill, BAR British Series 59 (Oxford: British Archeological Reports, 1978), 227–53, esp. 240–41.

74. *Ælfric's Catholic Homilies: The Second Series, Text,* ed. Malcolm Godden, EETS s.s. 5 (London: Oxford University Press, 1979) (hereafter *CH II*), p. 183, ll. 96–99; cited in Clayton, "Ælfric and Æthelred," 71; trans. my own.

75. *Heptateuch,* ed. Crawford, p. 71, ll. 1204–7. I have adopted Clemoes's dating of the *Letter:* "Chronology," 35.

76. *Old English Homilies,* ed. R. Morris, EETS o.s. 29 and 34 (London: Trübner, 1867–68,) 302; cited in Clayton, "Ælfric and Æthelred," 79–80.

77. Ælfric's Latin source is the *Hexameron of Saint Basil.*

78. *The Anglo-Saxon Version of the Hexameron of St. Basil . . . and the Anglo-Saxon Remains of St. Basil's Admonitio ad Filium Spiritualem,* ed. Henry W. Norman (London: Smith, 1849), 54.

79. The corresponding Latin phrase reads, "Et Achab propter avaritiam invasit vineam Naboth, et hujus rei gratiâ, in prælio vulneratus, defunctus est" (And because of his avarice, Ahab took possession of Naboth's vineyard and on account of that deed died, wounded in battle; *The Anglo-Saxon Version of the Hexameron of St. Basil,* ed. Norman, 54 note s).

80. Keynes, *The Diplomas of King Æthelred,* 176–86.

81. *Homilies of Ælfric: A Supplementary Collection,* ed. John C. Pope, 2 vols., EETS o.s. 259–60 (London: Oxford University Press, 1967), 1:380, ll. 32–35; cited in Clayton, "Ælfric and Æthelred," 81.

82. *Homilies of Ælfric,* ed. Pope, 1:380, ll. 46–47; cited in Clayton, "Ælfric and Æthelred," 81; trans. my own.

83. Keynes, *The Diplomas of King Æthelred,* 177–80, 193.

84. *Memorials of Saint Dunstan: Archbishop of Canterbury,* ed. William Stubbs, Rolls Series 63 (London: Longman, 1874; repr., Kraus Reprint, 1965), 356–57. Quoted in Janet L. Nelson, *Politics and Ritual in Early Medieval Europe* (London: Hambledon Press, 1986), 337.

85. *The Exeter Book,* ed. George Philip Krapp and Elliott Van Kirk Dobbie, ASPR 3 (New York: Columbia University Press, 1936), p. 158, ll. 58b–59.

86. Ælfric came to Winchester sometime during Æthelwold's episcopacy (963–984), and he left for Cerne Abbas ca. 987. On Æthelred's appropriation of lands from the Old Minster, Winchester, see Keynes, *The Diplomas of King Æthelred,* 180.

87. See Fred C. Robinson, "The Prescient Woman in Old English Literature," in *Philologia Anglica: Essays Presented to Professor Yoshio Terasawa on the Occasion of His Sixtieth Birthday,* ed. Kinshiro Oshitari et al. (Tokyo: Kenkyusha, 1988), 241–50; repr. in *The Tomb of Beowulf and Other Essays on Old English* (Oxford: Blackwell, 1993), 155–63. Also useful is Kees Samplonius, "From Veleda to the Völva: Aspects of Female Divination in Germanic Europe," in *Sanctity and Motherhood: Essays on Holy Mothers in the Middle Ages,* ed. Anneke B. Mulder-Bakker (New York and London: Garland, 1995), 68–99.

88. *The Exeter Book,* ed. Krapp and Dobbie, pp. 159–60, ll. 86a, 91b–92.

89. *The Life of King Edward Who Rests at Westminster, Attributed to a Monk of Saint-Bertin,* ed. and trans. Frank Barlow, 2nd ed. (Oxford: Clarendon Press, 1992), Latin at 22, trans. at 23. See also p. 6, where she is described as an "altius ingenium, conciliumque citum" (profound, intelligent, prompt counsellor); trans. at 7.

90. For the Old English, see *LS I,* ed. Skeat, p. 413, ll. 476–79.

91. *LS I,* ed. Skeat, p. 366, ll. 47–51; references to *De Auguriis* are hereafter cited parenthetically by line number.

92. On the extent to which the items and ordering of Julius E. vii may represent the work of Ælfric, see Joyce Hill, "The Dissemination of Ælfric's *Lives of Saints,*" 235–59.

93. *CH II,* ed. Godden, p. 232, ll. 68–70.

94. See *CH II,* ed. Godden, p. 167, ll. 200–207; and also *Homilies of Ælfric: A Supplementary Collection,* ed. Pope, 1:385, ll. 139–44.

95. *CH I,* ed. Clemoes, p. 361, ll. 179–82. See also p. 363, ll. 229–31, which further discuss the sevenfold gifts, drawing on Isa. 11:2–3. For the sources of these passages, I have relied on Godden, *Ælfric's Catholic Homilies: Introduction, Commentary and Glossary,* 507, 567.

96. On the powerful associations between sexual and spiritual fornication, see chap. 1 of this book, n. 57; Ziolkowski, *Jezebel: A Norman Latin Poem,* 10–12, is also useful.

97. *CH I,* ed. Clemoes, pp. 254–55, ll. 181–89.

98. The passage is of course not original to Ælfric. As Malcolm Godden points out, ll. 181–86 (up to *on clænnysse*) are a paraphrase of Luke 2:36–38. The detail *and on clænnysse* is Ælfric's, and it has been added to prepare for the subsequent comments (derived from Origen) on Anna's chastity rendering her worthy to prophesy about Christ: Godden, *Ælfric's Catholic Homilies: Introduction, Commentary and Glossary,* 75.

99. Yet it is worth noting that while exemplary habits of living (e.g., chastity and piety) were in theory equally available to either sex, women were less inclined to be viewed as having successfully achieved them, particularly during periods of heightened misogyny, as was the case during the Benedictine reforms.

100. Crawford, *Heptateuch,* 46.

101. Michael Winterbottom, ed. and trans., *Gildas: The Ruin of Britain and Other Works* (London and Chichester: Phillimore, 1978), 14.

Chapter 5   **Queenship and Social Reform in Ælfric's *Esther***

1. *Ælfric's Catholic Homilies: The Second Series, Text,* ed. Malcolm Godden, EETS s.s. 5 (London: Oxford University Press, 1979) (hereafter *CH II*), pp. 340–41, ll. 175–76, 187–91.

2. Ælfric's *Esther* was first published as Bruno Assmann, "Abt Ælfric's angelsächsische Bearbeitung des Buches Esther," *Anglia* 9 (1886): 25–38, and repr. in *Angelsächsische Homilien und Heiligenleben,* ed. Bruno Assmann, Bibliothek der angelsächsischen Prosa 3 (Kassel: G. H. Wigand, 1889); repr. with a supplementary introd. by Peter Clemoes (Darmstadt: Wissenschaftliche Buchgesellschaft, 1964), 92–101. References are to the 1964 edition by line number. Throughout this chapter, italics are used to distinguish Ælfic's *Esther* from the biblical book of Esther.

3. I have adopted the dating proposed by Peter Clemoes, "The Chronology of Ælfric's Works," *Old English Newsletter, Subsidia* 5 (1980): 34; originally published in *The Anglo-Saxons: Studies in Some Aspects of Their History and Culture Presented to Bruce Dickins*, ed. Peter Clemoes (London: Bowes and Bowes, 1959), 212–47.

4. The best study of *Esther* to date is Mary Clayton, "Ælfric's *Esther*: A Speculum Reginae?" in *Text and Gloss: Studies in Insular Learning and Literature Presented to Joseph Donovan Pheifer*, ed. Helen Conrad O'Briain, Anne Marie D'Arcy, and John Scattergood (Dublin: Four Courts Press, 1999), 89–101. Also useful is Timothy Alan Gustafson, "Ælfric Reads Esther: The Cultural Limits of Translation" (Ph.D. diss., University of Iowa, 1995). For an electronic edition that includes helpful commentary and bibliography, see *Ælfric's Homilies on Judith, Esther, and the Maccabees*, ed. Stuart D. Lee, 1999: http://users.ox.ac.uk/~stuart/kings/.

5. The question of precisely which Latin text(s) served as source material for Ælfric's *Esther* is vexed. For more on possible sources for Ælfric's biblical adaptations and on the problems of source study in general, see the discussion that opens chap. 4. For a detailed consideration of possible sources for *Esther*, see the important study by Stewart Brookes, "Ælfric's Adaptation of the Book of Esther: A Source of Some Confusion," in *Essays on Anglo-Saxon and Related Themes in Memory of Lynne Grundy*, ed. Jane Roberts and Janet Nelson (London: King's College London, Centre for Late Antique and Medieval Studies, 2000), 37–63. In this chapter, I have focused mainly on differences between the Vulgate and Ælfric's *Esther*, checking those differences against the Old Latin version of Esther contained in *Bibliorum sacrorum Latinae versiones antiquae, seu Vetus Italica*, ed. Pierre Sabatier, 3 vols. (Rheims: Reginaldus Florentain, 1743; repr., Turnhout: Brepols, 1976), 1:796–825. References to the Vulgate are to "Liber Hester," in *Biblia Sacra Iuxta Vulgatem Versionem*, ed. Robert Weber, 2 vols. (Stuttgart: Deutsche Bibelgesellschaft, 1983), 1:712–30; unless indicated otherwise, translations are from the Douay-Rheims.

6. "Esther quoque similiter reginam regina, in omni pietatis et sanctitatis actione imitabilem, vobis ante oculos cordis semper ponite": Hrabanus Maurus, "Expositio in librum Judith," PL 109, 539–92, quotation at 541; cited in Lois L. Huneycutt, "Intercession and the High-Medieval Queen: The Esther Topos," in *Power of the Weak: Studies on Medieval Women*, ed. Jennifer Carpenter and Sally-Beth MacLean (Urbana: University of Illinois Press, 1995), 126–46, at 140 n. 9; translation is also from Huneycutt, "Intercession," 129. The commentary on Esther is printed as "Expositio in librum Esther," PL 109, 635–70. For an insightful account of how Hrabanus's biblical commentaries were used, see Mayke De Jong, "The Empire as *Ecclesia*: Hrabanus Maurus and Biblical *Historia* for Rulers," in *The Uses of the Past in the Early Middle Ages*, ed. Yitzhak Hen and Matthew Innes (Cambridge: Cambridge University Press, 2000), 191–226.

7. Pauline Stafford, *Queens, Concubines, and Dowagers: The King's Wife in the Early Middle Ages* (Athens: University of Georgia Press, 1983), 20, 26. See also Gustafson, "Ælfric Reads Esther," 96–97.

8. "Et eritis pro Ecclesia Christi apud pium conjugem more sanctae illius Esther pro Israelitica plebe apud maritum": Pope John VIII, *"Ad Richildim Augustam,"* PL 126, 698–99; quotation at 698; cited in Huneycutt, "Intercession," 140 n. 11.

9. "Despondeo te uni viro virginem castam atque pudicam, futuram coniugem, ut sanctae mulieres fuere viris suis, Sarra, Rebecca, Rachel, Hester, Iudith, Anna, Noëmi": Hincmar of Rheims, "Coronatio Iudithae Karoli II. Filiae," ed. Alfred Boretius and Victor Krause, MGH, Legum Sectio II, Capitularia regum Francorum, 2 vols. (Hanover: Hahn, 1883–97), 2:426, ll. 9–11.

10. "Ut efferatum cor regis ad misericordiam et salvationem in te credentium ipsius precibus inclinares": Hincmar, "Coronatio Iudithae," 426, ll. 40–41; cited in Huneycutt, "Intercession," 140 n. 12; translation is also from Huneycutt, 129.

11. L'Isle's transcription of *Esther* is contained in Oxford, Bodleian Library, MS Laud Misc. 381, fols. 140v–48r. The lack of a contemporary copy of *Esther* necessitates caution when speaking of "Ælfric's changes" to his biblical sources. This essay proceeds on the cautious premise that L'Isle's transcription is a fairly accurate copy of Ælfric's *Esther* and that any changes L'Isle may have made to the text are confined to the omission of Ælfric's interpretive comments. This premise is based on an understanding of L'Isle's habits of transcription as presented in the following essays: Stuart Lee, "Oxford, Bodleian Library, MS Laud Misc. 381: William L'Isle, Ælfric, and the *Ancrene Wisse*," in *The Recovery of Old English: Anglo-Saxon Studies in the Sixteenth and Seventeenth Centuries,* ed. Timothy Graham (Kalamazoo, Mich.: Medieval Institute Publications, 2000), 207–42; and, in the same volume, Phillip Pulsiano, "William L'Isle and the Editing of Old English," 173–206. See also Timothy Graham, "Early Modern Users of Claudius B. iv: Robert Talbot and William L'Isle," in *The Old English Hexateuch: Aspects and Approaches,* ed. Rebecca Barnhouse and Benjamin C. Withers (Kalamazoo, Mich.: Medieval Institute Publications, 2000), 271–316. I am grateful to Timothy Graham for his assistance with William L'Isle.

12. The Vulgate, chaps. 1–8 (equivalent to the main portion of the text on which Ælfric relies), refers to Esther twenty-one times as "Hester," seven times as both "Hester" and *regina,* and six times as simply *regina.* Ælfric almost exactly reverses these figures, referring to Esther three times in *Esther* by name, twice as both "Hester" and *cwen,* and seventeen times as simply *seo cwen* or *cwen.*

13. *The Old English Version of the Heptateuch, Ælfric's Treatise on the Old and New Testament and His Preface to Genesis,* ed. S. J. Crawford, EETS o.s. 160 (London: Oxford University Press, 1922), 48, ll. 766–71.

14. On Esther's reception by the Christian Church, see Bernhard W. Anderson, "The Place of the Book of Esther in the Christian Bible," *Journal of Religion* 30 (1950): 32–43; repr. in *Studies in the Book of Esther,* ed. Carey A. Moore (New York: Ktav, 1982), 130–41.

15. Vulgate, 11:1. For more on the Additions, see Carey A. Moore, "On the Origins of the LXX Additions to the Book of Esther," *Journal of Biblical Literature* 92 (1973): 382–93; repr. in *Studies in the Book of Esther,* ed. Moore, 583–94.

16. Both Mary Clayton, "Ælfric's *Esther,*" 93, and Micheline M. Larès, *Bible et civilisation anglaise: Naissance d'une tradition* (Paris: Didier, 1974), 265–66, note that Ælfric's Esther converts the king. In this quotation and in those throughout this chapter, italics are used to indicate those portions of Ælfic's *Esther* which have no apparent source in, or are significantly expanded from, the Latin texts.

17. See Brookes, "Ælfric's Adaptation of the Book of Esther," 54.

18. See Pauline Stafford, "The King's Wife in Wessex, 800–1066," *Past and Present* 91 (1981): 3–27; repr. in *New Readings on Women in Old English Literature,* ed. Helen Damico and Alexandra Hennessey Olsen (Bloomington: Indiana University Press, 1990), 56–78; and also Stafford, *Queen Emma and Queen Edith: Queenship and Women's Power in Eleventh-Century England* (Oxford: Blackwell, 1997).

19. On Æthelred's date of birth and age at his accession, see Simon Keynes, *The Diplomas of King Æthelred "The Unready": 978–1016* (Cambridge: Cambridge University Press, 1980), 164, 174; on Ælfthryth's attestation of charters, see 104, 132 n. 163, 138, 174 n. 82, 176, 181–82.

20. For further discussion of Emma as a charter witness, see *Encomium Emmae Reginae,* ed. and trans. Alistair Campbell, with a supplementary introduction by Simon Keynes (Cambridge: Cambridge University Press, 1998), 55–65; and also Stafford, *Queen Emma and Queen Edith,* 221, 231–32, 254.

21. Clayton, "Ælfric's *Esther,*" 99.

22. The clearest example is Ælfric's *Judith,* which he offered as an exemplary narrative to both female religious and male warriors; see Mary Clayton, "Ælfric's *Judith:* Manipulative or Manipulated?" *Anglo-Saxon England* 23 (1994): 215–27.

23. In the *Letter to Sigeweard,* Ælfric claims, "Ðis gewrit wæs to anum men gediht ac hit mæg swa ðeah manegum fremian" (This text was composed for one man although it may nevertheless profit many): *Heptateuch,* ed. Crawford, 15.

24. For numerous examples, see *Ælfric's Prefaces,* ed. Jonathan Wilcox, Durham Medieval Texts 9 (Durham: Durham Medieval Texts, 1994), 70–71.

25. Stafford, "The King's Wife."

26. Relevant papal letters include Pope Gregory the Great's letter to Bertha (ca. 601), Pope Boniface V's letter to Æthelburh (ca. 625), and Boniface's letter to Æthelburh's husband, Edwin (ca. 625). For Gregory's letter, see *Councils and Ecclesiastical Documents Relating to Great Britain and Ireland,* ed. Arthur West Haddan and William Stubbs, 3 vols. (1871; repr., Oxford: Clarendon Press, 1964), 3: 17–18. For Boniface's letters, see *Bede's Ecclesiastical History of the English People,* ed. Bertram Colgrave and R. A. B. Mynors (Oxford: Clarendon Press, 1969), ii.10–11; ii.9 is also relevant. See also my chap. 1.

27. Paul Strohm, *Hochon's Arrow: The Social Imagination of Fourteenth-Century Texts* (Princeton: Princeton University Press, 1992), 95–96. See also John Carmi Parsons, "The Queen's Intercession in Thirteenth-Century England," in *Power of the Weak*, ed. Carpenter and MacLean, 147–77.

28. Strohm, *Hochon's Arrow*, 96.

29. On the misogyny of the reforms, with particular attention to Ælfric's writings, see Catherine Cubitt, "Virginity and Misogyny in Tenth- and Eleventh-Century England," *Gender & History* 12 (2000): 1–32.

30. Christopher A. Jones, *Ælfric's Letter to the Monks of Eynsham*, Cambridge Studies in Anglo-Saxon England 24 (Cambridge: Cambridge University Press, 1998), 43–49.

31. The *psalmi familiares* or *psalmi pro benefactoribus* were a set of devotions chanted after each of the liturgical hours for the monastery's friends and benefactors. See Jones, *Ælfric's Letter to the Monks of Eynsham*, 30. The omission of the queen from the *psalmi familiares* is noted by Lucia Kornexl, ed., *Die Regularis Concordia und ihre altenglische Interlinearversion*, Texte und Untersuchungen zur englischen Philologie 17 (Munich: Fink, 1993), lxiv n. 33.

32. See Robert Deshman, "*Christus rex et magi reges:* Kingship and Christology in Ottonian and Anglo-Saxon Art," *Frühmittelalterliche Studien* 10 (1976): 367–405; and Deshman, "*Benedictus Monarcha et Monachus:* Early Medieval Ruler Theology and the Anglo-Saxon Reform," *Frühmittelalterliche Studien* 22 (1988): 204–40.

33. *Regularis concordia Anglicae nationis monachorum sanctimonialiumque: The Monastic Agreement of the Monks and Nuns of the English Nation*, ed. and trans. Thomas Symons (London: Thomas Nelson and Sons, 1953), with prayers for the royal family prescribed at 7, 12, 13, 14, 16, and the roles of the king and queen outlined at 2.

34. *Regularis concordia*, xlvi.

35. See Antonia Gransden, "Traditionalism and Continuity During the Last Century of Anglo-Saxon Monasticism," *Journal of Ecclesiastical History* 40 (1989): 159–207, esp. 161–64, 180; Patrick Wormald, "Æthelwold and His Continental Counterparts: Contact, Comparison, Contrast," in *Bishop Æthelwold: His Career and Influence*, ed. Barbara Yorke (Woodbridge: Boydell Press, 1988), 38–41; and Jones, *Ælfric's Letter to the Monks of Eynsham*, 9, 47, and 51, although Jones points out at p. 51 that nostalgia for an early Anglo-Saxon golden age "find(s) only oblique expression" in Ælfric's *Letter to the Monks of Eynsham*.

36. See Malcolm Godden, "Apocalypse and Invasion in Late Anglo-Saxon England," in *From Anglo-Saxon to Early Middle English: Studies Presented to E. G. Stanley*, ed. Malcolm Godden, Douglas Gray, and Terry Hoad (Oxford: Clarendon Press, 1994), 130–62, esp. 130–42.

37. The complexities of these paradigms are discussed in Godden, "Apocalypse and Invasion."

38. *Ælfric's Lives of Saints,* ed. W. W. Skeat, EETS o.s. 76, 82, 94, 114 (London: Trübner, 1881–1900; repr., in 2 vols., London: Oxford University Press, 1966), 1:284, 286, ll. 30–35; trans. is from Godden, "Apocalypse and Invasion," 134. A similar linkage between national faith and political well-being appears again in this same homily at ll. 133–37.

39. Compare the early sixth-century anonymous *Vita Genovefae,* which explicitly spells out a contemporary political relevance for the Esther-narrative. The hagiographer likens the young virgin Genovefa (423–502) to Esther, detailing how Genovefa, through devotion to God, was able to ward off Attila the Hun and his invading troops, and thus save Paris, just as Esther's prayers saved the Jews; see *Sainted Women of the Dark Ages,* ed. and trans. Jo Ann McNamara and John E. Halborg, with E. Gordon Whatley (Durham, N.C.: Duke University Press, 1992), 23.

40. The idea is explored at length in Ælfric's homily "On the Dedication of a Church," *CH II,* ed. Godden, pp. 335–45, esp. ll. 191–92, and is also apparent in explanatory glosses contained in the Old English rendition of Psalm 44:10 as, for example, "And þær stent cwen þe on þa swyðran hand, mid golde getu[n]code and mid ælcere mislicre fægernesse gegyred (þæt ys, eall Cristnu gesamnung)" (And there stands the queen at your right hand, covered in gold and completely adorned with manifold fairness; that is the entire Christian congregation): *King Alfred's Old English Prose Translation of the First Fifty Psalms,* ed. Patrick P. O'Neill (Cambridge, Mass.: Medieval Academy of America, 2001), 155. Compare Douay-Rheims, which gives: "The queen stood on thy right hand, in gilded clothing; surrounded with variety." See also O'Neill, *King Alfred's Old English Prose Translation,* 254.

41. See, for example, the now classic discussion by Susan Stewart, who argues that nostalgia is a "social disease [in which] . . . the present is denied" and which seeks a past that "has never existed except as narrative": *On Longing: Narratives of the Miniature, the Gigantic, the Souvenir, the Collection* (Durham, N.C.: Duke University Press, 1993), 23. For an insightful account of nostalgia as a less pathological and more historically engaged strategy of remembrance, see Nicholas Dames, "Austen's Nostalgics," *Representations* 73 (2001): 117–43.

42. Sedulius wrote for the Carolingian court, which served as an important model for Anglo-Saxon ideologies of rule. For further discussion, see Deshman, *"Benedictus Monarcha et Monachus."*

43. *Sedulius Scottus: On Christian Rulers and the Poems,* trans. Edward Gerard Doyle (Binghamton, N.Y.: Medieval and Renaissance Texts and Studies, 1983), 61.

44. Both Icelandic sagas and early Anglo-Saxon secular law-codes suggest that native Germanic culture was not strongly opposed to divorce. For a lucid discussion of marriage in the sagas, see Roberta Frank, "Marriage in Twelfth- and Thirteenth-Century Iceland," *Viator* 4 (1973): 473–84. Relevant law-codes include Æthelberht, chaps. 31, 79, and 80: *English Historical Documents,* vol. 1, *c. 500–1042,* ed. Dorothy Whitelock, 2nd ed. (London: Eyre Methuen, 1979), 393; although

Carole A. Hough makes a strong case that chaps. 79 and 80 deal with the position of an Anglo-Saxon widow rather than divorce: Hough, "The Early Kentish 'Divorce Laws': A Reconsideration of Æthelberht, chs. 79 and 80," *Anglo-Saxon England* 23 (1994): 19–34. On possible points of contention between Germanic and Christian attitudes on divorce, see Michael Lapidge, "A Seventh-Century Insular Latin Debate Poem on Divorce," *Cambridge Medieval Celtic Studies* 10 (1985): 1–23; and Stephanie Hollis, *Anglo-Saxon Women and the Church: Sharing a Common Fate* (Woodbridge, Suffolk: Boydell Press, 1992), 46–74.

45. The three extant texts commonly identified as vernacular penitentials all contain provisions legitimating spousal separation, with the *Confessionale Pseudo-Egberti* or "Scriftboc" offering the most extensive range; see *Das altenglische Bussbuch (sog. Confessionale Pseudo-Egberti)*, ed. Robert Spindler (Leipzig: B. Tauchnitz, 1934), 179, 9g–h; 180–81, 14c; 181, 15c–d; 182, 16h; 182, 16k–l; 182–83, 17b; 183, 18d; 185, 19u; 185, 19zγ; cited by page and item number. The *Poenitentiale Pseudo-Ecgberti* or "Penitential" is closely related to, although slightly stricter than, the "Scriftboc": unlike the "Scriftboc," for example, the "Penitential" does not view adultery as an acceptable reason for separation, and it also prescribes harsh penalties, such as the withholding of the Eucharist and Christian burial, for individuals who abandon marriages; see *Die altenglische Version des Halitgar'schen Bussbuches (sog. Poenitentiale Pseudo-Ecgberti)*, ed. Josef Raith, Bibliothek der angelsächsischen Prosa 13 (Hamburg: Henri Grand, 1933), p. 19, item 7; pp. 20–21, item 8; p. 27, item 20; p. 65, item 52. The third penitential, known as the *Old English Handbook*, contains the same penalties as the "Penitential" for those who abandon their spouses and offers the confessor no guidance for advising laypeople who wish to remarry; see Roger Fowler, "A Late Old English Handbook for the Use of a Confessor," *Anglia* 83 (1965): 1–34, esp. p. 22, ll. 171–86.

46. *CH II*, ed. Godden, p. 185, ll. 159–62. As Godden points out, ll. 159–66 are indebted to Mark 10:11, Matt. 5:32, Mark 10:12, 1 Cor. 7:10–11, and Matt. 19:9: *Ælfric's Catholic Homilies: Introduction, Commentary and Glossary*, EETS s.s. 18 (Oxford: Oxford University Press, 2000), 525. Although Ælfric is generally opposed to spousal separation, he nevertheless concedes mutual desire for chaste living as a valid reason for this course of action: see *CH II*, ed. Godden, p. 185, ll. 166–68. For further discussion, see Peter Jackson, "Ælfric and the Purpose of Christian Marriage: A Reconsideration of the *Life of Æthelthryth*, Lines 120–30," *Anglo-Saxon England* 29 (2000): 235–60.

47. Ælfric's Latin and Old English letters are contained in *Die Hirtenbriefe Ælfrics in altenglischer und lateinischer Fassung*, ed. Bernhard Fehr, Bibliothek der angelsächsischen Prosa 9 (Hamburg: Henri Grand, 1914; repr., with a supplementary introd. by Peter Clemoes, Darmstadt: Wissenschaftliche Buchgesellschaft, 1966). References are to Fehr's 1966 edition by page and chapter numbers. For prohibitions against priests attending and blessing second marriages, see Fehr, p. 7,

chap. 26, and p. 49, chap. 114; for penances prescribed for remarriage, see Fehr, pp. 124–26, chap. 156. For Ælfric's Old English letter to Bishop Wulfsige of Sherborne, see Fehr, pp. 1–34, with the first quotation at p. 8, chap. 28, and the second at p. 7, chaps. 26–27.

48. See Ælfric's "Preface to Genesis," in *Ælfric's Prefaces*, ed. Wilcox, 116–19.

49. For more on this model, see Hollis, *Anglo-Saxon Women and the Church*, 46–51.

50. See Laws of Alfred, chaps. 1–1.7 in *English Historical Documents*, ed. Whitelock, 409. See also V Athelstan, prologues 1–3 in *English Historical Documents*, 422.

51. Important discussions of the gender implications of the reforms include Cubitt, "Virginity and Misogyny"; Pauline Stafford, "Queens, Nunneries and Reforming Churchmen: Gender, Religious Status and Reform in Tenth- and Eleventh-Century England," *Past and Present* 163 (1999): 3–35; and Jane Tibbetts Schulenburg, *Forgetful of Their Sex: Female Sanctity and Society, ca. 500–1100* (Chicago: University of Chicago Press, 1998), 107–18.

52. For sensitive accounts of the reforms' effects upon women religious, see Patricia Halpin, "Women Religious in Late Anglo-Saxon England," *The Haskins Society Journal* 6 (1994): 97–110; and Barbara Yorke, "'Sisters Under the Skin'? Anglo-Saxon Nuns and Nunneries in Southern England," *Reading Medieval Studies* 15 (1989): 95–117. On changing attitudes toward concubinage, see Margaret Clunies Ross, "Concubinage in Anglo-Saxon England," *Past and Present* 108 (1985): 3–34.

53. For further discussion, see Paul Beekman Taylor, "The Old English Poetic Vocabulary of Beauty," in *New Readings on Women*, ed. Damico and Olsen, 211–21, esp. 220–21 n. 26.

54. Latin translations here and in the remainder of this chapter are my own.

55. These examples are offered by Taylor, "Old English Poetic Vocabulary of Beauty," 213–14.

56. For a lucid discussion of the Old English term *fægere*, see Antonette diPaolo Healey, "Questions of Fairness: Fair, Not Fair, and Foul," in *Unlocking the Wordhord: Anglo-Saxon Studies in Memory of Edward B. Irving, Jr.*, ed. Mark C. Amodio and Katherine O'Brien O'Keeffe (Toronto: University of Toronto Press, 2003), 252–73.

57. It is worth noting Healey's point that *fægere* may occasionally refer to an outward beauty that does not map onto an internal reality, especially in descriptions of fair language in which eloquence and false words are used to cover a false or duplicitous nature. Nevertheless, as Healey reminds us, these cases are the exception rather than the rule and "except for these few passages depicting hollow language, the adjective 'fair' has wholly positive connotations in Old English": "Questions of Fairness," 263–64, quotation at 264.

Conclusion

1. One might note, for example, the collection of early medieval hagiographical materials entitled *The Age of Bede,* ed. D. H. Farmer, trans. J. F. Webb (New York: Penguin, 1983), or the recently constructed medieval heritage site at Jarrow that is named "Bede's World" and features a new permanent exhibition entitled "The Age of Bede."

2. *Encomium Emmae Reginae,* ed. and trans. Alistair Campbell, with a supplementary introduction by Simon Keynes (Cambridge: Cambridge University Press, 1998), 7.

3. Ibid.

Bibliography

Primary Sources

Ælfric. *Ælfric's Catholic Homilies: The First Series, Text*. Edited by Peter Clemoes. EETS s.s. 17. Oxford: Oxford University Press, 1997.

———. *Ælfric's Catholic Homilies: The Second Series, Text*. Edited by Malcolm Godden. EETS s.s. 5. London: Oxford University Press, 1979.

———. *Ælfric's Homilies on Judith, Esther, and the Maccabees*. Edited by Stuart D. Lee. 1999. http://users.ox.ac.uk/~stuart/kings/.

———. *Ælfric's Lives of Saints*. Edited by W. W. Skeat. EETS o.s. 76, 82, 94, 114. London: Trübner, 1881–1900. Reprinted as 2 vols. London: Oxford University Press, 1966.

———. *Ælfric's Prefaces*. Edited by Jonathan Wilcox. Durham Medieval Texts 9. Durham: Durham Medieval Texts, 1994.

———. *Esther*. Edited by Bruno Assmann. In "Abt Ælfric's angelsächsische Bearbeitung des Buches Esther," *Anglia* 9 (1886): 25–38. Reprint in *Angelsächsische homilien und heiligenleben*. Bibliothek der angelsächsischen Prosa 3. Kassel: G. H. Wigand, 1889. Reprinted with a supplementary introduction by Peter Clemoes, 92–101. Darmstadt: Wissenschaftliche Buchgesellschaft, 1964.

———. *Die Hirtenbriefe Ælfrics in altenglischer und lateinischer Fassung*. Edited by Bernhard Fehr. Bibliothek der angelsächsichen Prosa 9. Hamburg: Henri Grand, 1914. Reprinted with a supplementary introduction by Peter Clemoes. Darmstadt: Wissenschaftliche Buchgesellschaft, 1966.

————. *Homilies of Ælfric: A Supplementary Collection.* Edited by John C. Pope. 2 vols. EETS o.s. 259–60. London: Oxford University Press, 1967.

————. *The Old English Version of the Heptateuch, Ælfric's Treatise on the Old and New Testament and His Preface to Genesis.* Edited by S. J. Crawford. EETS o.s. 160. London: Oxford University Press, 1922.

Aldhelm. *Aldhelm: The Poetic Works.* Translated by Michael Lapidge and James L. Rosier. Cambridge: D. S. Brewer, 1985.

————. *Aldhelm: The Prose Works.* Translated by Michael Lapidge and Michael Herren. Cambridge: D. S. Brewer, 1979.

————. *Aldhelmi Malmesbiriensis prosa de virginitate cum glosa latina atque anglo-saxonica.* Edited by Scott Gwara. 2 vols. CCSL 124A. Turnhout: Brepols, 2001.

————. *Aldhelmi opera.* Edited by Rudolf Ehwald. MGH Auctores Antiquissimi 15. 1919. Reprint, Berlin: Weidmann, 1961.

Alfred. *King Alfred's Old English Prose Translation of the First Fifty Psalms.* Edited by Patrick P. O'Neill. Cambridge, Mass.: Medieval Academy of America, 2001.

Allen, Michael J. B., and Daniel G. Calder, eds. *Sources and Analogues of Old English Poetry.* Cambridge: D. S. Brewer, 1976.

Ambrose. *Epistola extra collectionem.* Edited by Michaela Zelzer. CSEL 82, pt. 10, pp. 141–311. Vienna: Hoelder-Pichler-Tempsky, 1982.

————. *De fuga saeculi.* Edited by Carolus Schenkl. CSEL 32, pt. 2, pp. 163–207. Vienna: F. Tempsky, 1897.

————. *De Nabuthae.* Edited by Carolus Schenkl. CSEL 32, pt. 2, pp. 469–516. Vienna: F. Tempsky, 1897.

————. *Sancti Ambrosii oratio de obitu Theodosii: Text, Translation, Introduction, and Commentary.* Edited and translated by Sister Mary Dolorosa Mannix. Patristic Studies 9. Washington, D.C.: Catholic University of America Press, 1925.

Asser. *Alfred the Great: Asser's Life of King Alfred and Other Contemporary Sources.* Edited and translated by Simon Keynes and Michael Lapidge. London: Penguin Books, 1983.

————. *Asser's Life of King Alfred Together with the Annals of St. Neot's.* Edited by William Henry Stevenson. Oxford: Clarendon Press, 1904.

Augustine. *De adulterinis coniugiis.* Edited by Joseph Zycha. CSEL 41, pp. 347–410. Vienna: F. Tempsky, 1900.

————. *Adulterous Marriages.* Translated by Charles T. Heugelmeyer. In *Saint Augustine: Treatises on Marriage and Other Subjects.* Edited by Roy J. Deferrari The Fathers of the Church 27, pp. 64–132. 1955. Reprinted with corrections, Washington, D.C.: Catholic University of America Press, 1969.

Bachrach, Bernard S., ed. and trans. *Liber historiae Francorum.* Lawrence, Kans.: Coronado Press, 1973.

Barlow, Frank, ed. and trans. *The Life of King Edward Who Rests at Westminster Attributed to a Monk of Saint-Bertin*. 2nd ed. Oxford: Clarendon Press, 1992.

Barmby, James, trans. *Gregory the Great, Ephraim Syrus, Aphrahat*. NPNF, 2nd ser., vol. 13, pt. 2. Edited by Philip Schaff and Henry Wace. New York: Christian Literature Co., 1898. Reprint, Peabody, Mass.: Hendrickson, 1994.

Bately, Janet, ed. *The Old English Orosius*. EETS s.s. 6. London: Oxford University Press, 1980.

Baudonivia. *Life of Radegund*. In *Sainted Women of the Dark Ages*, edited by McNamara, Halborg and Whatley, 86–105.

Bede. *Bede: A Biblical Miscellany*. Translated by W. Trent Foley and Arthur G. Holder. Liverpool: Liverpool University Press, 1999.

———. *Bede's Ecclesiastical History of the English People*. Edited by Bertram Colgrave and R. A. B. Mynors. Oxford: Clarendon Press, 1969.

———. *Bede's Letter to Egbert*. Translated by D. H. Farmer. In *Bede: Ecclesiastical History of the English People with Bede's Letter to Egbert and Cuthbert's Letter on the Death of Bede*, pp. 337–51. 1955. Revised ed., London: Penguin, 1990.

———. *Epistola Bede ad Ecgbertum Episcopum*. In *Venerabilis Baedae opera historica*, edited by C[harles] Plummer, 1:405–23.

———. *Explanatio Apocalypsis*. PL 93, 129–206.

———. *Homelia 23: In decollatione Iohannis Baptistae*. Edited by D. Hurst. CCSL 122, pp. 349–57. Turnhout: Brepols, 1955.

———. *In Regum librum: XXX quaestiones*. Edited by D. Hurst. CCSL 119, pp. 293–322. Turnhout: Brepols, 1962.

———. *Venerabilis Baedae opera historica*. Edited by C[harles] Plummer. 2 vols. 1896. Reprint, Oxford: Oxford University Press, 1946.

Bodden, Mary-Catherine, ed. and trans. *The Old English Finding of the True Cross*. Cambridge: D. S. Brewer, 1987.

Campbell, Alistair, ed. and trans. *Encomium Emmae Reginae*. Camden Third Series 72. London: Offices of the Royal Historical Society, 1949. Reprint, introduction by Simon Keynes. Cambridge: Cambridge University Press, 1998.

Crawford, S. J., ed. *The Old English Version of the Heptateuch, Ælfric's Treatise on the Old and New Testament and His Preface to Genesis*. EETS o.s. 160. London: Oxford University Press, 1922.

Cubbin, G. P., ed. *The Anglo-Saxon Chronicle: A Collaborative Edition*. Vol. 6, MS D. Cambridge: D. S. Brewer, 1996.

Cynewulf. *Cynewulf's "Elene."* Edited by P. O. E. Gradon. London: Methuen's Old English Library, 1958. Revised ed., Exeter: University of Exeter Press, 1977.

Dictionary of Old English: A to F on CD-ROM. Toronto: Pontifical Institute of Mediaeval Studies, 2003.

Dobbie, Elliott Van Kirk, ed. *The Anglo-Saxon Minor Poems*. ASPR 6. New York: Columbia University Press, 1942.

————. *Beowulf and Judith.* ASPR 4. New York: Columbia University Press, 1953.

Eddius Stephanus. *The Life of Bishop Wilfrid by Eddius Stephanus.* Edited and translated by Bertram Colgrave. 1927. Reprint, Cambridge: Cambridge University Press, 1985.

Fowler, Roger. "A Late Old English Handbook for the Use of a Confessor." *Anglia* 83 (1965): 1–34.

Garmonsway, G. N., and Jacqueline Simpson, trans. *Beowulf and Its Analogues.* London: J. M. Dent and Sons, 1968.

Gildas. *Gildas: The Ruin of Britain and Other Works.* Edited and translated by Michael Winterbottom. London: Phillimore, 1978.

Gregory the Great. *Gregorii I Papae registrum epistolarum.* Edited by Paul Ewald and Ludo M. Hartmann. MGH Epistolae 1 and 2. Berlin: Weidmann, 1887–99.

Gregory of Tours. *Glory of the Martyrs.* Translated by Raymond Van Dam. Liverpool: Liverpool University Press, 1988.

Haddan, Arthur West, and William Stubbs, eds. *Councils and Ecclesiastical Documents Relating to Great Britain and Ireland.* Vol. 3. 1871. Reprint, Oxford: Clarendon Press, 1964.

Henschen, G., and D. Papebroch, eds. *Acta sanctorum, Maius I.* Antwerp, 1680.

Herzfeld, George, ed. *An Old English Martyrology.* EETS o.s. 116. London: Kegan Paul Trench, Trübner, 1900.

Hincmar of Rheims. *Coronatio Iudithae Karoli II. Filiae.* Edited by Alfred Boretius and Victor Krause. MGH, Legum sectio II, Capitularia regum Francorum II. 2 vols. Vol. 2, pp. 425–27. Hanover: Hahn, 1883–97.

Holder, Alfred, ed. *Inventio Sanctae Crucis.* Leipzig: B. G. Teubner, 1889.

Hrabanus Maurus. *Expositio in librum Esther.* PL 109, 635–70.

————. *Expositio in librum Judith.* PL 109, 539–92.

Isidore of Seville. *Etymologiarum sive originum.* Vol. 1. Edited by W. M. Lindsay. Oxford: Clarendon, 1911.

John VIII. *Ad Richildim Augustam.* PL 126, 698–99.

Jonas of Bobbio. *Vitae Columbani.* Edited by Bruno Krusch. In *Ionae Vitae Sanctorum Columbani, Vedastis, Iohannis.* MGH, Scriptores rerum Germanicarum in usum scholarum, 1–294. Hanover: Hahn, 1905.

Keynes, Simon, ed. *The Liber Vitae of the New Minster and Hyde Abbey Winchester: British Library Stowe 944.* EEMF 26. Copenhagen: Rosenkilde and Bagger, 1996.

Klaeber, Friedrich, ed. *Beowulf and the Fight at Finnsburg.* 3rd ed., with 1st and 2nd supplements. Lexington, Mass.: D. C. Heath, 1950.

Krapp, George Philip, ed. *The Junius Manuscript.* ASPR 1. New York: Columbia University Press, 1931.

Krapp, George Philip, and Elliott Van Kirk Dobbie, eds. *The Exeter Book.* ASPR 3. New York: Columbia University Press, 1936.

Lapidge, Michael, ed. *Anglo-Saxon Litanies of the Saints.* Henry Bradshaw Society 106. London: Boydell Press, 1991.

Liebermann, Felix, ed. *Die heiligen Englands: Angelsächsisch und lateinisch.* Hanover: Hahn, 1889.

McNamara, Jo Ann, John E. Halborg, and E. Gordon Whatley, eds. and trans. *Sainted Women of the Dark Ages.* Durham, N.C.: Duke University Press, 1992.

Miller, Thomas, ed. *The Old English Version of Bede's Ecclesiastical History of the English People.* EETS o.s. 95–96, 110–11. London: Trübner, 1890–98.

Mitchell, Bruce, and Fred C. Robinson, eds. *Beowulf: An Edition with Relevant Shorter Texts.* 1998. Reprints, Oxford: Blackwell Publishers, 2000.

Morris, R., ed. *Old English Homilies.* EETS o.s. 29 and 34. London: Trübner, 1867–68.

Norman, Henry W., ed. *The Anglo-Saxon Version of the Hexameron of St. Basil . . . and the Anglo-Saxon Remains of St. Basil's Admonitio ad Filium Spiritualem.* London: Smith, 1849.

O'Keeffe, Katherine O'Brien. *The Anglo-Saxon Chronicle: A Collaborative Edition.* Vol. 5, MS C. Cambridge: D. S. Brewer, 2001.

Owen, Aneurin, ed. and trans. *Ancient Laws and Institutes of Wales.* London: Record Commissioners, 1841.

Percival, Henry R., ed. *The Seven Ecumenical Councils of the Undivided Church.* NPNF, 2nd ser., vol. 14. Edited by Philip Schaff and Henry Wace. New York: Charles Scribner's Sons, 1900. Reprint, Peabody, Mass.: Hendrickson, 1994.

Raith, Josef, ed. *Die altenglishche Version des Halitgar'schen Bussbuches (sog. Poenitentiale Pseudo-Egberti).* Bibliothek der angelsächsichen Prosa 13. Hamburg: H. Grand, 1933.

Rhodes, E. W., ed. *Defensor's Liber Scintillarum with an Interlinear Anglo-Saxon Version.* EETS o.s. 93. London: Trübner, 1889. Reprint, Millwood, N.Y.: Kraus Reprint, 1987.

Robb, Allan Phillipson. "The History of the Holy Rood-Tree: Four Anglo-Saxon Homilies." Ph.D. diss., University of Illinois at Urbana-Champaign, 1975.

Sabatier, Pierre. *Bibliorum sacrorum Latinae versiones antiquae, seu Vetus Italica.* 3 vols. Rheims: Reginaldus Florentain, 1743–49. Reprint, Turnhout: Brepols, 1976.

Sedulius Scottus. *Sedulius Scottus: On Christian Rulers and the Poems.* Translated by Edward Gerard Doyle. Binghamton, N.Y.: Medieval and Renaissance Texts and Studies, 1983.

Sisam, Celia, ed. *The Vercelli Book: A Late Tenth-Century Manuscript Containing Prose and Verse.* EEMF 19. Copenhagen: Rosenkilde and Bagger, 1976.

Spindler, Robert. *Das altenglische Bussbuch (sog. Confessionale Pseudo-Egberti).* Leipzig: B. Tauchnitz, 1934.

Stubbs, William, ed. *Memorials of Saint Dunstan: Archbishop of Canterbury.* Rolls Series 63. London: Longman, 1874. Reprint, Nendeln, Liechtenstein: Kraus Reprint, 1965.

Swanton, M. J. "A Fragmentary Life of St. Mildred and Other Kentish Royal Saints." *Archaeologia Cantiana* 91 (1975): 15–27.

Symons, Thomas, ed. and trans. *Regularis concordia Anglicae nationis monachorum sanctimonialiumque: The Monastic Agreement of the Monks and Nuns of the English Nation.* London: Thomas Nelson and Sons, 1953.

Turner, D. H., ed. *The Claudius Pontificals.* Henry Bradshaw Society 97. Chichester: Regnum Press for the Henry Bradshaw Society, 1971.

Webb, J. F., trans. *The Age of Bede.* Edited by D. H. Farmer. New York: Penguin, 1983.

Weber, Robert, ed. *Biblia Sacra Iuxta Vulgatem Versionem.* 2 vols. Stuttgart: Deutsche Bibelgesellschaft, 1983.

Whitelock, Dorothy, ed. and trans. *Anglo-Saxon Wills.* Cambridge: Cambridge University Press, 1930.

———, ed. *English Historical Documents.* Vol. 1, *c. 500–1042.* 2nd ed. London: Eyre Methuen, 1979.

Wormald, Francis, ed. *English Kalendars Before A.D. 1100.* Henry Bradshaw Society 72. London: Harrison and Sons, 1934. Reprint, Wolfeboro, N.H.: Boydell and Brewer, 1988.

Wulfstan. *The Homilies of Wulfstan.* Edited by Dorothy Bethurum. Oxford: Clarendon Press, 1957.

Secondary Sources

Anderson, Bernhard W. "The Place of the Book of Esther in the Christian Bible." *Journal of Religion* 30 (1950): 32–43. Reprinted in *Studies in the Book of Esther,* edited by Carey A. Moore, 130–41. New York: Ktav, 1982.

Anderson, Earl. "Cynewulf's *Elene:* Manuscript Division and Structural Symmetry." *Modern Philology* 72 (1974): 111–22.

Anson, John. "The Female Transvestite in Early Monasticism: The Origin and Development of a Motif." *Viator* 5 (1974): 1–32.

Appadurai, Arjun. "Introduction: Commodities and the Politics of Value." In *The Social Life of Things: Commodities in Cultural Perspective,* edited by Arjun Appadurai, 3–63. Cambridge: Cambridge University Press, 1986.

Armstrong, Dorsey. "Holy Queens as Agents of Christianization in Bede's *Ecclesiastical History:* A Reconsideration." *Medieval Encounters* 4 (1998): 228–41.

Auerbach, Erich. "Figura." In *Scenes from the Drama of European Literature,* 11–76. New York: Meridian, 1959. Reprint, Minneapolis: University of Minnesota Press, 1984.

Bennett, Helen. "The Female Mourner at Beowulf's Funeral: Filling in the Blanks/Hearing the Spaces." *Exemplaria* 4 (1992): 35–50.

Bjork, Robert E., ed. *Cynewulf: Basic Readings*. Basic Readings in Anglo-Saxon England 4. Garland Reference Library of the Humanities 1869. New York: Garland, 1996.

Blair, Peter Hunter. "The Letters of Pope Boniface V and the Mission of Paulinus to Northumbria." In *England Before the Conquest: Studies in Primary Sources Presented to Dorothy Whitelock*, edited by Peter Clemoes and Kathleen Hughes, 5–13. Cambridge: Cambridge University Press, 1971.

Bloomfield, Josephine. "Diminished by Kindness: Frederick Klaeber's Rewriting of Wealhtheow." *Journal of English and Germanic Philology* 93 (1994): 183–203.

Bremmer, Rolf H., Jr. "The Importance of Kinship: Uncle and Nephew in *Beowulf*." *Amsterdamer Beiträge zur Älteren Germanistik* 15 (1980): 21–38.

Brookes, Stewart. "Ælfric's Adaptation of the Book of Esther: A Source of Some Confusion." In *Essays on Anglo-Saxon and Related Themes in Memory of Lynne Grundy*, edited by Jane Roberts and Janet Nelson, 37–63. London: King's College London, Centre for Late Antique and Medieval Studies, 2000.

Bullough, Vern L. "Transvestism in the Middle Ages." In *Sexual Practices and the Medieval Church*, edited by Vern L. Bullough and James A. Brundage, 43–54. Buffalo, N.Y.: Prometheus, 1982.

Busse, W. G., and R. Holtei. "*The Battle of Maldon*: A Historical, Heroic and Political Poem." *Neophilologus* 65 (1981): 614–21.

Butler, Judith. *Bodies That Matter: On the Discursive Limits of "Sex"*. London: Routledge, 1993.

———. "The End of Sexual Difference?" In *Feminist Consequences: Theory for a New Century*, edited by Elisabeth Bronfen and Misha Kavka, 414–34. New York: Columbia University Press, 2001.

———. *Gender Trouble: Feminism and the Subversion of Identity*. New York: Routledge, 1990.

———. *The Psychic Life of Power: Theories in Subjection*. Stanford: Stanford University Press, 1997.

Bynum, Caroline Walker. *Jesus as Mother: Studies in the Spirituality of the High Middle Ages*. Berkeley: University of California Press, 1982.

Calder, Daniel. *Cynewulf*. Boston: Twayne Publishers, 1981.

———. "Strife, Revelation, and Conversion: The Thematic Structure of *Elene*." *English Studies* 53 (1972): 201–10.

Campbell, Jackson. "Cynewulf's Multiple Revelations." *Medievalia et Humanistica* 3 (1972): 257–77. Reprinted in *Cynewulf: Basic Readings*, edited by Robert E. Bjork, 229–50.

Campbell, James. "Bede I." In *Essays in Anglo-Saxon History*, edited by James Campbell, 1–27. London: Hambledon Press, 1986.

———. "The First Century of Christianity in England." *Ampleforth Journal* 76 (1971): 12–29. Reprinted in *Essays in Anglo-Saxon History*, edited by James Campbell, 49–67. London: Hambledon Press, 1986.

Campbell, James, Eric John, and Patrick Wormald, eds. *The Anglo-Saxons*. Oxford: Phaidon, 1982. Reprint, London: Penguin Books, 1991.

Castelli, Elizabeth. "'I Will Make Mary Male': Pieties of the Body and Gender Transformation of Christian Women in Late Antiquity." In *Body Guards: The Cultural Politics of Gender Ambiguity*, edited by Julia Epstein and Kristina Straub, 29–49. New York: Routledge, 1991.

Chadwick, H. M. *Early Scotland: The Picts, the Scots, & the Welsh of Southern Scotland*. Cambridge: Cambridge University Press, 1949.

Chadwick, Nora. "Pictish and Celtic Marriage in Early Literary Tradition." *Scottish Gaelic Studies* 8 (1955): 56–115.

Chamberlain, David. "*Judith:* A Fragmentary and Political Poem." In *Anglo-Saxon Poetry: Essays in Appreciation for John C. McGalliard*, edited by Lewis E. Nicholson and Dolores Warwick Frese, 135–59. Notre Dame, Ind.: University of Notre Dame Press, 1975.

Chambers, R. W. *Beowulf: An Introduction to the Study of the Poem with a Discussion of the Stories of Offa and Finn*. 3rd ed., with a supplement by C. L. Wrenn. Cambridge: Cambridge University Press, 1959.

Chance, Jane. *Woman as Hero in Old English Literature*. Syracuse: Syracuse University Press, 1986.

Chase, Colin. "Source Study as a Trick with Mirrors: Annihilation of Meaning in the Old English 'Mary of Egypt.'" In *Sources of Anglo-Saxon Culture*, edited by Paul E. Szarmach with Virginia Darrow Oggins, 23–33. Studies in Medieval Culture 20. Kalamazoo, Mich.: Medieval Institute Publications, 1986.

Clayton, Mary. "Ælfric and Æthelred." In *Essays on Anglo-Saxon and Related Themes in Memory of Lynne Grundy*, edited by Jane Roberts and Janet Nelson, 65–88. London: King's College London, Centre for Late Antique and Medieval Studies, 2000.

———. "Ælfric's *Esther:* A *Speculum Reginae?*" In *Text and Gloss: Studies in Insular Learning and Literature Presented to Joseph Donovan Pheifer*, edited by Helen Conrad O'Briain, Anne Marie D'Arcy, and John Scattergood, 89–101. Dublin: Four Courts Press, 1999.

———. "Ælfric's *Judith:* Manipulative or Manipulated," *Anglo-Saxon England* 23 (1994): 215–27.

———. *The Cult of the Virgin Mary in Anglo-Saxon England*. Cambridge: Cambridge University Press, 1990.

———. "Of Mice and Men: Ælfric's Second Homily for the Feast of a Confessor." *Leeds Studies in English* 24 (1993): 1–26.

Clemoes, Peter. "The Chronology of Ælfric's Works." In *The Anglo-Saxons: Studies in Some Aspects of Their History and Culture Presented to Bruce Dickins*, edited by Peter Clemoes, 212–47. London: Bowes and Bowes, 1959. Reprinted as *Old English Newsletter, Subsidia* 5. Binghamton, N.Y.: Center for Medieval and Renaissance Studies, 1980.

Clover, Carol J. "Regardless of Sex: Men, Women, and Power in Early Northern Europe." *Speculum* 68 (1993): 363–87.

Conner, Patrick W. "On Dating Cynewulf." In *Cynewulf: Basic Readings,* edited by Robert E. Bjork, 23–55.

Crane, Susan. *The Performance of Self: Ritual, Clothing, and Identity During the Hundred Years War.* Philadelphia: University of Pennsylvania Press, 2002.

Cross, J. E. "The Ethic of War in Old English." In *England Before the Conquest: Studies in Primary Sources Presented to Dorothy Whitelock,* edited by Peter Clemoes and Kathleen Hughes, 269–82. Cambridge: Cambridge University Press, 1971.

Cubitt, Catherine. "Virginity and Misogyny in Tenth- and Eleventh-Century England." *Gender & History* 12 (2000): 1–32.

Dames, Nicholas. "Austen's Nostalgics." *Representations* 73 (2001): 117–43.

Damico, Helen. *Beowulf's Wealhtheow and the Valkyrie Tradition.* Madison: University of Wisconsin Press, 1984.

de Jong, Mayke. "The Empire as *Ecclesia:* Hrabanus Maurus and Biblical *Historia* for Rulers." In *The Uses of the Past in the Early Middle Ages,* edited by Yitzhak Hen and Matthew Innes, 191–226. Cambridge: Cambridge University Press, 2000.

———. *In Samuel's Image: Child Oblation in the Early Medieval West.* Leiden: Brill, 1996.

Deshman, Robert. "*Benedictus Monarcha et Monachus:* Early Medieval Ruler Theology and the Anglo-Saxon Reform." *Frühmittelalterliche Studien* 22 (1988): 204–40.

———. "*Christus rex et magi reges:* Kingship and Christology in Ottonian and Anglo-Saxon Art." *Frühmittelalterliche Studien* 10 (1976): 367–405.

Discenza, Nicole Guenther. "Power, Skill and Virtue in the Old English *Boethius.*" *Anglo-Saxon England* 26 (1997): 81–108.

Drijvers, Jan Willem. *Helena Augusta: The Mother of Constantine the Great and the Legend of Her Finding of the True Cross.* Leiden: Brill, 1992.

Du Bois, Arthur E. "The Unity of *Beowulf.*" *PMLA* 49 (1934): 374–405.

Duggan, Anne J., ed. *Queens and Queenship in Medieval Europe: Proceedings of a Conference Held at King's College London, April 1995.* Woodbridge, Suffolk: Boydell Press, 1997.

Dumville, David N. "The Ætheling: A Study in Anglo-Saxon Constitutional History." *Anglo-Saxon England* 8 (1979): 1–33.

Eliason, Norman E. "Beowulf, Wiglaf and the Wægmundings." *Anglo-Saxon England* 7 (1978): 95–105.

Enright, Michael J. "Lady with a Mead-Cup: Ritual, Group Cohesion and Hierarchy in the Germanic Warband." *Frühmittelalterliche Studien* 22 (1988): 170–203. Reprinted in Michael J. Enright, *Lady with a Mead Cup: Ritual,*

Prophecy, and Lordship in the European Warband from La Tène to the Viking Age, 1–37. Portland, Ore., and Dublin: Four Courts Press, 1996.

Fell, Christine. *Women in Anglo-Saxon England*. London: British Museum Publications, 1984.

Fisher, D. J. V. *The Anglo-Saxon Age c. 400–1042*. London: Longman, 1973.

Fradenburg, Louise. *City, Marriage, Tournament: Arts of Rule in Late Medieval Scotland*. Madison: University of Wisconsin Press, 1991.

———, ed. *Women and Sovereignty*. *Cosmos* 7. Edinburgh: Edinburgh University Press, 1992.

Frank, Roberta. "The *Beowulf* Poet's Sense of History." In *The Wisdom of Poetry: Essays in Early English Literature in Honor of Morton W. Bloomfield*, edited by Larry D. Benson and Siegfried Wenzel, 53–65. Kalamazoo, Mich.: Medieval Institute Publications, 1982. Reprinted in *Beowulf: A Prose Translation*, 2nd ed., edited by Nicholas Howe, translated by E. Talbot Donaldson, 98–111. New York: Norton, 2002.

———. "Germanic Legend in Old English Literature." In *The Cambridge Companion to Old English Literature*, edited by Malcolm Godden and Michael Lapidge, 88–106. Cambridge: Cambridge University Press, 1991.

———. "Marriage in Twelfth- and Thirteenth-Century Iceland." *Viator* 4 (1973): 473–84.

Frantzen, Allen J. *Desire for Origins: New Languages, Old English, and Teaching the Tradition*. New Brunswick, N.J.: Rutgers University Press, 1990.

Fulk, R. D. "Cynewulf: Canon, Dialect, and Date." In *Cynewulf: Basic Readings*, edited by Robert E. Bjork, 3–21.

———. *A History of Old English Meter*. Philadelphia: University of Pennsylvania Press, 1992.

Gameson, Richard, ed. *St Augustine and the Conversion of England*. Stroud, Gloucestershire: Sutton, 1999.

Gatch, Milton McC. "The Office in Late Anglo-Saxon Monasticism." In *Learning and Literature in Anglo-Saxon England*, edited by Michael Lapidge and Helmut Gneuss, 341–62. Cambridge: Cambridge University Press, 1985.

———. *Preaching and Theology in Anglo-Saxon England: Ælfric and Wulfstan*. Toronto: University of Toronto Press, 1977.

Gerchow, Jan. "Prayers for King Cnut: The Liturgical Commemoration of a Conqueror." In *England in the Eleventh Century: Proceedings of the 1990 Harlaxton Symposium*, edited by Carola Hicks, 219–38. Stamford: Paul Watkins, 1992.

Glosecki, Stephen O. "*Beowulf* and the Wills: Traces of Totemism?" *Philological Quarterly* 78 (1999): 15–47.

Godden, Malcolm. *Ælfric's Catholic Homilies: Introduction, Commentary and Glossary*. EETS s.s. 18. Oxford: Oxford University Press, 2000.

———. "Anglo-Saxons on the Mind." In *Learning and Literature in Anglo-Saxon England*, edited by Michael Lapidge and Helmut Gneuss, 271–98. Cambridge:

Cambridge University Press, 1985. Reprinted in *Old English Literature: Critical Essays,* edited by R. M. Liuzza, 284–314. New Haven: Yale University Press, 2002.

———. "Apocalypse and Invasion in Late Anglo-Saxon England." In *From Anglo-Saxon to Early Middle English: Studies Presented to E. G. Stanley,* edited by Malcolm Godden, Douglas Gray, and Terry Hoad, 130–62. Oxford: Clarendon Press, 1994.

———. "Biblical Literature: The Old Testament." In *The Cambridge Companion to Old English Literature,* edited by Malcolm Godden and Michael Lapidge, 206–26. Cambridge: Cambridge University Press, 1991.

———. "Experiments in Genre: The Saints' Lives in Ælfric's *Catholic Homilies.*" In *Holy Men and Holy Women: Old English Prose Saints' Lives and Their Contexts,* edited by Paul E. Szarmach, 261–87. Albany: SUNY Press, 1996.

———. "Money, Power, and Morality in Late Anglo-Saxon England." *Anglo-Saxon England* 19 (1990): 41–65.

Goffart, Walter. "The *Historia Ecclesiastica:* Bede's Agenda and Ours." *Haskins Society Journal* 2 (1990): 29–45.

Goldsmith, Margaret E. *The Mode and Meaning of "Beowulf."* London: Athlone, 1970.

Graham, Timothy. "Early Modern Users of Claudius B. iv: Robert Talbot and William L'Isle." In *The Old English Hexateuch: Aspects and Approaches,* edited by Rebecca Barnhouse and Benjamin C. Withers, 271–316. Kalamazoo, Mich.: Medieval Institute Publications, 2000.

Gransden, Antonia. "Traditionalism and Continuity During the Last Century of Anglo-Saxon Monasticism." *Journal of Ecclesiastical History* 40 (1989): 159–207.

Grønbech, Vilhelm. *The Culture of the Teutons.* 2 vols. Translated from *Vor Folkeæt i Oldtiden* I–IV by William Worster. Copenhagen: Jespersen og Pios forlag, 1909–12. Reprint, London: Humphrey Milford, 1931.

Grundy, Lynne. *Books and Grace: Ælfric's Theology.* London: King's College London, Centre for Late Antique and Medieval Studies, 1991.

Gustafson, Timothy Alan. "Ælfric Reads Esther: The Cultural Limits of Translation." Ph.D. diss., University of Iowa, 1995.

Halpin, Patricia. "Women Religious in Late Anglo-Saxon England." *Haskins Society Journal* 6 (1994): 97–110.

Hansen, Elaine Tuttle. "Hrothgar's 'Sermon' in *Beowulf* as Parental Wisdom." *Anglo-Saxon England* 10 (1982): 53–67.

Harris, Joseph. "Beowulf's Last Words." *Speculum* 67 (1992): 1–32.

Healey, Antonette diPaolo. "Questions of Fairness: Fair, Not Fair, and Foul." In *Unlocking the Wordhord: Anglo-Saxon Studies in Memory of Edward B. Irving, Jr.,* edited by Mark C. Amodio and Katherine O'Brien O'Keeffe, 252–73. Toronto: University of Toronto Press, 2003.

Hermann, John P. *Allegories of War: Language and Violence in Old English Poetry.* Ann Arbor: University of Michigan Press, 1989.

Higham, N. J. *The Convert Kings: Power and Religious Affiliation in Early Anglo-Saxon England.* Manchester: Manchester University Press, 1997.

———. *An English Empire: Bede and the Early Anglo-Saxon Kings.* Manchester: Manchester University Press, 1995.

Hill, John M. *The Anglo-Saxon Warrior Ethic: Reconstructing Lordship in Early English Literature.* Gainesville: University Press of Florida, 2000.

Hill, Joyce. "The Dissemination of Ælfric's *Lives of Saints:* A Preliminary Survey." In *Holy Men and Holy Women: Old English Prose Saints' Lives and Their Contexts,* edited by Paul E. Szarmach, 235–59. Albany: SUNY Press, 1996.

———. "Þæt wæs geomuru ides! A Female Stereotype Examined." In *New Readings on Women in Old English Literature,* edited by Helen Damico and Alexandra Hennessey Olsen, 235–47. Bloomington: Indiana University Press, 1990.

Hill, Thomas. "Sapiential Structure and Figural Narrative in the Old English 'Elene.'" *Traditio* 27 (1971): 159–77. Revised and reprinted in *Cynewulf: Basic Readings,* edited by Robert E. Bjork, 207–28.

Hollis, Stephanie. *Anglo-Saxon Women and the Church: Sharing a Common Fate.* Woodbridge, Suffolk: Boydell Press, 1992.

Holum, Kenneth G. *Theodosian Empresses: Women and Imperial Dominion in Late Antiquity.* Berkeley: University of California Press, 1982.

Horner, Shari. *The Discourse of Enclosure: Representing Women in Old English Literature.* Albany: SUNY Press, 2001.

Hough, Carole A. "The Early Kentish 'Divorce Laws': A Reconsideration of Æthelberht, chs. 79 and 80." *Anglo-Saxon England* 23 (1994): 19–34.

Howe, Nicholas. "The Cultural Construction of Reading in Anglo-Saxon England." In *The Ethnography of Reading,* edited by Jonathan Boyarin, 58–79. Berkeley: University of California Press, 1993. Reprinted in *Old English Literature: Critical Essays,* edited by R. M. Liuzza, 1–22. New Haven: Yale University Press, 2002.

"Historicist Approaches." In *Reading Old English Texts,* edited by Katherine O'Brien O'Keeffe, 79–100. Cambridge: Cambridge University Press, 1997.

———. *Migration and Mythmaking in Anglo-Saxon England.* New Haven: Yale University Press, 1989.

Huneycutt, Lois L. "Intercession and the High-Medieval Queen: The Esther Topos." In *Power of the Weak: Studies on Medieval Women,* edited by Jennifer Carpenter and Sally-Beth MacLean, 126–46. Urbana: University of Illinois Press, 1995.

Hunter, Michael. "Germanic and Roman Antiquity and the Sense of the Past in Anglo-Saxon England." *Anglo-Saxon England* 3 (1974): 29–50.

Irving, Edward B., Jr. "Christian and Pagan Elements." In *A Beowulf Handbook*, edited by Robert E. Bjork and John D. Niles, 175–92. Lincoln: University of Nebraska Press, 1997.

———. "The Nature of Christianity in *Beowulf*." *Anglo-Saxon England* 13 (1984): 7–21.

———. "What to Do with Old Kings." In *Comparative Research on Oral Traditions: A Memorial for Milman Parry*, edited by John Miles Foley, 259–68. Columbus, Ohio: Slavica Publishers, 1987.

Jackson, Peter. "Ælfric and the Purpose of Christian Marriage: A Reconsideration of the *Life of Æthelthryth*, Lines 120–30." *Anglo-Saxon England* 29 (2000): 235–60.

Jones, Christopher A. *Ælfric's Letter to the Monks of Eynsham*. Cambridge Studies in Anglo-Saxon England 24. Cambridge: Cambridge University Press, 1998.

Karras, Ruth Mazo. "God and Man in Medieval Scandinavia: Writing—and Gendering—the Conversion." In *Varieties of Religious Conversion in the Middle Ages*, edited by James Muldoon, 100–114. Gainesville: University Press of Florida, 1997.

Kaske, R. E. "The *Eotenas* in *Beowulf*." In *Old English Poetry: Fifteen Essays*, edited by Robert P. Creed, 285–310. Providence: Brown University Press, 1967.

———. "'Hygelac' and 'Hygd.'" In *Studies in Old English Literature in Honor of Arthur G. Brodeur*, edited by Stanley B. Greenfield, 200–206. 1963. Reprint, Eugene: University of Oregon Press, 2001.

———. "*Sapientia et Fortitudo* as the Controlling Theme of *Beowulf*." *Studies in Philology* 55 (1958): 423–57. Reprinted in *An Anthology of Beowulf Criticism*, edited by Lewis E. Nicholson, 269–310. Notre Dame, Ind.: University of Notre Dame Press, 1963.

Ker, N. R. *Catalogue of Manuscripts Containing Anglo-Saxon*. Oxford: Clarendon Press, 1957.

Keynes, Simon. "The Æthelings in Normandy." *Anglo-Norman Studies* 13 (1990): 173–205.

———. *Anglo-Saxon History: A Select Bibliography*. 3rd rev. ed. *Old English Newsletter, Subsidia* 13. Kalamazoo, Mich.: Medieval Institute, 1998. Updated for second online publication at http://www.wmich.edu/medieval/research/rawl/keynesbib/home.htm.

———. "The Declining Reputation of King Æthelred the Unready." In *Ethelred the Unready: Papers from the Millenary Conference*, edited by David Hill, 227–53. BAR British Series 59. Oxford: British Archeological Reports, 1978.

———. *The Diplomas of King Æthelred "The Unready": 978–1016*. Cambridge: Cambridge University Press, 1980.

Kiernan, Kevin S. "Grendel's Heroic Mother." *In Geardagum* 6 (1984): 13–33.

Kirby, D. P. "Bede and Northumbrian Chronology." *English Historical Review* 78 (1963): 514–27.

———. *The Earliest English Kings*. London: Unwin Hyman, 1991.

Klinck, Anne L. "Anglo-Saxon Women and the Law." *Journal of Medieval History* 8 (1982): 107–21.

Kornexl, Lucia, ed. *Die Regularis Concordia und ihre altenglische Interlinearversion*. Texte und Untersuchungen zur englischen Philologie 17. Munich: Fink, 1993.

Lapidge, Michael. "A Seventh-Century Insular Latin Debate Poem on Divorce." *Cambridge Medieval Celtic Studies* 10 (1985): 1–23.

Laqueur, Thomas. *Making Sex: Body and Gender from the Greeks to Freud*. Cambridge: Harvard University Press, 1990.

Larès, Micheline M. *Bible et civilisation anglaise: Naissance d'une tradition*. Paris: Didier, 1974.

Lawson, M. K. *Cnut: The Danes in England in the Early Eleventh Century*. London: Longman, 1993.

Lebecq, Stéphane. "England and the Continent in the Sixth and Seventh Centuries: The Question of Logistics." In *St Augustine and the Conversion of England*, edited by Richard Gameson, 50–67.

Lee, Stuart. "Oxford, Bodleian Library, MS Laud Misc. 381: William L'Isle, Ælfric, and the *Ancrene Wisse*." In *The Recovery of Old English: Anglo-Saxon Studies in the Sixteenth and Seventeenth Centuries*, edited by Timothy Graham, 207–42. Kalamazoo, Mich.: Medieval Institute Publications, 2000.

Lees, Clare A. "At a Crossroads: Old English and Feminist Criticism." In *Reading Old English Texts*, edited by Katherine O'Brien O'Keeffe, 146–69. Cambridge: Cambridge University Press, 1997.

———. *Tradition and Belief: Religious Writing in Late Anglo-Saxon England*. Minneapolis: University of Minnesota Press, 1999.

———. "Working with Patristic Sources: Language and Context in Old English Homilies." In *Speaking Two Languages: Traditional Disciplines and Contemporary Theory in Medieval Studies*, edited by Allen J. Frantzen, 157–80. Albany: SUNY Press, 1991.

Lees, Clare A., and Gillian R. Overing. "Birthing Bishops and Fathering Poets: Bede, Hild, and the Relations of Cultural Production." *Exemplaria* 6 (1994): 35–65.

———. *Double Agents: Women and Clerical Culture in Anglo-Saxon England*. Philadelphia: University of Pennsylvania Press, 2001.

Lerer, Seth. "*Beowulf* and Contemporary Critical Theory." In *A Beowulf Handbook*, edited by Robert E. Bjork and John D. Niles, 325–39. Lincoln: University of Nebraska Press, 1997.

———. *Literacy and Power in Anglo-Saxon Literature*. Lincoln: University of Nebraska Press, 1991.

Lévi-Strauss, Claude. *Structural Anthropology*. Translated by C. Jacobsen and B. Grundfest Shoepf. Harmondsworth: Penguin, 1977.

Lionarons, Joyce Tally. "Cultural Syncretism and the Construction of Gender in Cynewulf's *Elene*." *Exemplaria* 10 (1998): 51–68.

Liuzza, R. M. "What the Thunder Said: Anglo-Saxon Brontologies and the Problem of Sources." *Review of English Studies* 55 (2004): 1–23.

Malone, Kemp. "Hygd." *Modern Language Notes* 56 (1941): 356–58.

Markus, Robert A. *Conversion and Disenchantment in Augustine's Spiritual Career.* Villanova, Pa.: Villanova University Press, 1989.

Marsden, Richard. *The Text of the Old Testament in Anglo-Saxon England.* Cambridge Studies in Anglo-Saxon England 15. Cambridge: Cambridge University Press, 1995.

Marx, Karl. *Capital.* Vol. 1, *A Critical Analysis of Capitalist Production.* Translated from the 3rd German ed. by Samuel Moore and Edward Aveling, edited by Frederick Engels. 1887. Reprint, Moscow: Progress Publishers, 1971.

Mauss, Marcel. *The Gift: The Form and Reason for Exchange in Archaic Societies.* Translated by W. D. Halls. New York: Norton, 1990. Originally published as "Essai sur le don. Forme et raison dans le societés archaïques" (1923–24), reprinted in Marcel Mauss, *Sociologie et Anthropologie,* 145–79. Paris: Presses Universitaires de France, 1968.

Mayr-Harting, Henry. *The Coming of Christianity to Anglo-Saxon England.* 3rd ed. University Park: Pennsylvania State University Press, 1991.

McCracken, Peggy. *The Romance of Adultery: Queenship and Sexual Transgression in Old French Literature.* Philadelphia: University of Pennsylvania Press, 1998.

McCulloh, John M. "Did Cynewulf Use a Martyrology? Reconsidering the Sources of *The Fates of the Apostles*." *Anglo-Saxon England* 29 (2000): 67–83.

Menzer, Melinda J. "*Aglæcwif* (*Beowulf* 1259a): Implications for *-wif* Compounds, Grendel's Mother, and Other *Aglæcan*." *English Language Notes* 34 (1996): 1–6.

———. "The Preface as Admonition: Ælfric's Preface to Genesis." In *The Old English Hexateuch: Aspects and Approaches,* edited by Rebecca Barnhouse and Benjamin C. Withers, 15–39. Kalamazoo, Mich.: Medieval Institute Publications, 2000.

Meyer, Marc Anthony. "Women and the Tenth-Century English Monastic Reform." *Revue Bénédictine* 87 (1977): 34–61.

Moore, Carey A. "On the Origins of the LXX Additions to the Book of Esther." *Journal of Biblical Literature* 92 (1973): 382–93. Reprinted in *Studies in the Book of Esther,* edited by Carey A. Moore, 583–94. New York: Ktav, 1982.

Morey, Robert. "Beowulf's Androgynous Heroism." *Journal of English and Germanic Philology* 95 (1996): 486–96.

Morrison, Karl F. *Understanding Conversion.* Charlottesville: University Press of Virginia, 1992.

Nelson, Janet L. "Early Medieval Rites of Queen-Making and the Shaping of Medieval Queenship." In *Queens and Queenship in Medieval Europe,* edited by Anne J. Duggan, 301–15.

———. *Politics and Ritual in Early Medieval Europe.* London: Hambledon Press, 1986.

———. "Queens as Jezebels: Brunhild and Balthild in Merovingian History." In *Medieval Women: Dedicated and Presented to Professor Rosalind M. T. Hill on the Occasion of Her Seventieth Birthday,* edited by Derek Baker, 31–77. Studies in Church History, Subsidia 1. Oxford: Basil Blackwell, 1978. Reprinted in *Politics and Ritual,* edited by Janet L. Nelson, 1–49.

———. "The Second English Ordo." In *Politics and Ritual,* 361–74.

———. "Women and the Word in the Earlier Middle Ages." In *Women in the Church: Papers Read at the 1989 Summer Meeting and the 1990 Winter Meeting of the Ecclesiastical Historical Society,* edited by W. J. Sheils and Diana Wood, 53–78. Oxford: Basil Blackwell, 1990.

Newman, Barbara. *From Virile Woman to WomanChrist: Studies in Medieval Religion and Literature.* Philadelphia: University of Pennsylvania Press, 1995.

Nicholson, Joan. "*Feminae Gloriosiae:* Women in the Age of Bede." In *Medieval Women: Dedicated and Presented to Professor Rosalind M. T. Hill on the Occasion of her Seventieth Birthday,* edited by Derek Baker, 15–29. Studies in Church History, Subsidia 1. Oxford: Basil Blackwell, 1978.

Niles, John D. *Beowulf: The Poem and Its Tradition.* Cambridge: Harvard University Press, 1983.

Nock, A. D. *Conversion: The Old and the New in Religion from Alexander the Great to Augustine of Hippo.* 1933. Reprint, Oxford: Oxford University Press, 1961.

Nolte, Cordula. "Gender and Conversion in the Merovingian Era." In *Varieties of Religious Conversion in the Middle Ages,* edited by James Muldoon, 81–99. Gainesville: University Press of Florida, 1997.

O'Keeffe, Katherine O'Brien. "*Beowulf,* Lines 702b–836: Transformations and the Limits of the Human." *Texas Studies in Language and Literature* 23 (1981): 484–94.

———. "Body and Law in Late Anglo-Saxon England." *Anglo–Saxon England* 27 (1998): 209–32.

———. "Heroic Values and Christian Ethics." In *The Cambridge Companion to Old English Literature,* edited by Malcolm Godden and Michael Lapidge, 107–25. Cambridge: Cambridge University Press, 1991.

Olsen, Alexandra Hennessey. "Cynewulf's Autonomous Women: A Reconsideration of Elene and Juliana." In *New Readings on Women in Old English Literature,* edited by Helen Damico and Alexandra Hennessey Olsen, 222–32. Bloomington: Indiana University Press, 1990.

———. "Gender Roles." In *A Beowulf Handbook,* edited by Robert E. Bjork and John D. Niles, 311–24. Lincoln: University of Nebraska Press, 1997.

Orchard, Andy. *Pride and Prodigies: Studies in the Monsters of the Beowulf Manuscript.* Cambridge: D. S. Brewer, 1995.

Otter, Monika. *Inventiones: Fiction and Referentiality in Twelfth-Century English Historical Writing.* Chapel Hill: University of North Carolina Press, 1996.

Overing, Gillian R. *Language, Sign and Gender in Beowulf.* Carbondale: Southern Illinois University Press, 1990.

Owen, Gale R. "Wynflæd's Wardrobe." *Anglo-Saxon England* 8 (1979): 195–222.

Parsons, John Carmi. "The Queen's Intercession in Thirteenth-Century England." In *Power of the Weak: Studies on Medieval Women,* edited by Jennifer Carpenter and Sally-Beth MacLean, 147–77. Urbana: University of Illinois Press, 1995.

Power, Eileen. *Medieval English Nunneries (ca. 1275–1535).* Cambridge: Cambridge University Press, 1922.

Pulsiano, Phillip. "William L'Isle and the Editing of Old English." In *The Recovery of Old English: Anglo-Saxon Studies in the Sixteenth and Seventeenth Centuries,* edited by Timothy Graham, 173–206. Kalamazoo, Mich.: Medieval Institute Publications, 2000.

Raw, Barbara. *Anglo-Saxon Crucifixion Iconography and the Art of the Monastic Revival.* Cambridge: Cambridge University Press, 1990.

Regan, Catharine A. "Evangelicalism as the Informing Principle of Cynewulf's *Elene.*" *Traditio* 29 (1973): 27–52. Reprinted in *Cynewulf: Basic Readings,* edited by Robert E. Bjork, 251–80.

Richards, Mary P. "A Reexamination of *Beowulf* ll. 3180–3182." *English Language Notes* 10 (1973): 163–67.

Ridyard, Susan J. "Anglo-Saxon Women and the Church in the Age of Conversion." In *Monks, Nuns, and Friars in Mediaeval Society,* edited by Edward B. King, Jacqueline T. Schaefer, and William B. Wadley, 105–32. Sewanee Mediaeval Studies 4. Sewanee, Tenn.: Press of the University of the South, 1989.

———. *The Royal Saints of Anglo-Saxon England: A Study of West Saxon and East Anglian Cults.* Cambridge: Cambridge University Press, 1988.

Robinson, Fred C. "The Afterlife of Old English: A Brief History of Composition in Old English After the Close of the Anglo-Saxon Period." In Robinson, *The Tomb of Beowulf and Other Essays on Old English,* 275–304.

———. *Beowulf and the Appositive Style.* Knoxville: University of Tennessee Press, 1985.

———. "The Prescient Woman in Old English Literature." In *Philologia Anglica: Essays Presented to Professor Yoshio Terasawa on the Occasion of His Sixtieth Birthday,* edited by Kinshiro Oshitari et al. Tokyo: Kenkyusha, 1988. Reprinted in *The Tomb of Beowulf and Other Essays on Old English,* edited by Fred C. Robinson, 155–63.

———. "The Significance of Names in Old English Literature." *Anglia* 86 (1968): 14–58. Reprinted in *The Tomb of Beowulf and Other Essays on Old English,* edited by Fred C. Robinson, 185–223.

————. "Teaching the Backgrounds: History, Religion, Culture." In *Approaches to Teaching Beowulf,* edited by Jess B. Bessinger and Robert F. Yeager, 107–22. New York: Modern Language Association of America, 1984.

————. *The Tomb of Beowulf and Other Essays on Old English.* Oxford: Blackwell Publishers, 1993.

Rollason, D. W. *The Mildrith Legend: A Study in Early Medieval Hagiography in England.* Leicester: Leicester University Press, 1982.

Ross, Margaret Clunies. "Concubinage in Anglo-Saxon England." *Past and Present* 108 (1985): 3–34.

Rubin, Gayle. "The Traffic in Women: Notes on the 'Political Economy' of Sex." In *Toward an Anthropology of Women,* edited by Rayna R. Reiter, 157–210. New York and London: Monthly Review Press, 1975.

Samplonius, Kees. "From Veleda to the Völva: Aspects of Female Divination in Germanic Europe." In *Sanctity and Motherhood: Essays on Holy Mothers in the Middle Ages,* edited by Anneke B. Mulder-Bakker, 68–99. New York: Garland, 1995.

Scheil, Andrew P. "Somatic Ambiguity and Masculine Desire in the Old English *Life of Euphrosyne.*" *Exemplaria* 11 (1999): 345–61.

Schlauch, Margaret. "The Allegory of Church and Synagogue." *Speculum* 14 (1939): 448–64.

Schulenburg, Jane Tibbetts. *Forgetful of Their Sex: Female Sanctity and Society, ca. 500–1100.* Chicago: University of Chicago Press, 1998.

————. "Women's Monastic Communities, 500–1100: Patterns of Expansion and Decline." *Signs: Journal of Women in Culture and Society* 14 (1989): 261–92.

Scragg, D. G. "The Compilation of the Vercelli Book." *Anglo-Saxon England* 2 (1973): 189–207.

Sedgwick, Eve Kosofsky. "The Character in the Veil: Imagery of the Surface in the Gothic Novel." *PMLA* 96 (1981): 255–70.

Sewell, William H., Jr. "The Concept(s) of Culture." In *Beyond the Cultural Turn: New Directions in the Study of Society and Culture,* edited by Victoria E. Bonnell and Lynn Hunt, 35–61. Berkeley: University of California Press, 1999.

Shipley, Joseph T. *The Origins of English Words: A Discursive Dictionary of Indo-European Roots.* Baltimore: Johns Hopkins University Press, 1984.

Smith, Julie Anne. "The Earliest Queen-Making Rites." *Church History* 66 (1997): 18–35.

Smyth, Alfred P. *King Alfred the Great.* Oxford: Oxford University Press, 1995.

————. *Warlords and Holy Men: Scotland A.D. 80–1000.* Edinburgh: Edinburgh University Press, 1984.

Stafford, Pauline. "The King's Wife in Wessex, 800–1066." *Past and Present* 91 (1981): 3–27. Reprinted in *New Readings on Women in Old English Literature,* edited by Helen Damico and Alexandra Hennessey Olsen, 56–78. Bloomington: Indiana University Press, 1990.

———. *Queen Emma and Queen Edith: Queenship and Women's Power in Eleventh-Century England*. Oxford: Blackwell Publishers, 1997.

———. "Queens and Treasure in the Early Middle Ages." In *Treasure in the Medieval West*, edited by Elizabeth M. Tyler, 61–82. Woodbridge, Suffolk: York Medieval Press, 2000.

———. *Queens, Concubines, and Dowagers: The King's Wife in the Early Middle Ages*. Athens: University of Georgia Press, 1983.

———. "Queens, Nunneries and Reforming Churchmen: Gender, Religious Status and Reform in Tenth- and Eleventh-Century England." *Past and Present* 163 (1999): 3–35.

Stancliffe, Clare. "The British Church and the Mission of Augustine." In *St Augustine and the Conversion of England*, edited by Richard Gameson, 107–51.

———. "Kings Who Opted Out." In *Ideal and Reality in Frankish and Anglo-Saxon Society: Studies Presented to J. M. Wallace-Hadrill*, edited by Patrick Wormald, with Donald Bullough and Roger Collins, 154–76. Oxford: Basil Blackwell, 1983.

Stepsis, Robert, and Richard Rand. "Contrast and Conversion in Cynewulf's *Elene*." *Neuphilologische Mitteilungen* 70 (1969): 273–82.

Stewart, Susan. *On Longing: Narratives of the Miniature, the Gigantic, the Souvenir, the Collection*. Durham, N.C.: Duke University Press, 1993.

Strohm, Paul. *Hochon's Arrow: The Social Imagination of Fourteenth-Century Texts*. Princeton: Princeton University Press, 1992.

Taylor, Paul Beekman. "The Old English Poetic Vocabulary of Beauty." In *New Readings on Women in Old English Literature*, edited by Helen Damico and Alexandra Hennessey Olsen, 211–21. Bloomington: Indiana University Press, 1990.

Tipton, Thomas. "Inventing the Cross: A Study of Medieval *Inventio Crucis* Legends." Ph.D. diss., Northwestern University, 1997.

Tolkien, J. R. R. "*Beowulf*: The Monsters and the Critics." *Proceedings of the British Academy* 22 (1936): 245–95. Reprinted in *An Anthology of Beowulf Criticism*, edited by Lewis E. Nicholson, 51–103. Notre Dame, Ind.: University of Notre Dame Press, 1963.

Ullén, Magnus. "Dante in Paradise: The End of Allegorical Interpretation." *New Literary History* 32 (2001): 177–99.

Wainwright, F. T. "Æthelflæd, Lady of the Mercians." In *New Readings on Women in Old English Literature*, edited by Helen Damico and Alexandra Hennessey Olsen, 44–55. Bloomington: Indiana University Press, 1990.

Wallace-Hadrill, J. M. "Bede and Plummer." In *Early Medieval History*, 76–95. Oxford: Basil Blackwell, 1975.

———. *Bede's Ecclesiastical History of the English People: A Historical Commentary*. Oxford: Clarendon Press, 1988.

————. *Early Germanic Kingship in England and on the Continent.* Oxford: Clarendon Press, 1971.

————. "War and Peace in the Earlier Middle Ages." *Transactions of the Royal Historical Society* 5th ser., 25 (1975): 157–74.

Webster, Leslie, and Janet Backhouse, eds. *The Making of England: Anglo-Saxon Art and Culture, A.D. 600–900.* Toronto: University of Toronto Press, 1991.

Weiner, Annette B. *Inalienable Possessions: The Paradox of Keeping-While-Giving.* Berkeley: University of California Press, 1992.

Whatley, E. Gordon. "Constantine the Great, the Empress Helena, and the Relics of the Holy Cross." In *Medieval Hagiography: An Anthology,* edited by Thomas Head, 77–95. New York: Garland, 2000.

————. "The Figure of Constantine the Great in Cynewulf's 'Elene.'" *Traditio* 37 (1981): 161–202.

Whitelock, Dorothy. *The Audience of Beowulf.* 1951. Reprint, Oxford: Clarendon Press, 1964.

Wilcox, Jonathan. "The Audience of Ælfric's *Lives of Saints* and the Face of Cotton Caligula A. xiv, fols. 93–130." In *Beatus Vir: Studies in Honor of Phillip Pulsiano,* edited by A. N. Doane and Kirsten Wolf. Tempe, Ariz.: Medieval and Renaissance Texts and Studies, forthcoming.

Wittig, Joseph. "Figural Narrative in Cynewulf's Juliana." *Anglo-Saxon England* 4 (1974): 37–55. Reprinted in *Cynewulf: Basic Readings,* edited by Robert E. Bjork, 147–69.

Wood, Ian. *The Merovingian Kingdoms, 450–751.* London: Longman, 1994.

————. "The Mission of Augustine of Canterbury to the English." *Speculum* 69 (1994): 1–17.

Woolf, Rosemary. "Saints' Lives." In *Continuations and Beginnings: Studies in Old English Literature,* edited by E. G. Stanley, 37–66. London: Nelson, 1966.

Wormald, Patrick. "Æthelwold and His Continental Counterparts: Contact, Comparison, Contrast." In *Bishop Æthelwold: His Career and Influence,* edited by Barbara Yorke, 13–42. Woodbridge, Suffolk: Boydell Press, 1988.

Yorke, Barbara. "Æthelwold and the Politics of the Tenth Century." In *Bishop Æthelwold: His Career and Influence,* edited by Barbara Yorke, 65–88. Woodbridge, Suffolk: Boydell Press, 1988.

————. "The Reception of Christianity at the Anglo-Saxon Royal Courts." In *St Augustine and the Conversion of England,* edited by Richard Gameson, 152–73.

————. "'Sisters Under the Skin'? Anglo-Saxon Nuns and Nunneries in Southern England." *Reading Medieval Studies* 15 (1989): 95–117.

Ziolkowski, Jan. *Jezebel: A Norman Latin Poem of the Early Eleventh Century.* New York: Peter Lang, 1989.

Index

STACY S. KLEIN is an associate professor of English at Rutgers University. She is the author of numerous scholarly articles on medieval literature and criticism.